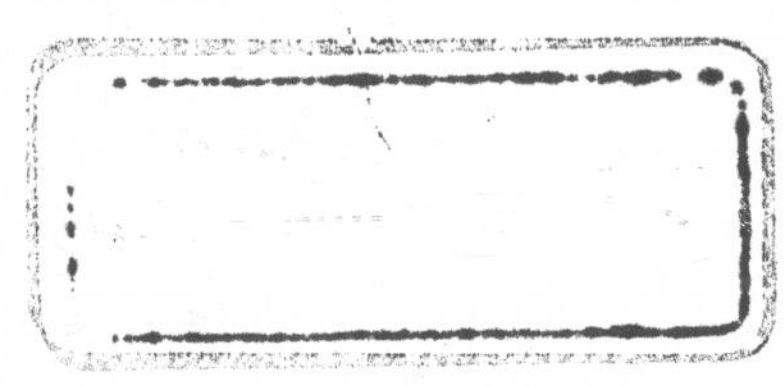

A Practical Guide to Spiritual Reading

revised edition

Susan Annette Muto

1995

Susan Annette Muto

Seek in reading and you will find in meditation Knock in prayer and it will be opened to you in contemplation —St. John of the Cross

with a Foreword by
Adrian van Kaam

St. Bede's Publications
Petersham, Massachusetts

Printed in the United States of America
6 5 4 3 2 1 99 98 97 96 95 94

Grateful acknowledgment is made to Doubleday & Company, Inc. for permission to quote excerpts from *The Jerusalem Bible*, Reader's Edition (New York, 1971). Copyright © 1966 by Darton, Longman & Todd, Ltd. and Doubleday & Company, Inc. and to the Institute of Carmelite Studies for permission to quote from *Counsels to a Religious On How to Reach Perfection* in *The Collected Works of St. John of the Cross*, translated by Kieran Kavanaugh and Otilio Rodriguez, Copyright © 1964 by Washington Province of Discalced Carmelites, Inc. Paperback edition published by Institute of Carmelite Studies, ICS Publications, Washington, DC, U.S.A.

Cover photo: THE OPEN MISSAL, c.1570, Ludger tom Ring, the Younger, German, 1522-1584; oil on panel, 24-7/8 x 24-1/8". The Frances Lehman Loeb Art Center, Vassar College, Poughkeepsie, NY. Purchase, 1956.6.

LIBRARY OF CONGRESS CATALOGING-IN-PUBLICATION DATA

Muto, Susan Annette.
A practical guide to spiritual reading / Susan Annette Muto : with a foreword by Adrian van Kaam. — Rev. ed.
p. cm.
Includes bibliographical references.
ISBN 1-879007-09-6
1. Spiritual life—Catholic Church. 2. Catholics—Books and reading. 3. Bibliography—Best books—Spiritual life—Catholic Church. 4. Spiritual life—Catholic Church—Bibliography. 5. Catholic Church—Doctrines. I. Title.
BX2350.2.M884 1994
248.4'82--dc20 94-19939
CIP

Published by St. Bede's Publications
P.O. Box 545
Petersham, Massachusetts 01366-0545

Contents

Foreword

After writing several excellent introductions to the art and discipline of spiritual reading, Dr. Susan Muto presents us now with a scholarly work that can guide us practically in this field. The following book fills a need felt deeply in Christianity since the reawakening of a genuine interest in the spiritual life. By now it has become clear that one of the fundamental sources of this life is to be found in Holy Scripture and the variety of devotional writings developed in Christianity over the centuries. Every serious group of Christians, and all Christians striving after the renewal of their inner lives, are convinced that they should engage in regular meditative reading. The only questions that may bother them are these: How can I do so most effectively? What readings should I choose? How do I distinguish between more and less essential texts? Where can I find the books I need? How can I devise for myself or for a group of like-minded Christians a practical reading program that would set us on the right path? Many retreat masters, directors of diocesan centers of spirituality, novice directors and directresses, heads of seminaries and houses of prayer, ministers and laity of many Christian churches have asked themselves these questions. Often they sought in vain for satisfying answers. I myself have been consulted repeatedly in regard to ideal reading programs for communities and individuals. I never felt quite sure that my answers objectively covered the best available literature in this field. Like others, I too looked in vain for one comprehensive guide that could assist me in my response to this recurrent problem. I myself am delighted, and I am sure others will feel as I do, that now at last this unique guide, so eagerly sought after, is available in a revised edition.

Guidelines for practical reading and sample programs are presented and it is made clear how they can be adapted to different audiences. The guidelines help us to read in the right way. Rooted in formational theology as developed by the great spiritual masters of the church, they stress and develop the formative dimension of spiritual reading. The author points out that the main approach to this art is not exegetical, informational, or literary but formative. This means we are to read Holy Scripture and spiritual literature in such a way that these texts help us to tune in to the inner life form or direction that God has meant for us from eternity. Because spiritual reading, done in the right way, helps us to find and unfold the mystery of this hidden life form, such reading is called formative, and spirituality approached from this perspective is called formative spirituality.

Dr. Muto is exceedingly well qualified to compose such a guide. Her specialization in pre- and post-Reformation spiritual literature, and her doctoral dissertation on Milton's *Paradise Lost* in the light of Paul Ricoeur's hermeneutics, developed in her a fine sense for tracing the foundational hermeneutic principles and themes that are basic to spiritual writing and reading. Many years of teaching the art and discipline of formative reading to future teachers of spirituality and directors of formation at the Institute of Formative Spirituality, and presently at the Epiphany Association, gave her an unusual opportunity to collect and expound many of the best classic and contemporary works available today. Her constant dialogue with a variety of students from many continents refined her perception of the essentials of spiritual formation. Added to this were the opportunities offered by alumni and others to test out her principles and programs with various religious and lay groups. This experimentation enabled the author to refine her program of reading to an eminently workable procedure that proved beneficial not only in the States but in many other countries as well.

Over the years, Dr. Muto directed her students in the composition of a variety of reading programs about different topics and themes of spiritual living. In the present book, a few of the best programs produced by her graduate students and thoroughly reworked and revised by herself are made available for the first time to a general audience.

We are most grateful for the tireless effort in research and experimentation that has gone into the production of this remarkable book. No other work of this scope on the topic of spiritual reading is at the moment available anywhere in the world in the field of formative spirituality. This book will foster not only the development of the new field of foundational human and Christian formation; it will also alleviate the task of the numerous spiritual directors, teachers and animators who have to initiate priests, ministers, religious, and lay people of various denominations in the art and discipline of in-depth spiritual reading. The book will prove to be an invaluable aid for those many individuals who cannot personally profit from spiritual teaching or private direction. These pages will teach them that they do not have to despair. Devotional reading, if done along the lines here proposed, can provide them with the direction Holy Providence may grant them through personal encounter with the message of scriptures and the masters.

Adrian van Kaam

Acknowledgments

This book emerges as a response to two practical questions: How do I do spiritual reading? How do I know which texts to use? In responding, my purpose has been to compile in a concise and concrete way main guidelines to this art and discipline and to select carefully themes and texts around which each reader can build a personal program of devotional reading alone or with a faith-sharing group. Complementing selected texts from Holy Scripture and the literature of spirituality found in each reading program is a Sample Bibliography of spiritual and informational texts from which the reader can make further selections. A book of this scope is, of course, never a product of the author alone. It has emerged over the years in courses and conferences given within and under the auspices of our graduate institute in spiritual formation at Duquesne University. Here I must acknowledge my lasting gratitude to the students of the Institute whose appreciation for spiritual reading is evidenced in their personal lives and scholarly work, in their research and class participation. I am deeply indebted to the spiritual writings and personal witness of Father Adrian van Kaam, who has offered excellent suggestions for improving the text and constant encouragement. Heartfelt gratitude is extended also to other colleagues and students, whose practical suggestions are incorporated throughout this guide, and to the members of the Epiphany Association for their enthusiastic support. For invaluable help with typing and proofreading, I am indebted to my aunt, Eve Bauer. For bibliographical research, thanks goes to Karen Holttum of our Epiphany staff, and to Marilyn Russell for detailed proofreading. Last, but not least, for understanding "where the time goes and why," I offer lasting thanks to my family and friends, and especially to Sr. Mary Joseph, O.S.B. and the wonderful staff at St. Bede's.

PART ONE

GUIDELINES

I

Guidelines for Spiritual Reading

In this book I will not be dealing with the ordinary reading we do to keep up with our profession, for example, a doctor's reading of medical journals, a teacher's preparation for classes, a writer's research project. I shall consider instead a special kind of reading, the words of which are directed primarily to our inner spiritual selves, a reading done outside the time we spend doing vocational or professional updating. This is the kind of reading that can console us in sorrow, deepen our joy, prompt a transformation, aid growth in reflection, and orient our whole being toward the Divine. It is the kind of reading, in other words, that nourishes the life of the spirit.

We are immersed in a busy round of duties and responsibilities. People and situations challenge us constantly. Understandably, under the pressure of daily preoccupations, we become distracted from dimensions of the spirit. The inner person in us does not, for all this activity, cease to cry out. Something in us is serious about living a spiritual life. We do not want to forget about ultimate concerns. That is why we know, deep down, that we must nourish this call to holiness by availing ourselves of certain religious practices that foster nearness to God, such practices as retreat, recollection, and prayer, meditation, examination of conscience, and spiritual reading. While our lifestyle may not allow us to do all of these things, we can at least do some of them.

In the course of my studies, teaching, and conferences, I have found that, of the above practices, one of the most attractive is spiritual reading. This is evident from a continually growing interest in Holy Scripture and the writings of spiritual masters. People do spiritual reading for a variety of reasons. Religious, for example, often do it because it is part of their rule and because it provides a prelude to meditative prayer. One housewife I met says she likes to read spiritual books late at night when the children are in bed and before her husband comes home from the night shift because "it quiets my mind from a million details and gives me that 'shot of inspiration' I often need." A businessman tells me that an unexpected side benefit of this "super slow reading" is an increase in efficiency. His explanation is that, by awakening reflective, intuitive levels of insight, spiritual reading balances the informational speed reading he must engage in at the firm.

Curiously enough, for all this interest in spiritual reading, there are few, if any, really handy guides for general readers or for retreat masters, spiritual directors, or directors of formation who want to know how to establish for themselves, or for those under their care, a practical, workable program of spiritual reading. What follows, therefore, is an attempt to give some practical guidelines for spiritual reading for individuals mainly but also for groups of people at different occasions, such as, for example, a reading group organized on the parish level, a retreat group of lay people or ministers, or a group of religious in various stages of initiation from pre-entrance to ongoing formation. The, so to speak, "meat on the bone of these guidelines" will be found in Part Two where three in-depth reading programs are outlined and where possible reading selections and themes are proposed for persons who want to start a spiritual reading program for themselves or others.

First Guideline[1]

Spiritual reading requires a careful selection of texts first of all from Holy Scripture and then from various sources in the literature of spirituality, preferably centered in and gathered around a fundamental theme of the spiritual life.

Let's take a closer look at each segment of this guideline. It is based on the simple presupposition that we cannot begin a program of spiritual reading without having appropriate texts available for this purpose.

1. Selection of Texts from Holy Scripture

The Bible is the basic text for spiritual reading. For our purposes, we assume that persons who do the planning of the reading program for themselves or others are enough imbued with the Church's teaching on Holy Scripture, its doctrine and tradition, that they can move from this doctrinal understanding toward personal spiritual application of the text to their own life or toward sharing life-meanings with others. Such background can be gained outside the time set aside for spiritual reading by a more informational type of reading in a commentary on Holy Scripture, by the study of introductions and references in scholarly editions of the Bible, and by consultation of commentaries on select books of the Bible. A helpful view of the relationship

[1]These guidelines are directed toward the average reader, especially the person who is beginning the practice of spiritual reading. There will always be exceptions to the rule and one has to allow for these. How the Holy Spirit may choose to move each reader who opens him- or herself sincerely to God's word is a mystery no mere guidelines can contain. Only the Divine Guide, the Holy Spirit, knows the true path each unique pilgrim is to follow.

between doctrinal understanding and personal application can be found in Chapter IV of Adrian van Kaam's book, *In Search of Spiritual Identity.*[2]

This kind of background reading (doctrinal, exegetical, historical) is to be done, as indicated, at a time other than that set aside for spiritual reading. However, even such informational reading can become spiritual to a degree because this kind of study often inspires the reader to learn more about spiritual living. The possibility is great, especially in the beginning, that reading is a mixture of the study approach and the spiritual approach. This mixture is not so bad, provided that slowly on we begin—during spiritual reading time—to center our attention more and more undividedly on what the text says to us.[3] True spiritual reading strives to eliminate gently and gradually all utilitarian (in the sense of information gathering) and ulterior motives in order to be solely intent on listening to the word of God as it manifests itself through the reading.

Let us consider a few suggestions regarding textual selections from the Bible to illustrate the first part of this guideline. As the most immediate word of God is given in Revelation, it seems advisable for the reader to choose, especially in the beginning, one of the Synoptic Gospels, that is, the Gospel of Matthew, of Mark, or of Luke.

Suppose we start to read the Gospel of Matthew which opens with the ancestry of Jesus given in three series of fourteen names. At first reading we may think, "What is so spiritual about that?" A little background reading, combined with the reading of this text in a slowed down, reflective way, may help us to realize that the evangelist in this balanced list of three times the same number of names from Abraham to Jesus must intend to communicate something.

God called Abraham to leave his own country and go to the land where later his descendants would settle. God promised the land to him, though Abraham himself would never own it and would remain a nomad. According to God's plan, Abraham was to be the father of a people—a people consisting not only of Jews but of a spiritual Israel of which Christ was the first born. In giving us this ancestry, Matthew wants to indicate that over hundreds of years God guided everything in accordance with the plan he had revealed successively through the prophets. This succession of ancestors is no haphazard

---

[2]Since all texts referred to in Part One are listed in Part Three, *Sample Bibliography*, I will not repeat full references here.

[3]The author hopes that the reader will bear with the fact that certain parts of the guidelines cannot be immediately clear, for instance, the matter of time. Earlier guidelines like this one presuppose what will be taken up in detail later. This chapter has to be read from beginning to end in order to be fully understood.

event but a record of how over the centuries God guided the history of the chosen people with infinite care and concern.

While reading, it may suddenly strike me that I, too, am part of this salvific history, that I, too, was included from the beginning in this divine plan, that God guides my history with the same infinite love with which he has guided all history. He has been with me up to this moment and he will be with me in the future, insuring by his presence my salvation and happiness. What an incredible perspective this seemingly dull list of names has opened up! The God who created me, the Infinite Love who died for me, is guiding me and calling me forth for my own good.

After the Synoptic Gospels, we may choose to read the Gospel of St. John. This book is the preferred reading of many spiritual persons. Once we start reading it, we shall soon see that it is not always easy to enter into the deeper meaning of the text. The same problem may come up, namely, instead of spiritual reading we start to do scripture study. Such study is, of course, valuable and ought to be done outside spiritual reading time. As a matter of fact, we may need to do a little more study before attempting a spiritual reading of this Gospel. But we should always remind ourselves that this kind of study is not the same as spiritual reading and ought not to take its place.

When we read the texts of St. John slowly and only a few at a time, we should not worry if there are elements that we do not understand as yet or fully. The purpose of spiritual reading is not to fully understand the text in that mode of mastery we need when, for instance, taking a course in scripture but to derive from it spiritual inspiration and nourishment. Peacefully and quietly, we read the text with an openness of mind and heart. In the parts we do understand, we will find a message that speaks meaningfully to us in our present situation.

As we grow more familiar with the New Testament and its wealth of spiritual treasures, we may be pointed backwards to the Old Testament accounts of creation, the calling of the chosen people, the binding of God's covenant with Israel, the prophets and their foretellings. Soon we may be including in our reading texts from the Old and New Testaments, thus following more and more faithfully the guideline of making Holy Scripture the first source for spiritual reading.[4]

2. Selection of Texts from Various Sources in the Literature of Spirituality

For spiritual reading, second to selections from Holy Scripture come sources in the literature of spirituality. Lists of source material from various

---

[4]Complementing regular reading of the Bible, in accordance with one's faith and formation tradition, can be readings from the liturgy of the day as well as from the Divine Office.

categories of spiritual literature can be found in the bibliographies of *Approaching the Sacred*, *Steps Along the Way*, *The Journey Homeward*, and in the present practical guide. I will first review what these categories are and then give a concrete example of spiritual reading from a notable classic by Thérèse of Lisieux. The categories are as follows: essential, secondary, edifying, and recreative.[5]

Essential. These include the writings of the Fathers, Doctors, and saints of the church, for example, Gregory of Nyssa, Bernard of Clairvaux, Catherine of Siena, John of the Cross. Included secondly in this category are autobiographical texts about the Christian spiritual life, classic and contemporary, for example, Augustine's *Confessions* and Merton's *Sign of Jonas*. Thirdly are treatises written to describe experientially the fundamentals of spiritual life as taught by the Church, an example being gentleness as described by Adrian van Kaam in *Spirituality and the Gentle Life*. Fourthly, I would include in this category standard texts in the literature of spirituality frequently used by spiritual directors and formation personnel, such as the spiritual letters of Francis Libermann or the conferences of Vincent de Paul.

Secondary. This category includes all biographical texts depicting or explaining the life of Christ, the saints, the spiritual masters, such as Butler's study of Western mysticism, Jörgensen's biography of Francis of Assisi, Athanasius' *Life of St. Anthony*, and so on. Secondly in this category are texts that explain objectively certain stages or fundamentals of spirituality, for example, Tanquerey's *The Spiritual Life*. Thirdly there are texts that clarify doctrines or practices of the church in its biblical, liturgical, sacramental, and prayerful life, such as commentaries on the scriptures or Johnston's exposition of the meditative life. Fourthly, there are texts that consider spirituality from a historical perspective and provide good background reading. Lastly, I list philosophical or psychological texts that focus on the search for meaning as pertaining to spiritual living, such as Frankl's books or Ricoeur's study of the symbolism of evil.

Edifying. Here I place first-person accounts by people of various faiths that touch reflectively upon aspects of human experience the reader can identify with, such as silence, solitude, having to face suffering and death, discipline, detachment, freedom, and so forth, exemplified in books by Thoreau, Lindbergh, Frank, and Bloom, to mention only a few. Found here are also texts written in a personal style to edify and inspire the reader to live the funda-

[5]The reader will find selected and annotated sources from each of these categories in the *Sample Bibliography*. These references have been selected mainly, but not exclusively, with the general reading public in mind rather than only specialists in spirituality or religious formation. I am aware that certain categories may overlap and my placement of certain books in these categories may be debatable. Nonetheless I feel that some principle of organization, however limited, has to be applied to this vast quantity of source material.

mentals of faith and the spiritual life, for example, Kierkegaard's edifying discourses and selections from Quaker spirituality.

Recreative. Placed here are fictional accounts of saints' lives, such as Kazantzakis' *St. Francis;* occasional essays dramatizing some aspect of spiritual living in the widest sense of that term, such as Benson's book on the relaxation response; novels, plays, poetry, and short fictional works that depict the spiritual nature of men and women as they struggle to find the meaning of life, as they meet their destiny with courage, celebrate creation, and so on, such as works by Silone, Bolt, Hopkins, Eliot, and others. Included lastly are essays of a highly literary nature, often biographically based, that present the natural underpinnings of spirituality. The writings of Loren Eiseley are a good example.

Generally, since the reader's time—outside that set aside for Holy Scripture—may be limited, it is wise to start with the essential texts and to move from there to edifying and perhaps recreative sources. For the most part, secondary texts provide good background reading in the informational sense.

This fourfold categorization can be illustrated briefly as follows, taking as an example Francis of Assisi. An essential text would be *The Little Flowers of St. Francis* in which are recorded his actual words to his brothers and anecdotes that have become familiar. A related and helpful secondary text would be the already mentioned biography of St. Francis by Jörgensen. Chesterton's reflections on the saint and his inspiring influence would be edifying. In the recreative category could be placed, also as mentioned, Kazantzakis' novel of that title. Taken together, these texts, on the side of information, give the reader a fine insight into the life and witness of St. Francis. Slowed down reading of selected texts in the essential or edifying category especially may provide, on the side of spiritual reading, many personally meaningful moments, more so if the reader is by temperament attracted to this poor troubadour of God.

A Concrete Example of Spiritual Reading from the Literature of Spirituality. One of the recurrent themes we are sure to find as we read St. Thérèse's autobiography slowly and meditatively is that perfection consists simply in doing God's will, in being the self God wants us to be, however humble our circumstances. "That's the whole of it," we may think. "It's so simple," but reflection tells us that simple does not mean easy. If we try every day to do what God asks of us, we will find many crosses on our path. The way was no easier for St. Thérèse, but what made it simple was her total reliance on God. The reason we so often feel frustrated may be because we follow our own will instead of God's. Reading leads us to ponder how much more peaceful we might be if we learned to accept ourselves as God does and to follow his directives from day to day.

Reading on, we find another recurrent theme: that the whole point of love is making ourselves small. This is a truth validated by scripture. Now in reading this text spiritually we become aware that in spite of our protestations of love for God, we attempt again and again to be the center of attention—powerful persons who can do all things for themselves. How often this obstacle of egoism blocks out the intimacy of love for God to which we are called. No longer is this admonition merely an objective fact; suddenly the text affects us personally; it lights up our life. It draws us into its meaning and becomes a message addressed to us here and now: we must grow smaller; Jesus must grow greater!

Since in this example we have focused on the finding of recurrent spiritual themes, let's turn now to the third segment of the first guideline, which concerns thematic spiritual reading.

3. Finding a Theme Around Which to Gather Our Reading

In addition to growing familiarity with Holy Scripture and the literature of spirituality, spiritual reading proves even more profitable when it is centered in and gathered around a fundamental or recurrent theme of spiritual living.[6] Reading widely without any particular guiding theme may be best at the beginning of spiritual reading when we are striving to become more at home with qualities and attitudes common to the interior life. However, steady reading, complemented by reflection and the jotting down of personal thoughts, may reveal to us certain themes that touch us personally again and again. These become, so to speak, life themes that we desire to personalize ever more deeply with the help of spiritual reading and God's grace.

God may be calling you, for example, to devote your life almost exclusively to the care of your husband and children. You spend a lot of time in kitchen and garden. You help the children with homework; you may even manage part of your husband's business. In those quiet moments, while doing spiritual reading and the reflection that flows from it, you may discover after some time how attracted you are to the theme of hiddenness. This attraction started with your reading of the New Testament. Perhaps because of your situation as a homemaker you could identify personally with Jesus during those years when he lived in a common family doing ordinary things while preparing himself for his public witness of total obedience to the Father's will.

In reading through some selections from the literature of spirituality, you might come across a book by Brother Lawrence entitled *The Practice of the Presence of God*. Quickly, perhaps because of the pots and pans you have in

[6]The reading programs in Part Two of this book exemplify this principle, being centered in and gathered around such themes as living the desert experience, blending life and labor, stepping aside and starting again.

common, you identify with this simple friar and his teaching that God is everywhere; you have only to turn to him to be reminded of his presence. He does not expect great things of you, that is, not by the world's standards of greatness. God loves all that you do, from preparing a good meal to painting the house, when you do it for his sake. Soon you may find yourself looking for other spiritual texts from scripture and literature that speak to you of the theme of hiddenness. This is one example of how a program of spiritual reading can begin to orient itself around a theme pertinent to the inner life.

This thematic approach is not only helpful to lay people; it is also an aid for those planning reading programs for various stages of religious formation. Formation personnel can direct the reading programs in Part Two toward the candidates or professed religious with whom they are working and in accordance with their phase of initiation or ongoing formation. Similar usage of these sample programs can be made by retreat masters or spiritual directors, depending on the situation and needs of the persons they are guiding. Those who will be introducing others to spiritual reading have a great responsibility. The formation they give initiates may have a lasting influence on their lives. In the unfortunate case of a poor formation in spiritual reading, the director may unwittingly close off an abundant source of divine inspiration.

Parallel with formation in spiritual reading, those in charge of initiation ought also to be formed in and prepared to form others in meditation, liturgical participation, the spiritual reading of Holy Scripture, private and common prayer, examination of conscience, and other such practices. The reading program is not intended to replace initiation in other areas of spiritual life; it is to supplement them. Clearly, introduction to spiritual reading will be most effective when the persons in charge are able themselves to participate in the reading program and to point out its harmony with what is being done in other areas. In this way, instead of each part of the formation program pulling in different directions, the various parts mutually enlighten and support one another. By bringing out this unified totality, candidates avoid starting off with a fragmented view of the spiritual life that may be harmful to their further growth.

Second Guideline

Spiritual reading is an art requiring the reader to develop attitudes more or less different from those required for informational reading.

1. Spiritual Reading as Art

Certain aspects of this second guideline are developed more thoroughly in Chapter One of my book *Steps Along the Way*. We see there that any art requires first of all a certain skill. For example, a practiced seamstress, because of her skill, can sew a difficult pattern, say a pleated skirt, whereas the unskilled seamstress, not yet proficient in the sewing arts, may feel confident with only a simple A-line. As she grows more skillful through regular practice in the art of sewing, she can turn to intricate designs. Growing proficient in a certain art also includes thoughtful observation of other artists in action. We learn an art by observing how others practice it. Even a skilled seamstress might attend an advanced sewing class once in a while to keep up with new developments and perfect her touch. Lastly, making a certain art one's own in the fullest sense means moving toward creative performance in the chosen media. Here the seamstress puts to use her native skill and talent plus what she has learned from others to create her own original product.

These same characteristics of art apply to spiritual reading. Reading as an art implies first of all that we develop our skill through regular practice. It is safe to say that nearly everyone in our culture learns early in life how to read. But merely because we know how to read does not mean we know how to do spiritual reading. This is a special skill that we can develop only through know-how and practice. Spiritual reading implies also that we develop our powers of observation. For instance, we may observe through reading itself how other authors have been inspired by a text. Testimonies of how a text affected them increase our motivation to read in the right way. Skill and observation must, of course, be put into action through the creative experience of fostering this art. The more regular our practice of reflective reading becomes, the more likely it is to nourish our spiritual life as a whole.

2. Attitudes of the Spiritual Reader

Growing in the art of spiritual reading requires that we develop attitudes more or less different from the attitudes we bring to informational reading. These two types of reading are complementary, as we saw in the relation between essential and secondary texts, but we have to develop a kind of "sixth sense" by which we know when to switch from level to level—when, so to speak, to take off our "student hat" and put on our "disciple hat." Often the same book will be in our hands for different purposes. For instance, in a scripture course, we can read the Synoptic Gospels for the sake of analyzing the variations from text to text. This is good training and may give some interesting new lights to familiar texts; but we have to take that "hat" off and put on our other "hat of spiritual reader" when we take up the same Gospel for inspirational reading. Thus we can use the same text on one occasion for study and on another for spiritual reading. The more we are able to sense interiorly when the shift has to be made, the more capable we will become as spiritual readers.

Attitudes do alter when we move from informational to inspirational reading. To clarify this change, the phrase "more or less" may be helpful because the attitudes are not totally distinct; they are just more or less different according to the emphasis one or the other type of reading requires.

Let me give a few examples of what I mean:

Digging/Dwelling. Informational reading is more digging for answers to questions and less dwelling on life meanings that may light up for us in the text. Spiritual reading is more a dwelling on such meanings and less a digging for full transparency. For instance, when a teacher is reading *The Way of Perfection* and preparing to use this text for her class, she has to dig into it for answers to the questions her students may have. When her "informational reading hat" is on, she may compare and contrast this text with others on the same subject of contemplative prayer written by contemporaries of St. Teresa or by spiritual writers closer to our time. When she puts on her "spiritual reading hat," her attitude toward the text becomes more dwelling—more a staying in one place and going deeper into the divine mystery St. Teresa addressed than a digging for answers to her questions. As a spiritual reader, she might take a few lines of one paragraph and stay with them, not at that moment looking for solutions to her problems with the comparative study of prayer experiences but letting the words of the text draw her into the mystery of God's love.

Dialectical/Docile. Informational reading is, of necessity, more dialectical and comparative whereas spiritual reading tends to be more docile. Another teacher preparing to use *The Way of Perfection* for his class has to place what he is reading in dialogue with what other spiritual writers teach about prayer. A lively dialogue ensues, for instance, when he reads along with this text two others that analyze the Lord's Prayer, Nicholas Grou's *How To Pray* and Alfred Delp's *Prison Meditations*. During spiritual reading time, however, wearing the "hat" of disciple, the teacher's reading becomes toned down academically and more docile to the text at hand. Now he is not so much teacher as one who seeks to be taught. He wants to receive the message of the master in whatever degree he is capable of opening up to it. What is the Holy Spirit offering him in the limited passage he is reading? His attitude as spiritual reader is clearly more docile and receptive, less dialectical and comparative.

Dissective/Dynamic. Informational reading tends also to be rather dissective, that is, taking pieces of spiritual knowledge from here and there to increase erudition; spiritual reading is more dynamic, that is, adroit at making connections between what we are reading and our life here and now. To use the same example, a teacher of spirituality studying *The Way of Perfection* may include in her approach an attempt to catalogue knowledge about the structure of the life of prayer that can be found in the text. This knowledge has to be put in some kind of line with the wisdom that has been communicated from generation to generation; it is important for the teacher of spirituality, who has to become familiar with various schools and their representative writers. It would be entirely mistaken for spiritual reading itself, however, if this attitude were in the foreground. The dissective approach has to recede to the background.

When we turn to spiritual reading, we have to let an attitude of personal concern emerge. Personal concern implies a receptive attention to the way in which this paragraph, this sentence, this word may connect with our life. How may the Holy Spirit be speaking to us through the text? Reading in this way becomes personally relevant in that it dynamically influences us and inspires us to grow in the practice of prayer. We derive from reading not just spiritual erudition but a deepening of our personal relation to God in prayer. Whereas informational reading may nourish one part of us—our analytical intelligence—spiritual reading sustains the deepest part, that inner spirit where God dwells and desires to permeate the whole of our life.

Third Guideline

Spiritual reading is a discipline requiring the reader to establish certain conditions to facilitate this practice.

1. Spiritual Reading as Discipline

In Chapter One of *Steps Along the Way*, there is a section on spiritual reading as discipline, which supplements what is presented here. For most of us discipline means a form of punishment or rigorous training like that received in an army, but the etymology of the word links it to disciple or learner, to one who seeks to be taught, in this case by the directives of the text. Therefore, spiritual reading as a discipline aims to help us become better listeners to God's guiding word.

What does spiritual reading require by way of facilitating conditions to foster this practice? Consider first of all the word "facilitate." Adrian van Kaam coined the expression "facilitating condition" to make clear that nothing we can do will in and by itself guarantee our sanctity. What such practices can do is to remove obstacles to the action of grace but in no way do they guarantee that we will become more holy, for that privilege is a pure gift of grace. Moreover, it is God's grace that prompts us to set these conditions in the first place. What are they?

2. Time

In order to expedite the regular practice of spiritual reading, we have to set time for it and adhere as much as possible to the rule of daily reading. A commonly agreed upon length is every day for fifteen minutes. Another suggested duration is at least three fifteen- to twenty-minute periods per week for the reading of Holy Scripture (over and above regular contact with the sacred word received in the liturgy and for some in praying the Office of the Hours) together with a minimum of three one-half hour periods per week for reading the literature of spirituality. It is important from the beginning that we try to determine beforehand at what time every day we are going to do our spiritual reading. Only when we make this practice a regular part of our daily program is there a chance that we will be faithful to it.

Time is at a premium for those of us who are busy professionals in the world. However, if growth in the spiritual life becomes a main priority for us, we have to make time to live out this value. At first we may think that this priority adds to our already heavy schedule more duties and responsibilities, but such is not the case. Perhaps we have to learn to say a polite "no" once in a while to extra unnecessary work, to social get-togethers, to TV programs, movies, and magazines. Our "no" to the latter is in effect a saying "yes" to something of greater value.

For example, we may say "no" to a fellow teacher who asks us to do something after hours for the sake of saying "yes" to the greater good of needing time for solitude and spiritual reading. Perhaps we need a quiet evening at home because we've had a hectic week. This response is not selfish; what we are doing is preserving a certain amount of time for privacy and in-touchness with the sacred word. We know in our heart that time spent this way readies us to participate more attentively in teaching and social life, attentive, that is, to God's presence and his call in each situation. Without such preparatory time, we risk being emptied out, becoming superficial and overly fatigued, thereby decreasing our effectiveness as competent teachers and, more than this, as witnesses for Christ.

Thus it seems wise that our days follow a certain rhythm and order if we are to be faithful to religious practices. This order includes being attentive to the bodies we have. For instance, some need more sleep than they get; others need less rest to be wakeful and alert. When we do set a time for spiritual reading, we want to bring our best self to this practice. We need to get in touch with our own bodily rhythms with their unique periods of rest and fatigue. What kind of persons are we in regard to our internal clock time —often different from the chronological ticking of the clock on the wall? In terms of our alertness and attentiveness, are we morning persons, afternoon, or late evening persons? All of us don't run on the same rhythm. I myself happen to be a "morning person." For me the optimum hours for spiritual reading and other creative endeavors are my morning hours. Others are "just about getting it together" around eleven or twelve o'clock. Still others feel that afternoon sag and need a short nap. After that they feel refreshed and are able to do personally recreative, spiritual work then or in the early evening. Whatever our bodily rhythms happen to be, it is easy to conclude that spiritual reading and like religious practices are best done when body and mind are rested and alert.

Setting the right time, choosing it in dialogue with our given pace, and sticking to it are thus important phases of this discipline. Each of us has a unique pace of spiritual progress that must be in tune with the given organic rhythms of our body. If we keep that correlation in mind, we are likely to choose an alert time for the main priority of our devotional practices rather than letting them go until the end of the day (unless, of course, that happens to be the best time for the kind of person you are) or pushing them off until everything else gets done.

3. Space

In addition to finding time for spiritual reading, it is also necessary to set aside a quiet space or place where we will not be disturbed and where we can be fully present to the text at hand. Why is this discipline important? Perhaps the deepest reason is that we humans, as bodily beings, are already in tune with the space we inhabit on a pre-reflective or preconscious level—the level below consciousness. Before we think about it, for instance, our body is already aware of having to step down the steps of the staircase. Automatically, as it were, our legs and feet find their way. Similarly, before we are, our body is aware of the chilly nip in the morning air. Without our thinking about it, our arms move to wrap the sweater more tightly around our shoulders. Our body picks up and registers before we do changes in temperature from cool to hot to humid. As bodily creatures, therefore, we live constantly on this pre-reflective level on which we receive information through our senses prior to channeling it through consciousness.

Consider the importance of this factor for spirituality and for such practices as spiritual reading. What may not have been too clear to us in the past, but what is becoming progressively known due to scientific studies, is the effect of environment on the self. Whether we know it or not on the conscious level, we are highly influenced by the space we inhabit. Take the space of a classroom. It gears us already prereflectively to the learning situation. The standard square shape is not distractive; the walls are relatively bare or covered with related teaching materials; it is built in such a way that the lecturer stands with her back to the board while students face front for maximum attentiveness. The response of teacher and student to one another and to the learning situation would shift considerably were class conducted on the lawn. Similarly, when walking into a gothic cathedral, the space does something to us that is different from what happens when we go to the bus depot or airport. The space of the cafeteria at lunch time affects us differently than going to an exquisite French restaurant for an elegant late supper.

All of these examples show how affected we are by the space we occupy. That is why every spiritual practice may become more fruitful if we take into account the facilitating condition of our surroundings. It is wiser, therefore, to do spiritual reading in the space of our private room, in the chapel, or in a familiar natural setting than, for instance, trying to get it done on the bus coming to work or while eating a quick cafeteria lunch. The space in which we read ought to be conducive to the meditative endeavor we are trying to participate in at the time. This is not to deny that some people who have become quite proficient in the art of formative reading may be able to do it fruitfully almost anywhere. It is only to suggest that the more we are mindful of spiritual priorities and their supportive devotional practices, the more we shall be in touch with the most conducive conditions of time and space to carry them out.

Something else may happen as we abide regularly by these conditions. The very act of following our set time and going to our favorite place with a well chosen text in hand already begins to slow us down. Even before the period of reading begins, we have been put in that more dwelling, docile, receptive mood that prepares us attitudinally for God's message.

4. Sticking to It

When we start to read in a peaceful, quiet way, we have to try for the duration of that reading to let everything else fall away from our mind and concern. Some days it will be easier to do this than others, but distraction and lack of discipline ought not to upset us unduly. It is amazing how fast the "honeymoon period" is over for any devotional practice. The excitement of newness lasts for only a short while. It is then that we must apply the principle of "stick-to-it-iveness." When the going gets rough, when routine and boredom set in, then comes the regular repetition of the practice. Days will dawn when, in spite of our willingness and openness, reading means little or nothing to us. Now is not the time to be discouraged. It is exactly the day-after-dayness of religious practice that matters. What God counts is our trying, our slow learning, not whether we always succeed. All we can do is to remain faithful to our reading and have the courage to go on, even though we feel inwardly arid and it is as if we are not accomplishing anything. It is precisely in going to our reading day after day that we show God our good will, no matter how we feel. We are willing to listen whenever it pleases God to speak. We say to God in effect, "Whatever you will is what I want to follow. The initiative is yours. I may create the right conditions, but it is up to you whether I shall experience consolation or dryness, awakening or aridity, in this practice."

There is another side to this story however. If such dryness happens constantly, it may be because the book we are using is not where we are. The purpose of spiritual reading is to nurture our unique inner life and, because it is unique, it has its own features and needs. That is why a friend of ours may consider a book we are both reading deeply inspiring while it leaves us steadily dry. In such a case the book we have selected may not be meeting our honest needs and we might be advised to read another. In making this decision there is, however, a new danger to consider.

Some people too quickly conclude that the book they are reading is not good for them while in fact the deficiency is not in the book but within themselves. We may pretend that we are truly open to the text, but are we? We may want only to be entertained or consoled by the writing. As soon as it demands effort, we reject it or run to something else. In that case the fault does not lie with the text. It is good, but we do not want to make the effort to penetrate to the heart of the matter. We get stuck instead on a superficial detail like the fact that the author's style does not appeal to us. Without further consideration, we may close ourselves off from a message that could be of value.

We may notice on another occasion that spiritual reading is becoming routine and on that basis alone move to another book. Is the discomfort we feel within us or is it because of the book? If after honest searching, we conclude that the deficiency is with the book, we may put it aside and look for another that addresses us at this moment. Though the book we have been reading says little or nothing to us now, it may offer much meaning at some future date. The idea is to put it aside, not to dismiss it totally. Perhaps the theme and subthemes suggested in Part Two, together with the literature selected for these reading programs, will be of assistance here. Keep in mind that the purpose of spiritual reading is not to read as much as possible—not to get through the whole list of reading topics and selections—but to read at a slow, reflective pace books that happen to be relevant to our situation so that the text can imprint its message on our heart.

5. Marking the Text

A final point about the discipline of spiritual reading regards marking the text. This condition applies mainly to those who are willing and able to invest in several basic and favorite texts as part of their personal library. If we do own a text for spiritual reading, marking it can be a helpful aid for two reasons. First of all, a mark in the margin, an underlining or circling, helps us to keep in mind what pops out spontaneously as meaningful. We find in the text something we have felt or thought ourselves; we are struck by the fact that it is said here so well. Since spiritual reading is aimed ultimately at our appropriating the text in a personal way, it may be good to mark this passage.

Marking makes the text more our own since its meaning ties in with our experience. Moreover, if we mark a particular text, we can go back to it in order to reflect upon its significance when—as will be discussed at length in the fourth guideline—we accompany our spiritual reading by the keeping of a spiritual reading notebook. It is also helpful to mark in the text those passages we feel a spontaneous resistance toward. Just as we may explore in our notebook what favorably impressed us, so too we can explore our resistances.

At this rate, it may take us a long time to read a spiritual book, but so what? It is better to stay with one or two texts that really speak to us, marking them and digesting them, than to pile up ten books that we "simply must read" and under pressure do so in speed fashion. Hearing the text, reading it, marking, learning, and inwardly digesting it—this is a good formula to follow, as the Book of Common Prayer recommends:

> Blessed Lord, who hast caused all holy Scriptures to be written for our learning: Grant that we may in such wise hear them, read, mark, learn, and inwardly digest them, that by patience and comfort of thy holy Word, we may embrace and ever hold fast the blessed hope of everlasting life, which thou has given us in our Savior Jesus Christ, Amen. (The Collect, the Second Sunday in Advent)

Fourth Guideline

Accompany spiritual reading by keeping a reflective reading notebook.

In the spiritual life such practices as spiritual reading, meditation, and contemplative prayer are above all works of love by which we manifest to God our dedication and fidelity. To these practices we may add another: that of the spiritual reading notebook. This notebook is by no means a record of noticeable results only. Success is not the norm that establishes the true value of religious practices. The person who for months is faithful to daily meditation in dryness ought not to say it is fruitless or that she is a failure just because she does not notice any salutary effect. What is apparently fruitless to her may be highly pleasing to God. If she has the right view of spiritual life, she remains faithful to daily meditation as a manifestation of her love. Though she may not derive from it emotional satisfaction, her meditation is all the more pure because it is a work of love. She is solely intent on pleasing God without demanding returns for her dedication and fidelity. Such inner purification of motive and desire prepares the way for a deepening intimacy through grace which is beyond our perception. In the light of faith, this person can be certain that God is at work in the depths of her soul, fostering at the same time divine glory and this person's good.

In a similar way, spiritual reading may seem to lack apparent success. "What," we may ask, "do I then do with my notebook?" First of all, remember that spiritual reading is fruitful also as a work of love and as a means of manifesting to God our dedication. We may not notice it on the feeling level, but we can be sure on the level of faith that God is at work to draw us closer to himself, despite the difficulties we may encounter. If we have done the best we could on our side to create the proper conditions, we can go on quietly with our reading, trusting that God will use this practice to lead us to deeper union—provided we do not give in to the temptation to stop reading just because what God asks of us is at times painful and demanding.

It is at this point that notebook keeping may be just what we need to spur us on. Spiritual reading necessarily becomes more effective if, at the end of every reading, we take a few minutes to ask ourselves what this reading meant to us today. On some days it will be easy to answer this question. Those are the days when what we read speaks to us with no dryness at all. We may not have read much, but what we did read stayed with us and we stayed with it. Now, in order to let the message penetrate even more deeply into us, to be inspired and encouraged by it, we may jot down in our notebook the text that evoked the response in us and write down a few reflections. Necessarily, we face the danger of being carried away by emotionalism or of getting lost in idealism, but this danger is mitigated through keeping a notebook of concrete reflections on the text. We try to see its message not as something up in the air but as linked with the concreteness of our everyday situation. How does it speak to where we really live and are?[7]

Spiritual living, as Thérèse of Lisieux so beautifully shows, does not mean doing only extraordinary things but living the common things of everyday as manifestations of God's will and as expressions of our fidelity. The message of the text as related to our personal life is better retained if we take the time to write it down. In writing and reflecting upon it, the meaning of the message becomes more clear as well as its place within the context of our daily life. At the same time, the fruit of our reading becomes available to us when later on we want to return to it to be refreshed and inspired anew. Written reflection thus becomes a further means of nurturing our spiritual life.

Despite faithful reading and notebook keeping, there may still come many days when all is without appeal. Reading, and after reading reflection, both seem tasteless. It is useful for us to write down this experience of distaste too, but rather than leaving it at that, it is wise to try to write out why we are feel-

---

[7]The reader might profit from knowing the difference between introspection and meditative reflection or transcendent self-presence as described by Adrian van Kaam in Chapter VII of his book, *In Search of Spiritual Identity*.

ing dry. Soon we may be well on the road to discovering what was wrong with our spiritual reading. Maybe we did not do it at the right time. Perhaps we failed to put our other tasks behind us so that during the reading period they preoccupied us and prevented us from being open to the text. Were we able to overcome the peculiarity of the author's style or did we allow it to block out communication of meaning? In this way we search for the cause of tastelessness within; we don't place the blame totally on the text.

Reflecting on the quality of our spiritual reading may prompt us to do better next time. There may be times, however, when nothing is wrong either within us or in the text and still everything seems dead. Such are the times of inner purification when reading is purely a work of love for God; as such it is of great value, though for us there is no consolation in it.

The value of keeping a spiritual reading notebook is not limited to the time immediately after spiritual reading. It may be good, say once a month, for us to read over the notes and reflections we have made. Reading our own notebook of spiritual reading not only provides new inspiration; it may also be a means to learn about ourselves. We may become aware, for example, that regularly when we speak about God we see him as the one who loves us. This recurrent life theme may indicate that in our personal relation with God intimacy is becoming a central experience to foster. Or we may see God time and again as the Good Shepherd, or as one who is always obedient to the Father's will. Through our notebook reflections and jottings, we may discover more about our unique spiritual identity and develop it further.

On the side of obstacles, we may become aware in reading our notes of a too self-assured and self-centered way of looking at persons and events. From then on, we could strive gently to overcome this fault. We must guard, however, against becoming too introspective, too harshly judgmental. In reading and writing these notes, we will become aware of our feelings and attitudes and in moderation this awareness can be helpful for spiritual growth, but we must always do so while placing ourselves serenely and humbly before God. In other words, when we look at ourselves, we must try not to do so within the narrow frame of our own plans and desires but in the light of God's love and concern for us. When we see ourselves in God's light and mercy, this loving look brings us closer to him in gratitude for all that he does to deepen our spiritual life. As soon as we notice ourselves losing this liberating perspective and becoming tense, we can place ourselves gently in God's presence, recalling that progress in spirituality comes about not by our own efforts but by the gift of grace. In this way writing and reading over our notes makes us more humble and helps us to cling closely to God.

In regard to faults illumined by the notebook, a few further cautions are necessary. Certain areas of spiritual life may require more attention. Here discretion is essential. Suppose that in reading over our notes and reflections we notice a certain arrogance in the way we formulate them. If this point recurs regularly, we can try to overcome it, at least to a degree. But what if we do not find such an obvious fault. One day we notice our laziness, the next our lack of charity. After that it is our envy, followed by our distractions in prayer. In other words, instead of one dominating deficiency, we discover in reviewing our notes a whole list of things that call for our attention and effort to improve. It would be a sign of indiscretion to try to tackle this list all at once. No one can cover all fronts at the same time. Hence, when we notice a variety of points that merit attention, we must make a prudent choice. It may be wise in such a situation to consult with someone versed in the ways of spiritual living. It is not always easy to judge our own situation. If such a person is not available—which is often the case—then we can pray for the guidance of the Holy Spirit and grow slowly to our own decision.

We thus see from the fourth guideline that reading the text in a slowed down way and then reflecting upon certain passages in a spiritual reading notebook are two interrelated practices. As a way of reviewing the value of notebook keeping and distinguishing it from other kinds of journals and diaries of a more intimate nature, we should consider briefly what the spiritual reading notebook *is not* and then what it *is*.[8]

1. Not Confessional

The spiritual reading notebook is not explicitly confessional but, as mentioned above, it may happen that in dialoguing with the text we become aware of certain failings. We may reflect on them, but our aim is not to write an intimate diary that details past sins or problems. Rather we let the text lead us to reflect on God's forgiveness and on the understanding that at times even the best intentions go awry. We try in the notebook to situate ourselves where we are at this moment, not to get imprisoned in the past.

2. Not for Publication

This is a facetious way of saying that when we keep a spiritual reading notebook, we do not have to "edit our copy." We may write what comes to us as it comes. It is mainly for ourselves that we are doing it. In a special case, like that of a novitiate, a novice directress may recommend the keeping of such a notebook by a novice, who agrees with her to use it as one basis for mutual interchange during periodic direction sessions. If the directress has a well planned reading program and has introduced along with it the practice of keeping a spiritual reading notebook, she can use these exercises to create an

---

[8]An example of this kind of notebook keeping can be found in Part Two of *Approaching the Sacred.*

atmosphere of sharing and trust between herself and the novices. The novitiate constitutes, of course, a special situation. Usually the practice is done in private for personal use only, not for current sharing or future posterity.

3. Not a Pious Collection

The notebook ought not to be merely a collection of "pious posies," a mere copying of lovely phrases that would look good on holy cards or posters. It is meant to be a reflective tool. If we find a pious phrase we do like, the idea is to stop there and try to get in touch with why it appealed to us. A related danger, especially for beginners, is that they start forcing their mind and imagination to produce pious thoughts and images on top of the ones that appealed to them. They proliferate piety and never come to personal reflection. Instead of listening to the Holy Spirit speaking to them through the word, they listen only to themselves thinking holy thoughts. Self-created piety takes the initiative whereas it should be God who gives us the inspiration we desire to follow.

4. Not a Record of Perfection

The keeping of a spiritual reading notebook is not meant to push us violently toward the perfection we may witness in the text we are reading. Often people say they are afraid to read certain books because they feel so far away from the spiritual goals set forth by the master. Behind this remark may be a kind of "if...then" mentality harmful to spiritual life. "If I were perfect, then I could read this book." Instead of accepting where we are now and deriving what we can from the text, we want to be all at once where God may be leading us after a number of years, if ever. The fact that we are in the valley of humility does not cut us off from the mountaintop of perfection. It is in the valley that we strive gently to remove the obstacles that prevent our climbing higher while gearing our quest for perfection to our unique pace and the grace we have received. If instead we read as if we have to be where the master is as quickly as possible, we may never have the courage to start. The way we approach a difficult work may so discourage us that we give it up altogether.

In other words, we may feel sure that we will never climb Mount Everest, but those who have can certainly give us advice that is valuable when we climb more modest precipices. By the same token, we may not be piano virtuosos, but those who are can undoubtedly help us to improve our playing. Similarly, we may never attain the state of mystical marriage granted to the likes of John of the Cross and Teresa of Avila, but they who have walked that path are reliable guides on our road to God. We are aware that we may never even remotely come near their depth of spirituality, but we know also that they can teach us the rights steps on the stage where we are.

We must, therefore, be wary of and try to avoid that spiritual arrogance by which we force ourselves in advance to where God wants us to go by slow and gradual steps. This forcing is a great obstacle to the spiritual life. People are afraid to read certain books because they are not where the writer of the text seems to have been; so they either force themselves beyond where they are or give up in dismay and close the text as setting an impossible goal. Linked to the forcing problem is the instant mentality that says in effect, "If I can't be a great mystic today, then by trying hard enough to be perfect, I'll be one tomorrow," as if perfection has to happen to us when and how we say it should.

The spiritual reading notebook, therefore, ought not to be a temptation to be ahead of ourselves. This is why, out of a whole spiritual text, we may take only a few thoughts and dialogue with them. In no way does this action represent a forced reaching for the heights of mystical life! Ours is a much more humble task.[9] We confine ourselves, for example, to such questions as how can we die daily to pride? If we can find an example of how, we may jot it in our notebook as a means of appropriating this part of the master's message. A few such examples, taken together, gradually form a pattern of daily detachment from self-centeredness, comprised of apparently insignificant actions. Showy holiness is not what counts for the spiritual life but those innumerable small events that comprise our day-to-day existence: no clanging cymbals and blasting trumpets but ordinary things made bright with love for God and neighbor. A steady record of these daily lights is more trustworthy than a forced search for so-called "spiritual highs."

To be where we are at the moment thus seems to be the "rule of thumb" for keeping a spiritual reading notebook. Spiritual life is not something static. We grow in it. We deepen our awareness of the spiritual realm and acquire new perspectives and needs. What appears to be a difficult book in the beginning of spiritual reading may turn out later to be a text that really inspires us. Or the same book read once may be read again and bring us a message and meaning we missed the first time because we were not ready for it. So, too, the spiritual reading notebook can show evidence of our spiritual growth. What else can it do? What else is it for?

5. A Record of Dialogue

If we have done spiritual reading faithfully and marked the text, there are available to us many lines, phrases, and words that have already spoken to us implicitly. Some we marked off because they spoke positively to us—we felt

[9]On the other hand, someone may be called by God undeservedly to experience mystical union and should not, out of fear or false humility, turn from these graces. One should consult a wise and experienced spiritual director, if possible, to prevent illusion or self-deception.

affirmed. Others we marked off because they addressed us negatively—we felt resistant. Now, in our spiritual reading notebook, we are going to try to make explicit what has implicitly appealed to us. We may not have thought why something appealed to us, but it did and so we spontaneously marked it off. Now, in service of growing as a deeper spiritual person, we want to make explicit our affirmations and our resistances. By exploring both responses, we learn more about where we are and who we are as spiritual persons.

The act of writing out this dialogue between us and the text makes reading more personal. Also, when we write out our thoughts, they gain in objectivity. They are now "out there" as a text in their own right and can be saved for later re-reading. The act of writing fixates in our notebook a thought that in the act of speaking or mere thinking would simply float away. The written word is, as it were, glued on the page; it sticks there and we can return to it. When we speak, our words drift off and we can't get them back. When we think, our thoughts float away and memory often cannot retrieve them. In writing we fixate them; we can go back to dwell further on them. Moreover, written words, that make fast our reflections, may draw out the multi-levels of meaning that are in the text. A text of any depth never has just one meaning; its richness cannot be fathomed on first reading but can emerge through re-reading and writing out the thoughts that come to us in reflective dialogue.

6. An Aid to Regular Reading

The reading notebook may prevent procrastination and encourage us to do spiritual reading on a regular basis. All of us are tempted to put off until tomorrow what we ought to do today. If notebook keeping becomes a familiar practice, it may remind us in turn that spiritual reading has to be done faithfully since it is a necessary support for our spiritual life.

7. A Mode of Self-Direction[10]

Lastly, the spiritual reading notebook can become a mode of self-direction. Periodic review of entries in our notebook, and the typical profile of likes and dislikes, strengths and weaknesses they reveal, helps us to gain insight into the direction God is leading us. Since regular spiritual direction on a one-to-one basis is neither always available nor needed, such practices as reflective reading and notebook keeping can serve as ways of discerning the direction of our life by the Divine. God guides us every step of the way by more and more clarifying what our life call is. According to Adrian van Kaam, each of us receives a specific call from God; from the beginning there is a particular

[10]For further insight into the meaning of this mode, see Adrian van Kaam's book *The Dynamics of Spiritual Self-Direction*. Of particular importance for understanding the Fifth Guideline is the section of this book on spiritual direction-in-common.

reason for our being in this world that is part of God's providential plan. We have to try to discover who God is calling us to be and how we can respond to this call in concrete circumstances, finding in the here and now what he is asking of us and not merely what it appears at first glance we can do.

Reflection on the text, while not guaranteeing clear answers, may help us discover directives for our spiritual life. As we grow in the sense of God's nearness at each turn, we may discover a firm thread of his providential care strung through seemingly unconnected events. God has been with us before, he is with us now, and he will be with us in all that is to come, if we but allow him personally to enter our hearts. The full unfolding of our life call cannot happen overnight. It is a lifelong endeavor, the steps of which we may find more surely by what is recorded in our reading notebook.

Fifth Guideline

Organize periods for shared spiritual reading.

This guideline is optional depending on the situation. Let's say a group of devout lay persons or a group of pastors decide to begin a reading program along the lines suggested in Part Two. In addition to doing all of the other things recommended thus far, the participants may decide that in the course of the reading program they want to set aside a period of time, convenient for all, in which they come together to share some reflections on the common texts they are reading. This get-together may last for forty-five minutes to an hour and can take place every three or four weeks. What this gathering presupposes, in order to be a fine exercise in spiritual sharing, is that the readers who comprise the group have already been reading the same texts and pursuing the same general theme. Then when they come together on a free basis, they gather not just to express their own opinions or ideas but to share some insights and reflections on the texts and themes that have begun to emerge in their reading. They want to do so in a devout way; they want also to encourage one another in the practice of spiritual reading and direction-in-common through a text.

In order for this guideline to work, the participants have to be reading in advance of the meeting the texts assigned for the reading program and dwelling upon the common theme and related subthemes. Secondly, one of the participants serves as group leader. The group leader begins the discussion by reading aloud a certain selected text that seems to have a lot of potential for discussion. Reading aloud aids the development of this practice because the group is immersing itself in the text and not in anyone's subjective ideas. It would seem commendable to follow this reading by a few minutes of silence so the participants can recollect their thoughts and try to orient them around the text that has been read aloud. Then the group leader can begin the discussion. If possible, in order for the discussion to proceed smoothly, the leader may distribute to the participants in advance of the meeting a spiritual reading direction sheet. This sheet is composed of four or five brief but interesting questions for discussion that have emerged out of the reading of the text and that give ample leeway for others' reflections. Such questions help to begin the discussion because sometimes people do not feel free to start talking. A question helps them to guide their thoughts and to formulate tentative answers that can be picked up and expanded upon by other members of the group. Frequent reference to the text being discussed is encouraged. Approximately eight people seems to be a good number for this kind of exercise, though it has been done effectively with as few as four and as many as sixteen.

As the participants grow familiar with one another and more trusting over the course of, say, a ten to twelve month period, they may begin to share on a limited basis some insights that at first seem personal but often turn out to be common problems of spiritual living. The members do not invade one another's privacy in any way; what they are looking at is not their personal lives but their common goal of growing in spirituality through imbibing the wisdom spiritual texts have to offer. Such shared reflection can inspire the members of the group and create an atmosphere of care and concern. A well delineated and faithfully followed spiritual reading program readies the participants for God's self-communication and places them in living contact with other pilgrims on the path to holiness.

II

Obstacles and Aids to Spiritual Reading

Not long ago I met one of my teachers—a philosophy professor from undergraduate days, a fine priest whose eighty plus years had not dimmed in the least his sharp wit and lively mind. At the time I met him he was working at a local seminary, translating some of the writings of the founder of his community. For a long time I had wanted to congratulate him on the translation he did of a book about the spiritual doctrine of St. Thérèse of Lisieux, a book I had found most helpful. Talking about her spirituality led me in a half serious, half playful moment to ask my former professor to share some of his wisdom regarding the spiritual life. Did he have any "secrets" he might be able to tell me? In characteristic fashion he took up the challenge and moved to illustrate his point. He held out to me his two hands. "On the left," he said, "you have the spiritual life and that is very simple: it means total abandonment in love and trust of my will to God. On the right, you have the obstacles to living such an inner life and these make the story most complex." Then he intertwined his fingers and added with a smile, "...and when you clasp your hands together like this you have the secret you are searching for: overcome the obstacles and abandon yourself to God."

"Overcome the obstacles and abandon myself to God." A simple formula but in the living how complex! The combination of our soul's yearning for the Divine and all that pulls us away from this goal is what makes the spiritual life such a challenge. How can we follow the path God is asking us to walk upon and not get sidetracked by a thousand detours? If only God's will were communicated in a "hot line from heaven" fashion, it would be so easy to follow. At least we would like to think so. But, alas, we have to struggle to uncover what God is asking of us in the here and now situation. God's will is not "out there" in some utopian community. It is appealing to us in the task we have to complete, in the person who sits across from us at the breakfast table, in the text we are reading quietly. We can be sure God is speaking to us through these events, persons, and things on a day-to-day basis.

One advantage of doing spiritual reading is that we can be confident that God's call is communicated to us through Holy Scripture and through the writings of spiritual masters. We find in such texts as St. Thérèse's autobiography the repeated counsel to listen to God's will in the simple revelations of daily reality. On our side, we need to remove obstacles that stand in the way of such listening and develop attitudes that aid our powers of appraisal. In what follows, we are going to explore a few common obstacles to encounter with the living word and some corresponding attitudes required to foster this encounter and therewith the art of spiritual reading. Undoubtedly, the removal of obstacles is a complex endeavor, but a first step to growing more simple involves recognition of them. If we don't know what is blocking us, we can hardly work to remove the obstacle. In this review of obstacles and aids we may meet "old friends," ideas we have considered implicitly in the previous chapter but which may resurface now with more force and prompt in us the awakening and transformation necessary for spiritual renewal.[1]

1. Timebound Elements vs. Timeless Truths

A first obstacle to overcome, especially in regard to the reading of classic texts in the literature of spirituality, is our inability as spiritual readers to distinguish between timebound elements and timeless truths. Consider, for example, the sometimes archaic imagery and symbolism used by spiritual writers of an earlier age. Take, as one illustration, St. Teresa of Avila's *Interior Castle*. She uses imagery from medieval times: the knight, the lady, the castle. The knight we learn is God; the soul is the maiden seeking him and being sought by him; the chambers of the castle represent the innermost recesses of the human heart where God wants to dwell everlastingly. The imagery of knight, lady, castle cannot be as meaningful to us as it was experientially to the people of St. Teresa's time who were used to seeing knights and ladies and castles. However, if we are put off by the imagery and cease our reading, we shall be unable to identify with the timeless truths being communicated through this imagery. Though St. Teresa's imagery is timebound, her message is timeless. Though the imagery used to convey this message may change under the pen of various authors from age to age, the message is changeless. And what is this message? It is the eternal seeking of the Bridegroom for the Bride, of Christ for the inner core of our soul—that inner core that longs for him because it belongs to him. Imagery, symbolism, points of style can and do change, but the message of surrender to God is timeless; spiritual language is timebound but not the attitude it implies. It is that attitude we must try to identify with when doing spiritual reading.

---

[1]See *Approaching the Sacred, Steps Along the Way,* and *The Journey Homeward* for further consideration of attitudes that hinder and help the spiritual reader.

A related danger concerns what I designate in *Approaching the Sacred* as the "compulsion to be current." This phrase signifies our craving for the new for its own sake with a consequent dislike for spiritual repetition. Spiritual writers regularly review certain fundamentals of the inner life as lived out in their own experience. They make no apology for this repetition but see it as a means of affirming such values as humility, patience, gentleness.

If such writing automatically "turns us off," perhaps it is because we are caught in the compulsion to value only what is "popular," "with it," "relevant for today," as if writings from the past lack any significance for the present and future. What might happen then is that we fall into the bad habit of labeling. We label the classic text, for example, as "old-fashioned," "archaic," "conservative," "traditional." Once we apply a label to something, it seems to fall under our control. We can then catalogue it and file it away. The text, thus reduced to our label, offers no meaning beyond it.

Notice how the same tactic works in human relationships. As soon as we apply a label to someone—for instance, Miss Holiness, the Superior Type, So Special—we can place these people carefully in our scheme and manipulate them accordingly. Our label means we no longer have to dialogue with them as unpredictable members of the human race. Something similar happens with the text. Say, because of this compulsion for the current, we label every classic text "conservative." Now that the label is applied we don't have to dialogue with the text. We don't have to consider the faults in us it may reveal. The answers are all in that well-organized file box of defenses and rationalizations. Such neat labels close us off from the latent meanings that may emerge when we read the "same old book" with the right attitude of discipleship. Under our caring look, the oldest of the old may suddenly become the newest of the new. It is as if we hear the message of the master anew. Freed from labels, with a caring look, we may be able to receive an old message and for the first time really make it our own.

2. Aesthetic Resistance vs. Personal Involvement

A second obstacle we have to deal with is that of aesthetic resistance. In considering spiritual notebook keeping, we saw that different kinds of resistances can emerge in our reading of the text and we pointed out our need to dialogue with them. For example, if the message of the master "turns us off," we need to find out why. Is it a language problem, as described above? Is it because the text just happens to come too close to the truth when we don't want our complacency to be disturbed?

There is another subtle resistance to be mentioned here, namely, the aesthetic. Far from being turned off by, say, medieval imagery and symbolism —perhaps because of a poetic or romantic tendency in our nature—we are entranced by this imagery. We feel poetically inspired. We revel in knights and ladies and castles. We enjoy a good trip back in time. The problem is that all the while we feel enraptured by the text, poetically, romantically, aesthetically on the level of emotion and feeling, we remain a spectator upon the text —appreciating it as we might a medieval painting but never becoming involved in its meaning for us. We remain in the stance of spectator and do not allow ourselves to get involved in the message the master is trying to communicate to us personally. We remain the interested connoisseur of this beautiful imagery and symbolism but deep down we are resisting, however subtly, applying that message to our lives. We are tempted to stay on the outside looking in; we never want to get down to the sober question of the challenge the text proposes to our spiritual life here and now. What is the quality of our surrender to God? Do we allow God's will to touch our heart? What in our lives might have to change if living for God becomes the first priority? Rather than face such questions, it is far easier to appreciate the text as a lovely historical artifact, as a delicate painting or a treasured relic. But, notice, it remains in the realm of "ancient interesting artifact." We have not allowed its message to touch us.

We have to watch out for this resistance, especially if we happen to be poetically inclined. If, for instance, we enjoy literature and language, we can be the victim of this obstacle before we know it. Unless we develop the corresponding attitude of personal appropriation, we may remain an impersonal spectator upon the text and never become personally involved in the message it is conveying.

3. Battle of the Wits vs. Respectful Abiding

This third obstacle is likely to affect especially the academicians among us. Persons with sharp, inquiring, polemic intellects do not always make the best spiritual readers. Difficulties arise when they carry over to the time of spiritual reading the same kinds of "academic games" that have to be played when pursuing degrees, conducting lively debates, preparing challenging classes. A few favorite "games" are these: one-upmanship (while someone is giving a rendition of her study and conclusions, we are already planning in our mind what to say that may top them slightly due to the studies we have made); name-dropping (while someone is reciting the list of authors he has read and quoted, we are forming our own list of whom we've read and he hasn't, but should); negative identity (we appear to be listening intently to another speaker, but we are only picking up what she is *not* saying so we can point out the missing pieces in her theory and thereby appear wise and bright ourselves). These "games" build up the informational intellect and may even be fun to play; there is nothing wrong with wearing my "debater hat." The trouble comes in when we carry this battle of wits into the arena of devotional practices like spiritual reading, a practice that calls not for witty repartee but respectful abiding.

Spiritual reading requires that we temper the tendency to go through spiritual books like a beaver in a lumber pile to get in all the religious erudition we can. Such voracious reading only serves to breed a shallow, quantitative approach to this practice. We may pile up academic credits, but have we done spiritual reading? We may round off our religious education, become spiritual reading connoisseurs, feel on a par with mystical scholars who can discuss in minute detail the stages of the dark night of the soul, but have we done spiritual reading? Have we respectfully abided with the text in that docile mode of discipleship—not out to teach the masters but humbly in need of being taught?

4. Non-Acceptance vs. Acceptance of Our Limited Self

This obstacle was touched upon when discussing the temptation to perfectionism in the context of the spiritual reading notebook. When we do formative reading, it is inevitable that we will experience moments of real discouragement in which we doubt if we are making any progress whatsoever. We may even feel at times that our spiritual life, in comparison to the witness given by the masters, has been a mockery and a waste. The key phrase here is "in comparison to" because it reveals that we have not grown in humble acceptance of the limited self that we are and the unique way that God is leading us. Instead we diminish this self by comparing it to that of another; we diminish this way by trying to follow what is right for someone else but forced when we try it. We may even desire God to raise us instantly to the status of saint instead of plodding slowly along the spiritual road at the pace God sets. Non-acceptance of the limited persons we are can, therefore, be a major obstacle to spiritual reading. Before even trying to dialogue with its essential truths as speaking to our unique pace of progress, we avoid the text for fear of discovering our failure and limitations.

Spiritual reading presupposes that we have grown in self-awareness and self-acceptance. We know that God's grace aims to fill each soul to its capacity; whether the soul is tiny as a thimble or large as a tumbler, we trust God to abide generously in each person. Growth in self-acceptance teaches us when reading a mystical text that we don't have to reach the mountaintop of perfection overnight. God may give us sudden, vivid tastes of what awaits us, but to try to snatch onto these graces before it is time would be an act of violence and pride, the exact opposite of accepting humbly where we are and trusting God to lead us where he wants us to go. We learn through spiritual reading that what God seeks in us is not constant proof of self-reliance but the holding out of empty hands—hands that symbolize our insufficiency, our vulnerability, our frailty. All of these weaknesses make for that inner void in which we are urged to turn to God in total dependency. Acceptance of limitations is thus at the same time what turns us to God with a plea for redemption.

A related example can be taken from the life of prayer. Often we experience the inability to pray because of too many distractions. As much as we try to return to meditation and let the buzzing mosquitoes buzz by, our minds keep following them. Perhaps at that moment, instead of forcing ourselves to meditate or feeling guilty because we cannot, it would be better to offer to God, so to speak, the "prayer of our distractions." This offering may be seen as a sign of accepting our limits, of realizing in this dry prayer, full of distractions, how dependent we are upon God. This attitude seems far better than that of applying to ourselves the whip of harsh criticism or the sting of envious comparison—both indications that we have not accepted our limits.

Encounter with the living word is thus blocked by our unwillingness to accept the frail, vulnerable, limited, imperfect beings we are. So often this obstacle is accompanied by a sense of discouragement. Then our failures in spiritual living loom up out of proportion. We feel too far away from our goal ever to make it. We dub ourselves failures before we even start. Such negative attitudes not only breed discouragement and despair; they violate the virtue of hope. They seem to imply that sin is greater than God's power to forgive. Such presumption is a close sister to pride—that prideful wanting to be where we are not yet, that impatient refusal to let God lead us there in his own good time.

5. Discouragement vs. Trust in God

Discouragement is itself another major obstacle to spiritual reading.[2] When we have no "aha" experiences, when we feel no consolation, we are tempted to give up. One remedy for avoiding discouragement might be remembering that in spiritual reading, in the life of the spirit, in our everyday experience, the following of God's will leads us to a time when, like it or not, the "honeymoon is over." The "honeymoon period" is usually short-lived in the spiritual life, not unlike that same period in married life.

Take the new bride. She revels in that first glorious week. Hair is perfect. Skin is perfumed. Nothing unaesthetic must mar her beauty. This first fervor is wonderful for both the bride and her beloved, but soon enough ordinary life sets in with its daily routines. Little irritating things come to the fore; each is aware that the romance has to be more than surface deep if the marriage is going to last.

Compare what happens in the beginning of such religious practices as

[2]See Francis de Sales, *Introduction to the Devout Life,* for an excellent analysis of this spiritual problem.

spiritual reading. There are those romantic honeymoon highs. The Divine Beloved may attract the person to himself by offering texts that give great consolation. The soul is encouraged to follow the spiritual path, but soon the harder work of transformation begins. There comes that routine time when nothing in reading seems to speak to us. We feel dried up. We want to get on with things but feel unable to move. We want to wrest some meaning from the text but nothing appeals to us. Everything seems to elude us; at times even God himself seems to disappear.

This can be an extremely painful time in the spiritual life but, seen from another perspective, truly blessed, for through it we may learn to trust wholly in God. Now we are no longer in control, no longer in the light, but waiting in the sidelines for God to take the initiative. The source of our security must now be God alone and not merely the gifts of consolation he sends. With the eyes of faith, we may be able to see that this experience of God's seeming absence may be, in regard to inner growth, the deepest gift of his presence. The spiritual masters even go so far as to say that it is only when we are completely without consolation that we may have our first real taste of God. Wherever God leads us, to desert or harvest, that is where we want to go.

If we are growing in the life of the spirit, as the spiritual masters testify, the Spirit may bring us to the point where neither the ebb of consolation nor the tide of desolation disturbs us any longer. When Christ starts to fill our life with his love, when he grants us the gift of his peace, what happens to us is only of secondary importance. Neither the aridity of the desert nor the fertile soil of the harvest makes that much difference to us spiritually. We see these experiences as relative in the light of the providential working of God in our lives. Rather than being discouraged when spiritual reading seems fruitless, we just keep on. Unlike the gourmet always craving for new food and tantalizing tastes, we are content to sit down and enjoy the lowly meal God places before us.

The seed has to go underground and be buried before the grain of wheat can spring forth. The cycle of dying and being reborn, of moving from discouragement to trust, is essential in the spiritual life. At the time of spiritual dying, we do encounter the darkness of discouragement, but it may be in that blessed darkness that we attain deep and lasting trust of God. Then we may be reborn to a new level of listening in which we experience God's allness and our nothingness. Through this dying to selfishness, we learn how to genuinely love.

III

A Concrete Example of Spiritual Reading

Once I made a three-day retreat at a Carmelite Center. The weekend was devoted to reading and reflecting upon some of the Carmelite masters, notably St. John of the Cross. Gathered together were a variety of lay people, married and non-married, religious, and members of the Third Order of Mount Carmel. One woman stands out in my mind.

Between conferences, we had quiet periods for walking, reading, and praying. There were also afternoon recreation hours where we could visit with the priests or with one another, if we chose to do so. Walking along, I met this woman whom I had seen the first day. We struck up a conversation and continued it while strolling together. I guess she felt trusting enough toward me to tell me something about her life. Perhaps our encounter was similar to those brief and occasionally intimate exchanges between two people sitting on a plane who dare to risk being more personal because, chances are, they will never see one another again.

I had asked her, as many of us did of one another, why she was here. Why had she come for this weekend of reflection? She went on to tell me that she had had the terribly painful experience of learning that her husband had been unfaithful to her. This crushed her completely, because she had seen herself as a model wife and mother, loving and generous. She did not have the slightest suspicion that this affair was occurring and it was shocking to her. Her first reaction was to turn completely against her husband. Then she began to look at herself for some reason why it had happened. She was torn between hatred and guilt. Her life was a mess. While she couldn't formulate it in these words then, she said, whatever a dark night was she felt she was in it. Nothing made sense anymore. All of her goals and hopes were dashed. She had to decide whether to go on with the marriage and, even more importantly, how to live together without making him feel pitied by her or unredeemably guilty for what he had done. The liaison had not continued and indeed was about to break off when she discovered it.

She felt as if she were in a dark tunnel. She couldn't see the beginning or the end. She tried to pray about it and by accident came in contact with a priest who was also a marriage counselor. He was a great help to her. One day as she was leaving his office, he mentioned to her that she might like to read *The Dark Night of the Soul* by St. John of the Cross. She was surprised that he would recommend such a lofty book to a simple person like herself but trusted his judgment and soon began reading a copy. This was her first contact with the mystical writer and, though she did not profess to understand in any great depth what St. John was saying, she was deeply touched. His image of the dark night spoke to her soul. For her it was a description of exactly what she had been going through. She could see that one of the roots of her suffering was the fact that her pride had been hurt. This led her to reflect on how much she valued the image she had created of the perfect wife and mother and what it meant to her when this image was shattered. St. John helped her to see that this perfect self-image was really an obstacle to God's love. In some way the suffering she had gone through was God's way of tempering her pride and bringing her closer to his redeeming love.

In the end she realized that all she could do was give everything over to God. For the first time in her life she didn't know what to do. She had to let God lead. She said it would be impossible to relate all that she had gone through, but that she would try to capture in a small example the transforming effect this nearness to God was exercising in her soul. Surrender to him was not a dramatic event, as she hoped I would see from this example.

"The way Christ is working in me," she said, "reminds me of what we heard in this morning's conference—about how he helps us to die to ourselves daily the more we give ourselves and all our cares over to him. Our children are raised now so both of us have a job. I pack the lunches in the morning. Recently I noticed what I was doing. On the counter were two brown bags, two apples, some chocolate chip cookies, lettuce, meat, and bread for the sandwiches. I looked at both ready-to-be-packed lunches and found myself quite spontaneously switching to my husband's bag the less wilted lettuce in the sandwich with more meat, the apple without the little worm hole, and the cookies with a richer amount of chips. Something inside made me do it—I never would have done it myself. Something—Someone made me put in my bag the sandwich with the soggier looking lettuce, the wormy apple, the cookies with fewer chips. I gave him the best lunch. There was something more loving than I, more generous and forgiving, at work in me that made me divide up those lunches in that way."

I was really struck by this example and told her so. It was so simple and yet so real an example of detachment. Not extraordinary, not grandiose, yet touching the very fiber of growth in spiritual living. This incident remains more real to me than many so-called mountaintop experiences. Even if genuine, they last only for a brief duration. What matters is how such experiences affect our daily lives. God seems to prefer the gentle breeze to the thunderclap. However we hear the Spirit's communication, what counts ultimately is its effect on our everyday lives. And if this effect is no more than giving a wormy apple to myself out of love for the other, then a great grace indeed has been granted to me.

1. Reading the Counsels of St. John

In this chapter I want to give a concrete example of how to read a difficult spiritual text that may on first reading appear somewhat cold and negative. I have found, however, that if we can get behind their apparent coldness and negativity and open ourselves as spiritual readers to the deep message they contain, St. John's *Counsels To A Religious On How To Reach Perfection* offer a valuable guide to spiritual living for all believers.

It seems to me that St. John is not speaking of reaching perfection as if it were my project or of trying to appear before God as an already completed self. He wants us to bring ourselves before God as we are with all our faults and failings and beg the Divine Beloved to lead us to a more perfect union of self with his indwelling spirit. What he proposes is an overall orientation of our lives toward the Father, rooted in the conviction that God hears us and dwells with us. The *Counsels* deal, therefore, with this overall turning of our lives Godward. They are directed especially to contemplative religious living in community, who desire to allow the Divine Beloved more and more to take over their lives, but their implications extend beyond this setting to encompass all true followers of Christ.

St. John wrote the *Counsels* for either a lay brother or a student for the priesthood sometime between 1585-87. He wrote them in a short time, probably under pressure, as the opening lines indicate, because he was occupied with business and travels as Vicar Provincial. It seems he wants to give the religious a short formula for learning the lifelong art of abiding always in God's presence, whatever the external circumstances may be. He wrote them also to ready the religious and, by implication, the Christian for the peaceful reception of God's word wherever it would lead the person. As St. John knew, where God's word leads us is along the way of the cross. The saint had no illusions on this point; he knew that if we want Christ as the center of our lives, we have to go through the narrow gate. We have to follow the way of the cross. We are not to spend our lives trying to justify to God our failures; what counts most for God is not the success we enjoy but the fact that we keep on trying no matter how often we fail. To live these counsels in inner peace is to accept that we are going to make mistakes over and over again on our spiritual journey. We may go off the track, but such counsels call us back to what matters ultimately when all this world has to offer passes away and only Christ's words remain.

The *Counsels* are not something we can expect to accomplish instantly. They present us with an ongoing task and challenge. The goal of the *Counsels* is not, therefore, the perfection of a perfectly self-sufficient personality but the sometimes clumsy, fault-ridden striving of a struggling self desiring to live in more perfect harmony with the Holy Trinity. We realize that on this earth we will never arrive at perfect union; we are always on the way. The perfection we strive toward in this world will always be imperfect or, in other words, only as perfect as our human condition and God's grace allows. In the life to come we will be confirmed in perfection according to our capacity when God brings to fulfillment and glory our earthly effort.

2. Introduction to the Counsels[1]

> 1. Your holy Charity with few words asked me for a great deal. An answer would require much time and paper. Seeing, then, that I lack both of these, I will try to be concise and jot down only certain points and counsels which in sum will contain much, so that whoever observes them perfectly will attain a high degree of perfection.
>
> He who wishes to be a true religious and fulfill the promises which by his state he has professed, advance in virtue, and enjoy the consolations and the delight of the Holy Spirit, will be unable to do so if he does not try to practice with the greatest diligence the four following counsels concerning resignation, mortification, the practice of virtue, and bodily and spiritual solitude.

In this opening passage, St. John gives four words—resignation, mortification, virtue, solitude—that invite us to reflection. These words, and the counsels surrounding them, imply a divine horizon against which we have to reflect on our unique situation. They are invitations to reflection on fundamental spiritual attitudes and challenges to put these attitudes into practice.

St. John says that these counsels aim first of all at helping the religious fulfill the promises which by his state he has professed. What are these promises? Poverty of spirit, that he may be empty of mere egoism and ready to seek God as his sole desire. Chaste love, that he may express a gentle, compassionate concern for his fellow religious and the people entrusted to his care. Obedience, that he may try with all of his capacities to listen to the immediacy of his situation and in and through that listening to perceive the transcendent source from which all particulars emerge.[2] Secondly, he says these counsels will help the religious advance in virtue, that is, in the practice of following Christ by fulfilling the Father's will. St. John further claims that practicing these counsels will help the religious to enjoy already on this earth

[1]All quotations of this text are from *The Collected Works of St. John of the Cross*.

[2]See Adrian van Kaam, *The Vowed Life*, in which the author describes in detail the "threefold path" of obedience, chaste love, and poverty of spirit.

the consolation and delight of the Holy Spirit, this being none other than the peace of heart oneness with Christ alone can give.

Though the *Counsels* are directed to contemplative religious, we can see, as we enter deeply into these attitudes, that they do apply to all Christians. St. John describes the concrete living out of these attitudes in terms of the vowed religious state, even more specifically for the contemplative priest, brother, or sister in a cloistered community, but they can be read and appreciated by participative religious as well as Christian lay people because they point to basic truths of spiritual deepening. As such, the Counsels are timeless in their validity. People of that time and today have found them invaluable for fostering spiritual life and bringing a wisdom and balance to communal living.

3. Resignation

> 2. In order to practice the first counsel, concerning resignation, you should live in the monastery as though no one else were in it. And thus you should never, by word or by thought, meddle in things that happen in the community, nor with individuals in it, desiring not to notice their good or bad qualities or their conduct. And in order to preserve your tranquillity of soul, even if the whole world crumbles, you should not desire to advert to this or interfere, remembering Lot's wife who was changed into hard stone because she turned her head to look at those who in the midst of much clamor and noise were perishing. [Gn. 19:26]
>
> You should practice this with great fortitude, for you will thereby free yourself from many sins and imperfections and guard the tranquillity and quietude of your soul with much profit before God and man.
>
> Ponder this often, because it is so important that many religious for not observing it not only failed to improve their other works of virtue and religious observance, but ever slipped back from bad to worse.

In this counsel, St. John points to the problem of human curiosity. All of us like to know what is going on, what others are doing, where they are going—not necessarily to meddle in their lives but just to know. He is against such curiosity because it brings the contemplative out of himself and thus breaks into his being with God. Once this curiosity is at work it can, as St. John indicates, lead to many sins and imperfections. In the secluded atmosphere of a contemplative monastery, religious can begin to focus more on their mutual attraction and aversion than on Christ. Gossip could spread like flies in an open air restaurant. In this situation, priests, brothers, or sisters could get overly involved in one another's business, meddling all the time, curious to know what is going on and why. Such scrutiny of one another could become a kind of local community sport.

For this reason, St. John cautions the religious to stay within himself, even if the whole world would crumble. This is what he means by the word resignation: we are dying to know what is going on, we are consumed with curiosity, yet we resign ourselves to not knowing. Our feverish imagination will propose a thousand reasons why we should know, but against this onslaught, we resign ourselves to not knowing. As long as we do not tackle this deeply rooted fault of undue meddling, other faults related to it will rise whenever we live in proximity to one another.

In family, dormitory, or community, problems of envy and jealousy will come up. All of us are tempted to meddle in the business of other people. We are prone to form little power groups and gossipy cliques, often in the name of friendship and encounter. We steal the other's right to privacy by our gossip; we can destroy the other's reputation by subtle innuendo. Even worse than this, we can mask our violence as love. We aim to put the other in his place "out of love," we say, "for the family, the school, the organization, the community."[3]

The practice of resignation, of not craving to know, is modulated by each person's situation. In some cases, for example, a person has to know—not to satisfy his curiosity but because of his profession (policeman), the practice of charity (social worker), and so on. St. John is not speaking here about paying legitimate attention to our business but about unwarranted curiosity, not tempered by spiritual resignation. All of us have experienced the nefarious consequences that may follow. We may be besieged by the buzzing flies of envy, jealousy, resentment, imprisoned by manipulative or seductive friendships, distracted by the prying and scrutiny that characterize so many relationships. The more we are busy about the business of others—seeing the sliver in their eyes and missing the plank in our own—the more likely we are to backslide from bad to worse, at peace neither with ourselves, nor others, nor God.

If we do not temper our curiosity, then our actions will be affected. We cannot possibly be as efficient nor as flexibly responsive to the real needs of the situation if we are living in inner tension, agitation, turmoil, or nervousness. We need, with God's grace, to find resignation of soul out of which we can radiate the love, joy, gentleness, peace, patience, and kindness that are the fruits of Christian living. If we are able, through grace and our own efforts, to find that inner core of peace, then life goes on in a more gracious manner. The same duties are done. The same efficient operation is accomplished, but there is a pervading atmosphere of gracious living among persons who are practicing charity and compassion toward one another rather than being

[3]For further clarification of the dynamics of envy, see Adrian van Kaam's, *Living Creatively.*

caught in sickly curiosity—in the restless atmosphere of in-groups fighting out-groups, of invasion of privacy, of meddling, envious comparison, back-biting, and other signs of turmoil found so often in family, professional, and communal life.

If we practice this inner discipline of overcoming curiosity, especially during trying circumstances, we may free ourselves from many imperfections and guard the tranquillity of our soul. The spiritual resignation of not knowing does not mean a forced retreat from facts; it is more a gentle catching of ourselves interiorly when we begin to feel caught in unnecessary worry, destructive gossip, and undue meddling or when we become so overly involved in this or that plan or project due to curiosity that we forget the primary relationship between ourselves and God. If we can grow gradually in the attitude of returning to him, humbly and quietly, then we can soon re-establish inner tranquillity. Out of that still center of spiritual resignation will flow our doing of the daily task in gentleness and peace without the interference of consuming curiosity. This balance of inner quietude and outer efficiency makes for more gracious living. Everyone feels happier in such a resigned and respecting atmosphere.

4. Mortification

> 3. To practice the second counsel, which concerns mortification and profit by it, you should engrave this truth upon your heart. And it is that you have not come to the monastery for any other reason than to be worked and tried in virtue, that you are like the stone which must be chiseled and fashioned before being used in the building.
>
> Thus you should understand that those who are in the monastery are craftsmen placed there by God to mortify you by working and chiseling at you. Some will chisel with words, telling you what you would rather not hear; others by deed, doing against you what you would rather not endure; others by their temperament, being in their person and in their actions a bother and annoyance to you; and others by their thoughts, neither esteeming nor feeling love for you.
>
> You ought to suffer these mortifications and annoyances with inner patience, being silent for love of God and understanding that you did not enter the religious life for any other reason than that others work you in this way, and that you become worthy of heaven. If this was not your reason for entering the religious state, you should not have done so, but should have remained in the world to seek your comfort, honor, reputation, and ease.

The contemplative religious comes to the monastery with the sole motivation to live out the call he feels to give himself in total fidelity to God. If he is in the cloister for any other reason, such as to receive praise, power, status, then, St. John says, it would have been better for him to stay in the world. The people in the monastery are part of God's plan for him, to mold and fashion him in such a way that he lives mainly for God.

It is easy to apply this counsel exclusively to contemplatives. And yet, does it not have universal implications for all Christians? All of us know from experience that human relations do chisel us; they fashion, mold, and grind us. We have no choice about where we are born or who our parents are going to be. We find ourselves surrounded by all kinds of people who seem to specialize in molding us from youth to old age. Parents, teachers, peers—all of them fashion us. So too are we formed by the community we inhabit. A grumpy morning face, a snide remark the other thinks we did not hear, a promise unkept—all of these experiences influence our possibilities for personal and spiritual growth. Christ uses others in our lives to help us find our true selves in him. Especially each failure in human relationships helps us to recognize anew our dependence on him. He allows the words of others to tell us what we hate to hear; the deeds of others to try our patience; the temperament of others to test our endurance; the admonitions of others to humble our arrogance and teach us that we are not perfect yet. Through these common interactions among people, Christ makes us more aware that he alone can offer full friendship and trust.

Through such actions and annoyances, we may die daily to our self-centeredness and center more in Christ. Such dying is what spiritual mortification means. Through the fashioning, molding, chiseling powers of others, whom God lets us encounter for his purposes, we become more the self he wants us to be. It is a necessary part of spiritual growth to be refined in the fire so that we can become the unique spiritual selves Christ lovingly wants to draw out. Spiritual mortification is a means of turning more and more to Christ, our first love and source of fulfillment.

Daily dying to self-centeredness diminishes unrealistic expectations of what our family or community should be or do for us. No human family or community in and by itself can ever fulfill us totally. No matter what we do to build community or create it, it can never be perfect. Human beings in all their unpredictability will always be there to chisel us with bad tempers, interpersonal conflicts, petty tensions. This is the human community St. John is talking about—a community of sinners not saints. The only solution in this situation, he says, is to suffer these annoyances with inner patience and to be silent for the love of God.

Inner patience implies an attitude of tolerance toward the faults of others because we know so well our own. It means not jumping too quickly to our own defense when something displeases us but bearing the wrong patiently for the sake of keeping the peace. If the issue is of major import, then something can be done about it in a calm and reasonable way when the time comes. But petty difficulties that rise inevitably when people live in proximity to one another can in many cases be best endured in inner, uncomplaining patience. This patient, gripe-free presence is aided by our free choice to be silent for the love of God, doing our part to preserve the peace. This silence implies not counter-attacking the foe at the first sign of opposition; it means not talking the annoyance over with anyone who will lend an ear but quietly letting small grievances pass by.

Such practices as inner patience and silence for God's sake are only possible when we center our attention not on the other and our relation to him but on Christ. Loving our Lord above all else allows other community relations to fall into place; this love tempers as well any utopian ideal we may have about the perfect community. It lets us affirm with St. John that others will work us in this way that we may become worthy of heaven.

Growth in inner patience is thus part of the dying process. We try to be patient when others annoy us, turning to Christ in the center of our heart instead of flying off the handle. Lacking patience, we refuse to suffer mortifications and annoyances in silence for the love of God. Instead we push to get our point across. We forget that God places us in this situation as part of his plan for our spiritual emergence. We can afford to be patient and trust God to take care of things.

St. John outlines some further fruits of this process of dying to self.

> 4. This second counsel is wholly necessary for a religious, that he fulfill the obligations of his state and find genuine humility, inward quietude, and joy in the Holy Spirit. If you do not practice this, you will neither know how to be a religious nor even why you came to the religious life. Neither will you know how to seek Christ (but only yourself), nor find peace of soul, nor avoid sinning and often feeling troubled.
>
> Trials will never be lacking in religious life, nor does God want them to be. Since he brings souls there to be proved and purified, like gold, with the hammer and the fire, it is fitting that they encounter trials and temptations from men and from devils, and the fire of anguish and affliction.
>
> The religious must undergo these trials, and he should endeavor to bear them patiently and in conformity to God's will, and not so sustain them that instead of being approved by God in his affliction he be reproved for not carrying the cross of Christ in patience.
>
> Since many religious do not understand that they have entered religious life to carry Christ's cross, they do not get along well with others. At the time of reckoning they will find themselves greatly confused and frustrated.

Humility, inward quietude, and joy in the Holy Spirit are the fruits of spiritual mortification; but to foster their emergence, we need to grow in the conviction that trials, anguish, affliction, and suffering are not deliberately mean or arbitrary tests God sends but truly signs of his love. God has always tried in the fire the ones he loves most so that their faith will be strong enough to inspire others. All Christians, in whatever way Christ decrees, have to carry the cross. To do so with patience, in conformity with what Christ is asking of us, is to grow more and more like him in humility, in peaceful acceptance of the Father's will, in the joy of the Holy Spirit. If in daily life, according to our state, we refuse the cross, we can expect that there will come a time of reckoning. How shall we find ourselves then? As good and faithful servants, as shepherds of Christ's word, as true followers in his flock or as "greatly confused and frustrated"? It is good to keep in mind that time of reckoning—not to frighten ourselves, as if God were an unmerciful judge but as a way of reflecting frequently on the faith we have been given and the demands it makes upon us.

5. Practice of Virtue

> 5. To practice the third counsel, which concerns the practice of virtue, you should be constant in your religious observance and in obedience, without any concern for the world, but only for God. In order to achieve this and avoid being deceived, you should never set your eyes upon the satisfaction or dissatisfaction of the work at hand as a motive for doing it or failing to do it, but upon doing it for God. Thus you must undertake all things, agreeable or disagreeable, for the sole purpose of pleasing God through them.
>
> 6. To do this with fortitude and constancy and acquire the virtues quickly, you should have care always to be inclined more to the difficult than to the easy, to what is rugged rather than to what is soft, to what is hard and distasteful in a work rather than to its delightful and pleasant aspects, and do not go about choosing what is less a cross, for that is a light burden, and the heavier a burden is, the lighter it becomes when borne for Christ.
>
> You should try, too, by taking the lowest place always, that in things bringing comfort your brothers in religion be preferred to you. This you should do wholeheartedly, for it is the way to becoming greater in spiritual things, as God tells us in his Gospel: *Qui se humiliaverit exaltabitur.* [Mt. 32:12]

The contemplative expects upon entering the community to forsake the concerns of ordinary life in the world and to take up a new life inside the monastery, oriented around the sole purpose of pleasing God through prayer and labor. If the religious is scrubbing the floor or singing in choir, answering the door or milking a cow, he can do it for the love of God whether it gives him personal satisfaction or not. We tend to apply this counsel to contemplatives only, but we can apply it also to ourselves.

The practice of virtue means dedicating ourselves to and strengthening our capacity for performing good deeds with ease. To do so we have to be constant in our religious observance and obedient to God's will in each situation. One way to practice virtue—a way Christ taught by word and deed—is to try to take the lowest place so as not to be preferred in things that bring comfort, honor, and ease. We facilitate this practice by doing what we do for God and not looking at the satisfaction we may attain (and doing it for that alone) or the dissatisfaction that is bound to come (and omitting it for that reason only). In order to promote this doing of what we do for God and not looking at the satisfaction or dissatisfaction we derive, we should be more inclined to do the difficult rather than the easy, the rugged rather than the soft, the distasteful rather than the delightful.

The third counsel directs us again to choose the goal of pleasing God and, for his sake, bearing joyfully the burdens he sends with fortitude and constancy. Growth in virtue implies becoming detached interiorly from such goals as satisfaction or dissatisfaction as our main motives. If these experiences come, they come, but we do not make them the main motive for what we do or omit to do. As we grow in the attitude of detaching ourselves from these feelings of lack or gain, we begin attaching ourselves more firmly to the attitude of doing what we do, pleasant or unpleasant, delightful or distasteful, solely for the love of God.

St. John says, "You should try, too, by taking the lowest place always, that, in things bringing comfort, your brothers...be preferred to you." How can we reconcile this counsel with the legitimate striving of persons in the world for promotion and bettering their position? How can we combine this passage with the aspiration and striving to get ahead in our field, to gain needed status and prestige? The word to emphasize in answering these questions is "legitimate." It is legitimate to better ourselves when we do so to provide for a family, to become a more dedicated contributor to the good of society, to find a more appropriate way to practice or expand our talents. Getting ahead is not legitimate when we want to reach the top even if it means injustice to others, or if we do our task only for the glory gained thereby, in short, if we are guided by pride instead of by the right motives mentioned above. These motives are rooted in humility, which is above all an inner attitude of not considering ourselves as more meritorious in God's eyes than we are. It is not our position that makes us proud or humble but the attitude we take in that position. In this humble attitude, we do not count the value of what we do by the measure of satisfaction we derive from it.

Hence, to take the lowest place always, that is, to be humble and to prefer others over ourselves, does not exclude striving after promotion that is legitimate and motivated by higher ideals. When something is offered that brings comfort to others, we are advised there, too, to take the lowest place so that others and not we ourselves receive this good. We don't begrudge them that honor. We are willing always to take the lowest place and to allow others to be preferred in our stead. Though such generosity is at odds with the gathering of worldly goods and personal gain as goals in themselves, it does pave the way for our becoming greater in spiritual things.

Christian spiritual life, therefore, with its emphasis on an incarnational spirituality, does not exclude the possibility that what we do gives us a great deal of pleasure and fulfillment; it only excludes making that motive count ultimately. Otherwise, to give only one example, persons might choose to care only for those rich in material goods and neglect those who are poor or the marginalized of humanity. Christian care extends to both classes. Once our motivation is rooted solely in our love for Christ, we are liberated interiorly to do whatever he asks of us without the provision of having to be praised for it or having to derive personal pleasure from it. If praise and pleasure come, we can thank God, but we do not make these rewards a condition for doing what we have to do.

When St. John writes that we are to follow the difficult rather than the easy road, he is writing to those who have chosen, whatever their state of life, to follow more closely after Christ, for he himself took the way that was rugged rather than soft, distasteful rather than delightful. However heavy the burden Christ asks us to bear, it becomes light when borne for him. If we follow Christ in what he taught and lived, we shall find sufficient crosses in daily life. By carrying them joyfully, by doing our task wholeheartedly, without the care for personal gain as ultimate, we become greater in spiritual things and, through God's grace, servants worthy of being named friends of the Lord.

6. Solitude

> 7. To practice the fourth counsel, which concerns solitude, you should deem everything in the world as finished. Thus, when (for not being able to avoid it) you have to deal with some matter, do so in as detached a way as you would if it did not exist.
>
> 8. Pay no heed to the things out in the world, for God has already withdrawn and released you from them. Do not handle any business yourself that you can do through a third person. It is very fitting for you to desire to see no one and that no one see you.
>
> And note carefully that if God will ask a strict account from all the

> faithful of every idle word, how much more will he ask it of the religious who has consecrated his entire life and all his works to him. And God will demand all of this on the day of reckoning.

The fourth counsel is a further development of the first one. There we were told not to be curious, not to get involved in what does not pertain to us. But, no matter how secluded one is, there are things in which one has to get involved either inside or outside the convent or monastery. How do we do so in a way that fosters rather than harms spiritual living? The key phrase here seems to be "do so in as detached a way as you would if it [the matter] did not exist." This phrase seems to be a warning, valid for all, against getting absorbed totally in our work to the exclusion of God, against allowing worldly cares to penetrate into the center of our lives where God alone should reign. To live and work in the world as if it did not exist does not mean ceasing to act but keeping out of the grip of over-involvement. In the world, we cannot avoid seeing people, but do we not often pursue others to avoid facing God? Are we not prone to increase our social involvements to the detriment of our spiritual life? Do we not use too many idle, damaging, uncharitable words, our tongue being like that small flame that sets fire to a huge forest? [Jm. 3:5-6]

We are not to confuse getting taken in totally—or not getting hooked on the world—with doing a sloppy job. St. John warns also against that possibility. Do well what you have to do but when it is finished, treat what you did as if it does not exist. How do we preserve such detachment? One condition, he suggests, is solitude.

While outer solitude is not built into the lives of us who live in the world—in the same fashion as contemplatives enjoy it—we can strive to preserve inner and, at least occasional, outer solitude, especially in regard to our business dealings with other people. The more mindful we become that God is appealing to us in persons, events, and things to heed his call, the more "second nature" becomes our habit of stepping aside from the work-a-day world and its pressures to find some place and time to be alone with God. Even without outer solitude, we can try wherever we are—in a busy bus depot or in the midst of a public meeting—to quiet ourselves inwardly so that we can listen to God's voice. Solitude means having a center within ourselves so that wherever we go we can be at one with the Lord.[4]

This attitude can also aid our dealings on a business level. In solitude, standing before God, we can deeply appreciate this world and the goodness of creation while at the same time acknowledging that for ourselves all is passing. By releasing our frantic hold on this world's goods, we can use them more

---

[4]See my book, *Celebrating the Single Life: A Spirituality for Single Persons in Today's World.*

wisely. Taking into account this larger view, we are not likely to base our business dealings solely on the criterion of what we can get out of them. Moreover, in order to conduct our business more objectively, it is wise not to get caught emotionally and thus risk losing that inner peace and contentedness so conducive to solitude. Such an approach may also have the side benefit of preventing impulsive or unwise decisions. If we can act in our business dealings in a way that tempers grasping, aggressive attitudes—as if we were standing back and viewing the decision to be made from a third-person perspective—we are more likely to discover the best course of action and also to take into account what Christ might do were he here.

What leads to solitude and provides some of the benefits described in the fourth counsel is prayer. Prayer does not mean we are to neglect our work; rather it gives us a ground of meaning out of which emerges the truest sense of what we are called to do.

> 9. I do not mean here that you fail to fulfill the duties of your state with all necessary and possible care, and any others that obedience commands, but that you execute your tasks in such a way that no fault is committed, for neither God nor obedience wants you to commit a fault.
>
> You should consequently strive to be incessant in prayer, and in the midst of your corporal practices do not abandon it. Whether you eat, or drink, or speak, or converse with lay people, or do anything else, you should always do so with the desire for God and with your heart fixed on him. This is very necessary for inner solitude, which demands that the soul dismiss any thought that is not directed to God. And in forgetfulness of all things that are and happen in this short and miserable life, do not desire to know anything in any way except how better to serve God and keep the observance of your institute.

Incessant or unceasing prayer does not mean mumbling prayers from dawn to dusk. It means the desire for God; it means having our heart fixed on Christ so that we do not become fixated on the things of this world as ends in themselves, thereby forgetting our journey's true end. Prayer in this sense is as necessary to the soul as breathing is to the body; it is the ceaseless lifting of our heart and mind always and everywhere to the Divine Master, who so gloriously manifests himself in all of creation. When we begin to live a life of prayer, we can better execute our tasks in such a way that no deliberate fault is committed. So in tune with God's will are we through prayer, that we respond to every situation in a way that gives glory to him. Whatever we do, our desire is for Christ and our heart is fixed on him. We loosen our grasp on this short and passing life and cling instead to the steady truth of his word in prayer and service.

7. Conclusion

St. John concludes the *Counsels* with this short sentence:

> 10. If Your Charity observes these four counsels with care, you will reach perfection in a very short time. These counsels are so interdependent that if you are lacking in one of them, you will begin to lose the profit and gain you have from practicing the others.

These four counsels are thus intertwined. If we overcome sickly curiosity by resigning ourselves not to know, we can be more objective in our dealings with others and less the victim of swiftly changing likes and dislikes or clouds of unreliable gossip. Learning to die daily to self-centeredness, we develop good habits of Christian living like taking the lowest place, being patient, and letting God alone determine our degree of exaltation. Living in inner solitude fosters prayer and prayer helps us to forget ourselves. In short, losing in one of these attitudes, we lose in the others; gaining in one we gain in the others.

We, on our own, would not be able to follow this rigorous road. What motivates and guides us is our love for God, the longing of our soul for him. Love alone is strong enough to motivate us, over a lifetime of trying, to empty ourselves of all those obstacles that block the fullness of God's presence. This love, together with the attitudes of resignation, mortification, practice of virtue, and bodily and spiritual solitude, gives us a sound plan for spiritual living. With God's grace guiding us, we can grow daily toward the gifts of genuine humility, inward quietude, and joy in the Holy Spirit. These precious gifts may then radiate through us and overflow the chalice of our heart into the hearts of all with whom we come in contact this day, and all the days of our life.

PART TWO

READING PROGRAMS

General Introduction

Part Two contains three reading programs, focusing on themes pertinent to spiritual living. These programs are adaptable to the needs of individual readers, but they can also be used for a group as part of a parish-organized reading plan, of a retreat, or of a program of formation.* This section is intended to serve persons who want to follow a workable program of spiritual reading over a period of time and in accordance with their needs, interests, and situations.

The duration of the readings is thus dependent on the persons doing this program and on the purposes they envision for it. No time limit is put on the reading programs, indicating that the reader may spend as much time with them as he or she deems necessary. A reading program may be finished once and gone back over again and still provide much nourishment. Especially biblical passages, rich in content and depth of meaning, can be read again and again in dialogue with various themes.

In these reading programs, selections from Holy Scripture are taken from the Reader's Edition of *The Jerusalem Bible*, a highly praised source that is within range of most budgets. Sources from the literature of spirituality have also been chosen from available texts, when possible in paperback editions, so as not to drain the reader's pocketbook. In all cases books are used rather than articles as books are for the most part easier to acquire and keep than periodical literature. If a recommended book has by chance gone out of print since this selection was made, the reader can choose a replacement from the *Sample Bibliography* or another appropriate source. From all that has been said, it may be clear that some initial expense is involved. Though the texts in the reading program have been kept to a minimum, some investment will still have to be made. My hope is that the serious reader, who desires to build up a personal library of spiritual literature, will allow these reading programs to serve as a good incentive for doing just that.

*These programs are meant for those already somewhat familiar with the practice of spiritual reading. Readers who do not yet have this experience are advised to review the guidelines in Part One of this book and to try out some of the principles found there before attempting an expanded reading program.

Reading selections have been made mainly with western Christians in mind. This choice in no way is meant to diminish the importance of the spiritual literature of the Far East nor the reader's appreciation for the literature of other spiritual traditions, such as that of the American Indian. Readers will realize that limits have to be set somewhere; these programs are thus directed in general toward a Christian audience in the West. Occasional references that fall outside this limit, such as those to orthodox spirituality, to Zen Buddhism, to the Hindu tradition, may be taken as clues to just how vast the field of spiritual literature really is.

We can now review a few introductory directives to be taken into account prior to the reader's beginning one or the other of these reading programs.

To choose the theme that appeals most to one or to one's group, it may be necessary for the reader to look in a cursory way at all of the suggested programs in Part Two. Based on each reader's needs, interests, and situation, he or she can then choose the one most suitable as a starting point.

It is advisable during the reading program that one read and keep a reading notebook following the guidelines given in Part One.

Remember that Holy Scripture is the first source of spiritual reading, though scripture reading may be mingled with readings from other sources once a regular reading and writing schedule is established.

Keep in mind that spiritual reading is slowed down and reflective, inspirational and not informational, qualitative not quantitative.

If readers are totally unfamiliar with a recommended text, outside of spiritual reading time, they may want to read that book through quickly to gain context so they can better understand where the excerpts are coming from. It seems best to do this background (and/or informational) reading outside of slowed down spiritual reading time.

The same advice applies to reading the Bible. If readers have never read the Bible through as a whole, they might plan to do so in conjunction with their reading program, doing such reading also outside of slowed down reading time.

On the basis of these formative programs, readers can develop additional ones in dialogue with their personal needs, using as a start the resources found in the *Sample Bibliography* and in the reading programs presented here.

I

Living the Desert Experience[1]

INTRODUCTION

The desert is first of all a physical place, usually associated with hot sun, dry sand and dust, sparse vegetation. From earliest times, within and outside of Christianity, it has been a place to which people retreated when they sought intense solitude, silence, and closeness to God. Secondly, desert is another word for place of spiritual retreat. This place can be the geographical desert, but it can also be a retreat center, a hermit's dwelling, or a house of prayer. Thirdly, and most importantly for our purposes, desert refers to an inner experience of detachment and letting go. In the desert of the heart one learns the true meaning of life. Man is a creature sustained by the breath of the Spirit—a fragile, limited being yet one infinitely precious in the eyes of God.

While few of us may have the occasion to go to a house of prayer, while fewer still may ever feel inclined or have the opportunity to go to a real desert like the Sahara, all of us in some way must occupy the desert of the heart if we want to become truly spiritual selves.

The desert theme appears throughout the Old and New Testaments, whether we recall the experience of the Israelites moving toward the promised

---

[1]This reading program was devised in accordance with principles given in spiritual reading courses to future formation personnel offered at the Institute of Formative Spirituality, under supervision of the author. A tentative version of this program, extensively modified and revised here, was done by Sr. Janice Fulmer, C.S.F.N .

Following this introduction to the overall theme is a brief listing of minor themes. After that comes the reading list of texts recommended for this program, according to their appropriate category: essential, secondary, edifying, recreative. Several small sections follow, introducing the reader to the minor themes that extend from the main branch. Around these minor themes are gathered suggested readings from Holy Scripture and from various sources in the literature of spirituality, including some supplementary readings. However, the reader should guard against a mere quantitative approach as indicated in the guidelines in Part One. The supplementary texts may also be read in informational fashion as a means of providing background to the theme. Supplementary selections fall most often within the secondary or recreative category. Generally introductions to texts provide good background reading and pertinent historical and biographical information which can be absorbed at the reader's discretion outside of the time one sets aside for slowed down spiritual reading. In regard to the overall duration of the reading program, readers must be faithful to their own pace of spiritual reading and notebook keeping. If a text is inspiring to them, they should stay with it as long as dwelling on the text keeps nourishing their heart and mind.

land or the preparatory forty days of our Lord prior to beginning his public life. For the chosen people, the desert experience was God's means of readying them for a more intimate encounter with him. They were his people and despite their recalcitrance and betrayal he would pursue them as the beloved does his bride. For Jesus, the time in the desert was spent alone and in prayer. He fasted and faced the tempter. When he said *no* to Satan's offer to give him earthly power and possessions, he said *yes* to the mission the Father had given him to lead all to oneness with the Divine Persons.

What happened spiritually in the desert experience of the Jews and of Jesus? On both occasions the comforts of life are left behind. There are no distracting, soothing pleasures in the desert, only the harshness of life stripped to its essentials. In the desert we have to fall back on ourselves; we realize then how weak and limited we are. It is only when we have deeply experienced and accepted our total helplessness that we may be willing to turn to God in trust and surrender. While the likelihood of our making a trip into the desert itself is doubtful, we, too, have to go through this experience spiritually. It takes courage to stand alone before God, to leave behind all human support—all proud claims to spiritual greatness—and face squarely the fact that of ourselves we are nothing in the order of grace. We are inclined to be unfaithful to God, to turn traitor, to sin. What an unsettling sight this can be. It means that if we want to come to God, we have to empty ourselves of all self-centeredness. We have to be willing to follow the divine call wherever it may lead, even if this following means foregoing the comforts we would like to maintain in our life.

When we stand thus defenseless in the desert of weakness and sin, when we are faced with the call to total surrender, temptation will come. We hear that subtle voice saying, "You can never make it. That is asking too much! Don't take the call so seriously. Others don't heed it and they are happy." The crisis of the desert is upon us. Our self protests. Inwardly all is darkness. It seems so attractive to let ourselves be lured away from this emptiness, to forget all about the call to surrender. It might not be so painful were this experience to last only a moment, but the aversion to suffering and the inclination to rebel may go on for days and days. It is the time of purification wherein our pride is being burned away. The experience of our vulnerability becomes so vivid that we have no illusions left about what we can do by ourselves in the order of salvation. We understand then that God's invitation to total surrender is not a stern demand but a manifestation of love, for only when we fully let go of our pride and surrender to the Lord in poverty of spirit can he lead us to true happiness.

The desert experience is thus a preparation for deeper union with the Trinity and a means of readying ourselves to cling to Jesus, without whose love and guidance life is only a sad procession of fleeting pains and pleasures. The desert experience brings us to a crisis. Left to our own resources, we could never cope with it. Mysteriously, in that deep darkness and spiritual dryness, the God of light and love descends to sustain our poor selves with divine grace. The Spirit stays with us until dawn breaks.

In imitation of the attitudes evolved in the desert experiences of the chosen people and of Jesus, we, too, should set aside time and space—inwardly if not outwardly—for desert-like experiences to deepen our presence to the Lord. In the desert of the heart, we begin to personalize the attitudes that characterized the chosen people in their best moments and that were epitomized by Christ—such attitudes as inner silencing, dwelling with the Divine, patient acceptance of suffering, self-emptying and detachment. These qualities and virtues can be developed in a reading program based on the theme of living the desert experience.

The desert is thus a place away from the bustle of noisy living and large numbers of people. To go there is to be shaken out of the ordinary humdrum acceptance of things and to reflect on their deeper meaning—a meaning conveyed only in solitude and silence. The desert is also a place of prayer as it was for the chosen people and for Jesus. And the desert is an inner ongoing experience of preparing a place in my heart for the coming of the Lord. There I must learn not to complain when things do not go my way—as many of the Israelites did. There I must learn to be content if at times certain conveniences are lacking—remembering that Jesus himself lacked a place where he could put his head and rest. There, in that interior desert, I have to wait patiently and trust that God will give me what I need if I but learn to depend on divine love more and more.

This dependence demands an emptying of self and its excessive attachment to persons and things; the reward of this desert experience is beyond measure. God comes out of the darkness to illumine our hearts with the light of faith; he relieves the dryness with living water that lasts forever. God grants us a gift of divine intimacy that calls for surrender of our whole self—body and soul, mind and heart. To come to live always in the divine presence from that deepest center of self is the purpose of desert experience. Readying us for this experience and its inestimable benefits is the aim of this reading program.

MINOR THEMES

I. The Desert: Without and Within
II. Silence and Solitude of Desert Experience
III. Reflective Dwelling and Desert Experience
IV. Prayer and Desert Experience
V. Self-Knowledge and Desert Experience
VI. Patience and Acceptance of Suffering in Desert Experience

VII. Trust and Dependence in Desert Experience
VIII. Self-Emptying and Detachment in Desert Experience
IX. Awakening through Desert Experience
X. Surrender and Commitment in Desert Experience

READING LIST

What follows is the list of books (annotated in the *Sample Bibliography*) to be assembled by the reader and used for this particular reading program. These books are certainly not the only ones available on the theme concerned nor necessarily the most outstanding written on this topic. They are, however, accessible to the general reader in current editions reasonably priced. Alternative and newer versions of some of the following books are also indicated in the *Sample Bibliography*. References to the same minor themes that readers may find more appropriate or available can be found in many cases as well in the *Sample Bibliography*. In each thematic section, the parts of the text the reader is advised to use for that specific subdivision will be indicated and briefly annotated. In case the reader should be using editions of the text different from those that appear on the Reading List, Chapters and/or Parts of the books, and occasionally page numbers, accompany each annotation.

HOLY SCRIPTURE

The Jerusalem Bible. Reader's Edition. Alexander Jones, General Editor. New York: Doubleday, 1985.

LITERATURE OF SPIRITUALITY

Essential

Carretto, Carlo. *Letters from the Desert*. Trans. Rose Mary Hancock. Maryknoll, NY: Orbis Books, 1982.

_______. *The God Who Comes*. Trans. Rose Mary Hancock. Maryknoll, NY: Orbis Books, 1974.

Caussade, Jean-Pierre de. *Abandonment to Divine Providence*. Trans. John Beavers. New York: Doubleday, 1993.

Merton, Thomas. *The Sign of Jonas*. New York: Hippocrene Books, 1983.

_______. *No Man Is an Island*. New York: Walker, 1986.

_______. *New Seeds of Contemplation*. New York: New Directions, 1972.

Teresa of Avila, St. *The Way of Perfection*. Trans. E. Allison Peers. New York: Doubleday, 1991.

van Kaam, Adrian. *On Being Involved: The Rhythm of Involvement and Detachment in Daily Life.* Denville, NJ: Dimension Books, 1970.

Secondary

Merton, Thomas. *The Wisdom of the Desert: Sayings from the Desert Fathers of the Fourth Century.* Boston: Shambhala, 1994.[2]

von Hildebrand, Dietrich. *Transformation in Christ.* Manchester, NH: Sophia Institute, 1990.

Waddell, Helen, trans. *The Desert Fathers.* Ann Arbor, MI: University of Michigan Press, 1957.

Edifying

Doherty, Catherine de Hueck. *Poustinia: Christian Spirituality of the East for Western Man.* Notre Dame, IN: Ave Maria, 1975.

Farrell, Edward J. *Prayer Is a Hunger.* Denville, NJ: Dimension Books, 1972.

Metz, Johannes Baptist. *Poverty of Spirit.* Trans. John Drury. Paramus, NJ: Newman, 1968.

Recreative

Dullard, Annie. *Pilgrim at Tinker Creek.* New York: Bantam Books, 1975.

Eiseley, Loren. *The Night Country.* Magnolia, MA: Peter Smith, 1988.

MINOR THEME I

THE DESERT: WITHOUT AND WITHIN

In the desert the chosen people received the revelation of God's majesty, of his love and care. Far from the familiar surroundings of Egypt and farther still from the promised land that would be theirs, they learned to rely on Yahweh, to overcome their resistance and to obey his commands. The desert fathers and mothers sought the same intimacy with God in the aridity of the wilderness, far from the comforts of a decaying civilization. Few of us can go to the physical desert to find God. Our desert is normally not found without; we have to create it within ourselves. We have to learn with the grace of God to let go of our worldly concerns, involvements and activities, and to stand before God in the nakedness and aridity of our sinful selves. It is a long and lonesome journey to that desert within where we have no other support than

[2] The actual sayings of the Fathers found in these texts can be placed in the category of essential literature of spirituality.

our faith. Yet it is in emptying ourselves that we open the way for the influx of God's grace and presence. Often this divine presence is experienced in darkness, but moments may come when God's light illumines our inmost being. Then we know, in a way words cannot explain, that being in the desert with our Lord is worth more than any worldly comfort or earthly gain.

READINGS FROM HOLY SCRIPTURE

Old Testament

Ex. 15:22-27; 16:1-36; 17:1-7—Israel in the desert.

Ex. 19:1-25; 20:1-21—The sons of Israel come to the wilderness of Sinai.

Nb. 11:1-35—The halts in the wilderness.

Nb. 13:25-33; 14:1-45—The sons of Israel grumble that it would have been better to die in the land of Egypt or at least in the wilderness than to fall by the sword of the powerful people who inhabit the land.

Nb. 20:1-13—At Meribah Yahweh makes water gush from the rock and proclaims his holiness.

Dt. 1:1-46; 2:1-37; 3:1-29—Yahweh instructs Moses at Horeb and Kadesh. Moses leads the people through the wilderness in obedience to Yahweh's commands.

Dt. 8:1-20; 9:1-29—The ordeal in the wilderness. Moses speaks of the promised land and its temptations and intercedes for the people when they sin.

Dt. 29:1-28; 30:1-2—Moses recalls the exodus and the covenant. He reminds the people that Yahweh sets before them two ways: life and prosperity or death and disaster. They must choose.

Ps. 29—"The voice of Yahweh sets the wilderness shaking."

Ps. 95—"Do not harden your hearts as at Meribah, as you did that day at Massah in the wilderness..."

Ps. 136—"Give thanks to Yahweh, for he is good.... He led his people through the wilderness..."

Is. 24:1-23; 25:1-12—"See how Yahweh lays the earth waste, makes it a desert." Yet at the time of the messianic banquet, he will remove the mourning veil covering all peoples and wipe away the tears from every cheek.

Is. 41:1-29—God is with Israel. He makes rivers on barren heights. He turns the wilderness into a lake.

Ho. 2:4-25—Yahweh and his unfaithful wife. "That is why I am going to lure her and lead her out into the wilderness and speak to her heart."

New Testament

Mt. 3:1-12; Mk. 1:1-8; Lk. 3:1-18; Jn. 1:19-34—John the Baptist preaches in the wilderness. He tells the people to repent for the kingdom of heaven is close at hand.

Mt. 4:1-11; Mk. 1:12-13; Lk. 4:1-13—Jesus is led by the Spirit into the wilderness to be tempted by the devil.

Mt. 11:1-19; Lk. 7:18-35—John the Baptist, now in prison, sends his disciples to ask Jesus if he is the one who is to come. Jesus commends John for preparing the way for him, but he condemns his contemporaries.

Mt. 13:53-58; Mk. 6:1-6; Lk. 4:16-30—During a visit to Nazareth, Jesus says to the people, "A prophet is only despised in his own country and in his own house."

Mt. 14:3-12; Mk. 6:17-29—John the Baptist is beheaded.

Mt. 14:13-21; Mk. 6:30-44; Lk. 9:10-17; Jn. 6:1-15—Jesus withdrew to a lonely place, but the people followed him. He took pity on them and fed them. After the miracle of the loaves, they wanted to take him by force and make him king, but he escaped back to the hills by himself.

Jn. 11:1-54—Jesus raises his friend Lazarus from the dead. The chief priests and Pharisees, fearing his power, decide that he must die. Jesus no longer went openly among the Jews. He left the district for a town called Ephraim, bordering on the desert.

Jn. 12:20-36—Jesus foretells his death and subsequent glorification.

Mt. 27:45-56; Mk. 15:33-39; Lk. 23:44-49; Jn. 19:28-37—The death of Jesus. *"My God, my God, why have you deserted me?"*

Ac. 7:1-54—In his address to the Sanhedrin, Stephen reviews the history of Israel from a Christian perspective, recalling that it was Moses who led the people across the Red Sea and through the wilderness for forty years.

Rm. 9:1-33; 10:1-21; 11:1-36—Paul describes the privileges of Israel, how God kept his promise, and the role of the "remnant."

1 Co. 10:1-33—Paul issues a warning and reminds his listeners of the lessons of Israel's history, how, despite God's favors, most of the people failed to please him and, consequently, their corpses littered the desert.

Heb. 8:1-13; 9:1-28; 10:1-18—Christ is the mediator of a greater covenant, whose sacrifice is superior to the sacrifices of the Mosaic Law.

* * * * *

As God led the Israelites into the desert, so, too, are we led at times through an inner desert so that we may become united with the Mystery more intimately. We must ready ourselves for such times and remain open to whatever experiences God allows, desolation as well as consolation. No matter what feeling prevails, the Lord is with us.

READINGS FROM THE LITERATURE OF SPIRITUALITY

Letters from the Desert, (Chapters 1, 2, and 3)—Carretto recalls that tract of desert between Tit and Silet, which is still the place of his purgatory.

The God Who Comes, (Chapter 4)—Carretto feels that the spirituality of man on earth is the spirituality of the Exodus.

The Sign of Jonas, (Part One)—Merton's solemn profession meant that he was consecrating his whole life to God in the monastery; he had to forget about going back to the world.

New Seeds of Contemplation, (Chapters 33 and 36)—Merton writes, "The man who does not permit his spirit to be beaten down and upset by dryness and helplessness, but who lets God lead him peacefully through the wilderness, and desires no other support or guidance than that of pure faith and trust in God alone, will be brought to the Promised Land."

Poustinia, (Part I)—"Poustinia" is the Russian word for "desert" and a "poustinik" is a person dwelling in a poustinia, someone in a secluded spot. Deserts are not necessarily places but states of mind and heart. They can be found in the midst of the city and in the everyday reality of our lives.

Prayer Is a Hunger, (Chapter 10)—The author asks, "What has happened to me in the desert?" The one clear thought that comes to him is that he has absorbed a vast silence from the desert, not a silence of emptiness but of fullness—a silence that is peace and communion and freedom.

SUPPLEMENTARY READING

The Wisdom of the Desert, (Introduction)—Of the Desert Fathers Merton says, "The flight of these men to the desert was neither purely negative nor purely individualistic.... What the Fathers sought most of all was their own true self, in Christ."

* * * * *

Desert living, as the phrase itself indicates, is a *way of living,* a way of being present to reality with our whole being and not merely with our body or mind. It involves an occasional distancing of ourselves from the immediacy of life situations and hectic involvements in daily tasks in order to center ourselves within the Divine. In this light, we gather our scattered selves together. Desert living thus implies a re-collecting of self and situation in the light of the Divine. In this re-collecting, we must not become centered on self. We should place ourselves instead in the caring presence of the Father and, against the background of this divine horizon, see who and where we are as part of a greater whole.

MINOR THEME II

SILENCE AND SOLITUDE OF DESERT EXPERIENCE

The desert as a geographical space offers an intensification of silence and solitude. Such profound stillness and aloneness is not easy to find for the average person. It may be tasted in a hermitage for longer periods of time or for shorter periods on retreat or at a house of prayer. For the most part, however, we live amidst noise and numbers of people. Thus we have to find within ourselves a place of quiet and solitary presence to the One who is present everywhere. Since most of us do not have an opportunity to enjoy lengthy experiences of outer silence and solitude, we have to learn to find the essence of these experiences within. Outer solitude and silence are only a means to facilitate inner stilling and aloneness before God. We can adopt these inner attitudes anywhere though, of course, in the midst of the world, doing so requires more discipline and resolve. We live in inner solitude when we put to rest agitation, tenseness, and needless concern. We try to silence our emotions and passions, our restless, searching minds. We shift the center of our attention from these concerns to God. We are alone with the Alone. In the beginning of our efforts, when we stand thus helplessly before God, we may only be able to say a simple prayer that expresses our love, adoration, and dedication. Repeating this prayer humbly and serenely may bring us to a state of inner quiet where we can simply be with Our Lord. If we are faithful to this practice, as time goes on, a day may come when we don't feel the need to say anything any more. We are totally silent; we simply love—and the deeper love is, the less words it needs.

READINGS FROM HOLY SCRIPTURE

Old Testament

Ex. 24:1-18—Yahweh ratifies the covenant and his glory settles on the mountain of Sinai. Moses stays there for forty days and nights.

Dt. 7:1-26—Israel is a people set apart by Yahweh, chosen to be his own out of all the peoples on the earth.

1 K. 19:1-18—Elijah walked for forty days and forty nights until he reached Horeb, the mountain of God. Yahweh was not in the wind, the earthquake or the fire but in the sound of a gentle breeze.

Ps. 32—"All the time I kept silent, my bones were wasting away..."

Ps. 39—"I will watch how I behave, and not let my tongue lead me into sin. "

Ps. 88—"I am numbered among those who go down to the Pit, a man bereft of strength: a man alone, down among the dead..."

Ws. 18:14-19—"When peaceful silence lay over all, and night had run the half of her swift course, down from the heavens, from the royal throne, leaped your all-powerful Word..."

Si. 19:4-17—Against loose talk. Do not trust everything you hear.

Si. 20:1-26—Silence and speech. A wise man will keep quiet until the right moment. "Better a slip on the pavement than a slip of the tongue."

Si. 22:27; 23:1-15—"Who will set a guard on my mouth, and a seal of prudence on my lips, to keep me from falling, and my tongue from causing my ruin?"

Is. 42:1-25; 43:1-28; 44:1-8—The servant of Yahweh "...does not cry out or shout aloud, or make his voice heard in the streets." The prophet recounts the liberation of Israel and the miracles of the new exodus.

Lm. 3:1-66—"It is good for a man to bear the yoke from youth onwards, to sit in solitude and silence when the Lord fastens it on him..."

Zc. 2:1-17—"Let all mankind be silent before Yahweh! For he is awaking and is coming from his holy dwelling."

New Testament

Mk. 1:35-39; Lk. 4:42-44—In the morning, long before dawn, Jesus got up and left the house, went off to a lonely place, and prayed there.

Mt. 8:1-4; Mk. 1:40-45; Lk. 5:12-16—Cure of a leper. Large crowds would gather to hear him and have their sickness cured, "...but he would always go off to some place where he could be alone and pray."

Lk. 6:12-16—Before choosing the twelve, Jesus went out into the hills to pray; he spent the whole night in prayer to God.

Mt. 14:22-33; Mk. 6:45-52—After sending the crowds away, Jesus went up into the hills by himself to pray. When evening came he was alone. He saw his disciples in a boat far out on the lake and went walking toward them.

Mt. 17:1-8; Mk. 9:2-8; Lk. 9:28-36—Jesus took Peter, James and John to a high mountain where they could be alone. In their presence he was transfigured. Peter wanted to stay there and make three tents, one for Jesus, one for Moses, and one for Elijah.

Lk. 21:37-38—In the daytime Jesus would be in the Temple teaching, but he would spend the night on the hill called the Mount of Olives.

Jn. 14:1-31—In his farewell discourses, Jesus says to his disciples: "If anyone loves me he will keep my word, and my Father will love him, and we shall come to him and make our home with him...I have told you this now before it happens, so that when it does happen you may believe. I shall not talk with you any longer, because the prince of this world is on his way."

Mt. 26:57-68; Mk. 14:53-65; Lk. 22:66-71—Jesus before the Sanhedrin. The high priest questions him, but Jesus remains silent.

Ep. 4:1-32; 5:1-20—A call to unity and new life in Christ. "There must be no coarseness or salacious talk and jokes...raise your voices in thanksgiving instead."

Col. 3:5-25—General rules of Christian behavior. "...but now you, of all people, must give all these things up: getting angry, being bad-tempered, spitefulness, abusive language and dirty talk; and never tell each other lies."

Jm. 3:1-18—Guard against uncontrolled language. "So is the tongue only a tiny part of the body, but it can...set fire to a huge forest..."

* * * * *

Absence of outer noise makes us vividly aware of the noise within. Inner noise only increases in volume the more we attempt to root ourselves ultimately in anything less than God. The desert can be a lonely experience unless we are able, with divine help, to convert this loneliness to solitude and this silence into greater communion with God and neighbor.

READINGS FROM THE LITERATURE OF SPIRITUALITY

Letters from the Desert, (Chapter 10)—Carretto reminds us that if we cannot go into the desert, we must nonetheless make some desert in our lives. Every now and then we must leave men and look for solitude to restore, in prolonged silence and prayer, the stuff of our soul.

The God Who Comes, (Chapters 5, 9, and 10)—The author is consoled by this thought: "I am a dwelling place. I am not alone. In the secret depths of my poor human substance is the presence of God."

The Sign of Jonas, (Part Six)—The peace Merton had found, the solitude of the winter of 1950, deepened and developed in him beyond measure.

No Man Is an Island, (Chapters 15 and 16)—Merton believes that a person is a person insofar as he has a secret and is a solitude of his own that cannot be communicated to anyone else. "Silence," he says, "is the strength of our interior life."

New Seeds of Contemplation, (Chapters 8, 9, and 11)—One goes into the desert not to escape other men but in order to find them in God. The truest solitude is not something outside us, not an absence of men or of sound, but an abyss opening up in the center of our soul.

Poustinia, (Part IV)—Through all her years of living in a poustinia, in silence and solitude, the author was pilgrimaging in search of her Desired One.

Prayer Is a Hunger, (Chapter 9)—In the beginning, when God spoke a word to Adam, he did not listen. When God spoke his final word, it was to a woman, to Mary, and through her listening, man came to know God as Abba, Father.

SUPPLEMENTARY READING

The Wisdom of the Desert—Read Sayings I to XXIV of the Desert Fathers.

The Desert Fathers—Read the introduction and the life of St. Paul, the first hermit. The author believes that solitude is the creative condition of genius, religious or secular, and the ultimate sterilizing of it.

* * * * *

In silence and solitude we step aside from our usual hectic pace and involvement. We come home to ourselves. Solitude provides the space we need to be present to who we are before God; silence makes us attentive to our inner world and to God's nearness. In silence and solitude we learn to live reflectively from our deepest center, to get in touch with the quality of our life, to abide by God's call.

MINOR THEME III

REFLECTIVE DWELLING AND DESERT EXPERIENCE

Desert experience implies at least a temporary withdrawal from worldly involvement, a quiet standing before God in inner silence and solitude. This stepping aside from activity presupposes also a change of inner attitude. There is no reason now to rush from one thing to another. All we can do, with

God's grace, is to stay still in quiet love and contemplation, waiting for the light. Now is the time to dwell with the Divine in peaceful presence. Especially in the beginning, we may notice that our mind or imagination has started to race again feverishly before we are even aware of its running away. This problem is quite normal. It takes long practice and experience before we are able to remain for a period of time in undistracted, dwelling presence to God. As our capacity for reflective dwelling increases, we shall discover that we are more relaxed, not only in moments of quiet meditation, but also in the midst of our task. We are more easily able to overcome the agitation that prevents us from being present where we are. Reflective dwelling as a mode of desert experience has thus to be carried over into daily living. Too often the mysterious meaning of things gets lost in the rushing stream of work and play. It is good to slow down once in a while and appraise what is going on, to abide in one place and dwell there, drinking in its richness as a nomad draws water from a desert oasis.

READINGS FROM HOLY SCRIPTURE

Old Testament

Gn. 32:23-33—At the place Jacob named Peniel, he was left alone. All night long he wrestled with God and then received his blessing.

Gn. 35:1-15—Jacob named the place Bethel where God had spoken with him.

Ex. 33:12-23; 34:1-35—On the mountain Moses prays to Yahweh. He sees his back but not his face. Yahweh renews the covenant after which Moses stays there for forty days and nights. So radiant is his face when he descends that he puts a veil over it.

Ps. 26—"I love the house where you live, the place where your glory makes its home."

Ps. 27—"One thing I ask of Yahweh, one thing I seek: to live in the house of Yahweh all the days of my life..."

Ps. 42-43—"Send out your light and your truth, let these be my guide to lead me to your holy mountain and to the place where you live."

Ps. 62—"Rest in God alone, my soul!"

Ps. 63—"On my bed I think of you, I meditate on you all night long..."

Ps. 65—"Happy the man you choose, whom you invite to live in your courts."

Ps. 78—"Listen to this Law, my people, pay attention to what I say..."

Ps. 84—"How I love your palace, Yahweh, Sabaoth!"

Si. 14:20-27; 15:1-10—"Happy the man who meditates on wisdom, and reasons with good sense, who studies her ways in his heart, and ponders her secrets."

Si. 18:19-29—"Learn before you speak, take care of yourself before you fall ill." Reflection and foresight are wise traits to cultivate.

Si. 39:1-35—The scholar "...devotes his soul to reflecting on the Law of the Most High." The gifts of creation invite praise of God.

Is. 2:1-5—"O House of Jacob, come, let us walk in the light of Yahweh."

Is. 59:1-20—"...our faults are present to our minds, and we know our iniquities..."

Zc. 9:1-17; 10:1-12; 11:1-3—Yahweh rewards faithfulness and promises to restore Israel despite its iniquity. "Near my house I will take my stand like a watchman on guard against prowlers; the tyrant shall pass their way no more, because I have now taken notice of its distress."

New Testament

Mt. 1:18-25—His name shall be Immanuel, which means "God-is-with-us."

Lk. 2:1-20—On the eve of Jesus' birth, an angel of the Lord appeared to the shepherds and bid them not to fear. They went to visit the babe. Mary, his mother, treasured all these things and pondered them in her heart.

Mt. 7:21-27; Lk. 6:46-49—The true disciple is like the man who built his house on rock. He listens to Jesus' words and acts on them.

Mt. 8:5-13; Lk. 7:1-10—Jesus is astonished by the centurion's faith, summed up in these words: "Sir, I am not worthy to have you under my roof; just give the word and my servant will be cured."

Mt. 9:14-17; Mk. 2:18-22; Lk. 5:33-39—Jesus says that his disciples do not fast because the bridegroom's attendants would never think of mourning as long as the bridegroom is still with them.

Mt. 13:1-23; Mk. 4:1-20; Lk. 8:4-15—Parable of the sower. "...the one who received the seed in rich soil is the man who hears the word and understands it..."

Mt. 13:24-30; 13:36-43—Jesus tells the parable of the darnel and explains it. "Listen anyone who has ears!"

Jn. 6:22-71—During his discourse in the synagogue at Capernaum, Jesus says to those who will listen, "I am the bread of life. He who comes to me will never be hungry; he who believes in me will never thirst."

1 Co. 3:5-17—The foundation on which the Christian is to build his life is Jesus Christ.

Ep. 3:1-21—Paul's prayer is that Christ may dwell lastingly in our hearts through faith.

Col. 1:15-20—Christ is the first-born of all creation; he holds all things in unity. All perfection is to be found in him and all things will be reconciled through him.

Col. 3:16-17—The message of Christ, in all its richness, is to find a home with us.

Heb. 4:12-16—"The word of God is something alive and active; it cuts like any double-edged sword but more finely..."

Heb. 5:11-14—The solid food of Christ's teaching is for mature men with minds trained by practice to distinguish between good and evil.

Rv. 21:1-8—In the heavenly Jerusalem God lives among men.

* * * * *

Though Jesus may be rejected by the world, we must try to make a dwelling place for him in our hearts. Enlightened by his spirit, we can better recognize the wrong and avoid it; we can see more clearly the right and choose it.

READINGS FROM THE LITERATURE OF SPIRITUALITY

Letters from the Desert, (Chapter 4)—Carretto says he is tired of arguing. He doesn't want to go on disputing any more. His belief in the ability to convince by words alone has gone. He is silent under African stars and prefers to worship his God and Savior.

The God Who Comes, (Chapters 6, 13, and 14)—God communicates with us and by communicating he gives us knowledge of himself, just as by communicating with him we can tell him about ourselves.

Abandonment to Divine Providence, (Chapter I)—On doing our part and leaving the rest to God.

The Sign of Jonas, (Part Three)—Merton had to find out that in the plans of Divine Providence there is no such thing as defeat and that every step is, or ought to be, a step forward into the wilderness.

No Man Is an Island, (Chapters 12 and 13)—Recollection fosters a change of spiritual focus, an attuning of our whole soul to what is beyond and above ourselves.

New Seeds of Contemplation, (Chapters 5 and 6)—To work out our own identity demands close attention to reality at every moment and fidelity to God as he reveals himself, however obscurely, in the mystery of each new situation.

Poustinia, (Part II)—The goal of the poustinia is "monasticism interiorized," which means that everyone is to live the life of the Trinity wherever they might be.

Prayer Is a Hunger, (Chapter 3)—The Word that God speaks is deposited deeply within us. The womb of mind and heart must be readied, waiting, responsive.

SUPPLEMENTARY READING

Transformation in Christ, (Chapters VI and VII)—Unless we rid ourselves of all illusory exaltation, unless we keep dwelling on the truth, we cannot attain to a veritable union with God. Thus we must relentlessly clear away whatever illusions still survive in us. Recollection, contemplation, and sobriety should form the basis of our life.

Pilgrim at Tinker Creek—This book has been described as "a mystical excursion into the natural world." By dwelling in the world of nature, in the environs of Tinker Creek, Annie Dillard learns through "stalking" to see the richness of the present and the awesome wonder, power, and beauty of God's world.

* * * * *

Reflective dwelling brings us in contact with the Divine in the core of our being. From this place of presence, we are called forth to respond to the concrete persons, events, and things that enter our daily life. These in turn take on a new value. In reflective awareness, we learn gradually to see them as invitations to face all revelations of reality in trust and care as part of God's plan for us.

MINOR THEME IV

PRAYER AND DESERT EXPERIENCE

The goal of desert experience is intimacy with God. When all else is taken away, we reach out to the Lord in love and seek to be united with him in prayer. Our prayer at such times may be no more than a peaceful telling of our love, an offering of adoration and dedication, a felt sorrow for sin. At moments of deepest intimacy, we may be united with God in total silence, in a bond of lasting communion. The deeper our union with the Beloved at these blessed times, the more we may stay united with him during the day. Christ becomes our dearest companion in labor and leisure. Perhaps the desert has been associated so closely with prayer because in the wilderness God is the only Person to whom we can speak. The same happens in daily life. However excellent our channels of human communication may be, there are times when all dialogue ceases save conversation with God. To whom can we go in our pain but him? Who else can we thank in our joy? Prayer is also the means by which we make room in our hearts for holy revelations. In a quiet unobtrusive way, we have to clear space inside so that our Divine Guest can find there an empty chamber he may occupy to the full.

READINGS FROM HOLY SCRIPTURE

Old Testament

Dt. 32:1-41—Moses offers a prayer of praise and thanksgiving to God, who in the wastelands adopts Jacob, who in the howling desert of the wilderness protects him, rears him, and guards him as the pupil of his eye.

Jos. 7:2-26—At Ai, Yahweh's anger flares out against the Israelites. Joshua and the elders of Israel prostrate themselves before the ark and pour dust on their heads as Joshua prays.

2 S. 7:1-29—Yahweh reveals to David through the prophet Nathan that his house and his sovereignty will always stand secure. David responds in prayer and promises to exalt the name of Yahweh forever.

1 K. 8:1-66—The ark of the covenant is brought to the Temple of Yahweh Solomon has built and the glory of Yahweh fills this place. Solomon prays for himself and for the people.

2 Ch. 5:1-14; 6:1-42—An account of the same.

Ps. 7—Prayer of the virtuous under persecution.

Ps. 17—"Yahweh, hear the plea of virtue, listen to my appeal, lend an ear to my prayer..."

Ps. 31—Prayer in time of ordeal.

Ps. 61—"God, hear my cry for help, listen to my prayer!"

Ps. 71—An old man's prayer.

Ps. 86—"Yahweh, hear my prayer, listen to me as I plead."

Ws. 9:1-18—A prayer for Wisdom.

Si. 51:1-30—A hymn of thanksgiving and a prayer for Wisdom.

Is. 35:1-10—The hopes and prayers of Israel will be answered when the glory of God shines forth. "...the tongues of the dumb sing for joy; for water gushes in the desert, streams in the wasteland..."

Ba. 1:16-22; 2:1-35; 3:1-8—The prayer of the exiles.

Hab. 3:1-19—Habakkuk the prophet prays to Yahweh for deliverance.

Zp. 3:9-20—Yahweh will restore the fortunes of the remnant of Israel and psalms of joy will ring in Zion.

New Testament

Lk. 1:5-25—Zechariah's prayer is answered in a vision. He and Elizabeth, though aged, shall receive a son.

Lk. 1:67-79—Zechariah foretells in prophetic prayer that this little child shall prepare the way of the Lord, who will give light to us who live in darkness and the shadow of death.

Mt. 5:20-48—The new standard Christ brings is higher than the old. "...love your enemies and pray for those who persecute you..."

Mt. 6:5-15; Lk. 11:1-4—Jesus teaches his disciples how to pray.

Mt. 7:7-11; Lk. 11:9-13—Effective prayer. "Ask, and it will be given to you."

Mt. 18:19-20—Prayer in common. "For where two or three meet in my name, I shall be there with them."

Mk. 9:14-29; Lk. 9:37-43—The demon Jesus drove out of the boy could only be driven out by prayer.

Mt. 21:18-22; Mk. 11:20-25—Passing by the withered fig tree, Jesus discourses on faith and prayer.

Lk. 18:9-14—The Pharisee and the publican pray, but it is the sinner who goes home at rights with God.

Jn. 17:1-26—The priestly prayer of Jesus. "I am not praying for the world but for those you have given me, because they belong to you..."

Mt. 26:36-46; Mk. 14:32-42; Lk. 22:39-46—Jesus prays in Gethsemane, "My Father...if this cup cannot pass by without my drinking it, your will be done!"

Rm. 8:1-39—The life of the spirit. "For when we cannot choose words in order to pray properly, the Spirit himself expresses our plea in a way that could never be put into words..."

2 Co. 13:1-10—"What we ask in our prayers is for you to be made perfect."

Ep. 6:10-20—The spiritual war. "Pray all the time, asking for what you need, praying in the Spirit on every possible occasion."

Ph. 1:3-11—"My prayer is that your love for each other may increase more and more..."

Col. 1:3-14—"...what we ask God is that through perfect wisdom and spiritual understanding you should reach the fullest knowledge of his will."

Col. 4:2-6—"Be persevering in your prayers..."

1 Th. 5:12-22—Paul appeals to the brothers to pray constantly.

1 Tm. 2:1-8—Liturgical prayer. "In every place, then, I want men to lift their hands up reverently in prayer, with no anger or argument."

* * * * *

Prayer is an intimate experience of the heart. We reach out to God because God has first reached out to us. These passages from Holy Scripture nourish our life of prayer and deepen our confidence in the God who hears.

READINGS FROM THE LITERATURE OF SPIRITUALITY

Letters from the Desert, (Chapters 6, 7, and 8)—Carretto came to the desert to learn how to pray. Prayer has been the Sahara's great gift to him, and he should like to share it with all his friends.

The God Who Comes, (Chapters 8 and 18)—If we don't pray, if we are not searching for a personal relationship with God, if we don't stay with him for long periods in order to know him, little by little we will start to forget him.

Abandonment to Divine Providence, (Chapter II)—Embrace the present moment as an ever-flowing source of holiness.

No Man Is an Island, (Chapter 3)—As Merton says, "All true prayer somehow confesses our absolute dependence on the Lord of life and death. It is, therefore, a deep and vital contact with him whom we know not only as Lord but as Father. It is when we pray truly that we really are."

New Seeds of Contemplation, (Chapters 1-3 and 29-30)—Merton describes contemplation as an awakening, an enlightenment, an amazing intuitive grasp by which love gains certitude of God's creative and dynamic intervention in our daily life. The secret of prayer is a hunger for God, for the vision of God, that lies far deeper than the level of language or affection.

The Way of Perfection, (Chapters 27-42)—St. Teresa's commentary on the Lord's Prayer, taken petition by petition, touches upon the themes of recollection, quiet, and union. In its few words are enshrined all contemplation and perfection; if we study it no other book seems necessary; in the Paternoster the Lord has taught us the whole method of prayer and of high contemplation, from the beginning of mental prayer to quiet and union.

Prayer Is a Hunger, (Chapters 1 and 2)—Prayer is a journey, a path created only by walking it; prayer is a hunger not easily quieted.

SUPPLEMENTARY READING

The Wisdom of the Desert—Read Sayings XXV to LXXXVII of the Desert Fathers.

The Desert Fathers—Read the history of the Monks of Egypt.

* * * * *

In prayer we encounter our Creator, our Redeemer, our Sanctifier while bringing to the most Holy Trinity our human strengths and weaknesses. We come to prayer to be with the Divine quietly, silently, and reflectively—attentive to the whispers of God's will, open to transcendent love and enlightenment, open to Father, Son and Holy Spirit.

MINOR THEME V

SELF-KNOWLEDGE AND DESERT EXPERIENCE

Life in the desert has a way of reducing needs to the bare essentials: water, food, shelter. The desert makes us vividly aware of how dependent we are. It is for this reason that it is a good teacher. It instructs us about our creaturehood. It helps us to accept the truth of who we are and to have no grandiose illusions. To walk in this truth is to know ourselves. Such knowledge of our limited condition instills humility. This means that we not only acknowledge our own misery but that we also rely on God's mercy. The humble heart seeks the desert to declare without shame its dependence and to praise without restraint God's power.

READINGS FROM HOLY SCRIPTURE

Old Testament

Gn. 3:1-24—The Fall. "For dust you are and to dust you shall return."

Lv. 19:1-37—Yahweh tells the people through Moses who they are and how they are to worship him. He commands Moses to say to them, "Be holy, for I, Yahweh your God, am holy."

Dt. 5:1-22—The limitations of men are summed up in the Ten Commandments.

1 S. 24:1-23—David spares Saul, who says to him, "Now I know you will indeed reign and that the sovereignty in Israel will be secure in your hands."

1 S. 26:1-25—David again spares Saul, who knows now that he, not David, is the one who has sinned. "Yes, my course has been folly and my error grave."

2 S. 22:1-51; 23:1-7—David knows that of his own power he can do nothing. "Yahweh is my rock and my bastion, my deliverer is my God."

Jb. 3:1-26; 4:1-21; 5:1-27—Job curses the day of his birth; Eliphaz of Teman tells him to have confidence in God.

Jb. 6:1-30; 7:1-21—Only the sufferer knows his own grief.

Jb. 36:1-33; 37:1-24—Elihu understands the real meaning of Job's sufferings.

Jb. 38:1-41; 39:1-30—Job must bow to the wisdom of Yahweh, who speaks to him from the heart of the Tempest.

Jb. 42:1-6—Job's final answer to Yahweh is to retract all he has said and in dust and ashes to repent.

Ps. 8—"...what is man that you should spare a thought for him..."

Ps. 16—"I bless Yahweh, who is my counselor, and in the night my inmost self instructs me..."

Ps. 119—"You yourself have made your precepts known, to be faithfully kept."

Ps. 139—"...I thank you: for the wonder of myself, for the wonder of your works."

Ps. 144— "Yahweh, what is man, that you should notice him? A human being that you should think about him?"

Pr. 18:1-24—"The heart of the discerning gains in knowledge, the ear of the wise man searches for knowledge.

Pr. 19:1-29—"Where reflection is wanting, zeal is not good; he who goes too quickly misses his way."

Si. 18:1-14—The greatness of God compared to the nothingness of man.

Si. 21:11-28—The wise man compared to the fool.

Si. 37:16-26—True wisdom compared to false.

Ba. 3:9-38; 4:1-4—Wisdom is the prerogative of Israel. "Learn where knowledge is, where strength, where understanding, and so learn where length of days is, where life, where the light of the eyes and where peace."

New Testament

Mt. 6:19-21—"For where your treasure is, there will your heart be also."

Lk. 6:39-45—"For every tree can be told by its own fruit..."

Mt. 7:13-14; Lk. 13:22-30—The two ways. "Enter by the narrow gate, since the road that leads to perdition is wide and spacious..."

Mt. 7:15-20—By their fruits you can tell a false from a true prophet.

Lk. 14:7-11—On choosing places at table. "For everyone who exalts himself will be humbled, and the man who humbles himself will be exalted. "

Lk. 23:26-32—The way to Calvary. "Daughters of Jerusalem, do not weep for me; weep rather for yourselves and for your children."

Jn. 16:1-15—Jesus tells his disciples all they need to know so that their faith will not be shaken.

Rm. 7:14-25—The inward struggle between what I want to do and what I in fact do gives me insight into "my inmost self."

1 Co. 1:10-31; 2:1-16—"...those whom the world thinks common and contemptible are the ones that God has chosen—those who are nothing at all to show up those who are everything."

1 Co. 12:1-31; 13:1-13; 14:1-40—The Spirit distributes different gifts to different people just as he chooses. We have to know and appreciate the gifts he gives us, especially the gift of love.

2 Co. 4:1-18; 5:1-10—Though our outer man may be falling into decay, our inner man is being renewed day by day.

2 Co. 10:1-18; 11:1-33; 12:1-21—Paul describes who he is and how God has used him. "If I am to boast, then let me boast of my own feebleness."

Ga. 2:15-21—The Good News is proclaimed by Paul. "...I live now not with my own life but with the life of Christ who lives in me."

* * * * *

Coming to true self-knowledge is impossible unless we are centered in the Divine. As long as we remain centered in self, we are blind to the true object of our desire. To love God and appreciate his goodness should be the goal of knowing who we are.

READINGS FROM THE LITERATURE OF SPIRITUALITY

Letters from the Desert, (Chapters 12 and 16)—The meeting between God's totality and man's nothingness is the greatest wonder of creation.

The God Who Comes, (Chapters 1, 2, and 7)—God makes himself known to man little by little; man knows himself in the light of the God who comes.

The Sign of Jonas, (Part Two)—Merton gains the insight that the things he had resented about the world when he left it were defects of his own that he had projected upon it. Now, on the contrary, he finds that everything stirs him with a deep and mute sense of compassion.

No Man Is an Island, (Prologue, Chapter 10)—We must be true to ourselves inside ourselves before we can know a truth that is outside us.

New Seeds of Contemplation, (Chapters 14 and 25)—In great saints we find that perfect humility and perfect integrity coincide.

The Way of Perfection, (Chapters 15, 17 and 18)—St. Teresa tells of the first steps in prayer and of the need for humility, love, and detachment as essential for contemplation. Humility is the principal virtue to be practiced by those who pray. True humility consists to a great extent in being ready for what the Lord desires to do with us and being happy that he should do it, in always considering ourselves unworthy to be called his servants.

SUPPLEMENTARY READING

Transformation in Christ, (Chapters III and VII)—The only fruitful self-knowledge is that which grows out of man's self-confrontation with God. Humility is a predisposition for the genuineness and truth of all our virtues—it is the central condition of our transformation and regeneration in Christ.

The Desert Fathers—Read the Sayings of the Fathers (Book I to Book VI).

* * * * *

The way of spiritual living contains many possibilities for self-deception. We can confuse gentleness with passivity. We may opt for an escapist attitude. A seeking for false security may turn out to be the motivation for meekness rather than the desire to be God-molded persons. To recognize these dangers and strive to grow beyond them is part of the process of self-discovery. However painful this process may be, it is a necessary phase of spiritual deepening. God guides us in this effort to know ourselves; it is his grace that awakens us to obstacles which make it difficult for us to see. Honest self-discovery must take place in a climate of gentleness lest we be overly harsh on ourselves. The Mystery does not intend such occasions of seeing to drive us to forceful perfectionism; it graces us with them mainly to help us grow in humility and greater confidence in the Triune God.

MINOR THEME VI

PATIENCE AND ACCEPTANCE OF SUFFERING IN DESERT EXPERIENCE

The faces of desert people—nomads and Indians—tell the story of great patience and the acceptance of suffering. Such wisdom awaits patiently the recurrent cycles of each year, counting on the Great Spirit to provide sufficient water and grain. The hardships of desert life leave no time for self-pity. Waking hours are spent in manual labor—planting and harvesting, tending sheep—and when night falls, with its sudden chill, one is grateful for sleep. The desert teaches patience; there is no rush when one waits upon the seasons. The desert leaves no room for complaint; hardship is part of this limited life, yet it is also a stepping stone to the Beyond. The desert experience can never be lived fully without great patience together with the willingness to undergo suffering. This journey to the depths of self intends to bring us to the presence of God but so often it seems to be aborted before we really begin. In spite of our good will, we get lost again and again in our own fantasy and imagination. That is why we need to be patient with ourselves, with our determined but deficient attempts to come to God. Only when we are patient may we find the courage to start our search again. With God's grace, we come to that still center where the Spirit speaks to us. We may hear this inner Voice today or tomorrow or for many days after that. To abide in the Eternal Now, we need patience—the patience to wait upon the Mystery knowing that its very silence speaks of God's love for us. If our love is true, then we are willing to wait. Our desire to do God's will does not make waiting less painful. The more intense it is, the more we suffer from delay. This kind of suffering is not the only one we meet in our desert experiences. The closer we come to God, and the more intense our love grows, the more we suffer from our sinfulness, our selfishness, our infidelity. We must also be patient with our failure and trust that God values our good intentions. Such attitudes aid us also in daily life. When we return to our task, we try to be patient with our own faults and those of others. Suffering in all its forms takes on a deeper meaning. We see it as a way to purify us of all traces of self-love, as a call to share with Christ in the work of redemption.

READINGS FROM HOLY SCRIPTURE

Old Testament

2 S. 1:1-27—When David learns of the death of Saul and Jonathan, he suffers this loss deeply. "How did the heroes fall in the thick of battle?"

2 S. 18:1-32; 19:1-15—Absalom dies and David mourns the loss of his son.

2 M. 6:18-31—The martyrdom of Eleazar "...though I might have escaped death, whatever agonies of body I now endure under this bludgeoning, in my soul I am glad to suffer, because of the awe which he inspires in me."

2 M. 7:1-42—The martyrdom of the seven brothers. Each brother met his end undefiled with perfect trust in the Lord.

Jb. 16:1-22; 17:1-16—Job is a patient man but he finds that those trying to justify his suffering speak only "airy words."

Jb. 19:1-29—Job feels deserted by God and man, a thing corrupt from whom everyone turns.

Jb. 29:1-20; 30:1-31; 31:1-40—In his lament and final defense, Job contrasts his former happiness to his present misery.

Ps. 22—The sufferings and hope of the virtuous man.

Ps. 38—Prayer in distress. "Your arrows have pierced deep, your hand has pressed down on me..."

Ps. 69—"...do not hide your face from your servant, quick, I am in trouble, answer me..."

Ps. 70—A cry of distress. "To me, poor wretch, come quickly God!"

Ps. 102—Prayer in misfortune. "Yahweh, hear my prayer, let my cry for help reach you..."

Si. 1:22-24—Patience and self-control. "The patient man will hold out till the time comes, but his joy will break out in the end."

Si. 2:1-18—"...if you aspire to serve the Lord, prepare yourself for an ordeal ...do not be alarmed when disaster comes."

Si. 40:1-27—"Much hardship has been made for every man, a heavy yoke lies on the sons of Adam..."

Si. 41:1-4—Death is the sentence passed on all living creatures by the Lord.

Is. 52:13-15; 53:1-12—Fourth song of the servant of Yahweh. "And yet ours were the sufferings he bore, ours the sorrows he carried."

Jr. 4:1-31; 5:1-31; 6:1-30—The prophet recounts the sufferings of those who do not listen to the voice of Yahweh and abide in his presence.

Lm. 2:1-22—"Oh, how Yahweh in his wrath has brought darkness on the daughter of Zion!"

Dn. 3:1-97—Those who will not worship the golden statue of King Nebuchadnezzar are thrown into the fiery furnace but do not burn. The king acknowledges the miracle and showers favors on Yahweh's faithful, who in the face of grave suffering rely wholly on him.

Jl. 1:2-20—The prophet laments the ruin of the country and calls the people to prayer and repentance.

New Testament

Lk. 2:33-35—Simeon foretells that a sword will pierce Mary's soul.

Mt. 12:15-21—Jesus is the suffering "servant of Yahweh."

Mt. 16:21-23; Mk. 8:31-33; Lk. 9:22—First prophecy of the Passion. "The Son of Man...is destined to suffer grievously, to be rejected...to be put to death, and to be raised up on the third day."

Mt. 17:22-23; Mk. 9:30-32; Lk. 9:44-45—Second prophecy of the Passion. "The Son of Man is going to be handed over into the power of men."

Mt. 20:17-19; Mk. 10:32-34; Lk. 18:31-34—Third prophecy of the Passion. "...he will be handed over to the pagans and will be mocked, maltreated and spat on..."

Mt. 24:4-44; Mk. 13:5-37; Lk. 21:5-38—Jesus foretells the onset of sorrows and the great tribulation of Jerusalem. The coming of the Son of Man will be evident if his disciples stay on the alert.

Jn. 14:1-31; 15:1-27—Jesus tells his disciples not to let their hearts be troubled or afraid; he will help them to bear with the hatred of the world.

Mt. 27:11-26; Mk. 15:1-15; Lk. 23:13-25; Jn. 18:28-40—Jesus is brought before Pilate but he makes no attempt to defend himself. He has fully accepted the Father's will.

Mt. 27:27-56; Mk. 15:16-39; Lk. 23:26-46; Jn. 19:1-37—Jesus is scourged, crowned with thorns, crucified and mocked. He accepts his suffering, though humanly he feels deserted.

Rm. 8:18-25—"...what we suffer in this life can never be compared to the glory as yet unrevealed, which is waiting for us." It is something we must wait for with patience.

1 Co. 13:1-13—"Love is always patient and kind..."

2 Co. 5:11-21; 6:1-10—"...we prove we are servants of God by great fortitude in times of suffering...by our purity, knowledge, patience and kindness..."

Ga. 5:1-26—"What the Spirit brings is...love, joy, peace, patience..."

Ep. 4:1-16—Paul exhorts the brothers to live in unity. "Bear with one another charitably, in complete selflessness, gentleness and patience."

2 Tm. 2:1-13—How Timothy should face hardships.

Heb. 10:32-39—The followers of Christ will need endurance to do God's will and suffer without complaint.

Jm. 1:2-11—Trials are a privilege to the man who walks with the Lord.

Jm. 5:7-20—Recall the patience of Job and wait for the Lord's coming.

* * * * *

Minor irritations make us impatient. Major suffering is an occasion of complaint. At times we would like to shake our fist at God rather than accept our fate. If such is our attitude, perhaps these passages from Holy Scripture will foster in us a change of heart. To endure patiently what God sends, confident that this way is the best, grants us inner peace and great contentment.

READINGS FROM THE LITERATURE OF SPIRITUALITY

Letters from the Desert, (Chapter 15)—The fact that Carretto's vocation leads him to seek the lowest place means nothing; what counts is forcing himself to stay in that place every day of his life.

The God Who Comes, (Chapters 12 and 16)—If God is great and comes to us with the immensity of creation, we must go to him with the dignity of being accepted in all dimensions of our creaturehood.

The Sign of Jonas, (Part Five)—Whatever may be the place in the Church to which a priest is called, he is bound to be purified by fire. That fire is the fire of divine charity in which his soul must become one with the soul of Jesus.

No Man Is an Island, (Chapter 5)—The Christian must not only accept suffering: he must strive to make it holy.

New Seeds of Contemplation, (Chapters 10 and 22)—The flight from the world is not an escape from conflict, anguish and suffering, but a flight from disunity and separation to unity and peace in the love of other men.

The Way of Perfection, (Chapter 11)—St. Teresa considers mortification and how it may be attained in times of sickness. To follow Christ one must renounce the world's standards of wisdom in order to attain the true wisdom accepting the cross brings.

SUPPLEMENTARY READING

The Wisdom of the Desert—Read Sayings LXXXVIII to CXXII of the Desert Fathers.

Transformation in Christ, (Chapters XII and XVI)—In the measure in which we live by our ties with the supernatural, we will sorrow, above all, over the sorrows of Christ. We will endure crucifixion with him and hail the cross as a possibility of expiation.

* * * * *

Christians see suffering as a blessing because it provides a possibility for growth in nearness to their Lord. Though our initial reaction may be one of rejecting pain, we may slowly come to see, upon reflection, that we are not in final control of our destiny. There is Someone greater than we who overshadows our life and leads us by "crooked lines" to the fulfillment of our call. Once we face the fact that no matter what we do we cannot expect to go through life without some suffering, we may come to see its salutary meaning. We begin to find strength and the courage of acceptance in prayerful presence to the sufferings of Christ. Through affliction, we become more at one with our Redeemer. Suffering can thus be a source of self-awareness and joy if we accept it in the right spirit—as one more phase of our desert call.

MINOR THEME VII

TRUST AND DEPENDENCE IN DESERT EXPERIENCE

Standing before the Lord in silence and inner emptiness, we sense in contrast to our weakness, his strength, in contrast to our inability to do anything in the order of salvation, his free and loving gift of redemption. We realize that if we ever do reach union with the Trinity, it will be a pure gift. We are wholly dependent on God. Our selfish pride has difficulty accepting such dependence. We all share in the desire of our first parents in Eden to be God's equals—to save ourselves by our own power. Only when we let go of illusions of self-salvation can we remove a formidable barrier to union. More, of course, remains to be done. Besides admitting that we cannot be our own savior, we have to turn to God in total trust. We have to have absolute confidence that he knows best how to lead us from sin to salvation. We have to say with Christ, "Not my will but yours be done." This kind of trust is not easy to attain in practice. Along the way we are more than willing to allow God to guide us in certain life situations but to give him the freedom to do with us what he wills, without reservation, is a frightening thought because we cannot foresee where it will lead us. Only in the trustful and free surrender of ourselves do we recognize the Father, as Jesus did, as wise and loving. To trust or not to trust in Love Divine is a fundamental decision each of us has to make. Once, with God's grace, we place ourselves in mightier hands in unlimited trust, we know that this step, hard as it was to take, was the best one after all. From the trust and dependence of desert experience our everyday life receives a deeper meaning. Hardships as well as joys acquire transcendent value. They become more obvious manifestations of divine care and a providential knowing of what is good for us. As sheep trust the shepherd who guides them, so must we trust God in the experience of desert living. Reliance on our own resources is not enough. We must turn to One greater than we for strength in the trials that beset us. As wanderers rely on an occasional oasis for a refreshing drink, so must we depend on the Divine to sustain us from day to day. Dependence on God is not a sign of weakness; it is the source of lasting strength. The One who made and redeemed us is wholly reliable. He never betrays our trust. In living the desert experience, we begin to discover that all things work together for our good.

READINGS FROM HOLY SCRIPTURE

Old Testament

Gn. 18:1-15—The angel of Yahweh promises Sarah that she will bear a son, though because of her age she is inclined to doubt.

Gn. 21:1-7—Yahweh keeps his promise and Sarah gives birth to a son, her trust in him totally restored.

Gn. 29:31-35; 30:1-24—God hears Rachel's plea for a son and seeing her utter dependence on him, he answers her prayer.

Ex. 2:23-25; 3:1-22—God remembers his covenant with Israel. He calls Moses and entrusts to him the mission of leading his people from slavery to freedom.

Ex. 14:1-31—Yahweh leads the sons of Israel across the Sea of Reeds. Witnessing this great act, the people put their trust in God and in Moses, his servant.

Jos. 5:13-15; 6:1-27—In perfect trust Joshua follows the Lord's commands and succeeds in taking Jericho.

Jos. 23:1-16; 24:1-28—Joshua sums up his work and sets forth once more the vocation of Israel. "...every promise of good made to you by Yahweh your God has been fulfilled for you..."

1 K. 17:1-24—Through the power of Yahweh and Elijah's dependence on him, the prophet performs two miracles.

1 K. 18:1-46—The sacrifice on Carmel is a testimony of trust in Yahweh.

2 K. 2:1-25—Elijah, God's trusted servant, is taken up by Yahweh and Elisha succeeds him. He performs two miracles.

2 K. 4:1-44; 5:1-27; 6:1-7—Some miracles of Elisha that manifest his trust in Yahweh's power.

Jdt. 8:1-36; 9:1-14—A portrait of Judith and her confident prayer to Yahweh for the protection of the house of Israel.

Jdt. 10:1-23; 11:1-23; 12:1-20; 13:1-20—Guided by Yahweh, in whom she places all her trust, Judith defeats Holofernes and avenges her people.

Jdt. 16:1-25—Her trust not betrayed, Judith sings to God a hymn of thanksgiving. She lives to old age and dies beloved by the House of Israel.

Ps. 23—"Yahweh is my shepherd, I lack nothing."

Ps. 25—"I rely on you, do not let me be shamed, do not let my enemies gloat over me!"

Ps. 37—"Commit your fate to Yahweh, trust in him and he will act..."

Ps. 44—"My trust was not in my bow, my sword did not gain me victory..."

Ps. 56—"I put my trust in you; in God, whose word I praise..."

Ps. 91—"I rescue all who cling to me, I protect whoever knows my name..."

Ps. 125—"Those who trust in Yahweh are like Mount Zion, unshakable, standing for ever."

Si. 11:12-28—Trust in God alone.

Is. 11:1-16—The virtuous king is totally trustworthy. "Integrity is the loincloth around his waist, faithfulness the belt around his hips."

Is. 12:1-6—"...he is the God of my salvation. I have trust now and no fear..."

Is. 64:1-11—"No ear has heard, no eye has seen any God but you act like this for those who trust him."

Jr. 17:5-11—"A curse on the man who puts his trust in man, who relies on things of flesh.... He is like dry scrub in the wastelands.... A blessing on the man who puts his trust in Yahweh.... He is like a tree by the waterside that thrusts its roots to the stream..."

Ezk. 34:1-31—The shepherds of Israel. "...it is Yahweh who speaks. I shall look for the lost one, bring back the stray, bandage the wounded and make the weak strong...I shall be a true shepherd to them."

Ho. 11:1-11—"When Israel was a child I loved him, and I called my son out of Egypt."

Ho. 14:2-10—The sincere conversion of Israel to Yahweh.

New Testament

Lk. 1:26-38—Responding in trust to the angel Gabriel, Mary says, "I am the handmaid of the Lord...let what you have said be done to me."

Mt. 6:25-34; Lk. 12:22-32—Trust in providence. "Now if that is how God clothes the grass in the field which is there today and thrown into the furnace tomorrow, will he not much more look after you, you men of little faith?"

Mt. 9:18-26; Mk. 5:21-43; Lk. 8:40-56—The faith of the woman who touches Jesus' cloak so touches him that he restores her to health. Jesus also raises the daughter of Jairus to life.

Mt. 11:25-27—The Good News is hidden from the learned and clever and revealed to mere children.

Mt. 14:22-33; Mk. 6:45-52—Jesus walks on the water and Peter, in an act of great trust, comes to meet him, but his faith wavers.

Mt. 18:1-14; Mk. 9:33-37, 42-50; Lk. 9:46-48; 17:1-3; 18:15-17—The disciples ask Jesus who is the greatest in the kingdom of heaven and he asks them to bring to him a little child. They are never to despise little ones or lead them astray, for it is the will of the Father that not one of them be lost.

Mt. 19:13-15; Mk. 10:13-16—Jesus asks that the children be brought to him, for the kingdom of heaven belongs to such as these.

Lk. 23:39-43—Jesus promises the good thief that, because of his trust, he will be with him in paradise.

Jn. 10:1-21—Jesus is the Good Shepherd, who lays down his life for his sheep.

Jn. 14:1-7—"Do not let your hearts be troubled. Trust in God still, and trust in me."

Ac. 17:23-34—In his speech before the Council of the Areopagus, Paul tells the men of Athens, "...it is in him that we live, and move, and exist..."

1 Co. 10:1-13—"You can trust God not to let you be tried beyond your strength..."

1 P. 1:3-21—The hope of the prophets has been realized in Christ. "Free your minds then, of encumbrances; control them, and put your trust in nothing but the grace that will be given you when Jesus Christ is revealed."

1 P. 2:1-10—We can rest our trust on the precious cornerstone, who is Christ.

* * * * *

Whenever our confidence in God wavers, we need only to turn to Holy Scripture to feel renewed. Holy men and women have rooted their trust not in the shifting winds of worldly success but in the firm soil of their Divine Source. We, too, must grow ever more trusting of the God who wills our good. We must depend on the Divine to insure our well being, remembering the words of Isaiah: "No ear has heard, no eye has seen any God but you act like this for those who trust him" (Is. 64:1-3).

READINGS FROM THE LITERATURE OF SPIRITUALITY

Letters from the Desert, (Chapter 17)—Our life on earth is a discovering, a becoming conscious of, a contemplating and loving this mystery of God's unique reality which surrounds us and in which we are immersed like meteorites in space.

The God Who Comes, (Chapters 11 and 22)—The God who is coming does not show himself to satisfy our curiosity; he unveils himself before our faithfulness, trust, and humility.

Abandonment to Divine Providence, (Chapter III)—To surrender to God is to practice every virtue.

No Man Is an Island, (Chapters 2, 11 and 14)—"He who hopes in God trusts in God, whom he never sees, to bring him to the possession of things that are beyond imagination."

New Seeds of Contemplation, (Chapters 16 and 17)—Men cannot trust anything if they cease to believe in God. Hell is where no one has anything in common except the fact that they all hate one another.

The Way of Perfection, (Chapters 21, 22 and 23)—St. Teresa describes the great importance of setting out upon the practice of prayer with firm resolution, surrendered to God, dependent wholly on him, and heeding no difficulties put in our way by the devil. She explains the meaning of mental prayer and describes the importance of not turning back once we have set out upon the way.

SUPPLEMENTARY READING

The Wisdom of the Desert—Read Sayings CXXIII to CL of the Desert Fathers.

Transformation in Christ, (Chapters VIII and XV)—One who is filled with true confidence in God clings, in the presence of all things that by themselves might justly arouse his anxiety, to the supreme reality and the omnipotent love and mercy of God.

* * * * *

An attitude of trust allows persons, events, and things to be what they are, to unfold in God's good time. Instead of manipulating life, our first choice is to listen to its message. Instead of forcing our solutions upon every situation, we remain open to all sides, trying to appraise the message God is communicating through apparently unconnected circumstances. A trustful attitude fosters reflection upon God's own fidelity, manifested age upon age in his concern for the Chosen People. Such trust confirms again our total dependence on the Holy Trinity.

MINOR THEME VIII

SELF-EMPTYING AND DETACHMENT IN DESERT EXPERIENCE

The sparseness of desert vegetation symbolizes the emptying or mortification of self-centered dispositions that must take place in the soul. We must free ourselves from the dominance of human powers and possessions to be freed for God's power over and possession of us. The remoteness of desert places symbolizes the detachment of the soul from temporal things as ends in themselves for the sake of appreciating them in the Eternal. Desert experience is intended to lead us to that center where we meet God to the degree that we leave everything else behind. This experience implies that self-emptying of which all spiritual writers speak. For instance, St. John of the Cross says we have to empty our intellect by faith, our memory by hope, our will by charity. This self-emptying can be effective only when it is accompanied by detachment. It is not enough that we put things aside, that we let go of them exteriorly. We must become interiorly disengaged from them as well as from our own self-centered needs and desires. Only in interior detachment can we focus first on God. In and through the Lord we see others, ourselves and things in their proper light. We are less inclined to make any of these limited goods absolute. The self-emptying and detachment of desert experience are part of the painful process of purification. The closer we come to God, the more we discover in our depths attachments we have not yet shed, though they are harmful to our inner growth. The roots of these attachments seem to sink deeper and deeper into our hearts. The process of purification has thus to begin anew. What is it that keeps us from becoming discouraged? It is, as St.

Paul says, the love of Christ that overwhelms us (2 Co. 5:14). That love, like the gift of intimacy, is so precious that no price is too high to pay—not even the pain of desert detachment.

READINGS FROM HOLY SCRIPTURE

Old Testament

Ex. 23:20-33—The chosen people must detach themselves from false gods and worship Yahweh only.

Lv. 16:1-34—The great Day of Atonement serves Yahweh's purpose to purify the people and cleanse them of their sins.

2 S. 24:1-25—Yahweh's anger blazes out against the Israelites because they break their promises to him. As punishment David chooses three days of pestilence. Yahweh takes pity on the people and turns the plague away from Israel.

1 Ch. 21:1-30—The days of pestilence come upon Israel but Yahweh takes pity on his people. David builds an altar to Yahweh and offers holocausts and sacrifices.

2 Ch. 29:1-36—The purification of the temple and the sacrifice of atonement.

2 Ch. 34:1-33; 35:1-27—During the reign of King Josiah, idols are demolished. The covenant is renewed and every member of the House of Israel serves their God.

Ne. 9:1-37—The ceremony of atonement.

Ps. 38—"My friends and my companions shrink from my wounds, even the dearest of them keep their distance..."

Ps. 51—"Purify me with hyssop until I am clean; wash me until I am whiter than snow."

Ps. 73—"I look to no one else in heaven, I delight in nothing else on earth."

Ps. 90—"Our days dwindle under your wrath, our lives are over in a breath..."

Si. 10:6-18—"The beginning of human pride is to desert the Lord, and to turn one's heart from one's maker."

Si. 38:16-24—Mourning. "Once the dead man is laid to rest, let his memory rest too, do not fret for him, once his spirit departs."

Si. 41:1-4—How bitter it is to remember death for a man at peace among his goods.

Is. 29:13-24—People honor Yahweh with lip service while their hearts are far from him; however, "...the lowly will rejoice in Yahweh even more and the poorest exult in the Holy One of Israel..."

Is. 54:1-17; 55:1-13—Yahweh renews his covenant with the poor who give up all lesser possessions for his sake.

Is. 61:1-11—The mission of the prophet is to comfort those who mourn and to give them instead of ashes a garland.

Jr. 10:1-25—The house of Israel must worship not idols but the true God.

Ezk. 14:1-23; 15:1-8—If the people persist in their idolatry, Yahweh will reduce the country to desert.

Jl. 2:12-27—A call to repentance and an answer to prayer. "...it is Yahweh who speaks—come back to me with all your heart, fasting, weeping, mourning."

New Testament

Mt. 5:1-12; Lk. 6:20-26—"How happy are the poor in spirit; theirs is the kingdom of heaven."

Mt. 10:37-39; Mt. 16:24-28; Mk. 8:34-38; Lk. 9:23-26—"Anyone who does not take up his cross and follow in my footsteps is not worthy of me."

Mt. 12:46-50; Mk. 3:31-35; Lk. 8:19-21—The true kinsmen of Jesus are those who empty themselves of their own will and do the will of his Father in heaven.

Lk. 12:13-21—What will the hoarding of possessions mean when God demands one's soul?

Lk. 13:1-5—Examples inviting repentance.

Lk. 14:25-33—"...none of you can be my disciple unless he gives up all his possessions."

Lk. 16:9-13—"You cannot be the slave both of God and of money."

Lk. 16:19-31—The rich man and Lazarus.

Mt. 19:16-30; Mk. 10:17-31; Lk. 18:18-30—The rich young man was not willing to sell what he owned and give the money to the poor. Jesus warns against the danger of riches and tells of the reward of renunciation.

Lk. 19:1-10—Zacchaeus promises to give half his property to the poor and Jesus promises in turn salvation to his house.

Mt. 22:15-22; Mk. 12:13-17; Lk. 20:20-26—Give to Caesar what belongs to Caesar and to God what belongs to God.

Mk. 12:41-44; Lk. 21:1-4—The widow put only a mite in the treasury but it was all that she possessed.

2 Co. 8:1-15—"Remember how generous the Lord Jesus was: he was rich, but he became poor for your sake, to make you rich out of his poverty."

2 Co. 9:6-15—God loves a cheerful giver. "Each one should give what he has decided in his own mind, not grudgingly or because he is made to..."

Ph. 2:1-11—"His state was divine, yet he did not cling to his equality with God but emptied himself to assume the condition of a slave, and became as men are..."

Ph. 3:1-21—Paul accepts the loss of everything if only he can have Christ.
Jm. 4:13-17; 5:1-6—A warning for the rich and self-confident.
1 Jn. 2:12-17—Detachment from the world. "You must not love this passing world or anything that is in the world."
1 Jn. 4:1-6—Be on guard against the enemies of Christ and against the world.

* * * * *

Letting go of our possessions means more than merely giving something away since, sadly, most of us only give from our abundance, from where it does not hurt. Few would imitate the widow who gave her last mite. Letting go means giving over to God all that we possess, including the pride of ownership, the abundant store out of which we give, the memory of what we gave, the inner image of ourselves as generous givers. We must empty our hearts of all these possessions—including our glorified self-image—if we want to prepare our inner chamber for the Divine Guest who desires to be our All in all.

READINGS FROM THE LITERATURE OF SPIRITUALITY

Letters from the Desert, (Chapters 5 and 9)—Our heart, with all its potential, loses its balance too easily when it holds on to the creature so passionately that it loses sight of its creator.

The God Who Comes, (Chapter 17)—"Without any doubt, one of the most dangerous enemies man has to combat in the spiritual life is pleasure."

Abandonment to Divine Providence, (Chapter IV)—Complete self-emptying and surrender to the will of God is the essence of spirituality.

No Man Is an Island, (Chapter 6)—"If we deny ourselves in order to think ourselves better than other men our self-denial is only self-gratification."

New Seeds of Contemplation, (Chapters 4, 5, 28, 32 and 35)—"We do not detach ourselves from things in order to attach ourselves to God, but rather we become detached from ourselves in order to see and use all things in and for God." Detachment is the secret of interior peace.

The Way of Perfection, (Chapters 8, 9 and 10)—St. Teresa considers the great benefit of self-detachment, both interior and exterior, from all created things, illustrating these blessings in regard to one's relations with relatives. She also shows how detachment and humility go together.

On Being Involved, (Chapters II and III)—Presence to the Divine in daily life is unattainable without detachment. True involvement calls for a vigilant distance that prevents less pure motives from gaining ascendance.

Poustinia, (Part II, Chapter 11)—The poustinia fosters a kenotic way of life. The very fact that one is in a poustinia means that he is tending toward a complete self-emptying.

Prayer Is a Hunger, (Chapter 8)—The Word, the Sacraments, the Incarnation—each is a kenosis, an emptying out, manifesting the poverty of Christ so that we may meet him.

Poverty of Spirit—In this meditative book, Metz reflects on how God empties himself to become man and how man in turn must empty himself to become who he truly is.

SUPPLEMENTARY READING

Transformation in Christ, (Chapter IV)—True meekness presupposes a soul detached from itself and touched by Christ's love, a love that softens and dissolves all hardened fibers of egoism.

The Night Country—Out of the shadows of a strange and lonely boyhood, issuing from the darkness of forgotten civilizations, welling from the obscurity of mankind's perplexing nature, Loren Eiseley weaves a tale of haunting fears and hopes, failures and triumphs. Through the life of one man is woven the story of all men in all times detached enough from the immediate to perceive in it the mystery of transcendent reality.

* * * * *

Detachment implies more than exterior distancing, for example, going to an actual desert or a place of retreat. It is mainly an interior experience in which we have to face our inordinate attachments to ideas, emotions, memories, dreams and whatever else hinders spiritual growth. In the desert we have to question our own self-centeredness as shown in a subtle clinging to little things. Detachment does imply a dying to self, a kenotic phase, but it occasions rebirth to a new level of consonance and spiritual living. The desert opens us to opportunities for spiritual deepening never known by us before this graced event.

MINOR THEME IX

AWAKENING THROUGH DESERT EXPERIENCE

Desert experience teaches us with God's grace both to go beyond the things of this world as ultimate and to let go of our selfish preoccupation with power, pleasure, and possession. It thrusts us beyond the limits of temporal goods to the Eternal One who transcends creation and in whom all that is finds its source. The God beyond all and yet in all cannot be grasped by our senses, our imagination, our intellect. As we near the end of our desert experience, we face a Mystery no natural faculty can master. We paradoxically experience this fullness as emptiness, this nearness as distance. In our effort to push against the pace of grace, we may set in motion our imagination and overwork our reason, but such moves represent a regression on the spiritual path. We forget that neither our images nor our concepts can contain God as God. All we can do in the face of this not knowing is to rest attentively, to wait lovingly upon God until he makes himself known in whatever way he chooses. When grace lifts the veil from our eyes, we see that the emptiness we feared affects only our natural faculties—not our faith. Through grace there awakens in us an awareness of a different kind. A mysterious "dark light" dawns in the center of our soul. It is light insofar as we *know* God, but it is also darkness because the Godhead is ungraspable to us. At this moment of awakening to deeper union—to a depth of presence only those who have experienced it can know—God is no longer a vague force but a Loving Person who calls us by name, the Lord and Savior whom we are invited to love with our whole heart and soul.

READINGS FROM HOLY SCRIPTURE

Old Testament

Nb. 22:1-41; 23:1-30; 24:1-2—Balak summons Balaam to curse the people coming from Egypt. Yahweh opens his eyes. Instead of cursing the people, he blesses them.

Is. 11:12-15; 12:1-25—When Samuel gives way to Saul, he says to all Israel, "Only reverence and serve Yahweh faithfully with all your heart, for you see the great wonder he has done among you."

1 K. 3:4-28—An account of Solomon's dream at Gibeon and an example of his wise judgment.

1 K. 9:1-9—Yahweh appears to Solomon a second time and says to him, "I consecrate this house you have built: I place my name there for ever; my eyes and my heart shall be always there."

Ps. 3—"Now I can lie down and go to sleep and then awake, for Yahweh has hold of me..."

Ps. 66—"Come and see what marvels God has done..."

Ps. 77—"I reflect on all that you did, I ponder on all your achievements. God, your ways are holy!"

Ps. 119—"...your word is a lamp to my feet, a light on my path."

Ws. 6:1-25—Cultivate Wisdom. "...be on the alert for her and anxiety will quickly leave you."

Ws. 8:1-20—From Wisdom comes all that is desirable. "...she is an initiate in the mysteries of God's knowledge..."

Is. 9:1-6—"The people that walked in darkness has seen a great light...." A child is born for us and the name they give him is "Wonder Counselor, Mighty God, Eternal Father, Prince of Peace."

Is. 50:4-11—Third song of the servant of Yahweh. "Each morning he wakes me to hear, to listen like a disciple."

Is. 51:9-23; 52:1-12—The awakening of Yahweh and of Jerusalem.

Is. 60:1-22—The glorious resurrection of Jerusalem.

Is. 62:1-12—A second poem on the glorious resurrection of Jerusalem.

Jr. 31:1-40—Yahweh will pardon his people in the wilderness and restore their fortunes. "For I will refresh the wearied soul and satisfy every sorrowing soul. And hence: I awoke and was refreshed and my sleep was peaceful."

Zc. 12:1-14; 13:1-9; 14:1-21—The deliverance and restoration of Jerusalem.

New Testament

Mt. 2:13-23—In a dream Joseph is told to take the child and flee into Egypt. He awakens and does as he is told. After Herod's death, an angel appears in a dream and assures him it is safe to return to Israel.

Lk. 2:22-32—Jesus is presented in the Temple. Simeon, setting his eyes upon the child, says he can go in peace because he has seen the salvation God has prepared for all nations.

Mt. 3:13-17; Mk. 1:9-11; Lk. 3:21-22—As soon as Jesus is baptized, the heavens opened and he saw the Spirit of God descending like a dove. A voice spoke frown heaven, "This is my Son, the Beloved; my favor rests on him."

Mt. 6:22-23—Since the lamp of the body is the eye, it follows that if the eye is sound, the whole body will be filled with light.

Mk. 4:21-23; Lk. 8:16-18; Lk. 11:33-36—Parable of the lamp. "For there is nothing hidden but it must be disclosed, nothing kept secret except to be brought to light."

Mt. 8:23-27; Mk. 4:35-41; Lk. 8:22-25—The storm was violent. The disciples woke Jesus, asking him to save them. He questioned their faith.

Lk. 12:35-48—On being ready for the Master's return. "It may be in the second watch he comes, or in the third, but happy those servants if he finds them ready."

Mt. 20:29-34; Mk. 10:46-52; Lk. 18:35-43—Jesus felt pity for the blind. He touched their eyes and immediately their sight returned.

Mt. 22:23-33; Mk. 12:18-27; Lk. 20:27-40—The resurrection of the dead. "God is God, not of the dead, but of the living."

Mt. 24:37-51; Mk. 13:33-37; Lk. 21:34-36—"...stay awake, because you do not know the day when your master is coming."

Mt. 25:1-13—The foolish bridesmaids brought no oil for their lamps. They arrive late and the Lord does not know them. Jesus cautions us to stay awake, for we do not know the day or the hour of his coming.

Jn. 3:1-21—Jesus' conversation with Nicodemus. "You must be born from above."

Jn. 8:12-20—"I am the light of the world; anyone who follows me will not be walking in the dark; he will have the light of life."

Jn. 9:1-41—The cure of the man born blind. "As long as I am in the world I am the light of the world."

Lk. 24:13-35—Jesus walked with two men on the way to Emmaus, but they did not recognize him. Only when he broke bread with them were their eyes opened. Then he vanished from their sight.

Jn. 21:1-23—Jesus shows himself to the disciples on the shore of Tiberias.

Ep. 4:17-32; 5:1-20—The new life in Christ. "Wake up from your sleep, rise from the dead, and Christ will shine on you."

1 Th. 5:1-11—Watchfulness while awaiting the coming of the Lord.

Rv. 7:9-17—The rewarding of the saints. The Lamb will be their shepherd; he will lead them to springs of living water and wipe away all their tears.

Rv. 21:1-27; 22:1-15—In the heavenly Jerusalem, "It will never be night again and they will not need lamplight or sunlight, because the Lord God will be shining on them."

* * * * *

Though we have physical sight, we may still walk like people who are blind. Our eyes may be open, but we are closed to Christ. We give him only lip service when he wants to awaken our hearts to the fullness of love and new life in him. We must pray that our eyes will be opened and able to behold in persons, events, and things the imprint of the Living God.

READINGS FROM THE LITERATURE OF SPIRITUALITY

Letters from the Desert, (Chapter 11)—A breath from the Spirit is animating and awakening the whole universe. An old world is dying, and a new one is being born.

The God Who Comes, (Chapters 20 and 21)—To be able to live in Jesus' love, to do everything in his love, is the key to wakeful living, the most authentic summary of being Christian.

Abandonment to Divine Providence, (Chapter V)—Only complete and true faith enables the soul to awaken to God's goodness and to accept with joy everything that happens to it.

No Man Is an Island, (Chapters 4 and 9)—The will of God is more than a concept; it is a transcendent reality, a secret power given to us from moment to moment, that awakens us to the life of our life, the soul of our soul's life.

New Seeds of Contemplation, (Chapters 21, 31, 34 and 38)—The mystery of Christ in the Gospel concentrates the rays of God's light to a point that sets fire to the spirit of man. The utter simplicity and obviousness of the infused light contemplation pours into our soul suddenly awakens us to a new level of awareness. Tides of joy are concentrated into strong touches, contacts of God that wake the soul with a bound of wonder and delight and sometimes burn with a wound that is delectable although it gives pain.

The Way of Perfection, (Chapters 24, 25 and 26)—St. Teresa describes how vocal prayer may be practiced with perfection and explains its alliance to mental prayer. She goes on to describe a method for recollecting our thoughts that leads to further awakening to the divine reality.

Prayer Is a Hunger, (Chapters 4 and 6)—When we return to God in penance, we begin to discover truths we had never really known and yet they were there awaiting our discovery, our reverent awakening to their being.

SUPPLEMENTARY READING

Transformation in Christ, (Chapters I, II and IV)—Christian life begins with a deep yearning to become a new man in Christ. "The inward progress in the Christian's life is linked to a process of awakening to an ever increasing degree of consciousness."

The Desert Fathers—Read the Sayings of the Fathers (Book VII to Book XXI).

* * * * *

The capacity to see anew, as if through the eyes of a child, to marvel at the wonders of creation, to stand in awe before the Divine, are characteristic qualities of the desert experience. We slow down to see what is really there. We look again and again. Through this wakeful approach, we grow to appreciate the mysterious Beyond in the midst of the everyday, the epiphany of the Divine that remains invisible to the utilitarian eye alone.

MINOR THEME X

SURRENDER AND COMMITMENT IN DESERT EXPERIENCE

When we awaken through desert experience to a deeper awareness of the Divine, we see God as an infinitely loving Person who invites us to union and communion—to a oneness only possible when we truly surrender. To abandon ourselves to the Mystery means that we allow this infinitely wise and loving Lord to be the goal and main source of our life direction. We turn in moments of doubt to the Spirit, and attune our ears to his voice speaking in every situation. We make an ongoing commitment to appraise and affirm God's will not just theoretically but practically in our day-to-day circumstances, in the persons we meet, in relation to the things we possess. Our surrender to the Divine Will, our renewed *Yes*, happens in the sufferings we have to face as well as in the joys the Mystery sends our way. Once we learn to live in renunciation, we may experience an inner liberation that will surprise us. The first step is difficult, but once we take it we are freed from many useless concerns. We live in the assurance that God cares for us always and everywhere. The desert of the heart is thus the site of our abandonment to the "More Than." This surrender may happen freely at the height of our prosperity or it may happen when we have reached the end of our strength in a moment of ego-desperation. Nothing we do suffices to relieve our plight until at last we fling ourselves into the outstretched arms of Christ. Whether our motivation for surrender is gratitude or desperation, he embraces us tenderly. Initial surrender to the Triune God must then grow into lasting commitment. The desert moment, in its peculiar intensity, will pass, but its transforming traces will linger in daily concrete commitment to the life task God has commissioned us to do. Then the formative dispositions we learn during our desert experience may invade our whole being and make us radiant witnesses to Christ's way and truth in this world.

READINGS FROM HOLY SCRIPTURE

Old Testament

Gn. 12:1-20; 13:1-8—Because Abram has always been committed to Yahweh, he becomes the chosen one through whom Yahweh will establish a covenant and create a great nation.

Gn. 15:1-21—The divine promises and the covenant.
Gn. 17:1-27—Yahweh gives Abram a new name, Abraham, father of a multitude, and in his old age promises him a son by Sarah.
Gn. 22:1-19—God puts Abraham to the test. He asks him to sacrifice his son Isaac. Abraham does not refuse and God delights in his surrender.
Lv. 26:1-46—Yahweh bestows his blessings and his curses upon the House of Israel whom he has ordained to uphold his covenant.
Nb. 30:1-17—Moses conveys Yahweh's laws concerning vows.
Dt. 10:12-22; 11:1-32—Moses tells the people that they must love Yahweh and always keep his injunctions. "Let these words of mine remain in your heart and in your soul...a blessing, if you obey the commandments of Yahweh...a curse, if you disobey..."
Dt. 26:16-19; 27:1-26; 28:1-69—Together with the writing of the Law, Yahweh issues his promised blessings and curses.
Jos. 1:1-9—When Moses was dead, Yahweh spoke to Joshua and promised to be with him as he was with Moses—provided he would be strong and stand firm.
Jg. 6:1-40; 7:1-25; 8:1-35—Yahweh calls Gideon whose clan is the weakest in Manasseh. Because Yahweh is with him, he shall crush single-handedly the power of the Midian.
1 S. 3:1-21—God calls Samuel, who answers "Speak, Yahweh, your servant is listening."
Ps. 50—"...fulfill the vows you make to the Most High..."
Ps. 55—"Unload your burden onto Yahweh, and he will support you..."
Ps. 61—"You, God, accept my vows, you grant me the heritage of those who fear your name."
Ps. 106—"Who can count all Yahweh's triumphs? ... Happy are we if we exercise justice and constantly practice virtue!"
Ps. 112—"Happy the man who fears Yahweh by joyfully keeping his commandments!"
Ws. 1:1-15—Wisdom prompts man to seek the Lord in simplicity of heart and to reject evil.
Ws. 3:1-12—"...the souls of the virtuous are in the hands of God; no torment shall ever touch them."
Si. 5:9-15; 6:1-4—"Be steady in your convictions..."
Is. 6:1-13—God calls Isaiah, "a man of unclean lips." Isaiah offers himself to be sent as a prophet.
Is. 40:1-11—The calling of the prophet.
Is. 61:1-11—The mission of the prophet.
Jr. 1:4-19—The call of Jeremiah. Yahweh tells him that before he was born he had been consecrated by God and appointed to be a prophet to the nations. He need not be afraid, for through him Yahweh will speak.

Jr. 11:1-17—Jeremiah on observance of the covenant. "Listen to my voice, I told them, carry out all my orders, then you shall be my people and I will be your God..."

Jr. 15:10-21—The call of Jeremiah renewed.

Jr. 18:1-12—Jeremiah visits the potter and the word of Yahweh addresses him saying, "...as the clay is in the potter's hand, so you are in mine, House of Israel."

Jr. 31:31-34—Yahweh will make a new covenant with the House of Israel.

New Testament

Mt. 4:18-22; Mk. 1:16-20; Lk. 5:1-11; Jn. 1:35-51—The first disciples are called. "At once, leaving the boat and their father, they followed him."

Jn. 5:24-47—"...whoever listens to my words and believes in the one who sent me, has eternal life..."

Mt. 7:21-27; Lk. 6:46-49—The true disciple is not one who says, "Lord, Lord," but everyone who listens to Jesus' words and acts on them. He who builds his house on Jesus' words has a sound foundation.

Mt. 8:18-22; Lk. 9:57-62—Hardships of the apostolic calling.

Lk. 10:1-20—The mission of the seventy-two disciples.

Mt. 10:1-33; Mk. 6:7-13; Lk. 9:1-6; Lk. 12:1-12—The mission of the disciples. Anyone who welcomes them, welcomes Jesus. Anyone who declares himself for Jesus in the presence of men, Jesus will declare him in the presence of his Father.

Mt. 15:1-20; Mk. 7:1-23—Jesus condemns the Pharisees who honor God with only lip service and are not truly committed. What makes a man unclean is not what goes in from the outside but what comes out from the inside.

Mt. 16:13-20; Lk. 9:18-21—Peter's profession of faith.

Mt. 19:27-30; Mk. 10:28-31; Lk. 18:28-30—The reward of renunciation. "...you will yourselves sit on the twelve thrones to judge the twelve tribes of Israel...be repaid a hundred times over, and also inherit eternal life."

Mt. 20:1-16—Parable of the vineyard laborers. "Thus the last will be first, and the first, last."

Mt. 20:20-23; Mk. 10:35-40—The sons of Zebedee make their request. Jesus asks them, "Can you drink the cup that I must drink, or be baptized with the baptism with which I must be baptized?"

Mt. 23:1-39; Mk. 12:38-40; Lk. 11:37-54—Jesus condemns the scribes and Pharisees for their hypocrisy and vanity.

Mt. 28:16-20; Mk. 16:9-20; Lk. 24:44-49; Jn. 20:19-29—The risen Jesus meets his disciples and tells them about their mission to the world.

Ac. 12:1-19—Peter's arrest and miraculous deliverance.

Ac. 16:16-40—The imprisonment of Paul and Silas and their miraculous deliverance.

Ac. 22:1-30; 23:1-11—Paul is arrested and asks the Jews of Jerusalem to listen to his defense. The Lord appears to Paul and tells him to have courage. As he has witnessed for him in Jerusalem, so must he do in Rome.

Rm. 3:21-31; 4:1-25; 5:1-11—Faith, not mere obedience to the Law, guarantees salvation.

2 Co. 5:11-21; 6:1-10—The apostolate in action.

Ph. 3:1-21; 4:1-9—All Paul wants to know is Christ; he is still running, trying to capture the prize for which Jesus captured him. He is racing for the finish, for the prize to which God calls us, and exhorts his brothers to do likewise.

Jm. 2:14-26—Faith and good works.

2 P. 1:12-18—The apostolic witness.

2 P. 3:1-18—Live holy and saintly lives while you wait and long for the Day of God.

* * * * *

Christ's way is not to demand sacrifice but to show us mercy if we but surrender ourselves to the Father's will. Though we may fail the test of faith on many occasions, the Lord is always ready to offer us forgiveness. Christ lifts from us the burden of self-salvation and repays in full the debt of our redemption. He gives us new life in abundance.

READINGS FROM THE LITERATURE OF SPIRITUALITY

Letters from the Desert, (Chapters 13 and 14)—Carretto became a Little Brother of Jesus because God called him to this commitment. He says he never doubted his call. He sees also that if God hadn't called him he couldn't have survived for long.

The God Who Comes, (Chapters 3, 15 and 19)—"Early on we understand that faith is a risk; much later we learn the price of this risk." We must not make the mistake of identifying the gospel message with the evolution of history or with social revolution. "Only the Holy Spirit is capable of building the Church with such badly hewn stones as ourselves!"

Abandonment to Divine Providence, (Chapter VI)—All will be well if we abandon ourselves to God.

The Sign of Jonas, (Part Four)—Nothing is of any value except insofar as it is transformed and elevated by my commitment to the charity of Christ. The smallest thing, touched by committed love, is through Christ immediately transfigured.

No Man Is an Island, (Chapters 1, 7 and 8)—"True happiness is found in unselfish love, a love which increases in proportion as it is shared."

New Seeds of Contemplation, (Chapters 18, 19 and 37)—"If we experience God in contemplation, we experience him not for ourselves alone but also for others."

The Way of Perfection, (Chapters 4-7)—Three things are important for the spiritual life, of which the first of these is love of one's neighbor. St. Teresa speaks of why confessors should be learned men and then returns to the subject of perfect love, giving certain counsels for gaining it.

On Being Involved, (Part I)—When I live a spiritual life in surrender and commitment, I become aware of the relevance of really being with whatever I am doing.

Poustinia, (Part III)—When one goes into a poustinia, he goes for others as well as for himself—but predominantly for others.

Prayer Is a Hunger, (Chapter 5 and 7)—Only the Eucharist enables us to change ourselves into Another, to give ourselves over wholly into his hands.

SUPPLEMENTARY READING

Transformation in Christ, (Chapters XI and XIII)—Our hunger and thirst for justice and the kingdom of God necessarily involves our imitation of Christ and our transformation in him; this transformation involves in turn a commitment to peace, a concord of hearts, and a horror of all forms of discord, disunion and dissension.

The Desert Fathers—Read the Sayings of the Fathers.

* * * * *

Self-surrender is not a once-and-for-all experience but one that requires repeated commitment. There is much in us—in our still unspiritual self—that rebels against abandoning ourselves wholly to God. We must do what we can to overcome these obstacles and hesitations, trusting that the Lord will grace our efforts. We must be patient with ourselves and not expect to make more than just noticeable improvements. We must try to surrender to God constantly in the desert of our heart. The Master himself will bless our efforts.

CONCLUSION

The journey into the desert is risky. It requires a guide lest we get lost and succumb to the dangers that beset the inexperienced explorer. So, too, our spiritual journey cannot progress to its true end without the guidance of the Holy Spirit. We are led into the darkness and dryness of desert spaces for a reason. We are to emerge from this experience as transformed people, ready to serve God whenever and wherever the need arises. We await the coming of the Lord in the ordinary events of daily life that now announce his presence. At every moment, we prepare the way of the Lord. We are never alone, for our Beloved lives with us in the hermitage of our heart as well as within the community of faith.

II

Here I am, Send Me[1]

INTRODUCTION

Christian lay persons and religious as well as clergy and ministers of many faith groupings share a common problem: how to blend the side of their life that would sit at the feet of the Lord like Mary with the side of their life that must be busy building the reign of God on earth like Martha. It seems at first glance that being and doing align themselves as foes on a battlefield, and yet life does not have to be this tense. Ultimately the two sides of our nature—that bent toward recollection and that straining to participate—can be in perfect harmony. Being without doing, contemplation without the fruits of action, might deteriorate into pure passivity. Doing without being, action lacking the firm roots of listening in quiet contemplation to the Divine, might lose its direction and become mere activism. The phrase "Here I am, send me" (Is. 6:9) seems to capture the right relationship between being and doing.

Isaiah had been apart with the Lord during the time of his vision. The experience of the Mystery in its awesome majesty had overwhelmed him. He felt so inadequate, so sinful. Then in a blinding moment of ecstatic surrender,

---

[1]This reading program was devised in accordance with principles given in spiritual reading courses to future formation personnel offered at the Institute of Formative Spirituality, under supervision of the author. A tentative version of this program, extensively modified and revised here, was done by Sr. Gemma Pepera, C.S.F.N. Following this introduction to the overall theme is a brief listing of minor themes. After that comes the reading list of texts recommended for this program, according to their appropriate category: essential, secondary, edifying, recreative. Several small sections follow, introducing the reader to the minor themes that extend from the main branch. Around these minor themes are gathered suggested readings from Holy Scripture and from various sources in the literature of spirituality, including some supplementary readings. However, the reader should guard against a mere quantitative approach as indicated in the guidelines in Part One. The supplementary texts may also be read in informational fashion as a means of providing background to the theme. Supplementary selections fall most often within the secondary or recreative category. Generally, introductions to texts provide good background reading and pertinent historical and biographical information which can be absorbed at the reader's discretion outside of the time one sets aside for slowed down spiritual reading. In regard to the overall duration of the reading program, readers must be faithful to their own pace of spiritual reading and notebook keeping. If a text is inspiring to them, they should stay with it as long as dwelling on the text keeps nourishing their hearts and minds.

he had been purified by the touch of a live coal upon his lips. This man of unclean spirit was now one of God's chosen. There was no turning back. The experience of apartness and its consequent gifts of self-knowledge and purification had prepared him for the task awaiting him. He heard the voice of the Lord saying, "Whom shall I send? Who will be our messenger?" (Is. 6:8) With a strength emerging from a source beyond himself, Isaiah was able to respond, "Here I am, send me." He was available for service because he had first submitted himself in quiet self-presence to the Lord. He thus becomes a good model for the blending of contemplation and action in daily life.

The minor themes of this reading program will delve into various ways of living the two main parts of the title. "Here I am" speaks of abandonment to the Mystery as echoed in such themes as centering, silencing, and repentance for sin. "Here I am" is a gentle reminder that we must bring ourselves before the Lord, hiding nothing, and an insistent call not to neglect the contemplative dimension of Christian living, no matter how active our lives become. "Send me" refers to the readiness of Isaiah to accept the mission God gave him. Readiness implies such attitudes as a willingness to suffer, to trust, and to surrender. In God's divine plan for our lives, we each have a mission to perform. Will we hear our call? Will we participate to the fullest in this unfolding? The answers depend upon the depth of our relationship to God, for how can we expect to follow the Lord if we never take time to listen?

MINOR THEMES

I. Blending of Life and Labor
II. Living from My Deepest Center
III. Being Present in the Here and Now
IV. Here I am in Solitude and Silence
V. Here I am in Inner Peace
VI. Here I am in Repentance for Sin
VII. Here I am in Prayer
VIII. Send Me on My Mission in Gentleness
IX. Send Me though I May Have to Suffer
X. Send Me in Trust and Surrender

READING LIST

What follows is the list of books (annotated in the *Sample Bibliography*) to be assembled by the reader and used for this particular reading program. These books are certainly not the only ones available on the theme concerned nor necessarily the most outstanding written on this topic. They are, however, easily accessible to the general reader in current editions reasonably priced. Alternative and newer versions of some of the following books are indicated also in the *Sample Bibliography*. References to the same minor themes that readers may find more appropriate or available can be found in many cases as well in the *Sample Bibliography*. In case the reader should be using editions of the text different from those that appear on the Reading List, Chapters and/or Parts of the books, and occasionally page numbers, accompany each annotation.

HOLY SCRIPTURE

The Jerusalem Bible. Reader's Edition. Alexander Jones, General Editor. New York: Doubleday, 1985.

LITERATURE OF SPIRITUALITY

Essential

Anonymous. *The Cloud of Unknowing.* Ed. William Johnston. New York: Doubleday, 1973.

Boylan, Dom Eugene. *This Tremendous Lover.* Paramus, NJ: Newman Press, 1964.

Chautard, Dom Jean-Baptiste. *The Soul of the Apostolate.* Trans. A Monk of Our Lady of Gethsemani. Trappist, KY: Abbey of Gethsemani, 1946.

Lawrence of the Resurrection, Brother. *The Practice of the Presence of God.* Trans. Donald Attwater. Springfield, IL: Templegate, 1974.

Merton, Thomas. *Thoughts in Solitude.* New York: Doubleday, 1968.

van Kaam, Adrian. *Spirituality and the Gentle Life.* Denville, NJ: Dimension Books, 1974. Rpt. Pittsburgh, PA: Epiphany Books, 1994.

Secondary

Muggeridge, Malcolm. *Something Beautiful for God: Mother Teresa of Calcutta.* San Francisco: Harper, 1976.[2]

Pieper, Josef. *Leisure, The Basis of Culture.* Trans. Alexander Dru. New York: New American Library, 1963.

Sertillanges, A.D. *The Intellectual Life: Its Spirit, Conditions, Methods.* Trans. Mary Ryan. Washington, DC: Catholic University Press of America, 1987.

---

[2]The actual sayings of Mother Teresa found in this text can be placed in the category of essential literature of spirituality.

Edifying

Hammarskjöld, Dag. *Markings.* New York: Ballantine Books, 1985.
Nouwen, Henri J.M. *Out of Solitude: Three Meditations on the Christian Life.* New York: Walker, 1986.
Steere, Douglas V. *On Being Present Where You Are.* Pendle Hill Pamphlet, #151. Lebanon, PA: Sowers Printing, 1967.
van Breemen, Peter G. *As Bread That Is Broken.* Denville, NJ: Dimension Books, 1974.
van Kaam, Adrian. *Personality Fulfillment in the Spiritual Life.* Denville, NJ: Dimension Books, 1966.
van Zeller, Hubert. *The Current of Spirituality.* Springfield, IL: Templegate, 1970.

Recreative

Lynch, John. *A Woman Wrapped in Silence.* New York: Paulist, 1976.

MINOR THEME I

BLENDING OF LIFE AND LABOR

"...end of a tiring day...my feet are sore...I feel irritable...there must be more to life than this...." All of us have played and replayed this scene. The questions inevitably posed are: How can I blend my inner life of meaning with the work I have to do so that my being with God and my doing for God are more intimately related? How can I overcome this apparent split between life and labor? Does this integration happen of itself after a lapse of time or does it require some special discipline on my side? Slowly I may come to realize that action has to be rooted in the fertile soil of presence to the Eternal and not merely in the shifting sands of this or that period of the day. When what I do is an expression of who I am, I may be able at every moment to hear and respond to the invitations of the Spirit in many different situations. Isaiah could go forth to serve because he had first been subservient to God. His spiritual self and his mission were rooted in the same divine source. His life and labor were in perfect harmony and God made him a prophet. To foster this consonance with the Mystery, Holy Scripture stresses the importance of keeping the Sabbath. If one is a doer six days a week, then at least a day ought to be set aside to be with God for worship and praise. The Sabbath symbolizes the need to free ourselves from the pressures of work so that we can regain the perspective. True action emerges from quiet presence to the Divine, who is the source and origin of our life.

READINGS FROM HOLY SCRIPTURE

Old Testament

Gn. 1:1-31; 2:1-4—According to the first account of creation, God rested on the seventh day after all the work he had been doing.

Ex. 31:12-17—The sons of Israel must keep Yahweh's sabbaths carefully. "Work is to be done for six days, but the seventh day must be a day of complete rest, consecrated to Yahweh."

Ex. 35:1-3—The sabbath rest.

Lv. 23:26-36—Yahweh tells Moses that the tenth day of the seventh month shall be a Day of Atonement. Anyone who works that day shall be removed from his people. On the feast of Tabernacles—a day of solemn meeting—neither must there be any heavy work.

Nb. 15:32-36—Here is what happens to one who breaks the sabbath.

Dt. 15:1-11—Yahweh asks the people to keep a sabbatical year. He commands that no one harden his heart or close his hand to the poor.

Ps. 8—Yahweh made man lord over the work of his hands.

Ps. 85—"I am listening. What is Yahweh saying?"

Ps. 134—"Come bless Yahweh, all you who serve Yahweh, serving in the house of Yahweh...."

Ps. 139—"God...make sure I do not follow pernicious ways, and guide me in the way that is everlasting."

Si. 10:26-31—"Do not try to be smart when you do your work, do not put on airs when you are in difficulties."

Is. 29:13-24—People who honor him with lip service only do not please Yahweh. He blesses the lowly who live and labor with him.

New Testament

Lk. 2:41-50—Jesus among the doctors of the Law. "Why were you looking for me?" he replied. "Did you not know that I must be busy with my Father's affairs?"

Mt. 6:1-4—"Be careful not to parade your good deeds before men to attract their notice...."

Mt. 12:1-8; Mk. 2:23-28; Lk. 6:1-5—The Pharisees notice that the disciples pick ears of corn to eat on the sabbath. Jesus rebukes them, reminding them that he is master of the sabbath and that what God wants is mercy not sacrifice.

Mt. 15:1-9; Mk. 7:1-13—Jesus calls the Pharisees and scribes hypocrites—people, as Isaiah prophesied, who honor him with lip service only while their hearts are far from him.

Mt. 20:1-16—Parable of the vineyard laborers. "Thus the last will be first, and the first last."

Mt. 23:13-32; Lk. 11:37-54—Jesus rebukes the Pharisees and lawyers because they load on men burdens that are unendurable, burdens they themselves do not move a finger to lift.

Lk. 13:10-16—Healing of the crippled woman on a sabbath.

Lk. 14:1-6—Healing of a dropsical man on the sabbath.

Mt. 24:45-51—Parable of the conscientious steward who takes care of the master's household as he would.

Mt. 25:14-30; Lk. 19:11-27—Parable of the talents. "...to everyone who has will be given more; but from the man who has not, even what he has will be taken away."

Lk. 10:29-37—Parable of the good Samaritan. He who was a neighbor to the man who fell into the hands of the brigands took pity on him. We must go and do the same.

Lk. 10:38-42—Martha served the Lord; Mary sat at his feet. Jesus said it was Mary who had chosen the better part.

Lk. 17:7-10—On humble service.

Jn. 2:1-12—During the wedding feast at Cana, Mary told the servants, "Do whatever he tells you."

2 Co. 5:11-21; 6:1-10—The apostolate in action. "We do nothing that people might object to, so as not to bring discredit on our function as God's servants."

1 Th. 5:12-28—"We appeal to you, my brothers, to be considerate to those who are working among you and are above you in the Lord as your teachers. Have the greatest respect and affection for them because of their work."

2 Th. 3:6-15—Against idleness and disunity. "...we urge you, brothers, to keep away from any of the brothers who refuses to work or live according to the tradition we passed on to you."

Jm. 2:14-26—Faith and good works. "You see now that it is by doing something good and not only by believing, that a man is justified."

Jm. 3:13-18—"If there are any wise or learned men among you, let them show it by their good lives, with humility and wisdom in their actions."

1 P. 2:4-12—The new priesthood. Christians are obliged to behave honorably among pagans so that they can see their good works for themselves.

* * * * *

Whether building a church or serving its members, the people of God must worship and work with great care. What we do ought to be an expression of who we are. As God's children, made in the Divine likeness, we cooperate at every moment in the unfolding of creation. There is to be no split between life and labor, being and doing, recollection and action. The "Mary" in us is the ground out of which the "Martha" emerges.

READINGS FROM THE LITERATURE OF SPIRITUALITY

The Cloud of Unknowing, (Chapters 8 and 16-23)—The author distinguishes between the degrees and parts of the active and contemplative life. He reflects on the Gospel story of Martha and Mary and explains why Mary has chosen the best part.

This Tremendous Lover, (Chapters 15 and 16)—To love God in practice means to do his will, no matter how ordinary it is. The merit of our life and the efficacy of our apostolate is proportionate not to the amount of trouble we take, but to our holiness.

The Soul of the Apostolate, (Parts One and Two)—Good works should be nothing but an overflow from the inner life. "Action relies upon contemplation for its fruitfulness; and contemplation, in its turn, as soon as it has reached a certain degree of intensity, pours out upon our active works some of its overflow."

The Practice of the Presence of God, (Conversations)—The most absorbing work did not divert Brother Lawrence from God. "...he gave thought neither to death nor to his sins, neither to Heaven nor to Hell, but only to the doing of small things for the love of God—small things because he was incapable of big ones."

Spirituality and the Gentle Life, (Chapters III and IX)—Spiritual life leaves ample room for involvement in society.

Markings, (1941-1942: *The middle years*)—Hammarskjöld believed that the more faithfully we listen to the voice within us, the better we will hear what is sounding outside. Only he who listens can speak.

As Bread That Is Broken, (Chapter 14)—We, like Christ, must identify with these least of our brothers, for as we do to them we do to Christ.

Personality Fulfillment in the Spiritual Life, (Part Two)—Being a Christian means that I am called with other Christians to be in the world with the sensitivity of Christ himself.

The Current of Spirituality, (Chapter 15)—"If labor is a punishment laid upon fallen man, it is also an act of worship."

SUPPLEMENTARY READING

Something Beautiful for God, (pp. 15-63)—The work Mother Teresa and her Missionaries of Charity do is in service of Christ; it is his work, of which she and her sisters are instruments.

Leisure, The Basis of Culture, (The Philosophical Act: I, II)—To blend being and doing, we must bring our philosophy of life into our world of work.

The Intellectual Life, (Chapter 9)—Work maintains the balance of the soul and brings about interior unity.

* * * * *

The art of spiritual living is to integrate contemplation and action, prayer and participation, profession of faith and expression of fidelity. Living an integrated life in the world depends on our being integrated within ourselves. We need to become reservoirs of spiritual strength that overflow into the world. We ought to minister from our abundance, not from our want. Since all that we have to give comes from God, there is no cause to boast. The fruits of Christian living may be hidden from the eyes of a worldly person, but they are beheld in minute detail and blessed by God.

MINOR THEME II

LIVING FROM MY DEEPEST CENTER

The deepest center of our life is Christ. He gives us firm anchorage however furious the storm. Anchored in him, we can venture forth without fear of going astray. Returning to him, we see things in their proper order. The more Christ-centered we become, the more attuned we are to his challenges and appeals in daily life. To flow with the Father's will becomes our major concern. Such fidelity harmonizes leisure and labor. Scattered fragments of life group together like iron slivers around a magnet. Our sojourn on earth has purpose and meaning. No longer do we panic about where we are going or what we are doing. As long as we look to Jesus, we will find our way. God becomes our rock, our shelter, our protection in the midst of life's most terrible ordeals. Christ is our redeemer, our comforter, our divine companion. The Father reveals himself through Jesus as infinite, caring nearness—nearer to us than we are to ourselves, so near in fact that the Holy

Spirit dwells in the center of our being, drawing us through grace in the direction decreed for us from the beginning to the end of time.

READINGS FROM HOLY SCRIPTURE

Old Testament

Ex. 19:1-25; 20:1-21—Yahweh promises to live with the sons of Israel in a covenant relationship. He tells them through Moses what they must do to honor his presence.

Ex. 34:1-3—Yahweh reveals to Moses that he is a God of tenderness and compassion. He renews his covenant and Moses is radiant after speaking with him.

Lv. 19:1-37—Yahweh speaks to Moses about how the sons of Israel are to worship him. He commands Moses to say to them, "Be holy, for I, Yahweh your God, am holy."

Dt. 3:18-29; 4:1-4—In his last instruction, Moses assures the people that if they keep the laws of Yahweh he will live with them forever.

Dt. 5:1-31; 6:1-25—Moses proclaims the Ten Commandments and explains to the people that love of Yahweh is the essence of the law. Right living means to observe these commandments as he has directed.

Jos. 24:1-28—Joshua sets forth the vocation of Israel once more. Yahweh is a jealous God. He is with the people and expects them to be with him.

2 Ch. 15:1-15—The people pledge an oath of fidelity to Yahweh.

Ps. 7—God is the shield that protects his people under persecution.

Ps. 27—In God's company there is no fear.

Ps. 46—"God is our shelter, our strength, ever ready to help in time of trouble...."

Ps. 80—When the face of the Shepherd of Israel smiles on his chosen, they are safe.

Ps. 91—Yahweh rescues all who cling to him; he protects whoever knows his name.

Ps. 14—"He, Yahweh, is merciful, tenderhearted, slow to anger, very loving and universally kind; Yahweh's tenderness embraces all his creatures."

Ws. 7:15-30; 8:1-29; 9:1-18—Within Wisdom is a spirit beneficent and loving towards man. The man who lives with her makes God his center.

Si. 2:1-18—Cling to God and do not leave him.

Si. 32:14-24; 33:1-3—Watching ourselves in what we do is what keeping the commandments means. "If a man fears the Lord, evil will not come his way...."

Is. 45:1-25—"Truly, God is hidden with you, the God of Israel, the savior." To those who are centered in him, he expresses himself with clarity.

Is. 51:1-16—The integrity of Yahweh remains for ever. He is the all-powerful consoler to his people.

Is. 63:7-19; 64:1-11--"Let me sing the praises of Yahweh's goodness, and of his marvelous deeds..."

Jr. 30:1-24; 31:1-40—The Book of Consolation. "Yahweh has saved his people, the remnant of Israel."

Ho. 2:4-25—Yahweh and his unfaithful wife. "I will say to No-People-of-Mine, 'You are my people,' and he will answer, 'You are my God.' "

Ho. 14:1-10—The sincere conversion of Israel to Yahweh.

New Testament

Jn. 1:1-18—God has been with us from the beginning.

Jn. 3:1-21—Jesus converses with Nicodemus and explains that he must be born-again of the spirit. He must find his center in God.

Jn. 4:1-42—Jesus reveals himself as savior of the world to the Samaritans. He offers the woman at the well "living water," explaining that anyone who drinks the water he shall give will never be thirsty again.

Mt. 5:1-48; Lk. 6:20-45—The Christian whose center is the Lord is to be the salt of the earth and the light of the world, compassionate, generous, and full of integrity. He is to live by a new standard which is higher than the old.

Mt. 6:19-21—Jesus knows that where our treasure is, there will our heart be also.

Mt. 6:25-34; Lk. 12:22-32—When God is our center, we have no reason not to trust him. Our heavenly Father knows what we need, so why worry?

Mt. 7:7-11; Lk. 11:9-13—For those who live in the Father, prayer is always effective. "If you, then, who are evil, know how to give your children what is good, how much more will your Father in heaven give good things to those who ask him."

Mt. 11:28-30—We can rest in Jesus, for he is gentle and humble of heart.

Mt. 22:1-4; Lk. 14:15-24—The Lord calls many to his wedding feast but only those are chosen for whom he is the center. Those who make excuses or come uninvited are sent away.

Mt. 26:26-29; Mk. 14:22-25; Lk. 22:19-20—The Eucharist seals our covenant with Christ. "Drink all of you from this," he said, "for this is my blood, the blood of the covenant...."

Rm. 12:1-2—Paul recalls the history of the chosen people—of the remnant who made God their center—and sings a hymn to his mercy and wisdom.

Ga. 4:1-11—"The proof that you are sons is that God has sent the Spirit of his

Son into our hearts: the Spirit that cries, 'Abba, Father,' and it is this that makes you a son...."

Ep. 2:1-10—"We are God's work of art, created in Christ Jesus to live the good life as from the beginning he had meant us to live it."

Col. 1:15-20—Jesus is the Beginning. All things are reconciled through him and for him.

Jm. 4:1-12—Disunity among Christians must be overcome. "The nearer you go to God, the nearer he will come to you."

1 Jn. 4:7-21—"My dear people, let us love one another since love comes from God and everyone who loves is begotten by God and knows God."

Rv. 22:1-21—The river of life rises from the throne of God and of the Lamb. He is the Alpha and the Omega, the First and the Last, the Beginning and the End.

* * * * *

Although the rebellion of Israel angers him, Yahweh is still a tender God, full of kindness and compassion. He is "God-with-us." The fullness of divine mercy, the epitome of divine gentleness, is Christ. When he comes to us in Holy Communion, we partake in a special way of God's saving love. At this moment of utmost nearness, the gentle grace of God may pervade our being and wipe from our eyes every tear.

READINGS FROM THE LITERATURE OF SPIRITUALITY

The Cloud of Unknowing, (Chapters 3-7)—The author describes the "work of contemplation." "Think only of God," he says, "the God who created you, redeemed you, and guided you to this work. Allow no other ideas about God to enter your mind. Yet even this is too much. A naked intent toward God, the desire for him alone, is enough."

This Tremendous Lover, (Chapters 12 and 13)—If we would be truly happy, and find all that our heart longs for, we must live in complete abandonment to the will of him who comes as our tremendous lover. We must belong to Christ and not to ourselves.

The Practice of the Presence of God, (Spiritual Maxims)—The most holy, general, and necessary practice of the spiritual life, according to Brother Lawrence, is the practice of the presence of God. Since we know that God is with us in all our actions, that he is at the depth and center of our soul, we ought to pause an instant in our external occupations and in our prayers to worship him inwardly, to praise him, to petition him, to offer him our heart and to thank him.

Spirituality and the Gentle Life, (Chapter XXI)—Gentle communion with the Divine Mystery in whom all reality is anchored is the heart of human life.

Markings, (1952-1953)—To live in faith is to be both humble and proud; it is to know that though I am nothing, God is in me.

As Bread That is Broken, (Chapters 1, 2 and 3)—Faith is to discover that God is the deepest ground and center of my being.

Personality Fulfillment in the Spiritual Life, (Chapters 1 and 2)—Presence to the Holy is an inescapable reality deeply rooted in the structure of my being. "The more I am present to the Holy, the more I experience that the Holy is the foundation of the sacredness of all people and things."

The Current of Spirituality, (Chapters 1 and 2)—From the human point of view, the way to true spirituality is desiring God's will more than one's own. We need to be one with the unceasing current of the spirit of God.

SUPPLEMENTARY READING

Something Beautiful for God, (pp. 83-129)—Mother Teresa speaks of her calling to serve the poorest of the poor in whom the suffering Jesus lives.

Leisure, The Basis of Culture, (The Philosophical Act: IV)—To live Christianity is to reflect upon the deepest origins of our being. Such reflection occupies especially the Christian philosopher.

A Woman Wrapped in Silence, (I-VI)—Mary lives with God as her deepest center and she becomes the mother of God.

* * * * *

When we live from our deepest center, we turn our attention always toward the Divine. With our attention thus centered, we can see from a transcendent perspective. We are open to the revelations of God's will as we seek occasion after occasion to manifest our love. Centering in Christ is the means by which we come home to our deepest self. Only in him can we be at one with the Trinity and aware, however dimly, of the destiny the Divine has in waiting for us.

MINOR THEME III

BEING PRESENT IN THE HERE AND NOW

There is a common fallacy, when wanderlust seizes us, that the grass is greener on the other side—that the life of meaning for which we are looking is not in the here and now situation but in some other far away place. In our mind's eye, we imagine doing great things for the kingdom, meeting fascinating masters, unlocking with their help life's ultimate secrets. How dull by comparison is our daily routine. Yet it is in this ordinariness that we have to find the meaning of our life and its divine direction.

To grow in the life of the Spirit means to be present where we are—in this concrete situation, at this particular time, whenever and however Christ calls us to be his disciples. God is omnipresent. The Spirit is not in some distant place. God speaks in and through our present situation. Coming home to the Holy in daily life is the only way in which we can spiritualize our activities. Without this sense of presence to the Divine everywhere—in all people, events, and things, however ordinary—we risk living a "floating" spiritual life, inflated with grand ideas but lost to the needs of everyday people. We must try to serve God in our daily work. Faith tells us we have been placed here for a reason; hope readies us for whatever changes God may decree; love lets us give the best that is in us to the task at hand.

READINGS FROM HOLY SCRIPTURE

Old Testament

Gn. 30:1-43; 31:1-54—God hears Rachel's plea and gives her a son. Jacob works hard where God places him and prospers greatly.

Ex. 15:22-27; 16:1-36; 17:1-16—In the desert Yahweh takes care of the daily needs of his people.

Ex. 39:1-43; 40:16-33—Work on the vestments of the high priest, the tabernacle, the Tent, and all its furnishings is carried out exactly as Yahweh has directed. He himself takes possession of the sanctuary and guides the House of Israel on every stage of their journey.

Dt. 10:1-22; 11:1-32—Moses tells the people that they must love Yahweh and keep his injunctions as worthy disciples would. If his words are inscribed on their souls, their work will be pleasing to Yahweh and the rewards of obedience will be theirs.

Is. 3:1-21—When God calls Samuel, he responds with these obedient words, "Speak, Yahweh, your servant is listening."

Is. 9:1-27; 10:1-27—Samuel makes known to Saul the word of God. Saul undergoes a change of heart and is chosen king.
Is. 11:12-15; 12:1-25—Saul is proclaimed king and Samuel gives way to him. It is now Saul's duty to serve Yahweh faithfully every day of his life.
Is. 15:10-35—When Saul does not carry out his orders, Yahweh regrets having made him king of Israel.
Is. 16:1-23; 17:1-57; 18:1-16—The spirit of Yahweh comes upon David and he is anointed as God's servant. David takes up service with Saul and accepts the challenge to face Goliath. When David defeats the giant, Saul becomes jealous.
Is. 23:19-28; 24:1-33—Saul tries to kill David, but David, who is under Yahweh's protection, in the end spares Saul.
1 K. 1:28-40—Solomon is consecrated king at David's nomination.
1 K. 8:1-66—When the Lord takes possession of the Temple Solomon has built, Solomon relates the history of his own and his forefathers' service to Yahweh. He prays for himself and for his people.
Ps. 95—Psalm for daily use. "If only you would listen to him today..."
Ps. 103—Yahweh's love lasts forever as long as his children remember to listen to his precepts and be attentive day by day to his word of command.
Ps. 134—"Come bless Yahweh, all you who serve Yahweh, serving in the house of Yahweh...."
Si. 44:1-25; 45:1-26; 46:1-20; 47:1-25; 48:1-25; 49:1-16; 50:1-29—The glory of God and his power over the daily life of his people is recorded in this lengthy eulogy of illustrious men "...whose good works have not been forgotten."
Is. 28:14-29—"Listen to the word of Yahweh, you scoffers...or your bonds will be tightened further.... Listen closely to my words, be attentive and understand what I am saying."
Is. 50:4-11—Yahweh opens the ear of his servant to listen like a disciple.
Jon. 1:1-16; 2:1-11; 3:1-10; 4:1-11—Yahweh's dealings with the prophet Jonah exemplify the demands of discipleship as well as its rewards.

New Testament

Mt. 3:1-12; Mk. 1:1-8; Lk. 3:1-18; Jn. 1:19-34—John the Baptist is God's true servant, preparing a way for the Lord, making his paths straight.
Jn. 3:22-36—John bears witness for the last time.
Mt. 10:1-42; Mk. 6:7-13; Lk. 9:1-6—As servants of God, the twelve will have to suffer persecution but their reward will be great.
Mt. 11:2-19; Lk. 7:18-35—Jesus commends John the Baptist and names him a true prophet, but he condemns his contemporaries.
Lk. 10:1-20—The mission of the seventy-two disciples.

Mt. 20:24-28; Mk. 10:41-45—Leadership with service. "...anyone who wants to become great among you must be your servant..."

Lk. 14:7-11—Choose the lowest place, for God exalts the humble.

Mt. 23:1-12—"The greatest among you must be your servant."

Lk. 17:7-10—"We are merely servants..."

Jn. 13:1-20—Jesus washes his disciples' feet. "I tell you most solemnly, no servant is greater than his master, no messenger is greater than the man who sent him."

Mt. 24:45-51—The conscientious servant receives his master's trust; the dishonest one is cut off from his favor.

Mt. 25:14-30; Lk. 19:11-27—The wicked and lazy servant buries his talents and is thrown by his master out into the dark.

1 Co. 10:31-33—"Whatever you eat, whatever you drink, whatever you do at all, do it for the glory of God."

2 Co. 4:1-18; 5:1-10—"Whether we are living in the body or exiled from it, we are intent on pleasing him."

Ep. 4:1-16—"If we live by the truth and in love, we shall grow in all ways into Christ..."

Ep. 5:1-20—"Try, then, to imitate God, as children of his that he loves, and follow Christ by loving as he loved you..."

1 Th. 4:1-12—The brothers are to live in holiness and charity, attending to their own business and earning their living.

2 Th. 3:1-15—The brothers are to keep away from those who refuse to work or to live according to the tradition that has been passed on to them.

Jm. 4:1-17; 5:1-20—As servants of the Lord, the brothers are to be as kind and compassionate as he was while they await his coming.

* * * * *

In and through our daily environment, we are presented with a multitude of ways and means to meet God. An important condition for spiritual living is thus the growing capacity to be wholly present where we are. This quality of presence requires an inner readiness to listen to what is latent in each situation, namely, God's voice, and to respond in a way that fosters spiritual unfolding. Whether our task is meditation or a mundane cleaning chore, we must try to be really there, to gather our thoughts, feelings, and efforts around this particular involvement. We must be ready to heed God's command in the present moment.

READINGS FROM THE LITERATURE OF SPIRITUALITY

The Cloud of Unknowing, (Chapters 51-54 and 57-62)—The author explains the problems of pseudo-contemplation that arise when we are not present where we are. He describes by contrast the wisdom and poise that grace a person when contemplation is true.

This Tremendous Lover, (Chapters 14 and 20)—Every act of the spiritual life, performed in full presence to the Father, is performed in partnership with Jesus, but there is no comparison between his share and ours. What we contribute is but a tiny drop of water in a chalice full of the rich wine of his immeasurable love.

The Practice of the Presence of God, (Letters I-VIII)—If he were a preacher, writes Brother Lawrence, he would preach nothing else but the practice of the presence of God. If he were a director, he would recommend it to everybody: so necessary and even so easy does he believe it to be.

Thoughts in Solitude, (Part One)—Merton shows that there is no greater disaster in the spiritual life than to be immersed in unreality. "When our life feeds on unreality, it must starve." Therefore, growth in the spiritual life implies being present to the self we are in Christ and following him wherever he leads—from desert to harvest.

Spirituality and the Gentle Life, (Chapters V and VI)—Meditative reflection directs me primarily toward the mysterious presence of God in all that is and especially in ordinary life.

Markings, (1945-1949: *Towards new shores*)—"Here and now—only this is real: The good face of an old man, Caught naked in an unguarded moment, Without past, without future."

On Being Present Where You Are—The author asks what does it mean to be really present in any given place or at any given time? "To be present is to be vulnerable, to be able to be hurt, to be willing to be spent—but it is also to be awake, alive, and engaged actively in the immediate assignment that has been laid upon us."

As Bread That Is Broken, (Chapter 11)—"We can live in the presence of God, the sacrament of the present moment. There we can find God day by day."

Personality Fulfillment in the Spiritual Life, (Chapter 3)—The "religious presence which I already am" does not spontaneously arise and fill my life. Many barriers hinder, prevent, or delay this emergence. The author explores these obstacles in this chapter.

SUPPLEMENTARY READING

Something Beautiful For God, (A Door of Utterance)—The daily life of Mother Teresa exemplifies the art of living in the here and now.

The Intellectual Life, (Chapters 1 and 2)—A Christian worker should live constantly in the concrete here and now.

A Woman Wrapped in Silence, (VII-IX)—Mary relives each event surrounding the birth of her son. The Holy Family must now flee to Egypt.

* * * * *

The spiritual life is seldom lifted to the plane of the extraordinary. It is lived for the most part amidst the common ways of everyday existence, with ordinary people who do ordinary things. It is like the life of Jesus in Nazareth. Together with the people of his time, he went to the temple for worship; he attended wedding feasts; he walked the dusty roads around the Sea of Galilee; he went out in fishing boats. These are ordinary events yet they bear symbolic significance because of the way Jesus lived them. He never lost an opportunity to respond to the will of the Father as manifested in the here and now situation. When his parents found him in the temple, he reminded them gently that he had to fulfill the mission ordained for him by his heavenly Father. At Cana he showed gentleness toward his mother and did as he was asked, though the time of his public witnessing had not yet come. When the crowds of wounded people followed him on each walk, he did not push them away, as some of the disciples were inclined to do. He chose instead to feed them with fish and bread and to nourish their souls with the living water of his word. Following Jesus' example, we, too, must strive to hear and obey the Father's will in the common people and events he sends our way.

MINOR THEME IV

HERE I AM IN SOLITUDE AND SILENCE

Alone and in silence, I present the whole of my being to God. To say, "Here I am," is to place at his disposal the unique creation he has made. It is to give God this body of mine, with its weaknesses and strengths; this intellect, with its confusion and clarity; this heart, with its hardness and pliability. To say, "Here I am," is to offer Christ the talents he has entrusted to me, using them to their fullest potential. It is to follow him wherever he leads, to stand ready in all situations to be his servant. To prepare myself for such a commitment, I have to find frequent occasions when I stand peacefully and quietly before the Lord—alone and at the same time at one with him. In this aloneness, I try gently to quiet the many voices that besiege me in the pressures of daily life; I want to listen only to God's voice in the depths of my being. Outer silence may be sought to foster inner stillness, but it is not necessary. The closer I grow to God, the more I am able to be with him in all circumstances. Whenever the Beloved calls, I am able to say, "Here I am."

READINGS FROM HOLY SCRIPTURE

Old Testament

Dt. 7:1-26—Israel is a people set apart by Yahweh, chosen to be his own out of all the peoples on the earth.

Dt. 8:1-20—Yahweh led Israel for forty years in the wilderness to humble and test his chosen. Now he is bringing the people to a prosperous land, but they must not neglect his commandments nor become proud of heart.

1 K. 19:1-18—Elijah journeys through the wilderness to Horeb, the mountain of God. There he encounters Yahweh in the sound of a gentle breeze.

Jb. 1:1-22; 2:1-12; 3:1-26—Satan tests Job but throughout all this misfortune he never utters a sinful word. In the end, it is Job who breaks the silence and curses the day of his birth.

Jb. 6:1-21—The sufferer alone knows his own grief.

Jb. 19:1-29—Job finds faith at its height when he feels deserted by God and man.

Ps. 39—"I will watch how I behave, and not let my tongue lead me into sin..."

Ps. 88—"I am numbered among those who go down to the Pit, a man bereft of strength: a man alone, down among the dead..."

Ps. 94—"...Yahweh has not abandoned or deserted his hereditary people..."

Ps. 119—"I mean to observe your statutes; never abandon me."

Ws. 18:14-19—When peaceful silence lay over all, and night had run the half of her swift course, down from the heavens, from the royal throne, leaped your all-powerful Word..."

Si. 19:4-17—"...which of us has never sinned by speech?"

Si. 20:1-31—A wise man will keep quiet until it is time to speak.

Si. 22:27; 23:1-15—"Who will set a guard on my mouth, and a seal of prudence on my lips, to keep me from falling, and my tongue from causing my ruin?"

Is. 41:1-29—Islands, keep silence before me, let the people renew their strength."

Is. 42:10-25; 43:1-28; 44:1-8—"From the beginning I have been silent, I have kept quiet, held myself in check." Now a new hymn to Yahweh must be sung, celebrating the liberation of Israel and the miracles of the new Exodus.

Lm. 3:1-66—"It is good for a man to bear the yoke from youth onwards, to sit in solitude and silence when the Lord fastens it on him..."

Ba. 1:16-22; 2:1-35; 3:1-8—The prayer of the exiles.

Ho. 9:1-17—The sorrows of exile.

Zc. 1:1-17; 2:1-17—A summons to conversion. "Let all mankind be silent before Yahweh! For he is awaking and is coming from his holy dwelling."

New Testament

Mt. 4:1-11; Mk. 1:12-13; Lk. 4:1-3—Jesus is led into the wilderness by the Spirit. Though weakened by his forty-day fast, he resists the tempter. Man is to worship and serve God alone.

Mk. 1:35-39—"In the morning, long before dawn, he got up and left the house, and went off to a lonely place and prayed there."

Lk. 4:40-44—All the suffering were brought to Jesus and he cured them. When daylight came, he made his way to a lonely place to pray.

Mt. 8:1-4; Mk. 1:40-45; Lk. 5:12-16—Jesus cures a leper.... Large crowds gathered to hear him and have their sickness cured, "but he would always go off to some place where he could be alone and pray."

Lk. 6:12-16—Before choosing the twelve, "...he went out into the hills to pray; and he spent the whole night in prayer to God."

Mt. 14:22-33; Mk. 6:45-52—After sending the crowds away, Jesus went up into the hills by himself to pray. When evening came he was alone. He saw his disciples in a boat far out on the lake and went walking toward them.

Mt. 14:13-21; Mk. 6:30-44; Lk. 9:10-17; Jn. 6:1-15—Jesus and his disciples withdrew to a lonely place, but a large crowd followed them. Jesus fed the multitude with a few loaves and some fish. Following the miracle, the people wanted to take Jesus by force and make him king, but he escaped back to the hills by himself.

Mt. 17:1-8; Mk. 9:2-13; Lk. 9:28-36—Jesus took Peter, James, and John to a high mountain where they could be alone. In their presence he was transfigured. Peter wanted to stay there and make three tents.

Lk. 21:37-38—"In the daytime he would be in the Temple teaching, but would spend the night on the hill called the Mount of Olives."

Mt. 26:36-46; Mk. 14:32-42; Lk. 22:39-46—Jesus is alone in his agony. Sadness comes over him and great distress.

Mt. 26:57-68; Mk. 14:53-65; Lk. 23:66-71—Jesus remains silent before the Sanhedrin.

Mt. 27:45-56; Mk. 15:33-39; Lk. 23:44-46; Jn. 19:28-30—Jesus is alone in his death. About the ninth hour, he cries out in a loud voice, "*My God, my God, why have you deserted me?*"

Rm. 8:1-39—God has called us to share his glory. The Spirit expresses our plea in a way that could never be put into words.

1 Co. 1:10-31; 2:1-16—Words cannot contain the hidden wisdom of God.

Jm. 3:1-18—We must guard against uncontrolled language. The tongue may be only a tiny part of the body, but it can set fire to a huge forest.

* * * * *

As we begin to set aside time for silence and solitude, we may be afraid to face that in us that has to change. We may feel like a failure. Christ, who was himself tempted in the wilderness, will help us to persevere. As he experienced the need to distance himself from the clamor of the crowd, so we need to find a "lonely place." There, in a posture of listening, we can prepare for our mission to make straight his way in this world.

READINGS FROM THE LITERATURE OF SPIRITUALITY

The Cloud of Unknowing, (Chapters 9, 25, 31 and 32)—The author explains that the most sublime thoughts are more a hindrance than help during the time of contemplative prayer. We must strive with God's grace to silence them all. "For surely if you are seeking God alone, you will never rest contented with anything less than God."

Thoughts in Solitude, (Part Two)—"A man becomes a solitary at the moment when, no matter what may be his external surroundings, he is suddenly aware of his own inalienable solitude and sees that he will never be anything but solitary."

Spirituality and the Gentle Life, (Chapter XX)—A hindrance to the fullness of Divine Presence is my lack of silence.

Markings, (1925-1930: *Thus it was* and 1950-1951: *Night is drawing nigh*)—Hammarskjöld writes of himself: "He is one of those who has had the wilderness for a pillow, and called a star his brother. Alone. But loneliness can be a communion."

Out of Solitude, (First Meditation)—"To live a Christian life means to live in the world without being *of* it. It is in solitude that this inner freedom can grow."

The Current of Spirituality, (Chapter 6)—"People naturally shrink from anything that brings them face-to-face with themselves—which is exactly what the spiritual life does."

SUPPLEMENTARY READING

Something Beautiful for God, (Mother Teresa's Way of Love)—Of silence Mother Teresa says, "God is the friend of silence.... The more we receive in silent prayer, the more we can give in our active life."

The Intellectual Life, (Chapter 3)—"In the organization of life, the essential point to safeguard, in view of which all the rest is necessary, is the wise provision of solitude, exterior and interior.... It is in view of retirement, silence, and inner solitude that action and outer contacts are admissible, and by them they must be regulated."

A Woman Wrapped in Silence, (X-XII)—The Holy Family resumes life in Nazareth. Mary holds all the events of her life in her heart and ponders them in silence.

* * * * *

In climates conducive to reflection—such as vacation, a relaxed evening at home, a quiet walk—it is easier to get in touch with ourselves than when we are juggling a variety of tasks. At such times we can think without strain; our mind may drift spontaneously toward the Transcendent; we shed our cares in beachcomber fashion and listen peacefully to the ebb and flow of life. Such occasions of relaxed listening are necessary for spiritual living, but their duration is usually brief. All too soon it's time to pack our things and return home. The telephone rings or a companion catches up with us and turns our quiet stroll into a time of conversation. Thus we must learn to carry over into daily life and our relations with others what we have learned in these solitary times of deeper listening. When we feel ourselves regressing into a tight task-and-other-oriented schedule, we must listen to the pressures felt within and try to silence their demands. This attitude of inner quieting will in turn effect the quality of our work and gentle the way we are with others.

MINOR THEME V

HERE I AM IN INNER PEACE

Often in the midst of strenuous activity, when the pressures of life seem too great to bear, I turn to the Lord in longing and pray to receive the gift of his peace. This gift is not something I can produce at will. It is a graced condition of inner tranquillity only Jesus can give. It helps at times to seek a peaceful place in which to reflect upon my life. The peace for which I pray may then well up from deep within. I then understand how much Christ cares for me. To appreciate where I am at this moment of my life and why I need the gift of Christ's peace, it helps at times to reflect on where I have been. In this retrospective look, I may pick up a thread of meaning. I see God's hand guiding me on the right path. By peacefully reflecting on past and present, I become aware of God's loving direction. Occasions that may have seemed negative now speak of his nearness. When I ponder the mystery of God's providential care, when I dwell on Christ's personal love for me, I am filled with inner peace. Each situation of my life radiates with his light. At no time has he left me alone. He has known of my need and responded in the right way—with an increase of self-knowledge here, a feeling of consolation there. On other occasions the Lord has given me the strength to bear suffering. Each situation shows me his love when I see it from all sides. I can dwell with Christ in peace because he abides so near to me. From this place of peaceful inwardness, I may, with God's grace, become a peacemaker in daily life. I may radiate to others something of the loving care that went forth from the Lord.

READINGS FROM HOLY SCRIPTURE

Old Testament

Nb. 6:22-27—The form of blessing. "May Yahweh uncover his face to you and bring you peace."

Nb. 25:1-18—At Peor the people bow down before false gods. Phinehas does not and so Yahweh grants to him his covenant of peace.

1 M. 14:1-15—Simon established peace in the land and Israel knew great joy.

Ps. 4—"In peace I lie down, and fall asleep at once..."

Ps. 29—"Yahweh blesses his people with peace."

Ps. 34—"...never yield to evil, practice good, seek peace, pursue it."

Ps. 72—"In his days virtue will flourish, a universal peace till the moon is no more..."

Ps. 122—"Pray for peace in Jerusalem..."

Ws. 3:1-12—The souls of the virtuous are in the hands of God; they are in peace.

Si. 1:11-20—"The fear of the Lord is the crown of wisdom; it makes peace and health to flourish."

Is. 9:1-6—"Wide is his dominion in a peace that has no end..."

Is. 11:1-16; 12:1-6—When the virtuous king comes, the wolf will lie down with the lamb.

Is. 32:1-20—Salvation is from Yahweh. "...integrity will bring peace..."

Is. 52:7-12—"How beautiful on the mountains are the feet of one who brings good news, who heralds peace, brings happiness, proclaims salvation..."

Is. 66:5-24—An apocalyptic poem. "Now toward her I send flowing peace, like a river..."

Jr. 14:1-22—"We were hoping for peace—no good came of it!"

Jr. 33:1-26—Another promise of recovery for Jerusalem and Judah. "...I will cure them and let them know peace and security in full measure."

Ba. 3:9-38; 4:1-4—Wisdom is the prerogative of Israel. "Had you walked in the way of God, you would have lived in peace for ever."

Ezk. 34:1-31—Yahweh, the Shepherd of Israel, shall make a covenant of peace with his flock.

Ezk. 37:15-28—"I shall make a covenant of peace with them, an eternal covenant with them."

Zc. 8:1-23—The prospect of messianic salvation. "For I mean to spread peace everywhere.... I am going to bestow all these blessings on the remnant of this people."

Zc. 9:1-17; 10:1-12; 11:1-3—The new promised land and the Messiah. "He will proclaim peace for the nations. His empire shall stretch from sea to sea, from the River to the ends of the earth."

New Testament

Lk. 2:1-20—The birth of Jesus and the visit of the shepherds. "Glory to God in the highest heaven, and peace to men who enjoy his favor."

Mt. 5:1-12—"Happy the peacemakers: they shall be called sons of God."

Mt. 10:1-16; Mk. 6:7-13; Lk. 9:1-6—Jesus instructs his disciples, "As you enter his house, salute it, and if the house deserves it, let your peace descend upon it; if it does not, let your peace come back to you."

Mt. 18:5-10; Mk. 9:42-50; Lk. 17:1-3—"Have salt in yourselves and be at peace with one another."

Mk. 11:1-11; Lk. 19:28-38—The Messiah enters Jerusalem. "Peace in heaven and glory in the highest heavens."

Mt. 23:37-39; Lk. 19:41-44—Lament for Jerusalem. "If you in your turn had only understood on this day the message of peace!"

Jn. 14:1-31—"Peace I bequeath to you, my own peace I give you, a peace the world cannot give, this is my gift to you."

Jn. 16:16-33—Jesus says to his disciples, "I have told you all this so that you may find peace in me."

Lk. 24:36-43; Jn. 20:19-29—Jesus appears to his disciples and says "Peace be with you." He then shows them his hands and his side.
Rm. 2:1-11—"...renown, honor and peace will come to everyone who does good..."
Rm. 14:1-23; 15:1-13—The kingdom of God means righteousness, peace, and joy brought by the Holy Spirit.
Ep. 2:11-22—Christ is the peace between us.
Ep. 6:10-20—Be eager to spread the gospel of peace.
Ph. 4:2-9—The peace of God is so much greater than we can understand.
Jm. 3:13-18—"Peacemakers, when they work for peace, sow the seeds which will bear fruit in holiness."
2 P. 3:11-18—"...while you are waiting, do your best to live lives without spot or stain so that he will find you at peace."

* * * * *

Because we lead fragmented lives, torn between labor and leisure, functional needs and transcendent desires, menial tasks and meritorious deeds, it is difficult for us both to attain and maintain inner peace. By our own efforts alone, the harmony we seek escapes us. Christ knew we could not find lasting peace by means of worldly pursuits. Such peace is only possible when we dwell in his presence, when we open our hearts in humble receptivity to the gift he alone can give.

READINGS FROM THE LITERATURE OF SPIRITUALITY

This Tremendous Lover, (Chapters 7, 17, 23 and 24)—The spiritual life is a life of intimacy with Jesus in which peace is found through humility, obedience, and poverty of spirit.
Spirituality and the Gentle Life, (Part Two)—The author describes in these chapters the many barriers aggression and anger pose to gentleness and inner peace. He shows us ways in which, with God's guidance and grace, we can work these volatile emotions through and regain the peace and tranquillity characteristic of a person whose center is not self but Christ.
Markings, (1956)—In Christ's hand, every moment has its meaning, its greatness, its glory, its peace, its co-inherence.
As Bread That Is Broken, (Chapter 15)—How to find peace.
Personality Fulfillment in the Spiritual Life, (Chapter 4)—The author describes another obstacle to inner peace and religious presence, that of addiction. His aim is to show us how to spot the dangers of spiritual

addiction before we grow in the wrong direction so that we can experience in ourselves a deep receptive openness to the whole and Holy.

The Current of Spirituality, (Chapters 10 and 11)—"Does a failure leave me in a state of peace with a greater desire for prayer, or does it make me restless, ready to take advantage of my exhaustion, less disposed to offer myself for God's work in the future if that is the way he is going to treat me?"

SUPPLEMENTARY READING

A Woman Wrapped in Silence, (XIV)—Mary witnesses the beginning of Jesus' public life and realizes that her peace will always be accompanied by pain.

* * * * *

Christ's gift of peace is his farewell gesture of care for us, his followers. This is a peace the world cannot fathom. He knows we will need this gift to be gentle instead of violent; to be compassionate rather than scornful; to radiate hope though surrounded by despair; to be tranquil even when chaos threatens. As spiritual persons, we must guard our serenity of soul. As long as we are rooted in Christ, no matter how our situation changes, we shall find the strength we need to be other Christs in this world.

MINOR THEME VI

HERE I AM IN REPENTANCE FOR SIN

Growth in the spiritual life implies an ever deepening intimacy with the Trinity. As Christ-centered persons, we are aware of our sinfulness as well as of the general fallibility of humankind. At the same time we sense an inner call to draw near to Christ and to live in the light of our divine likeness. For this reason we need to die to sin in all its forms. Death to sin is possible only because Christ has redeemed us with the total sacrifice of himself. He has loved us without reserve. This love, however, does not give us the license to presume on Christ's forgiveness. We must try to do better each time we fail—not out of fear or stern self-condemnation but out of love for God, knowing that sin in any form separates us from God and causes Christ to suffer. As true followers of Jesus, we pray not to be put to the test. We ask the Father to deliver us from all that is evil. Each time we miss the mark, we return, as did the Prodigal Son, to ask the Father's forgiveness. This generous gift is granted to us when we sincerely repent. We try in turn to extend it to others, forgiving them as we have been forgiven, and helping them, as we ourselves have been helped, to go and sin no more.

READINGS FROM HOLY SCRIPTURE

Old Testament

Gn. 3:1-24—Adam and Eve are banished from the garden of Eden because they eat the fruit of the forbidden tree.

Gn. 9:1-17—Through Noah, the man who has not displeased God by sin, a new world order is established.

Ex. 32:1-35; 33:1-23; 34:1-35—When the people bow down to the golden calf, despite their apostasy, Yahweh relents. He hears the repentant prayers of Moses and he renews his covenant.

Lv. 4:1-35; 5:1-26—The sacrifice of reparation for sin is described by Yahweh through Moses, his spokesman.

Lv. 6:17-23; 7:1-6—Another description of the sacrifice for sin and reparation.

Lv. 16:1-34—The great Day of Atonement. "...once a year the rite of atonement must be made over the sons of Israel for all their sins."

Lv. 23:26-32—Another description of the Day of Atonement.

Ne. 9:1-37—The ceremony of atonement. "Standing, each man in his right position, they read from the Book of the Law of Yahweh their God for one quarter of the day; for another quarter they confessed their sins and prostrated themselves before Yahweh their God."

Jb. 42:1-17—Job's final answer to Yahweh, whose marvels are beyond him, is to retract all he has said and, in dust and ashes, to repent. Yahweh then restores Job's fortunes.

Ps. 32—Candid admission of sin.

Ps. 36—The wickedness of the sinner compared to the goodness of God.

Ps. 37—The fate of the virtuous and the wicked.

Ps. 102—"Ashes are the bread I eat, what I drink I lace with tears..."

Ps. 106—National confession.

Si. 17:25-32—Exhortation to repentance.

Is. 35:1-10—Yahweh is coming to ransom those who repent.

Is. 42:1-25—The servant of Yahweh "...does not cry out or shout aloud, or make his voice heard in the streets. He does not break the crushed reed, nor quench the wavering flame."

Is. 52:13-15; 53:1-12—The servant of Yahweh is despised and rejected by men, pierced through for our faults, crushed for our sins, surrendering himself to death while bearing the faults of many.

Is. 59:1-20—A psalm. "For our faults in your sight have been many and our sins are a witness against us."

Ba. 1:16-22; 2:1-10—Confession of sins. "...we have been disobedient to the Lord our God, we have been disloyal, refusing to listen to his voice."

Ezk. 6:1-14; 7:1-27—The sins of Israel. "...they will all carry on sinning and be none the stronger for it."

Ho. 6:1-6—Israel's short-lived and shallow repentance.

Ho. 6:7-11; 7:1-16—The past and present sins of Israel, the ingratitude this people has shown, warrant punishment.

Ho. 11:1-11—God's love proves stronger than his vengeance.

Ho. 13:4-15; 14:1-10—The repentance and reconciliation of Israel.

Jl. 1:2-20—The prophet laments the ruin of the country and calls the people to prayer and repentance.

Mi. 7:8-20—A plea for God's forgiveness. "What god can compare with you: taking fault away, pardoning crime, not cherishing anger for ever but delighting in showing mercy?"

Hab. 3:1-19—A plea to Yahweh for deliverance. "You have marched to save your people, to save your own anointed..."

Zp. 3:9-20—Yahweh awaits the return of the exiles. "Yes, I will then give the people lips that are clean, so that all may invoke the name of Yahweh and serve him under the same yoke."

New Testament

Mt. 4:12-17; Mk. 1:14-15; Lk. 4:14-15—Jesus preached this message: "Repent, for the kingdom of heaven is close at hand."

Lk. 7:36-50—The woman who was a sinner. "For this reason I tell you that her sins, her many sins, must have been forgiven her, or she would not have shown such great love."

Mt. 6:7-15; Lk. 11:1-4—"...and forgive us our debts, as we have forgiven those who are in debt to us."

Mt. 9:1-8; Mk. 2:1-12; Lk. 5:17-26—Cure of a paralytic. "Courage, my child, your sins are forgiven."

Mt. 9:10-13; Mk. 2:15-17; Lk. 5:29-32—Eating with sinners. "...indeed I did not come to call the virtuous but sinners."

Lk. 13:1-5—Examples inviting repentance.

Lk. 15:1-32—Three parables of God's mercy: the lost sheep, the lost drachma, the lost son.

Mt. 18:21-35—I must forgive my brothers not seven but seventy-seven times. Jesus makes this lesson clear in the parable of the unforgiving debtor.

Mt. 21:28-32—Parable of the two sons. "I tell you solemnly, tax collectors and prostitutes are making their way into the kingdom of God before you."

Jn. 8:1-11—One by one all who had accused the woman walked away and she was alone with Jesus. There was no one to condemn her and neither did he.

Jn. 8:21-59—Jesus warns the unbelieving Jews. "I am going away; you will look for me and you will die in your sin." He adds, "I tell you most solemnly, everyone who commits sin is a slave."

Lk. 23:39-43—The good thief. "...we are paying for what we did. But this man has done nothing wrong."

Jn. 20:19-29—Jesus appears to his disciples and says, "Receive the Holy Spirit. For those whose sins you forgive, they are forgiven; for those whose sins you retain, they are retained."

Rm. 5:12-21; 6:1-23; 7:1-25—Paul explains our deliverance from sin and death through Jesus and defines the true function of the law.

2 Co. 6:11-18; 7:1-4—"...let us wash off all that can soil either body or spirit, to reach perfection of holiness in the fear of God."

Ep. 1:3-14—God's plan of salvation."...through his blood, we gain our freedom, the forgiveness of our sins."

1 Jn. 1:8-10; 2:1-2—"I am writing this, my children, to stop you sinning..."

1 Jn. 3:3-9—"...anyone who lives in God does not sin..."

* * * * *

The further we advance in the life of the spirit, the closer we desire our relationship with God to become. With his grace we want to cast off any intentional or unintentional acts that displease the Beloved or separate us from his goodness. With a generosity beyond our capacity to grasp, he offers us the free gift of intimacy with himself. We must become worthy receivers of this gift by repenting for sin and living in thanksgiving.

READINGS FROM THE LITERATURE OF SPIRITUALITY

The Cloud of Unknowing, (Chapters 10-12, 28, 33-34, 40, 43-50)—The author describes how beginners in contemplation should conduct themselves in regard to their thoughts and inclinations to sin. He instructs his disciple to keep in mind this general principle: If he possesses God, he will be free of sin and when he is free of sin he will possess God.

This Tremendous Lover, (Chapters 1-5 and 11)—God himself, with his infinite power, knowledge, and wisdom became man and took upon himself the sins of the human race. He became man to atone for the sins of mankind, to win for men the supernatural life they had lost in Adam.

Spirituality and the Gentle Life, (Chapter XIX)—The kingdom of selfish desires is nothing like the gentle Kingdom of God; it is an anarchy of lust, greed, envy and anger—the reign of the isolated self, seeking its own salvation.

Markings, (1957)—We can reach the point where it becomes possible for us to recognize and understand original sin, that dark counter-center of evil in our nature. Though it is not our nature, it is of it; something within us which rejoices when disaster befalls the cause we are trying to serve or misfortune overtakes even those whom we love.

As Bread That Is Broken, (Chapters 6, 7 and 8)—Jesus did not come to call the virtuous but sinners. We can be saved provided we confess our need to be saved. Part of true repentance is thus learning our place.

SUPPLEMENTARY READING

As Bread That Is Broken, (Appendix)—A Penance Service. "With you, O Lord, there is forgiveness and on this we live."

Leisure, The Basis of Culture, (Chapter III)—Sloth, one of the capital sins that calls for repentance, is the despairing refusal to be oneself.

* * * * *

Jesus taught with utmost clarity that God is love. His love enveloped all who believed in him, even those who were public sinners. He was not a stern judge but a shepherd who would spare nothing to find one lost lamb and return it to the fold. On the cross Christ drew repentant sinners to himself. Repentance heals the separation from God sin has caused in our soul; it is a foundational disposition of the heart that anchors us firmly in the forgiving love of our Redeemer.

MINOR THEME VII

HERE I AM IN PRAYER

Prayer offers us the opportunity, time and again, to slow down our usual pace. During this pause, we may feel refreshed in body, mind and spirit. Quietly resting in God fosters not only trustful openness to the wonders that surround us but also relaxed in-touchness with ordinary life. The world is no longer merely the place in which we work; it is also the arena in which we worship. In humble, quiet prayer we recognize our personal need for God. We ready ourselves to receive any manifestation of his presence by humbly waiting upon the Mystery rather than babbling many words. We ask the Spirit who prays in us to refine our sensitivity to the Father's will. At times this means praying in the darkness of not knowing. Our experience of God remains dim and obscure. We believe he is there, we continue to love and adore him, though we do not feel his presence. Ours is a prayer of attentive desire—an aspiration of love reaching toward the Beloved as he is in himself. It is a prayer of openness to God as God, a mode of presence that remains as steady and true in consolation as in desolation.

READINGS FROM HOLY SCRIPTURE

Old Testament

Ex. 33:12-23—Moses prays on the mountain. "...please show me your ways, so that I can understand you and win your favor."

Nb. 11:10-30—The prayer of Moses and Yahweh's reply. "If only I had found favor in your eyes, and not lived to see such misery as this!"

Jos. 7:6-15—Joshua's prayer and Yahweh's answer: "What are you going to do for your great name?"

1 S. 1:9-28; 2:1-11—The prayer of Hannah before and after the birth of Samuel.

2 S. 7:1-29—The prophecy of Nathan and David's prayer. "Who am I, Lord Yahweh, and what is my House that you have led me as far as this?"

2 S. 22:1-51—A psalm of David.

1 K. 8:22-61—Solomon's prayer for himself and for the people. "Listen to the prayer and entreaty of your servant, Yahweh my God; listen to the cry and to the prayer your servant makes to you today."

1 Ch. 17:1-27—The prophecy of Nathan and David's prayer.

2 Ch. 6:1-42—Solomon's prayer for himself and for the people.

Ps. 5—Morning prayer. "Yahweh, let my words come to your ears, spare a thought for my sighs."

Ps. 20—Prayer for the king. "May Yahweh grant all your petitions!"

Ps. 31—Prayer in time of ordeal. "Yet you heard my petition when I called to you for help."

Ps. 40—Song of praise and prayer for help. "May your love and faithfulness constantly preserve me."

Ps. 50—Worship God in spirit and truth.

Ps. 71—An old man's prayer. "Be a sheltering rock, a walled fortress to save me!"

Ws. 9:1-18—A prayer for wisdom.
Si. 36:1-17—Prayer for the deliverance and restoration of Israel.
Si. 51:1-30—A hymn of thanksgiving and a poem on the quest for Wisdom.
Is. 25:1-12; 26:1-21—A prayer of thanksgiving and song of victory.
Ba. 2:11-35; 3:1-8—The prayer of the exiles. "Almighty Lord, God of Israel, hear the prayer of the dead of Israel, of the sons of those who have sinned against you..."
Jl. 2:18-27—The prayer answered. "I am Yahweh your God, with none to equal me. My people will not be disappointed any more."

New Testament

Lk. 1:46-56—Mary's prayer. "My soul proclaims the greatness of the Lord..."
Lk. 1:67-79—Zechariah's prayer. "Thus he shows mercy to our ancestors..."
Mt. 6:5-18; Lk. 11:1-4—Jesus teaches his disciples how to pray.
Mt. 7:7-11; Lk. 11:9-13—Effective prayer. "Ask, and it will be given to you..."
Lk. 10:38-42—Martha serves Jesus while Mary sits at his feet. Jesus says that Mary has chosen the better part.
Mt. 17:14-20; Mk. 9:14-29; Lk. 9:37-43—Upon curing the epileptic demoniac, Jesus answers his disciples, "...if your faith were the size of a mustard seed you could say to this mountain, 'Move from here to there,' and it would move; nothing would be impossible for you."
Lk. 17:5-6—The power of faith.
Mt. 18:19-20—Prayer in common. "For where two or three meet in my name, I shall be there with them."
Mt. 21:18-22; Mk. 11:20-25—"...if you have faith, everything you ask for in prayer you will receive."
Lk. 18:9-14—The Pharisee and the publican. The prayer of the publican is beheld with great favor by God.
Jn. 17:1-26—The priestly prayer of Jesus. "I pray not only for these, but for those also who through their words will believe in me. May they all be one."
Rm. 8:1-39—The life of the spirit. "For when we cannot choose words in order to pray properly, the Spirit himself expresses our plea in a way that could never be put into words..."
Col. 1:3-14—"...we have never failed to pray for you, and what we ask God is that through perfect wisdom and spiritual understanding you should reach the fullest knowledge of his will."
Col. 4:2-6—"Be persevering in your prayers and be thankful as you stay awake to pray."
1 Th. 5:12-22—"Be happy at all times; pray constantly; and for all things give thanks to God..."

1 Tm. 2:1-8—Liturgical prayer. "In every place, then, I want the men to lift their hands up reverently in prayer, with no anger or argument."

* * * * *

Prayer must not be confined to an occasional visit with God; it is meant to be an all-encompassing orientation of our being toward his. We believe that God remains near to us, though we may at times distance ourselves from him due to sin. Prayer enables us to turn swiftly to Jesus and to ask for forgiveness. Praise, petition, and thanksgiving are all modes of prayer. God is with us always, but his nearness to us is especially manifest when we pray.

READINGS FROM THE LITERATURE OF SPIRITUALITY

The Cloud of Unknowing, (Chapters 2, 13-15, 26-27, 35-42, 71-75)—The author identifies humility as the basic attitude of the one who prays. He explains that contemplative prayer is possible only with grace, for it is the work of God; he describes the kinds of personal prayer common to contemplatives and suggests certain signs by which we may determine whether or not God is drawing us to contemplation.

This Tremendous Lover, (Chapters 8-10, 19)—"In practice, we start to pray by bringing God before our mind, or more properly, by turning our mind to God. He is everywhere; and by putting aside other thoughts and adverting to his presence, we can always pray to him."

The Soul of the Apostolate, (Part Five)—The author explains why mental prayer and participation in liturgical life are absolutely necessary to the apostolic worker. The keystone of the interior life, hence essential to the apostolate, is what he calls "custody of the heart." In the appendix he gives ten aids to mental prayer.

Spirituality and the Gentle Life, (Chapter XXII)—Gentleness and playfulness are aids to prayer.

As Bread That Is Broken, (Chapters 4, 5, and 18)—The heart of prayer is the realization of God's love for me and my response in total surrender to his love.

The Current of Spirituality, (Chapter 12)—"Being able to pray is a gift from God, but if the gift is to lead to further gifts of the same kind there has to be regularity, which means that there must be set times for prayer, and that they must be safeguarded as far as possible from interruption..."

SUPPLEMENTARY READING

Leisure, The Basis of Culture, (Chapter I, II, IV and V)—Reflections on the relation between contemplation and play, feast and worship, lead the author to conclude that leisure is a singularly human activity made possible through worship of the Divine.

* * * * *

Whether we offer prayer in repentance or gratitude, we do so in faith. In matters of grace, God has the initiative. He shows us the way by which we must go to him. To pray is to acknowledge that we are, from the beginning, grasped by God who desires to make us into a new creation in Christ. A mistaken notion about the spiritual life is to think of it as merely a moral code of do's and don'ts. Like the Pharisees Jesus condemns, we seek to draw attention to ourselves by outward manifestations of holiness. Jesus sees in these external shows of piety the worst possible pride. Hence he praises the prayer of the publican, for his unassuming presence manifests the humble, childlike approach so pleasing to God.

MINOR THEME VIII

SEND ME ON MY MISSION IN GENTLENESS

Isaiah's response to the Lord's question of who will speak for him is a resounding, "...send me." This acceptance of God's call is not an impulsive self-willed reaction but a response rooted in the sense of mission instilled in us by God. To be thus called is not a privilege reserved for prophets; each of us has a special destiny. We are to be active members of Christ's body. No Christian is excluded from discipleship, whether the field of one's witnessing is as private as a kitchen or as public as an office building. In accordance with the situation, each Christian is sent by God to bear good fruit on this earth. Once we sense that the work we do is not merely ours but God's, we can become attuned to the sacred implications of each act. Nothing is unimportant in the Kingdom. God's gentle care pervades all realms. He invites us to be his partners. One quality that defines the Christian, who is actively witnessing for his Divine Lord in the world, is gentleness. This attitude is expressed in the care and concern we show for each person who crosses our path. The gentle way tempers the tendency toward harshness of heart. It softens the admonishing voice and stills the angry response. To be and become gentle in what we say and do, we need to be with Christ, the master of gentleness. He will show us the way to serve the Father so that others may be drawn to him through us.

READINGS FROM HOLY SCRIPTURE

Old Testament

Gn. 12:1-9—The call of Abraham. "Leave your country, your family and your father's house, for the land l will show you."

Ex. 2:23-25; 3:1-22; 4:1-31—The mission of Moses.

Ex. 6:2-13; 6:28-30; 7:1-7—Another account of the call of Moses.

Nb. 22:1-41; 23:1-30; 24:1-25—The king of Moab appeals to Balaam to curse this people coming from Egypt, but God has other plans for Balaam. The spirit of God comes upon him and he heaps blessings upon the enemy.

Nb. 27:12-23—Joshua is appointed head of the community "...so that the community of Yahweh may not be like sheep without a shepherd."

Dt. 31:1-8—Joshua and his mission.

Jos. 1:1-18—When Moses was dead, Yahweh spoke to Joshua and promised to be with him as he was with Moses—provided he would be strong and stand firm.

Jg. 6:1-40; 7:1-25; 8:1-35—Yahweh calls Gideon whose clan is the weakest in Manasseh. Because Yahweh is with him, he shall crush single-handedly the power of the Midian.

1 K. 19:19-21—The call of Elisha.

2 K. 2:1-25—Elijah is taken up and Elisha succeeds him. Elisha performs two miracles.

2 K. 4:1-44; 5:1-27; 6:1-7—Some miracles of Elisha that manifest how he carries on his mission in gentleness, justice, and care.

Ezr. 7:1-26—The mission and personality of Ezra.

Ne. 1:1-11; 2:1-20—The call of Nehemiah and his mission to Judah: the decision to rebuild the walls of Jerusalem.

Ne. 13:1-31—The second mission of Nehemiah.

Ps. 23—"Yahweh is my shepherd, I lack nothing."

Ps. 30—"Yahweh, my God, I cried to you for help, and you have healed me."

Pss. 42-43—"Send out your light and your truth, let these be my guide, to lead me to your holy mountain and to the place where you live."

Si. 3:17-24—"My son, be gentle in carrying out your business..."

Is. 40:1-11—The calling of the prophet.

Is. 49:1-26—Second song of the servant of Yahweh. "It is not enough for you to be my servant, to restore the tribes of Jacob and bring back the survivors of Israel; I will make you the light of the nations so that my salvation may reach to the ends of the earth."

Is. 61:1-11—The mission of the prophet.

Jr. 1:4-19—The call of Jeremiah.

Jr. 15:10-21—The call of Jeremiah renewed.

Ezk. 34:1-31—Yahweh foretells trouble for the shepherds who feed themselves when they ought to feed their flock. He shall rescue his flock from wherever they have scattered. He shall look for the lost one and bring back the stray.

New Testament

Jn. 1:1-18—"A man came, sent by God. His name was John. He came as a witness, as a witness to speak for the light, so that everyone might believe through him."

Mt. 4:18-22; Mk. 1:16-20; Lk. 5:1-11; Jn. 1:35-51—The first disciples are called.

Jn. 3:22-36—John bears witness for the last time.

Mt. 7:12—The golden rule.

Mt. 9:9—The call of Matthew.

Mt. 11:28-30—The gentle mastery of Jesus.

Mt. 18:12-14; Lk. 15:4-7—The lost sheep.

Jn. 10:1-21—Jesus is the good shepherd who lays down his life for his sheep. He knows his own and his own know him.

Jn. 13:1-20—Jesus washes his disciples' feet. "I have given you an example so that you may copy what I have done to you."

Jn. 13:33-35—"I give you a new commandment: love one another; just as I have loved you, you also must love one another."

Mt. 20:24-28; Mk. 10:41-45—"...anyone who wants to be great among you must be your servant..."

Mt. 26:31-46—The Last Judgment. "...as you did this to one of the least of these brothers of mine, you did it to me."

Mt. 28:16-20; Mk. 16:9-20; Lk. 24:13-49; Jn. 20:19-29—Jesus appears in Galilee and speaks to his disciples about their mission to the world.

Jn. 21:1-23—Jesus appears to his disciples on the shore of Tiberias. "Feed my lambs," he says. "Look after my sheep."

Rm. 14:1-23; 15:1-13—"If a person's faith is not strong enough, welcome him all the same without starting an argument.... It can only be to God's glory, then, for you to treat each other in the same friendly way as Christ treated you."

1 Co. 12:1-31; 13:1-13; 14:1-40—Spiritual gifts and their order of importance in the community. "...without love, I am simply a gong booming or a cymbal clashing."

2 Co. 1:12-24; 2:1-17—"When I wrote to you, in deep distress and anguish of mind, and in tears, it was not to make you feel hurt but to let you know how much love I have for you."

2 Co. 5:11-26; 6:1-10—The apostolate in action. "We do nothing that people might object to, so as not to bring discredit on our function as God's servants."

Col. 2:16-23—Christians follow the example of Jesus' gentleness not the way of a false asceticism based on the principles of this world with their self-imposed devotions, their self-abasement, and their severe treatment of the body.

1 Th. 2:1-20—Paul's example in Thessalonika. "You are witnesses, and so is God, that our treatment of you, since you became believers, has been impeccably right and fair."

1 Th. 4:1-12—Live in holiness and charity.

2 P. 1:3-18—The Christian ought to have a generous supply of goodness, self-control, patience, true devotion, kindness, and love."

1 Jn. 2:3-11—Keep the commandments, especially the law of love.

1 Jn. 3:10-24—"This is the message as you heard it from the beginning: that we are to love one another..."

* * * * *

Though the gifts God gives to each person are unique, the mission we share is the same: to be faithful to our call to live as holy and harmonious a life as possible. In whatever situation God places us, we must be channels of his grace. At times we may falter; we may offer God only lukewarm service; but, if we persevere, a transformation may occur. We may become messengers of the Mystery, who, through gentle and loving mediation, invite others to follow Jesus.

READINGS FROM THE LITERATURE OF SPIRITUALITY

This Tremendous Lover, (Chapters 6 and 21)—To be a living member of the Mystical Body of Christ, a Christian must do God's will and act for the good of his fellow members. The Christian is to imitate Christ's gentle love in all relations, especially in marriage.

The Soul of the Apostolate, (Part Three)—The interior life, and its gentling effect, is the foundation of sanctity in the active worker, renewing his strength, multiplying his energies and merits, giving him joy and consolation, refining his purity of intention, and offering him a firm defense against discouragement.

Spirituality and the Gentle Life, (Chapters I, II and IV)—The gentle person has time to listen, time to be quiet, to think without strain, to work without pressure.

Markings, (1954-1955)—Many personal failures are due to a lack of faith in the harmony between human beings that can be at once strict and gentle.

Out of Solitude, (Second Meditation)—Care is the basis and pre-condition of all cure. "To care means first of all to empty our own cup and to allow the other to come close to us. It means to take away the many barriers which prevent us from entering into communion with the other."

As Bread That Is Broken, (Chapter 9)—The sign of being a holy person is to give people the good feeling of being themselves. There is no pressure, no uneasiness. Pressure always implies a lack of respect, a lack of love, a lack of gentleness.

Personality Fulfillment in the Spiritual Life, (Chapter 5)—Chaste, gentle love is part of the path to full religious presence.

The Current of Spirituality, (Chapters 5, 7, 8 and 13)—The touchstone of the Christian spiritual life is charity. From this love flow the qualities of kindness, patience, gentleness—the marks of one who lives in God and witnesses to his care.

SUPPLEMENTARY READING

The Intellectual Life, (Chapter 8)—We are being gentle with ourselves when we proportion our task to our powers of creativity.

* * * * *

To look upon each moment of life as a gift from God gentles our response in even the most trying of circumstances. If we believe that Christ is risen and truly present in us and in all of creation, we will keep his commandments of love. It will become second-nature to show others the respect, tolerance, and concern we wish them to show us. By this response of love, everyone will know that we are Jesus' disciples, eager to imitate the gentle compassion of our Lord.

MINOR THEME IX

SEND ME THOUGH I MAY HAVE TO SUFFER

We only need to see the lives of the prophets and of Jesus himself to know that everyone who is sent into the world as God's servant will inevitably incur suffering. Suffering may be experienced when we come up against personal limitations, when we have to admit our inability to fulfill cherished plans, when we are the brunt of misunderstanding. It stings us in the sheer routine of daily living, in our powerlessness to help certain people, and in our incapacity to change ourselves. Some form of suffering will accompany us if we walk the way Christ has chosen. No true disciple can avoid taking up the cross. Acceptance of this suffering makes us sharers in Christ's redeeming gift of love.

READINGS FROM HOLY SCRIPTURE

Old Testament

Dt. 33:1-29; 34:1-12—Before he dies, Moses blesses the tribes. He sees the promised land but is not allowed to cross into it.

Tb. 1:1-22; 2:1-14; 3:1-6—Tobit, the exile, is blinded. Sad at heart, he sighs and weeps. "Lord, I wait for the sentence you will give to deliver me from this affliction."

Tb. 11:1-18; 12:1-21; 13:1-17—Tobit's sight is restored. He praises God with a hymn of thanksgiving. "Blessed be God who lives for ever.... By turns he punishes and pardons; he sends men down to the depths of the underworld and draws them up from supreme destruction..."

2 M. 6:18-31—The martyrdom of Eleazar. "...in my soul I am glad to suffer, because of the awe which he inspires in me."

2 M. 7:1-42—The martyrdom of the seven brothers. "We are suffering for our sins; and if, to punish and discipline us, our living Lord vents his wrath upon us, he will yet be reconciled with his own servants."

Jb. 3:1-26—Job curses the day of his birth.

Jb. 6:1-30; 7:1-21—Only the sufferer knows his own grief.

Jb. 16:1-22; 17:1-16—Job is a patient man but he finds that those trying to justify his suffering speak only "airy words."

Jb. 19:1-29—Job feels deserted by God and man, a thing corrupt from whom everyone turns.

Jb. 29:1-20; 30:1-31—Job's lament and final defense. His former happiness in contrast to his present misery.

Jb. 36:1-33; 37:1-24—The real meaning of Job's suffering. Elihu's hymn to God's wisdom and omnipotence.
Ps. 22—"My God, my God, why have you deserted me?"
Ps. 69—"...when I was thirsty they gave me vinegar to drink."
Ps. 70—"To me, poor wretch, come quickly, God!"
Ps. 86—"...take pity on me, Lord, I invoke you all day long..."
Ps. 118—"It was the stone rejected by the builders that proved to be the keystone..."
Ps. 130—"From the depths I call to you, Yahweh, Lord, listen to my cry for help!"
Si. 2:1-18—"My son, if you aspire to serve the Lord, prepare yourself for an ordeal...do not be alarmed when disaster comes."
Is. 52:13-15; 53:1-12—Fourth song of the servant of Yahweh. "...ours were the sufferings he bore, ours the sorrows he carried."
Jr. 4:1-31; 5:1-31; 6:1-30—The sufferings of those who do not listen to the voice of Yahweh our God.
Lm. 3:1-66—"I am the man familiar with misery under the rod of his anger; I am the one he has driven and forced to walk in darkness, and without any light."
Ba. 4:5-37; 5:1-9—"Take courage, Jerusalem: he who gave you that name will console you...take off your dress of sorrow and distress, put on the beauty of the glory of God for ever..."
Ezk. 24:15-27—The personal ordeals of the prophet.
Dn. 3:1-97—The song of Azariah and the three young men in the furnace. In the heart of the furnace, Azariah and his companions praised Yahweh and the fire did not cause them any pain or distress.
Dn. 6:1-29—Daniel in the lion pit.

New Testament

Mt. 5:1-12—The Beatitudes. "Happy those who are persecuted in the cause of right: theirs is the kingdom of heaven."
Mt. 8:18-22; Lk. 9:57-62—Hardships of the apostolic calling.
Mt. 10:1-36; Mk. 6:7-13; Lk. 9:1-6—The mission of the Twelve and the persecutions they will have to undergo.
Mt. 10:37-42; Mt. 16:24-28; Mk. 8:34-38; Lk. 9:23-26—Renouncing self to follow Jesus. "Anyone who does not take up his cross and follow in my footsteps is not worthy of me."
Lk. 10:1-20—The mission of the seventy-two disciples.
Lk. 12:1-12—Open and fearless speech may bring persecution.
Mt. 12:15-21—Jesus is the "servant of Yahweh."
Mt. 13:53-58; Mk. 6:1-6; Lk. 4:16-30—Jesus is not accepted in Nazareth

because a prophet "...is only despised in his own country and in his own house."

Mt. 14:3-21; Mk. 6:17-29—John the Baptist is beheaded.

Mt. 21:20-23; Mk. 10:35-40—The mother of Zebedee's sons makes her request. "Can you drink the cup that I am going to drink?"

Mt. 21:33-46; Mk. 12:1-12; Lk. 20:9-19—Parable of the wicked husbandmen. The stone rejected by the builders became the keystone.

Mt. 24:4-25; Mk. 13:5-23; Lk. 21:5-28—Jesus foretells the onset of sorrows and the great tribulation of Jerusalem.

Jn. 12:20-36—Jesus foretells his death and subsequent glorification.

Jn. 15:1-27; 16:1-33—In his farewell discourses, Jesus comforts his disciples by saying, "If the world hates you, remember that it hated me before you."

Mt. 26:36-46; Mk. 14:32-42; Lk. 22:39-46—Gethsemane. "My Father...if this cup cannot pass by without my drinking it, your will be done."

Mt. 26:57-68; Mk. 14:53-63; Lk. 22:66-71—Jesus goes before the Sanhedrin and his long ordeal begins.

Mt. 27:11-26; Mk. 15:1-15; Lk. 23:2-25; Jn. 18:28-40—Jesus is brought before Pilate, but he makes no attempt to defend himself. He has fully accepted the Father's will.

Mt. 27:27-56; Mk. 15:16-39; Lk. 23:26-46; Jn. 19:1-37—Jesus is scourged, crowned with thorns, crucified and mocked. He accepts his suffering, though humanly he feels deserted.

Ac. 7:55-60; 8:1-3—The stoning of Stephen.

Ac. 12:1-25—Peter is arrested and miraculously delivered. Herod, the persecutor, dies.

Ac. 16:16-40—Paul and Silas are imprisoned, and they too are miraculously delivered.

Rm. 8:18-39—"...what we suffer in this life can never be compared to the glory as yet unrevealed, which is waiting for us."

Col. 1:24-29—Paul's labors in service of the pagans. "It makes me happy to suffer for you, as I am suffering now, and in my own body to do what I can to make up all that has still to be undergone by Christ for the sake of his body, the Church."

2 Tm. 2:1-13—How Timothy should face hardships.

Heb. 10:32-39—"Remember all the sufferings that you had to meet after you received the light..."

Jm. 1:2-12—"My brothers, you will always have your trials but, when they come, try to treat them as a happy privilege..."

1 P. 3:13-17—"...if it is the will of God that you should suffer, it is better to suffer for doing right than for doing wrong."

* * * * *

Every true follower of Christ has to expect affliction in this life and welcome it as an opportunity to share in the cross. When suffering comes, our first reaction is to overcome it. With the help of the Holy Spirit, our first response may be instead prayerful abandonment to God's will out of love for him. In this way we further the work of redemption. We do not seek suffering as an end in itself, but we do try to accept it in surrender. We believe that Christ will give us the strength we need to see this crisis through with fortitude and constancy.

READINGS FROM THE LITERATURE OF SPIRITUALITY

The Cloud of Unknowing, (Chapters 67and 70)—Though our sinful nature suffers because of the contemplative work, we must abide patiently in this darkness, for, as the author says, the suffering we endure now is not hell at all but our purgatory.

This Tremendous Lover, (Chapters 18 and 22)—Every grace that comes to us from God had to be merited by Jesus; it comes to us from him. He has associated his mother, the Mother of Sorrows, with him in the work of Redemption, so that, at least in the application of its fruits, she always has a part.

The Practice of the Presence of God, (Letters XI-XVI)—Suffering will be a happiness, a balm and a consolation while we are occupied with God.

Spirituality and the Gentle Life, (Chapter XXIII)—Sharing the suffering of the Lamb of God that was slain, we will share in his glory.

Markings, (1958-1959)—Hammarskjöld reflects on how incredibly great is what he has been given and how meaningless what he has had to sacrifice.

As Bread That Is Broken, (Chapters 10 and 16)—The servant's life, because of suffering, will be fruitful. We will all have to face the cross someday.

The Current of Spirituality, (Chapters 3 and 9)—The purpose of the Christian life is to know Christ crucified. Few of us are called upon to suffer as Christ did, but there must be in us the willingness to abandon our self-sufficiency and accept whatever trials God sends.

SUPPLEMENTARY READING

A Woman Wrapped in Silence, (XV-XVI)—A sword pierces Mary's heart as she witnesses the crucifixion and death of her son.

* * * * *

Jesus suffered in many ways. He knew physical pain, mental anguish, disappointment with his disciples, the apparent failure of his mission. He showed us that suffering, weakness and powerlessness, if accepted in faith, open us to God's mercy and might. It is our littleness the Lord loves, not our grandiosity. Pain in its myriad forms can become an occasion for joy if it promotes prayerful living and surrender to Christ, the compassionate healer.

MINOR THEME X

SEND ME IN TRUST AND SURRENDER

"Send me" is a response that can only be given by one who has come to trust in a loving God who allows what is best for us and grants us the grace to endure all things graciously. Without such confidence, our chances of growing in spiritual living atrophy quickly. We need to trust because we cannot see immediately what God has in mind. Often we have to follow blindly, confident that the divine purpose will be revealed in the long run. Living trustfully is itself the best proof that God will not fail us. He gives us the courage to face risk and uncertainty as well as the unfailing ability to say "yes" in gratitude for and in relaxed acceptance of all God gives or allows to happen. This surrender results in serenity and peace. Letting go of our narrow understanding lets the Spirit elevate us to a higher level of loving knowledge. In trust and surrender we play our part in the divine plan, the fullness of which no human mind can fathom.

READINGS FROM HOLY SCRIPTURE

Old Testament

Gn. 22:1-19—God puts Abraham to the test. He asks him to sacrifice his son Isaac. Abraham does not refuse and God delights in his surrender.

Ex. 14:1-31—Yahweh leads the sons of Israel across the Sea of Reeds. Israel witnesses this great act and puts its trust in Yahweh and in Moses, his servant.

Dt. 18:1-22—"You must be entirely faithful to Yahweh your God."

Dt. 31:14-30; 32:1-52—Moses' final song of witness testifies to the trust and surrender Yahweh expects of his chosen people.

1 K. 18:1-46—The sacrifice on Carmel. Elijah's trust in Yahweh triumphs over the peoples' faith in Baal.

Jdt. 10:1-23; 11:1-23; 12:1-20; 13:1-20—Judith places her trust in Yahweh. Guided by his hand, she defeats Holofernes and avenges her people.

Ps. 1—The man who trusts Yahweh is like a tree planted by water streams; success attends all he does.

Ps. 32—"Many torments await the wicked, but grace enfolds the man who trusts in Yahweh."

Ps. 40—"Happy the man who puts his trust in Yahweh...."

Ps. 56—"Raise me up when I am most afraid, I put my trust in you..."

Ps. 91—"My refuge, my fortress, my God in whom I trust!"

Ps. 121—"Yahweh guards you from harm, he guards your lives..."

Ps. 125—"Those who trust in Yahweh are like Mount Zion, unshakable, standing for ever.

Ps. 127—Trust in providence.

Ps. 131—Childlike trust in God.

Ws. 3:1-12—The souls of the virtuous are in the hands of God; they surrender to him and are in peace.

Si. 11:12-28—Trust in God alone.

Is. 12:1-6—"See now, he is the God of my salvation. I have trust now and no fear...."

Is. 63:7-19; 64:1-11—A psalm. "No ear has heard, no eye has seen any god but you act like this for those who trust him."

Jr. 11:1-14—"Listen to my voice, I told them, carry out all my orders, then you shall be my people and I will be your God...."

Jr. 17:5-18—"...the man who puts his trust in Yahweh...is like a tree by the waterside that thrusts its roots to the stream...."

New Testament

Lk. 1:26-38—Mary surrenders to God's will without hesitation. "...let what you have said be done to me."

Mt. 6:25-34; Lk. 12:22-32—Trust in providence. "Set your hearts on his kingdom first, and on his righteousness, and all these other things will be given you as well."

Mt. 8:5-13; Lk. 7:1-10—Because the centurion has trusted in the power of Jesus, his servant is cured.

Mt. 9:18-26; Mk. 5:21-43; Lk. 8:40-56—The woman trusts that if she touches the fringe of Jesus' cloak, she will be cured. The official believes that his daughter will rise to life if Jesus so wills.

Mt. 15:21-28; Mk. 7:24-30—The daughter of the Canaanite woman is healed because of her mother's great faith.

Mt. 17:14-20; Mk. 9:14-29; Lk. 9:37-43—The father of the boy possessed by the devil cries out, "I do have faith. Help the little faith I have!"

Jn. 11:1-51—The resurrection of Lazarus. Martha said to Jesus, "If you had been here, my brother would not have died, but I know that, even now, whatever you ask of God, he will grant you."

Jn. 14:1-31—"Do not let your hearts be troubled. Trust in God still, and trust in me."

1 Co. 10:1-13—"You can trust God not to let you be tried beyond your strength, and with any trial he will give you a way out of it and the strength to bear it."

Ph. 3:1-21; 4:1-9—All Paul wants to know is Christ. He is racing for the finish, for the prize to which God calls those who surrender to him.

1 P. 1:13-21—"Free your minds, then, of encumbrances; control them, and put your trust in nothing but the grace that will be given you when Jesus Christ is revealed."

1 P. 2:1-10—We can rest our trust on the precious cornerstone, who is Christ.

Rv. 4:1-11; 5:1-14—God entrusts the future of the world to the Lamb.

* * * * *

Jesus' surrender to the Father's will should be the model of our own trustful response. The Lord may test us in times of inner trial, but not beyond our strength. Our main attitude at such times must be one of loving cooperation, ready when Christ calls to surrender our will fully to his. Such self-surrender is not a quietistic stance but an active invitation to fidelity. We must be as faithful to God as God has been faithful to us.

READINGS FROM THE LITERATURE OF SPIRITUALITY

The Soul of the Apostolate, (Part Four)—A eucharistic interior life is the only hope of apostolic success. The apostle who surrenders to Christ becomes an "...accumulator of supernatural life, and condenses in himself a divine current which is diversified and adapted to all conditions and all the needs of the sphere in which he is working."

The Practice of the Presence of God, (Letters IX and X)—We must turn with complete trust to that Father of mercies who is always ready to receive us affectionately.

Spirituality and the Gentle Life, (Chapters VII and VIII)—We must have deep faith and trust in the Divine Master who is present to us in the Church, in our life situation, in our soul. The poorer we become in spirit, the more freely we can surrender to him.

Markings, (1960-1961)—At some moment Hammarskjöld answered *Yes* to Someone or Something and from that hour he was certain that existence had a meaning and, therefore, that his life, in self-surrender, had a goal.

Out of Solitude, (Third Meditation)—"Care born out of solitude can hardly last unless undergirded by a hopeful expectation for the day of fulfillment when God will be all in all."

As Bread That Is Broken, (Chapters 12, 13, 17, 19, 20)—Poverty of spirit, trust, surrender—these are the treasures of spiritual life. Christ lived these treasures to the full at the Last Supper, when he emptied himself into a small piece of bread and a little wine. By this act he lives on forever and his love is everlasting. Our witness to him is full of hope and a manifestation to others of the fruits of the Spirit.

The Current of Spirituality, (Chapters 4, 14, 16, 17)—"Faith and trust are not emotional reflexes but willed responses.... The inwardness of faith and the inwardness of hope should come to mean the same thing, the trust of one being indistinguishable from the trust of the other."

SUPPLEMENTARY READING

Leisure, The Basis of Culture, (The Philosophical Act: III)—The structure of hope (trust) and the structure of wonder are similar.

The Intellectual Life, (Chapter 6)—The right spirit of work is to perceive in wonder and trust the mystery of all things.

* * * * *

Christ asks us to remain like little children who trust their parents and at no moment doubt their nearness. And yet, before we know it, our aggressive, angry defenses threaten to break down this trust. To fail in trust and simplicity ought to be no cause for alarm. We are human. Christ knows of our good will, though our actions seem to declare the contrary. What matters is that we are trying to be present to God in faith and surrender. We trust that the gift of peace will enter into the deepest recesses of our heart, though on the surface of life we may feel only turmoil. We trust that when our burdens become too much to bear we can lay them at Christ's feet and rely totally on the grace that flows to us without cease from his sacred heart.

CONCLUSION

Starting with the event of Isaiah's encounter with God and his acceptance of the call, these readings have guided us to new depths of self-knowledge and surrender. Each of us, no matter what our state of life may be, must say to God, "Here I am." Bright or opaque, strong of body or weak, task-oriented or contemplative, we can hide nothing from God. He who made us knows us. He who loves us saves us. We have a distinct place in the divine plan. Merciful God that he is, he forgives our failures and uses them to reveal many formation opportunities. God cannot send us to do his work if we are hard of heart. Jesus needs disciples who are pliable and eager to live in his light. A servant is not greater than his master. Our master is Christ. He was totally at the disposal of the Father's will. So, too, are we whenever we go to him with a pure heart and say, "Here I am, send me."

III

Stepping Aside and Starting Again*

INTRODUCTION

Into each of our lives may come times and places in which we seem to have reached a plateau. For some reason there is little movement. We don't retreat, but neither do we advance. We seem to be at a standstill. Generally speaking, we may be happy, cooperative, enthusiastic persons. Were someone to describe us, they might use such words as "reliable," "a good sport," "humble yet not afraid to speak her mind." Until now we have managed to flow easily with the current of life. There may have been occasional moments of questioning, a few ups and downs but, for the most part, life has been good to us. Now, for whatever reason, our zeal begins to wane. We catch ourselves growing pensive. There is an uneasy feeling in the pit of our stomachs. Why do we feel dissatisfied? There is no concrete cause to which we can point—just the feeling that things are not as they used to be. The old "get up and go" is gone. It becomes difficult to face the new day.

Though this experience leaves us desolate, without realizing it, we may be on the verge of tasting a deeper draught of life. Christ may be allowing us to

*This reading program was devised in accordance with the principles given in spiritual reading courses to future formation personnel offered at the Institute of Formative Spirituality, under supervision of the author. A tentative version of this program, extensively modified and revised here, was done by Sr. Una Agnew, S.S.L., with supplementary material from the reading program of Sr. Joan Michael Carboy, S.S.J. Following this introduction to the overall theme is a brief listing of minor themes. After that comes the reading list of texts recommended for this program, according to their appropriate category: essential, secondary, edifying, recreative. Several small sections follow introducing the reader to the minor themes that extend from the main branch. Around these minor themes are gathered suggested readings from Holy Scripture and from various sources in the literature of spirituality, including some supplementary readings. However, the reader should guard against a mere quantitative approach as indicated in the guidelines in Part One. The supplementary texts may also be read in informational fashion as a means of providing background to the theme. Supplementary selections fall most often within the secondary or recreative category. Generally introductions to texts provide good background reading and pertinent historical and biographical information which can be absorbed at the reader's discretion outside of the time one sets aside for slowed down spiritual reading. In regard to the overall duration of the reading program, readers must be faithful to their own pace of spiritual reading and notebook keeping. If a text is inspiring to them, they should stay with it as long as dwelling on the text keeps nourishing their hearts and minds.

undergo this malaise, this bout of meaninglessness, to lead us from the shallows of life toward greater depths of divine intimacy. Thus, from time to time, we have to step aside from daily activity to review our life in quiet presence to the Trinity. From this perspective, we may, with God's grace and light, come to the resolve to be more at his disposal. The Lord knows we need periods of stillness to hear his call and to find the inner strength to respond. Stepping aside, for whatever duration we can spare, enables us to start again as disciples of the Most High. Days of recollection and periods of retreat have always been necessary and helpful conditions for spiritual growth. Perhaps an example from ordinary life will clarify the need for exploring the theme that comprises this reading program.

Suppose you have had a hard day shopping in town. The weather is hot and you are burdened with bags. You have been buying school clothes and supplies for your children who are soon to return to the classroom after summer vacation. You bought a dress for your daughter, some shoes for your son, a few books, and still the list is not complete! You decide to stop for a rest at a small cafe. You are parched with thirst and need a cup of coffee. The packages are cumbersome and you can't remember what remains on your list. It must be buried somewhere in the bundles or in your purse. You sit down at a quiet table in the corner of the restaurant. Thank goodness you can get away from the milling crowd! You rearrange your packages as the waitress approaches to receive your order: coffee and a sweet roll. You suddenly ache all over. Coffee is served and it tastes good. You sip it slowly; it seems to reach down to the tips of your aching toes. You savor the roll. As the last bite disappears, you realize you cannot linger here much longer. You find the list and see that there are still three items to be purchased, even though this morning you tried all the likely stores. You sort the packages and fit them together in the largest shopping bag, pay your bill, and go. You feel refreshed and ready for the remainder of the day's work. You sense a new surge of energy to finish your shopping. You had not really wasted time after all. Rather by means of this pause you gained stamina for the task you still had to do.

Here, in this everyday description of the "stepping aside" experience, we find the basic ingredients that help us to "start again." We go to someplace special, a little cafe, for refreshment, only to find that it may become for us a place of retreat in the transcendent sphere. We draw away from the crowd. In the same way, the need for solitude may emerge when we want to pursue a spiritual life. We take time out to reset our course, as when we reviewed our shopping list and put our packages in order. This action may be compared in the life of the spirit to redefining our priorities. At the cafe we enjoyed a good cup of coffee. Similarly, renewal of a spiritual nature may be granted to us by grace following a day of recollection or a more prolonged retreat.

In the end we left the cafe with renewed energy, ready to start our work again. The same is true for spiritual living. Stepping aside, far from being a waste of time, is often what we need to find the energy and inner peace to go forth in the world as witnesses to Christ's way. We are ready to renew the covenant relationship made with us, the chosen people. When we take up again the Christian service entrusted to us, we try to do so in deeper awareness of God's will, in respectful love for those entrusted to our care, and in a spirit of poverty that imitates the self-emptying of Jesus for our sake.

To foster the living of this basic rhythm is the intention of this reading program. It is organized around the following minor themes:

MINOR THEMES

I. Stepping Aside to Someplace Special
II. Stepping Aside—Away from the Crowd
III. Stepping Aside to Reset My Course
IV. Stepping Aside Grants Spiritual Refreshment
V. Stepping Aside Enables Me to Start Again
VI. Starting Again in a Covenant Relationship
VII. Starting Again as Servants of the Lord
VIII. Starting Again in Obedience to God's Will
IX. Starting Again in Respectful Love
X. Starting Again in Poverty of Spirit

READING LIST

What follows is the list of books (annotated in the *Sample Bibliography*) to be assembled by the reader and used for this particular reading program. These books are certainly not the only ones available on the theme concerned nor necessarily the most outstanding written on this topic. They are, however, easily accessible to the general reader in current editions reasonably priced. Alternative and newer versions of some of the following books are also indicated in the *Sample Bibliography*. References to the same minor themes that readers may find more appropriate or available can be found as well in many cases in the *Sample Bibliography*. In each thematic section, the parts of the text that the reader is advised to use for that specific subdivision will be indicated and briefly annotated. In case the reader should be using editions of the text different from those that appear on the Reading List, Chapters and/or Parts of the books, and occasionally page numbers, accompany each annotation.

HOLY SCRIPTURE

The Jerusalem Bible. Reader's Edition. Alexander Jones, General Editor. New York: Doubleday, 1966.

LITERATURE OF SPIRITUALITY

Essential

Anonymous, *The Way of a Pilgrim*. Trans. R.M. French. San Francisco: Harper, 1991.

Ciszek, Walter J. with Daniel L. Flaherty. *He Leadeth Me*. New York: Doubleday, 1973.

de Sales, Francis, St. *Introduction to the Devout Life*. Trans. Michael Day. New York: E.P. Dutton, 1961.

Merton, Thomas. *The Climate of Monastic Prayer*. Kalamazoo, MI: Cistercian Publications, 1969.

Teresa of Avila, St. *The Book of Her Life* in *The Collected Works of St. Teresa of Avila*. Vol. One. Trans. Kieran Kavanaugh and Otilio Rodriguez. Washington, DC: Institute of Carmelite Studies (ICS), 1976.

Thérèse of Lisieux, St. *Story of a Soul: The Autobiography of St. Thérèse of Lisieux*. Trans. John Clarke. Washington, D.C.: Institute of Carmelite Studies, (ICS), 1976.

Secondary

Higgins, John J. *Thomas Merton on Prayer*. New York: Doubleday, 1975.

Edifying

Bloom, Anthony. *Beginning to Pray*. Ann Arbor, MI: Servant, 1993.

Frank, Anne. *The Diary of a Young Girl*. Trans. B.M. Mooyaart-Doubleday. New York: Bantam Books, 1993.

Lindbergh, Anne Morrow. *Gift from the Sea*. New York: Random House, 1991.

Nouwen, Henri J.M. *Reaching Out: The Three Movements of the Spiritual Life*. New York: Doubleday, 1986.

Thoreau, Henry David. *Walden and Civil Disobedience*. Ed. Sherman Paul. Boston: Houghton Mifflin, 1957.

van Kaam, Adrian. *The Vowed Life*. Denville, NJ: Dimension Books, 1968.

van Kaam, Adrian, Bert van Croonenburg, and Susan Muto. *The Participant Self*. Denville, NJ: Dimension Books, 1969.

Recreative

Eiseley, Loren. *The Immense Journey*. New York: Random House, n.d.

West, Jessamyn. *Hide and Seek: A Continuing Journey*. New York: Harcourt Brace, 1987.

MINOR THEME I

STEPPING ASIDE TO SOMEPLACE SPECIAL

Stepping aside involves stepping into a style of life differing in varying degrees from my daily routine. For example, when I go on retreat or vacation, it is usually to a place away from my professional or familial setting. I may seek a spot that offers some quiet and an opportunity for recollection, if possible in a naturally beautiful atmosphere like that of the mountains or the shore. The object of going there is not only to relax outwardly but to create conditions for growing inwardly. This intention is what makes the stepping aside experience different from, say, merely taking a holiday with family or friends. What renders where I go so special is my intention to engage, with the help of grace, in an experience conducive to spiritual renewal. This may affect my way of prayer or lead to the simple rediscovery that I, too, am a dwelling place of the Divine. Remembering in prayer and presence that I am a temple of the Trinity strengthens me to return to my daily task.

READINGS FROM HOLY SCRIPTURE

Old Testament

Gn. 26:15-25—At Beersheba,Yahweh appears to Isaac and says, "Do not be afraid, for I am with you."

Gn. 32:23-33—Jacob named the place Peniel, for there he had seen God face to face and survived.

Gn. 35:1-15—Jacob named the place where God had spoken with him Bethel.

Ex. 24:12-18—Yahweh invites Moses to join him on the mountain of Sinai; he stays there for forty days and forty nights.

Ex. 34:29-35—When Moses comes down from the mountain, his face is so radiant that he puts a veil over it.

Dt. 1:1-46—At Horeb and Kadesh, Moses reviews for Israel the instructions of Yahweh. He assures them: "Do not take fright, do not be afraid...

Yahweh your God goes in front of you and will be fighting on your side as you saw him fight for you in Egypt. In the wilderness, too, you saw him: how Yahweh carried you, as a man carries his child, all along the road you traveled on the way to this place."

Dt. 12:1-31—These are Yahweh's instructions regarding the place of worship and the regulations governing sacrifice.

1 K. 19:1-18—The angel of Yahweh comes to Elijah and gives him strength to walk forty days and nights until he reaches Horeb, the mountain of God. There he encounters Yahweh in the sound of a gentle breeze.

Ps. 26—"Yahweh, be my judge! ...I love the house where you live, the place where your glory makes its home."

Ps. 27—"One thing I ask of Yahweh, one thing I seek: to live in the house of Yahweh all the days of my life..."

Ps. 42-43—"Send out your light and your truth, let these be my guide, to lead me to your holy mountain and to the place where you live."

Ps. 84—"How I love your palace, Yahweh Sabaoth!"

Ps. 132—"Let us go where he is waiting and worship at his footstool."

Is. 66:1-24—"Thus says Yahweh: With heaven my throne and earth my footstool, what house could you build me, what place could you make for my rest?"

Jr. 7:1-34; 8:1-3—"Do you take this temple that bears my name for a robber's den?...it is Yahweh who speaks. Now I go to my place in Shiloh where at first I gave my name a home..."

Mi. 4:1-14; 5:1-14—"Come, let us go up to the mountain of Yahweh, to the Temple of the God of Jacob so that he may teach us his ways and we may walk in his paths..."

New Testament

Mt. 4:1-11; Mk. 1:12-13; Lk. 4:1-13—Jesus is led into the wilderness by the Spirit. Though weakened by his forty-day fast, he resists the Tempter, for he knows that man is to worship and serve God alone.

Mt. 6:1-18—Though we give alms secretly, though we pray and fast in a secret place, the Father sees what we are doing and rewards us.

Mk. 1:32-39; Lk. 4:40-44—All the suffering were brought to Jesus and he cured them, but he would always make his way to a lonely place and pray.

Mt. 14:13-21; Mk. 6:30-44; Jn. 6:1-15—Jesus said to his apostles, "You must come away to some lonely place all by yourselves and rest for a while...," but the people followed him like sheep and he fed them.

Jn. 4:1-42—"On the way he came to a Samaritan town called Sychar, near the land that Jacob gave to his son Joseph. Jacob's well is there and Jesus, tired by the journey, sat straight down by the well."

Jn. 6:22-66—Jesus teaches in the synagogue at Capernaum. "It is the spirit that gives life, the flesh has nothing to offer. The words I have spoken to you are spirit and they are life."

Mt. 17:1-8; Mk. 9:2-8; Lk. 9:28-36—Jesus goes up to the mountain to pray. There in the presence of Peter, James and John he is transfigured. A voice from out of the cloud says to them, "This is my Son, the Beloved; he enjoys my favor. Listen to him."

Mt. 26:36-46; Mk. 14:32-42; Lk. 22:39-46—In the place called Gethsemane Jesus endures his great agony. There he surrenders wholly to his Father's will.

1 Co. 3:1-23—"Didn't you realize that you were God's temple and that the Spirit of God was living among you?"

Heb. 3:1-6—"...we are his house, as long as we cling to our hope with the confidence that we glory in."

* * * * *

Jesus wants our hearts to become an oasis where we can rest with him wherever we are, a center from which his presence can be revealed to the world. Periodically we have to step aside from places of work-a-day preoccupation and return to holy ground. There we can enter the house of God where the faithful glimpse something of the treasures of grace held in store for those who pray unceasingly.

READINGS FROM THE LITERATURE OF SPIRITUALITY

The Way of a Pilgrim, (Chapter 1)—The pilgrim learns that there was a village between two and three miles from the monastery. He goes there to look for a place to live, and to his great joy God shows him the exact thing he needs. "A peasant hired me for the whole summer to look after his kitchen garden, and what is more gave me the use of a little thatched hut in it where I could live alone. God be praised! I had found a quiet place."

He Leadeth Me, (Chapters 1 and 2)—Father Ciszek knew he had to volunteer for the Russian mission. He experienced his desire to go to this land almost like a direct call from the Lord. In the end he was fully convinced that God was sending him, that Russia was his destination in his providence.

The Climate of Monastic Prayer, (Introduction)—The monk is a Christian who has responded to a special call from God and has withdrawn from the more active concerns of a worldly life to the monastery in order to devote himself completely to repentance, conversion, renunciation, and prayer. The monastery, in turn, symbolizes for all Christians retreat to a place in which one may enter into communion with the silence of the praying and meditating Church.

Story of a Soul, (Chapters I and II of Manuscript "A")—Thérèse sees spiritual meaning in her youthful visits to such places as Le Mans (her first train ride there and trip alone with her mother); Les Buissonnets (the new home of the Martins); and Trouville (where she sees the sea for the first time).

Beginning to Pray, (Chapter IV)—In order to step aside to someplace special, it is necessary as well to set aside the time for this sojourn. "I will spare you any description of the way in which one can make time: I will only say that if we try and waste a little less of it, there will be more of it. If we use crumbs of wasted time to try to build short moments for recollection and prayer, we may discover that there is quite a lot of it."

The Diary of a Young Girl, (Sunday, 14 June 1942 to Thursday, 29 October 1942)—Due to the Nazi purge of Jews in Holland, Anne Frank was forced to retreat with her own family and another one to a hiding place. Though she did not choose to go there, she soon found in this stepping aside experience a new Anne and a new relation to God. The hiding place served to release deep thoughts and feelings she might otherwise not have known—all faithfully recorded in her diary. "Who, three months ago, would ever have guessed that quick-silver Anne would have to sit still for hours—and, what's more, could?"

Gift from the Sea, (Chapter I)—The beach is the place where Anne Morrow Lindbergh learns to be patient, to wait upon the sea to surrender its treasures of self-insight and openness to the Beyond.

Walden, (Chapters I and II)—Of his special place, Thoreau says, "I went to the woods because I wished to live deliberately, to front only the essential facts of life, and see if I could not learn what it had to teach, and not, when I came to die, discover that I had not lived. I did not wish to live what was not life, living is so dear; nor did I wish to practice resignation, unless it was quite necessary. I wanted to live deep and suck out all the marrow of life, to live so sturdily and Spartan-like as to put to rout all that was not life, to cut a broad swath and shave close, to drive life into a corner, and reduce it to its lowest terms, and, if it proved to be mean, why then to get the whole and genuine meanness of it, and publish its meanness to the world; or if it were sublime, to know it by experience, and be able to give a true account of it in my next excursion."

SUPPLEMENTARY READING

Hide and Seek: A Continuing Journey—Jessamyn West deliberately sought to step aside and so for three months chose to live in a travel trailer on a remote bank of the Colorado River. In this lonely place she was hiding from one phase of life (the active) in order to seek another (the contemplative). Here she discovers that "...solitude, like a drug, can be addictive. The more you have it, the more you want it. Solitude is an unending colloquy between you and yourself and such persons as inhabit your memory or are called forth by your imagination. It is painful to have this colloquy interrupted by the voices of real people. 'Be still, be still,' you want to say to them. 'I can't hear what's being said.' In the heart of solitude, when barriers between yourself and the world melt, your body becomes as Thoreau said, 'the organ and channel of a melody, as a flute is of the music that is breathed through it.' "

* * * * *

If we do come to a haven of rest, retreat, and renewal, we must try to be attentive to where we are, physically as well as spiritually. We need to direct our attention to the landscape around us, for God can display his grandeur as fully in a star as in a speck of dust. Once the meditative mood is upon us, we may move from creature to Creator, finding traces of sheer beauty in the most obscure places.

MINOR THEME II

STEPPING ASIDE—AWAY FROM THE CROWD

When too much activity fatigues me, when I feel drained of energy, it is time to step into a "little cafe," to be alone for a while, away from the crowd, in order to think. Such solitude can evoke two possible experiences: either the fear of loneliness or the faith that I can grow in oneness with self, with others, and with God. Because loneliness can be frightening, I may try to avoid it, to lose myself in the crowd. Casual chatter, empty laughter, idle gossip block reflection. As long as I'm snared in the rush of things, I don't have to face the possible barrenness of my inner life. If I can grow beyond the fear of loneliness, I may savor the blessing of solitude. I welcome times of being alone with the Lord, away from the lure of the masses. Such aloneness helps me to create an inner horizon of receptive openness to God's will. I can face my daily duties and responsibilities, knowing that the strength I need comes not from my own efforts but from divine grace. Love of solitude gradually weans me away from the crowd toward the true center of my life in God. Sustained by the gift of his gracious presence, I come to life again.

READINGS FROM HOLY SCRIPTURE

Old Testament

Ex. 15:22-27; 16:1-36; 17:1-7—In their solitude Yahweh comforts his people. He feeds them manna and quail and gives them water from desert rock.

Lv. 26:1-46—Yahweh will bless his people if they live according to his laws and do not listen to worldly wisdom.

Dt. 7:1-26; 8:1-20; 9:1-29—Israel is a people set apart by God from all the peoples on the earth to enjoy his favor, provided they obey his commandments and do not follow the idolatrous crowd.

Dt. 30:1-20—Yahweh sets before his people two ways: life and prosperity or death and disaster. The choice is theirs: to follow the ways of the world or to obey his commands.

Jos. 1:1-9—When Moses was dead, Yahweh spoke to Joshua and promised to be with him as he was with Moses—provided he would be strong and stand firm, following Yahweh alone and not worldly ways.

Jos. 24:1-24—At the end of his life, Joshua gathers the tribes of Israel together and sets forth once again their vocation: they belong not to the world but to God. All alien gods must be cast away.

1 M. 2:1-70—Mattathias and his sons cannot tolerate the blasphemies being committed in Judah and Jerusalem; they draw apart from the crowd and follow instead the covenant of their ancestors.

2 M. 6:18-31—Eleazar stands alone, choosing to die with honor rather than follow the urgings of his friends to pretend to eat portions of sacrificial meat prescribed by the king.

2 M. 7:1-42—The seven brothers and their mother prefer to accept outcast, torture, and death rather than betray the covenant.

Ps. 7—"Yahweh my God, I take shelter in you..."

Ps. 11—"In Yahweh I take shelter."

Ps. 12—Against a deceitful world where the wicked prowl on every side.

Ps. 25—"To you, Yahweh, I lift up my soul..."

Ps. 31—"In you, Yahweh, I take shelter..."

Ps. 57—"...I take shelter in the shadow of your wings until the destroying storm is over. "

Ps. 59—Against the wicked who prowl through the town, the wise take shelter in Yahweh.

Ps. 62—"In God alone there is rest for my soul..."

Ps. 71—"In you, Yahweh, I take shelter..."

Ps. 141—Against the attractions of evil. "To you, Yahweh my Lord, I turn my eyes. I take shelter in you..."

Pr. 2:1-22—Wisdom is a safeguard against bad company.

Si. 11:1-34—The ways of the world are wicked, but we must trust in God alone.

Si. 31:1-31; 32:1-24—Riches, dinner parties, wine, banquets—contrast to these activities of the crowd the fear of God in the vigilant soul.

Is. 2:1-22—The prophet foresees that when Yahweh comes the arrogance of the crowd will be humbled, all idols will be thrown down, and Yahweh alone will be exalted.

Is. 29:15-24—When that day comes, "Woe to those who hide from Yahweh to conceal their plans, who scheme in the dark and say, 'Who can see us? Who can recognize us?' "

Is. 48:1-22—Yahweh is not subservient to human schemes of greatness. He acts alone and is sole master of the future.

Jr. 23:9-40—A tract against false prophets who want to please the crowd rather than listen to Yahweh's commands.

New Testament

Mt. 5:13-16; Lk. 6:24-45—Jesus tells his followers in effect that they cannot melt into the crowd. They are to be with him in solitude and then become a light to the world, living by a new standard that is higher than the old.

Mt. 7:13-14; Lk. 13:22-30—The road that leads to perdition is wide and spacious; that is why the Christian must leave the crowd and enter by the narrow door.

Mt. 7:21-27; Lk. 6:46-49—The true disciple builds his house not on the sand of worldly wisdom but on the rock of Jesus' words.

Mt. 8:18-22; Lk. 9:57-62—Anyone who follows Jesus cannot at the same time follow the crowd. One has to accept the hardships of an apostolic calling.

Mt. 13:4-23; Mk. 4:1-20; Lk. 8:4-15—The lure of worldly riches chokes the word, but the man who hears and understands it yields a harvest of God's wisdom in his heart.

Lk. 17:11-19—Jesus cleansed the ten lepers but only the one who was a Samaritan returned to praise and thank him.

Mt. 19:16-30; Mk. 10:17-31; Lk. 19:18-30—The rich young man wants to follow Jesus, but he goes back to the world when he finds out what he must do and the solitude he must endure.

Lk. 19:1-10—Zacchaeus could not see Jesus, because he was too short to peer above the crowd, so he ran ahead and climbed a sycamore tree to catch a glimpse of him.

Mt. 21:12-17; Lk. 19:45-46; Jn. 2:13-25—Jesus, angered at what the crowd of dealers has done to his Father's house, drives them from the Temple.

Jn. 15:18-27; 16:1-15—Jesus tells his disciples of the hostile world they will have to face, but he shall send the advocate to be with them in their aloneness and to help them so that their faith may not be shaken.

Mt. 26:69-75; Mk. 14:66-72; Lk. 22:54-62; Jn. 18:12-27—Peter's faith is not yet strong enough to resist the taunts of the crowd and so, as Jesus predicted, he betrays him.

1 Co. 1:17-31; 2:1-16—Paul compares true wisdom to that which is false and concludes, "A spiritual man...is able to judge the value of everything, and his own value is not to be judged by other men."

Col. 2:9-15—Christ alone is the true head of men and angels.

1 Jn. 2:12-29; 3:1-2—Detachment from the world is essential for Christian discipleship.

* * * * *

As God set the Chosen People apart from all nations, so by his call he draws us away from the crowd—with its ungrateful, slovenly ways, and its false teachings—toward the community of the faithful. He asks us to live holy and saintly lives, though the world may hate us for the witness we give. To hear his call and respond as true disciples, to start again, we must at times step aside from the many, both outwardly and inwardly, to be alone with the One.

READINGS FROM THE LITERATURE OF SPIRITUALITY

The Way of a Pilgrim, (Chapter 2)—After many journeys and meetings with other people, the pilgrim feels at last that it would be better for him to stay in one place, in order to be alone more often, so as to be able to keep by himself and study *The Philokalia*.

He Leadeth Me, (Chapters 3 and 4)—Father Ciszek feels cut off from everyone who has supported him—from his superiors, his colleagues and family, his church and country. He writes of this experience of going away: "For a moment I thought with sorrow and regret about the possibility of never returning to Europe, to the United States, to Shenandoah. Yet the strong realization rushed over me that I was not cut off from God, that he was with me, indeed that I was dependent only on him in a new and very real way."

Introduction to the Devout Life, (Part III, Chapters 24 and 25; Part IV, Chapter 1)—St. Francis counsels Philothea, "Over and above that spiritual retirement which you can practice in the midst of even important affairs, have a love for true solitude, not to the extent of going into the desert like St. Mary of Egypt, St. Paul, St. Anthony, and the other fathers of the desert, but by spending some time alone, in your room, garden, or anywhere else where you can the more easily enter into your soul."

The Climate of Monastic Prayer, (Chapter I)—According to Merton, "The climate in which monastic prayer flowers is that of the desert, where the comfort of man is absent, where the secure routines of man's city offer no support, and where prayer must be sustained by God in the purity of faith. Even though he may live in a community, the monk is bound to explore the inner waste of his own being as a solitary."

The Book of Her Life, (Chapters 1-3)—Already in childhood, the Lord awakened in St. Teresa a love of virtue and a desire to associate with people of virtue. She sought good companionship and, if this could not be found, she preferred to be alone rather than waste time on useless gossip or vain flattery.

Story of a Soul, (Chapter III of Manuscript "A")—By the age of nine St. Thérèse knew that it was for God alone that she wished to be a Carmelite. She did not wish to live in the world but only for him in the solitude of the cloistered life.

The Diary of a Young Girl, (Saturday, 7 November 1942 to Thursday, 1 April 1943)—In the secret annex, though surrounded by her family and friends, Anne comes to know inner solitude. "I've drawn myself apart from them all; I am my own skipper and later on I shall see where I come to land." Her only companion, besides God, is her diary, which she affectionately calls "Kitty." "Still, I can't refrain from telling you [Kitty] that lately I have begun to feel deserted. I am surrounded by too great a void."

Gift from the Sea, (Chapter III)—In a quiet moment by the sea, Anne Morrow Lindbergh acknowledges, "We are all, in the last analysis, alone. And this basic state of solitude is not something we have any choice about. 'It is,' as the poet Rilke says, 'not something that one can take or leave. We are solitary...' "

Reaching Out, (Chapters 1, 2 and 3)—"By slowly converting our loneliness into a deep solitude, we create that precious space where we can discover the voice telling us about our inner necessity—that is, our vocation. Unless our questions, problems and concerns are tested and matured in solitude, it is not realistic to expect answers that are really our own."

Walden, (Chapters III-VI)—"Sometimes, in a summer morning, having taken my accustomed bath, I sat in my sunny doorway from sunrise till noon, rapt in a reverie, amidst the pines and hickories and sumacs, in undisturbed solitude and stillness, while the birds sang around or flitted noiseless through the house, until by the sun falling in at my west window, or the noise of some traveler's wagon on the distant highway, I was reminded of the lapse of time. I grew in those seasons like corn in the night, and they were far better than any work of the hands would have been."

The Participant Self, (Book I, Chapters II and IV)—At times we must leave the world of people and appointments to refind our reason for living. While ways of retreat differ from person to person, abiding in solitude is as beneficial as communing with others. There is a time for withholding and a time for participating, a time to preserve privacy, a time to welcome intimacy.

SUPPLEMENTARY READING

The Immense Journey—Eiseley's journey through nature and time puts him in touch with "...such miracles as can be evoked from common earth." He discovered for himself that common place of all religious thought: "...that the man seeking visions and insight must go apart from his fellows and live for a time in the wilderness."

* * * * *

To become truly spiritual persons, we must learn to stand alone before God. We may experience initially some loneliness since it takes a while to be weaned away from the crowd with its endless gossip and cheap promises of togetherness but, at some point, we have to meet God in solitude. We have to converse with Christ. If we continue to sacrifice our integrity to the crowd and its way, we cannot come to the solitary obedience essential for the spiritual life. Solitude may imply an outer state of aloneness, but more often it means an inner state of readiness in which the soul rids itself of images of God in order to discover the invisible depths of faith. To find the deepest center of our being where we are most ourselves and at the same time most at one with others offers us an experience of profound renewal.

MINOR THEME III

STEPPING ASIDE TO RESET MY COURSE

Recall the initial experience of shopping. When you arrive at the cafe and settle into a quiet corner, you realize that your parcels are in disarray. What does this incident mean in the spiritual life? We have reached a haven of solitude. We have separated ourselves from the crowd. What next? In anticipation of the spiritual growth for which we have come to this place, we may begin to see that many facets of our personal life are also in disarray. An essential part of the stepping aside experience is to try, with God's grace, to put our life in some kind of order. As long as disharmony prevails, as long as we are not sure of our priorities, it is difficult for real growth to occur. The first step toward resetting our course is to face the disorder of our life—to see in what disarray our parcels are. The next step is to take distance in order to regain our perspective on the whole instead of feeling lost in fragmented parts and parcels. From this perspective a new sense of mission and purpose may emerge. We notice that whenever we shift from God as our center to lesser values, our life again becomes disoriented. Resetting our course means choosing God as our focal point. To choose thusly is a lifelong challenge. We must pause in prayer to appraise the direction in which the Spirit is now asking us to go. Our chances of making the right move improve to the degree that God is our guide. They lessen whenever we choose idols of our own making or listen to the counsel of false teachers.

READINGS FROM HOLY SCRIPTURE

Old Testament

Ex. 2:11-25; 3:1-22—Moses escapes to Midian where Yahweh calls him and instructs him for his mission.

Ex. 6:2-13—The course of Moses' life is set when God sends him to Pharaoh with the request to release his people from slavery.

Nb. 22:1-41; 23:1-30; 24:1-25—Yahweh changes Balaam's course and through him blesses rather than curses the people.

Dt. 31:1-18—Moses passes on his mission to Joshua.

Jg. 6:1-40—God calls Gideon to deliver Israel, despite his weakness; he works many signs to convince Gideon that this call is his true destiny.

1 S. 3:1-21—Samuel's destiny is unveiled when he responds positively to Yahweh's call.

1 K. 3:4-15—Yahweh tells Solomon that because he has not asked for long life

for himself or for riches or for the lives of his enemies but for a discerning heart, he will give him a heart wise and shrewd, as none before him has had.

1 K. 19:19-21—Elisha receives Elijah's call and runs after him.

2 K. 2:1-25—When Elijah is taken up, Elisha succeeds him.

Ne. 1:1-11; 2:1-20—Nehemiah hears God's call, prays to him for guidance, and decides to rebuild the walls of Jerusalem.

Ps. 40—Song of praise and prayer for help. "I waited and waited for Yahweh, now at last he has stooped to me and heard my cry for help."

Ps. 51—"God, create a clean heart in me, put into me a new and constant spirit..."

Ps. 55—"Unload your burden on to Yahweh, and he will support you..."

Ws. 9:1-18—A prayer for Wisdom.

Ws. 13:1-19; 14:1-31; 15:1-19—Naturally stupid are men who have not known God, who cultivate instead the worship of idols.

Si. 5:9-15; 6:1-4—We must be straightforward and self-possessed, steady in our convictions, if we hope to follow the right course.

Is. 6:1-13—Isaiah heard God's call and allowed the Holy One to change the course of his life.

Is. 40:1-11—The prophet's mission is to make a straight highway for God across the desert.

Is. 61:1-11—Yahweh sends the prophet to bind up hearts that are broken, to proclaim liberty to captives, to announce a year of favor from the Lord.

Jr. 1:4-19—Jeremiah assents to Yahweh's call, though he himself feels like a child.

Jr. 10:1-16—To guide the people on the right course, the prophet compares idols and the true God.

Jr. 14:1-22—Jeremiah warns against false prophets who try to sway the people from following Yahweh's truth. They promise peace where none is to be found.

Jr. 15:10-21—Jeremiah asks Yahweh to remember him and renew his call.

Ezk. 13:1-23; 14:1-11—False prophets promise peace when there is no peace and watch while the people worship idols, but Yahweh will use even these false prophets for his own purpose and rescue his chosen from their evil ways.

New Testament

Mt. 3:1-12; Mk. 1:1-8; Lk. 3:1-18; Jn. 1:19-34—John the Baptist comes out of the wilderness of solitude and prayer to take up his mission to make straight the paths of the Lord.

Mt. 4:18-22; Mk. 1:16-20; Lk. 5:1-11; Jn. 1:35-51—Jesus calls the first disciples and they at once leave what they are doing to follow him.

Mt. 7:15-27; Lk. 6:43-45—False prophets, compared to the true disciple, are like trees that yield rotten fruit.

Mt. 9:9—The call of Matthew.

Mt. 10:1-42; Mk. 6:7-13; Lk. 9:1-6—Jesus describes the course his apostles will have to follow in order to fulfill the divine mission for which he has chosen them.

Lk. 10:1-20—The mission of the seventy-two disciples.

Mt. 16:13-20—"Simon...You are Peter and on this rock I will build my Church."

Mt. 16:24-28; Mk. 8:34-38; Lk. 9:23-26—The condition of following Christ.

Mt. 22:1-14; Lk. 14:15-24—The wedding feast is ready but the invited guests make excuses not to come. "For many are called, but few are chosen."

Lk. 14:25-33—One main condition of following Christ is the renunciation of all that one holds dear.

Ac. 9:1-30—The conversion of Saul.

Ac. 13:17-52—Paul's preaching before the Jews is a testimony to God's power to alter the course of human history.

Ac. 22:1-30; 23:1-11—Paul is arrested and asks the Jews of Jerusalem to listen to his defense. The people want to kill him but fear to do so because he is a Roman citizen. The Lord appears to Paul and tells him to have courage. As he has witnessed for him in Jerusalem, so he must do in Rome.

Ph. 2:19-30—The mission of Timothy and Epaphroditus.

Col. 2:6-23; 3:1-4—Paul cautions the brothers to live according to the true faith in Christ, not according to false teaching.

1 Th. 3:1-5—Timothy's mission to Thessalonika.

1 Tm. 1:12-20—Paul writes about his own calling and Timothy's responsibility.

1 Tm. 4:1-16—The brothers must learn to recognize the lies of false teachers and resist their deceit.

2 Tm. 2:1-26—Timothy will have to face the hardship of standing against false teachings that belie the truth Christ brings if he wants to follow the right course.

2 P. 2:1-22; 3:1-18—Peter cautions against false teachers whose aim is to dissuade the brothers from their chosen course. He advises them to live holy and saintly lives while they wait and long for the Day of the Lord.

1 Jn. 4:1-6—The disciple must be on guard against the enemies of Christ.

* * * * *

When something tells us we are off course in regard to the direction of our life, we may experience a combination of inertia and fear. We would like to maintain the status quo, secure the possessions we thought would make us happy, seek the shallow compliments and self-deceptive slogans of the crowd. If we can get past this inertia and listen to the invitation of God to reexamine our life as a whole, we may feel fearful of the implications this refocusing will entail. At such moments, we must fall back on our faith in a loving God who wants the best for us. We must believe in the mission God is asking us to perform. The question is: Do we want to live life in its depth dimension or to be lived by it. God wants to free us from the trap of egoism so we can participate fully in the unfolding of creation.

READINGS FROM THE LITERATURE OF SPIRITUALITY

The Way of a Pilgrim, (Chapter 3)—In speaking of his past, the pilgrim begins to sense the providential working of God in his life and the path He is asking him to follow in the present and future. He can do no better than place his life wholly in God's hands.

He Leadeth Me, (Chapters 5 and 6)—In prison Father Ciszek has to "reset his course" in regard to many dimensions. He learns to purify his prayer and to remove from it the elements of self-seeking. He learns to pray for his interrogators, "...not so they would see things my way or come to the truth so that my ordeal would end, but because they, too, were children of God and human beings in need of his blessing and his daily grace." He learns to stop asking for more bread for himself and instead to offer up his sufferings for others in the world and in Russia enduring the same agony. He tries not to worry about what tomorrow will bring but rather to seek the kingdom of God and his will for himself and all humankind.

Introduction to the Devout Life, (Part IV, Chapters 2-9; Part V, Chapters 1-8)—Many new paths open up for one who chooses to live the devout life. "It may well happen, Philothea, that having embarked on this new life, your soul may feel ill at ease and that you experience a sense of sadness and discouragement in bidding farewell to the follies and vanities of the world; be patient a little while, it is of no importance, only the discomfort of unfamiliarity; as soon as it has worn off you will experience abundant consolation."

The Climate of Monastic Prayer, (Chapter III)—"...as we determine to face the hard realities of our inner life, as we recognize once again that we need to pray hard and humbly for faith, he draws us out of darkness into light—he hears us, answers our prayer, recognizes our need, and grants us the help we require..." God is with us as we turn our lives in the direction of his truth.

The Book of Her Life, (Chapters 4-7)—The Lord has chosen a path for St. Teresa which she has to follow often against her will. This course will include "grievous infirmities" but God will bring good out of evil and grant her the grace of spiritual resignation—provided she travels with him and follows the hard road of the cross however tempted she might be to take the easy way.

Story of a Soul, (Chapter IV of Manuscript "A")—At first communion, St. Thérèse chose the course she would follow from that moment on. "Ah! How sweet was that first kiss of Jesus! It was a kiss of love; I felt that I was loved, and I said: 'I love You, and I give myself to You forever!' There were no demands made, no struggles, no sacrifices, for a long time now Jesus and poor little Thérèse looked at and understood each other. That day, it was no longer simply a look, it was a fusion; they were no longer two. Thérèse had vanished as a drop of water is lost in the immensity of the ocean. Jesus alone remained; He was the Master, the King. Had not Thérèse asked him to take away her liberty, for her liberty frightened her? She felt so feeble and fragile that she wanted to be united forever to the divine Strength!"

Diary of a Young Girl, (Friday, 2 April 1943 to Saturday, 19 February 1944)—Anne had plenty of time to think about her life: looking back, living now, and projecting ahead, she could begin to make some serious decisions. For example, she tells "Kitty": "I shall not shrink from the truth any longer, because the longer it is put off the more difficult it will be for them when they do hear it." She faces other truths at this time: the truth of her emerging womanhood, of her love for Peter, and of her identification with all suffering Jews.

Gift from the Sea, (Chapter VII)—Anne asks how she can resist the onslaught of the world once she leaves the beach. Can she maintain the reflective path she has pursued here? Yes, through conscious selectivity, through taking with her a "few shells" to mark the way: "Balance of physical, intellectual, and spiritual life. Work without pressure. Space for significance and beauty. Time for solitude and sharing. Closeness to nature to strengthen understanding and faith in the intermittency of life: life of the spirit, creative life, and the life of human relationships."

Reaching Out, (Chapters 4, 5 and 6)—The movement from loneliness to solitude enables us to reset the course of our lives in another way:

now we can move from hostility to hospitality. "It is there that our changing relationship to ourself can be brought to fruition in an ever-changing relationship to our fellow human beings. It is there that our reaching out to our innermost being can lead to a reaching out to the many strangers whom we meet on our way through life."

Walden, (Chapters VII-X)—"In our trivial walks, we are constantly, though unconsciously, steering like pilots by certain well-known beacons and headlands, and if we go beyond our usual course we still carry in our minds the bearing of some neighboring cape; and not till we are completely lost, or turned round...do we appreciate the vastness and strangeness of Nature.... Not till we are lost, in other words, not till we have lost the world, do we begin to find ourselves, and realize where we are and the infinite extent of our relations."

The Vowed Life, (Part Two)—"I experience that I, like others before me, am called to something in life but I cannot yet know what my call will be. I can accept it or reject it when it comes but I cannot choose it. And even if I come to know my call, the contents will by far exceed my grasp; they will reach beyond what I can foresee. The call is beckoning, too, for I realize somehow that if I do not direct or vow my life in some meaningful way, my life is in danger of becoming meaningless, scattered, inconsistent, dispersed and imprisoned in functional everydayness."

The Participant Self, (Book I, Chapters V and VI)—Experience is excellent, but it calls for evaluation if I am not to lose the way God chooses for me.

SUPPLEMENTARY READING

Beginning to Pray—Archbishop Bloom discusses the providential direction of his life thus far. (Interview with Archbishop Anthony Bloom by Timothy Wilson)

Thomas Merton on Prayer, (Chapter 2)—If man is to discern where God is asking him to go, he must have some realization of who he is. In this chapter the author discusses Merton's conviction that only in finding God can man find himself and the lasting direction of his life.

* * * * *

One aid to putting order into our life may entail the outward shedding of superfluous activity. Certain plans and projects can be left aside. We can still our overly busy approach to life. Such simplifying and stilling are helpful as we strive to reset our course on a path that will facilitate spiritual unfolding. Crucial for this growth is also the transformation of our will. We have to detach ourselves from inordinate desires if we want to direct the restlessness of our heart toward the One who alone can still it. Freed from inner divisiveness, we are more ready to be led by grace along the way of transformation.

MINOR THEME IV

STEPPING ASIDE GRANTS SPIRITUAL REFRESHMENT

Once you are relaxed, you see that your unwieldy bundle of packages will fit nicely into a large shopping bag. So, too, we discover that the fragments of our life (disorderly affections, undigested experiences of the past, unchristian attitudes and fads borrowed from a secular society) need to be reordered to be compatible with the new graced self we are becoming. As long as we are trying to reorder our affections and attitudes around the Divine as our center, we need not fear. This total offering or rededication of self may result in an imperfect mosaic, made up of scattered pieces, but the pieces will fall more and more into place as we bring ourselves to God with the intention of loving and serving him. Thus the time of stepping aside is not all painful. In the wayside cafe, you put your bundles in order, but you also have a cup of delicious coffee. You experience definite refreshment. You feel revitalized down to the tips of your aching toes. So, too, during the time of stepping aside, we will experience arid moments of awakening from illusion. These will be complemented, however, by periods of spiritual refreshment—by comforting thoughts and prayers, by substantial locutions to treasure, by tiny beams of eternity peeping through the surface of everyday existence. Such is the "sabbath rest" God often grants in the midst of activity. The spiritual rest we take enables us to imbibe the living water God wants to give us with its power to heal our body and soul.

READINGS FROM HOLY SCRIPTURE

Old Testament

Gn. 1:1-31; 2:1-4—God created heaven and earth and on the seventh day he rested.

Ex. 23:10-13—A description of the sabbatical year and the sabbath.

Ex. 31:12-17 and 35:1-3—Yahweh says to Moses that the sons of Israel must keep the sabbath.

Lv. 23:3-4—"...the seventh day must be a day of complete rest...on which you do no work at all."

Lv. 25:1-7—"...in the seventh year the land is to have its rest, a sabbath for Yahweh."

Nb. 15:32-36—The penalty for breaking the sabbath is severe.

Nb. 20:1-11—At Meribah Yahweh refreshed his people with water from the rock.

Dt. 15:1-11—The sabbatical year is an occasion for remission of debt.

Ps. 23—The Good Shepherd leads us to the waters of repose.

Ps. 42-43—"As a doe longs for running streams, so longs my soul for you, my God. My soul thirsts for God..."

Ps. 62—"In God alone there is rest for my soul..."

Ps. 95—"Do not harden your hearts as at Meribah, as you did that day at Massah in the wilderness..."

Ps. 107—"...he turned rivers into desert, springs of water into arid ground..."

Is. 25:1-12; 26:1-19—A prayer of thanksgiving. "...awake, exult, all you who lie in the dust, for your dew is a radiant dew and the land of ghosts will give birth."

Is. 35:1-10—"...let the wasteland rejoice and bloom..."

Is. 41:8-29—"The poor and needy ask for water, and there is none...I, the God of Israel, will not abandon them. I will make rivers well up on barren heights..."

Ezk. 36:1-38—Oracle on the mountains of Israel. "I shall pour clean water over you and you will be cleansed...I shall give you a new heart, and put a new spirit in you..."

Ezk. 37:1-11—Yahweh led the prophet to a valley full of bones and made the dry bones live.

Jl. 4:15-21—The day of Yahweh. "When that day comes, the mountains will run with new wine and the hills flow with milk, and all the river-beds of Judah will run with water."

New Testament

Mt. 5:1-12—"Happy are those who hunger and thirst for what is right: they shall be satisfied."

Mt. 9:18-22; Mk. 5:21-34; Lk. 8:43-48—Cure of the woman with a hemorrhage. "Courage, my daughter, your faith has restored you to health."

Mt. 11:28-30—Jesus who is gentle and humble of heart will give us rest.

Mt. 15:21-28; Mk. 7:24-36—Jesus heals the daughter of the Canaanite woman; her wish is granted because of her great faith.

Jn. 5:1-23—Jesus cures a sick man at the Pool of Bethzatha, though it happens to be the sabbath. He teaches that whoever listens to his words and believes in the one who sent him has eternal life.

Mt. 15:32-39; Mk. 8:1-10; Lk. 9:10-17; Jn. 6:1-15—Jesus takes pity on the large crowd of people. He heals their sick and feeds them with a few loaves and fishes.

Mk. 8:31-37—Jesus restores hearing and speech to the deaf man.

Mt. 20:29-34; Mk. 12:46-52—Jesus hears the blind man's plea for pity and opens his eyes.

Lk. 13:10-17—Jesus heals the crippled woman on a sabbath because his love rises above the letter of the law.

Mt. 26:26-29; Mk. 14:22-25; Lk. 22:19-20—The institution of the Eucharist.

Jn. 6:35-66—Jesus is the bread of life. Whoever comes to him will never be hungry; whoever believes in him will never thirst.

Jn. 7:37-39—"If any man is thirsty, let him come to me!"

Jn. 10:1-21—Jesus is the Good Shepherd who lays down his life for his sheep.

Jn. 14:23-31—Jesus grants us the gift of his own peace, a peace the world cannot give.

Jn. 16:16-33—Jesus has told his disciples all of this so that they may find peace in him amidst a world that persecutes them.

Rm. 8:1-39—The children of God receive peaceful refreshment from the Holy Spirit.

1 Co. 11:17-34—The Lord's Supper quenches spiritual hunger and thirst.

Heb. 3:7-19; 4:1-11—How to reach God's land of rest.

* * * * *

To draw us away from our need for comfort and consolation as ends in themselves, the Lord may allow, for a short or long duration, periods of spiritual dryness. At such times we may be tempted to give up prayer but that is no solution. Especially during those "watershed" times when God is helping us to change the course of our life, we need to remain in constant contact with him, no matter how we feel. If we trust in the God of consolation rather than in consolations from God, we can be sure, when the time is right, the Lord will grant us all we need to feel renewed and spiritually refreshed. Beyond mere human comfort, we will receive the gift of inner peace.

READINGS FROM THE LITERATURE OF SPIRITUALITY

The Way of a Pilgrim, (Chapter 4)—Interior prayer more than anything else offers light and refreshment to the pilgrim's soul. "And that can be done by anyone. It costs nothing but the effort to sink down in silence into the depths of one's heart and call more and more upon the radiant Name of Jesus. Everyone who does that feels at once the inward light, everything becomes understandable to him, he even catches sight in this light of some of the mysteries of the Kingdom of God."

He Leadeth Me, (Chapters 7 and 14)—Meditation on our Lord's agony in the garden became for Father Ciszek a wonderful treasure and source of strength and consolation. He knew that he must abandon himself entirely to the will of the Father and live from now on in the spirit of self-abandonment to God. "I can only describe the experience as a sense of 'letting go,' giving over totally my last effort or even any will to guide the reins of my own life."

Introduction to the Devout Life, (Part II, Chapters 1-21; Part III, Chapters 31-34; Part IV, Chapters 13-15)—"Since prayer opens our mind to the brightness of divine light and our will to the warmth of heavenly love, nothing so purges our mind of ignorance and our will of evil desires; its sacred waters freshen the soul, wash away our imperfections, revive the flowers of our good desires and quench the thirst of our heart's passions."

The Climate of Monastic Prayer, (Chapters II, V and IX)—Meditation and contemplative prayer are not so much ways to find God as ways of resting in him whom we have found, who loves us, who is near to us, who comes to us to draw us to himself. In the "sabbath" of contemplation, the soul rests in God and God works in the soul.

The Book of Her Life, (Chapters 8-10)—In these chapters St. Teresa speaks of the great benefits she derived from prayer and the means the Lord used to awaken her soul and give her light amid darkness. She begins to describe in detail the favors granted her by the Lord.

Story of a Soul, (Chapter V of Manuscript "A")—St. Thérèse experienced already on earth the spiritual refreshment God reserved for those who love him (not with the eye but with the heart), and "...seeing the eternal rewards had no proportion to life's small sacrifices, I wanted to love, to love Jesus with a passion, giving him a thousand proofs of my love while it was possible."

Beginning to Pray, (Chapter III)—Prayer is not an exhausting chore. "Simply turn your eyes Godwards, smile at him and go into it. There are moments when you can tell God, 'I simply must have a rest, I have no strength to be with You all the time,' which is perfectly true. You are still not capable of bearing God's company all the time. Well, say so. God knows that perfectly well, whatever you do about it. Go apart, say for a moment, 'I'll just have a rest. For a moment I accept to be less saintly.' "

The Diary of a Young Girl, (Wednesday, 23 February 1944 to Monday, 3 April 1944)—Though confinement causes her to suffer the ache of an adolescence cut off from the world of beauty and freedom, Anne does experience occasionally deep consolation. "I looked out of the open window too, over a large area of Amsterdam, over all the roofs and on to the horizon, which was such a pale blue that it was hard to see the dividing line. 'As long as this exists,' I thought, 'and I may live to see it, this sunshine, the cloudless skies, while this lasts, I cannot be unhappy'...As long as you can look fearlessly up into the heavens, as long as you know that you are pure within...you will still find happiness."

Reaching Out, (Chapters 7, 8 and 9)—Each movement thus far, from loneliness to solitude and from hostility to hospitality, has deepened in some way our relationship to God. If we cannot reach out to God, the source and giver of our own and our neighbor's life, then solitude and hospitality remain vague ideals, good to speak about but unreal in daily life. "The movement from illusion to prayer, therefore, is the most crucial movement of the spiritual life undergirding all that has been said thus far." It is prayer alone that ultimately refreshes the soul and slakes all thirst.

Walden, (Chapters XI-XVI)—Spiritual refreshment comes to Thoreau in the form of reflection on the higher laws that govern man and nature. Though in our eyes certain actions may appear brutal, nature is never wasteful. Even in winter, when all seems to die, nature is merely refreshing herself for the burgeoning of new life that will come in the spring.

The Participant Self, (Book II, Chapters V-VIII)—To experience the world creatively, we must abide in occasional retreat, attuned to the truth which speaks in silence to our uniqueness. Restored by recollection, we can unveil the real value of culture and civilization, its aim and origin.

SUPPLEMENTARY READING

The Book of Her Life, (Chapters XI-XXI)—St. Teresa describes the four degrees of prayer she experienced and the spiritual refreshment God granted to her through them, comparing these stages to four different ways of watering a garden.

Thomas Merton on Prayer, (Chapter 3)—According to Merton, "...man's search for God lies essentially in his becoming aware of himself as a person possessed by God. And so, he must learn to rest in God, to listen in silence to the God Who has already found him."

* * * * *

When the Lord leads us to the wellspring of refreshment that is his love, we feel renewed on all levels of our being. His gentle guidance has led us from rough to restful waters, far beyond the pressures of daily demands. Water from the well of Jesus' peace transforms monotonous tasks into acts of loving fidelity. Such moments of deep communion are a source of strength in times of stress, a dawning light filtering through the shadows of earthly concerns.

MINOR THEME V

STEPPING ASIDE ENABLES ME TO START AGAIN

Having rearranged your parcels and enjoyed a refreshing drink, you step outside the cafe and go on with your shopping. The crowd seems to feel less suffocating than it was previously. As a matter of fact, you feel compassion for your companion shoppers. They, too, have aching feet; they, too, need to find their way to a cafe as you did. Also your shopping task seems less burdensome; you can focus your attention once again on your original purpose for coming to town. Through this experience, we may see that transcendence is not an avenue of escape from the concrete situation. You did not stay in the little cafe all day, but you were refreshed by stopping there. You were filled with new energy to complete your task. After a time of stepping aside, we feel more inclined to start again. Applying this experience to our spiritual life, we see that each task we do takes on a new depth of meaning when we place it in the context of our spiritual life as a whole. We are less inclined to confine action and contemplation to air-tight compartments. We see that peaceful presence to the Divine is the ground of effective activity. Daily action is less wearisome to us when it radiates the love of the Lord whom we have met in our "little cafe" of recollection.

READINGS FROM HOLY SCRIPTURE

Old Testament

Gn. 6:1-22; 7:1-24; 8:1-22; 9:1-29—When the flood subsides, the world order is begun anew by Yahweh through Noah and his family.

Ex. 19:1-25; 20:1-21—When Moses comes down from the mountain, he tells the people what they must do to begin a life of dedication to Yahweh's law.

Nb. 9:15-23—The sons of Israel pitch camp when the Cloud rests on the tabernacle; they set out again only when it lifts.

Jb. 38:1-41; 39:1-30; 40:1-32; 41:1-26; 42:1-17—After Yahweh takes Job aside and conveys to him the mystery of his ways, the poor sufferer repents for having questioned his power. Then Yahweh restores Job's fortunes and his life begins again.

Ps. 78—Israel learns from its history that each falling away from Yahweh marks at the same time the occasion of return.

Ps. 80—The psalmist prays for the restoration of Israel.

Ps. 89—God's faithfulness has always given his people the courage to start anew.

Ps. 105—The wonder-filled history of Israel proves that God always gives his chosen a chance to regain his favor.

Jr. 3:1-25; 4:1-31—"If you wish to come back, Israel—it is Yahweh who speaks —it is to me you must return..."

Jr. 30:1-24; 31:1-40—"For see, the days are coming—it is Yahweh who speaks—when I will restore the fortunes of my people Israel...and bring them back to possess the land I gave to their ancestors."

Ba. 1:16-22; 2:11-35; 3:1-8—The prayer of the exiles shows their longing to return to the promised land.

Ba. 4:5-37; 5:1-9—"As by your will you first strayed from God, so now turn back and search for him ten times as hard..."

Ho. 1:1-9; 2:4-25; 3:1-5—Hosea takes back his unfaithful wife and tests her fidelity.

Ho. 6:7-11; 7:1-16; 8:1-14; 9:1-17—The prophet recounts the past and present sins of Israel and the sorrows of exile.

Ho. 11:1-11; 12:1-15; 13:1-15; 14:1-10—Since God's love proves stronger than his vengeance, he will take Israel back.

Am. 9:11-15—Prospects of restoration and of idyllic prosperity. "I mean to restore the fortunes of my people Israel; they will rebuild the ruined cities and live in them..."

Zc. 8:1-23; 9:1-17—A prospect of messianic salvation. "I am going to save my people...I will bring them back to live inside Jerusalem."

Zc. 10:1-12; 11:1-3—"I am going to restore them, because I have taken pity on them..."

Zc. 12:1-14; 13:1-9; 14:1-21—The deliverance and restoration of Jerusalem.

New Testament

Mt. 4:12-17; Mk. 1:14-15; Lk. 4:14-30—Following his period of preparation in the desert, Jesus begins his preaching with the message, "Repent, for the kingdom of heaven is close at hand."

Jn. 3:1-21—Jesus tells Nichodemus that he must be born again of the Spirit.
Jn. 11:1-54—Prior to raising Lazarus from the dead, Jesus reveals that he is the resurrection and that whoever lives and believes in him will never die.
Lk. 15:1-32—Three parables of God's mercy in one of which the prodigal son is welcomed home by his father and given a second chance.
Mt. 28:16-20; Mk. 16:9-20; Lk. 24:13-49; Jn. 20:11-29—Jesus' last instructions to his disciples encourage them to begin their ministry.
Jn. 21:1-23—Jesus instructs Peter on the shore of Tiberias to feed his lambs and to look after his sheep.
Ac. 12:1-25—Peter's arrest and miraculous deliverance.
Ac. 16:16-40—The imprisonment of Paul and Silas and their miraculous deliverance.
Rm. 6:1-23—"...we believe that having died with Christ we shall return to life with him..."
Rm. 8:1-13—"...if the Spirit of him who raised Jesus from the dead is living in you, then he who raised Jesus from the dead will give life to your own mortal bodies through his Spirit living in you."
2 Co. 4:1-18; 5:1-10—The brothers can carry on the apostolate because they live in Christ. "...and for anyone who is in Christ, there is a new creation; the old creation has gone, and the new one is here."
Ga. 2:15-21—"...I live now not with my own life but with the life of Christ who lives in me."
Ep. 4:1-32; 5:1-20—The new life in Christ.
Col. 3:5-17—"You have stripped off your old behavior with your old self, and you have put on a new self which will progress toward true knowledge the more it is renewed in the image of its creator..."

* * * * *

The life of the Christian never implies *only* sitting in quiet contemplation; it always calls for active participation in the everyday world, provided this is nourished by the life of prayer. Every occasion of stepping aside has as its intention to start again. Christians return to the world to share the wisdom they have received in recollection. They nurse the sick, teach rich and poor, engage in social work or scientific research, care for their friends and family members with a depth of love that signifies God's care for them. The sacrifices we make to step aside are nothing in comparison to the graces God gives us to start again.

READINGS FROM THE LITERATURE OF SPIRITUALITY

He Leadeth Me, (Chapter 8)—Father Ciszek did not know how he would react in the world into which he had been so rudely thrust and in which his future life would be lived. He only knew he was to be a laborer in a vineyard in which the laborers might be very few indeed. The harvest, however, would not depend on him but on God's providence, even as had the sowing of the seed. That is precisely why he had resolved to accept all things, come what may, as from his hands.

Introduction to the Devout Life, (Part IV, Chapters 10, 11 and 12)—It takes courage to start again, so St. Francis tells Philothea how to strengthen her heart and how to overcome two obstacles to Christian action: anxiety and sadness.

The Climate of Monastic Prayer, (Chapter IV)—Rooted in contemplative prayer, "...more and more our efforts attain a new orientation: instead of being directed toward ends we have chosen ourselves, instead of being measured by the profit and pleasure we judge they will produce, they are more and more directed to an obedient and cooperative submission to grace, which implies first of all an increasingly attentive and receptive attitude toward the hidden action of the Holy Spirit."

The Book of Her Life, (Chapters 22 and 23)—St. Teresa insists that contemplatives are not to uplift their souls to lofty things if they are not so uplifted by God. She resumes description of the course of her life and tells how and by what means she began to aim at greater perfection in prayer and action.

Story of a Soul, (Chapter VI of Manuscript "A")—"How beautiful is the vocation...which has as its aim the *preservation* of the *salt* destined for souls! This is Carmel's vocation since the sole purpose of our prayers and sacrifices is to be the apostle of the apostles."

The Diary of a Young Girl, (Tuesday, 4 April 1944 to Tuesday, 1 August 1944) —Even though Anne, along with the other occupants of the secret annex, was captured and later died in a concentration camp, she confided to her diary her constant hope of being able to start life over again after the war. "I must work, so as not to be a fool, to get on, to become a journalist, because that's what I want!... I must have something besides a husband and children, something that I can devote myself to!... I want to go on living even after my death! And therefore I am grateful to God for giving me this gift, this possibility of developing myself and of writing, of expressing all that is in me."

Gift from the Sea, (Chapter VIII)—This time of reflection has taught Anne that she must return to the here and now. "The waves echo behind me. Patience—Faith—Openness, is what the sea has to teach. Simplicity—Solitude—Intermittency...but there are other beaches to explore. There are more shells to find. This is only a beginning."

Walden, (Chapters XVII and XVIII)—"I learned this, at least, by my experiment; that if one advances confidently in the direction of his dreams, and endeavors to live the life which he has imagined, he will meet with a success unexpected in common hours. He will put some things behind, will pass an invisible boundary; new, universal, and more liberal laws will begin to establish themselves around and within him; or the old laws be expanded, and interpreted in his favor in a more liberal sense, and he will live with the license of a higher order of beings. In proportion as he simplified his life, the laws of the universe will appear less complex, and solitude will not be solitude, nor poverty, poverty, nor weakness, weakness. If you have built castles in the air, your work need not be lost; that is where they should be. Now put the foundations under them."

The Vowed Life, (Part Two)—The transition from the prevowed to the vowed life marks a new beginning for us with all the crises inherent in such a move. "...the vow signals my birth as a free human being who himself chooses his life orientation. It is a new birth for which I alone am responsible; its consequences will shape my unique destiny."

The Participant Self, (Book I, Chapters III and VII)—"The rhythm of participation and recollection is like listening to life before speaking, pondering before acting, plowing before sowing. While I may flee from solitude to action, only in the blending of both is human life enhanced."

SUPPLEMENTARY READING

The Vowed Life, (Part Five)—"True and lasting accomplishment is always a manifestation of active strength sustained and supported by my capacity to distance myself from activity for its own sake. Passive strength in this sense implies a quiet, receptive evaluation of the immediate and transcendent dimensions of every life situation. The dispassionate insight thus gained is the best vantage point for adequate action..."

* * * * *

Eventually the time comes when we must leave our place of retreat and return to the needs and demands of everyday living. We realize that our lives must become a rhythm of *stepping aside* from the community and starting again. These are the ebb and flow movements of a mature spiritual life. Stepping aside enables us to see the eternal order behind each temporal part. Because we have tasted the waters of transcendence, we can approach our functional tasks with a new sense of purpose and meaning. Going apart has brought us peace and joy, but we do not want to leave these precious gifts behind. They must come with us as we try, with courage and fidelity, to meet the challenges God sends.

MINOR THEME VI

STARTING AGAIN IN A COVENANT RELATIONSHIP

When you step outside the cafe to resume your shopping, you feel less tired and taken-for-granted. Spiritually, it feels as if we have drunk from the living waters of Divine Love and enjoyed the deep refreshment they give. Now we feel ready to take up our task in a responsible way, aware that between God and us there exists a special relationship. This relationship is no ordinary encounter we can take or leave; it is a consecrated covenant that touches our life in its deepest center. For reasons unbeknown to us, because we feel so unworthy, God has chosen us to be his people.

Baptism secures this covenant. In the name of the Father, and the Son, and the Holy Spirit, we are initiated into the community of the faithful where we begin to unfold the life-direction God has decreed for us. Baptism seals the covenant, but it is not the end of the story, for we must embrace ever anew the call God has invited us to follow. In making a covenant with his chosen, the Lord pledged himself also to remain faithful to his promises. The covenant is not a one-sided relationship in which the burden of faithfulness falls upon us. God is with us every step of the way. Though we are recalcitrant people who betray his favor, though we rebel and disobey, God beckons us to return to the fold. He remains faithful to us even if only a remnant remain faithful to him. Whatever happens, once God has chosen us, we will always be a covenanted people. We can refuse this choice; we can live as if it did not exist, but that does not change the fact that the covenant is there. We must treasure it and renew it day by day, pledging fidelity to the divine will and repenting when we disobey, living the challenge of being his people and asking for pardon when we fall away.

READINGS FROM HOLY SCRIPTURE

Old Testament

Gn. 15:1-21—The divine promises and covenant.
Gn. 17:1-27—The covenant and circumcision.
Ex. 24:1-18—The covenant is ratified.
Ex. 32:1-35; 33:1-23; 34:1-35—Israel's apostasy and the renewal of the covenant.
Dt. 29:1-28; 30:1-20—Moses recalls the exodus and the covenant and tells of the generations to come.
2 K. 22:1-20; 23:1-30—The renewal of the covenant during Joshiah's reign.
2 Ch. 34:1-33—During the reign of Joshiah every member of Israel served their God.
Ps. 25—"All Yahweh's paths are love and truth for those who keep his covenant and his decrees."
Ps. 44—"All this happened to us though we had not forgotten you, though we had not been disloyal to your covenant..."
Ps. 50—"Assemble my faithful before me who sealed my covenant by sacrifice!"
Ps. 74—"Respect the covenant!"
Ps. 103—Yahweh's love lasts as long as his children keep his covenant.
Ps. 111—"...he never forgets his covenant."
Is. 55:1-13—"With you I will make an everlasting covenant out of the favors promised to David."
Jr. 11:1-17—"Cursed be the man who will not listen to the words of this covenant..."
Ezk. 11:14-21—The new covenant promised to the exiles.
Mi. 5:6-7—The future role of the remnant among the nations.
Zp. 3:9-20—The humble remnant of Israel.

New Testament

Mt. 1:1-17—The ancestry of Jesus reveals that from generation to generation God has kept the covenant he made with his people.
Mt. 6:25-34; Lk. 12:22-32—God never neglects his little flock.
Mt. 11:25-27; Lk. 10:21-22—The Good News is revealed to the simple, who never betray God's covenanted trust.
Mt. 18:1-4; Mk. 9:33-37; Lk. 9:46-48—Unless we become like little children we can never enter God's kingdom and enjoy the fullness of his covenant.

Mt. 19:13-15; Mk. 10:13-16; Lk. 18:15-17—"...it is to such as these that the kingdom of God belongs."

Mt. 22:34-40; Mk. 12:28-34; Lk. 10:25-28—The covenant is fulfilled when we follow the greatest commandment of all: love of God and love of neighbor for his sake.

Jn. 8:31-59—Jesus is the light of the world who brings to mankind a new covenant.

Mt. 24:1-44; Mk. 13:1-37; Lk. 21:5-38—The sermon on the end. Those who live for God in the covenant relationship will enjoy great happiness; those who live only for themselves will suffer.

Jn. 13:33-38; 14:1-31; 15:1-27; 16:1-33—Jesus' farewell discourses confirm that the covenant will last forever.

Mt. 26:26-29; Mk. 14:22-25; Lk. 22:19-20—The institution of the Eucharist. "...for this is my blood, the blood of the covenant, which is to be poured out for many for the forgiveness of sins."

Ac. 7:1-54—In his speech before the Sanhedrin, prior to his stoning, Stephen reveals the history and meaning of God's covenant with their ancestors.

1 Co. 11:17-34—The Lord's Supper.

Rm. 9:1-33; 10:1-21—Paul explains how Israel failed to see the true meaning of the promises made by God to his people.

Rm. 11:1-32—The remnant of Israel and the conversion of the Jews.

Ga. 4:21-31—The two covenants.

Heb. 8:1-13; 9:1-28—Christ is the mediator of a greater covenant, which he seals with his blood.

Heb. 12:14-29—The two covenants.

1 Jn. 2:1-11—"We can be sure that we know God only by keeping his commandments."

1 Jn. 3:10-24—"Whoever keeps his commandments lives in God and God lives in him."

* * * * *

Only because the Lord has consecrated himself to us in a covenant of love can we pledge ourselves in full trust to him. In his fidelity to us resides the possibility of our being faithful to him. Such is the strength of God's covenant relation that not even our sin and selfishness can break it. God renews this covenant by never withholding his grace from a humble heart. God judges justly while being exceedingly generous in granting us forgiveness.

READINGS FROM THE LITERATURE OF SPIRITUALITY

He Leadeth Me, (Chapters 11 and 13)—The function of the priesthood is to help people renew their covenant relationship with God, especially through participation in Holy Mass.

Introduction to the Devout Life, (Part I, Chapters 1-24)—To embrace the devout life is to affirm without doubt that we want to renew our covenant relationship to cooperate with charity, and to keep generally and universally all of God's commandments. St. Francis counsels Philothea in regard to purification from sin and instructs her in meditation as an aid to renewing her relationship with God.

The Climate of Monastic Prayer, (Chapters XVII and XVIII)—"This [defenselessness] is at once the heart of meditation and of liturgical sacrifice. It is the sign of the Spirit upon the Chosen People of God, not the ones who 'have' an inner life and 'deserve' respect in the gathering of an institution notorious for its piety, but who have simply surrendered to God in the desert of emptiness where he reveals his unutterable mercy without condition and without explanation in the mystery of Love."

Story of a Soul, (Chapter VII of Manuscript "A")—St. Thérèse's covenant relationship is affirmed when her confessor declares that she has never committed a mortal sin.

Beginning to Pray, (Chapters I and V)—Even when God is apparently absent, he is still related to us; whenever and however we pray, we establish a relationship with the living God.

Gift from the Sea, (Chapters IV and VI)—The marriage relationship is in many ways comparable to the covenant relationship God has offered to us—even when we have been unfaithful. "In a growing relationship, however, the original essence is not lost but merely buried under the impedimenta of life. The core of reality is still there and needs only to be uncovered and reaffirmed."

The Participant Self, (Book I, Preface and Chapter I)—The covenant is an invitation to communion and consecration. "In moments of meditative presence communion may become consecration: I abide in my deepest self where the Holy invites me to see in his light all that I am and encounter."

SUPPLEMENTARY READING

Thomas Merton on Prayer, (Chapter 1)—"Although Merton is offering to the man of today what one might call an inward-looking spirituality or a spirituality of 'being,' nonetheless, it is a spirituality that is intended to give meaning and direction, not only to man's understanding of God, of others, of himself, but also to his very life and to his work. Above all, it is a spirituality that underscores the intimate relationship that should exist between man and God. Because of this, one could say that the focus of such spirituality consists in revealing to contemporary man the double experience that he himself continually must undergo in the spiritual life: the experience of himself and his own destitution, and the experience of God whose mercy gives him salvation in Christ."

* * * * *

Through Baptism we experience the beginning of a lifelong covenant relationship. Our birth becomes a rebirth in Christ. Because of this bond, we are destined to seek first the kingdom of God. Our life in the most profound sense is not our own. It is God's to do with as he wills. Once we say *yes* to God with all our heart, we need not fear the consequences of this covenant response. The Lord never fails to keep his pledge of faithfulness to his chosen. To live in faith is to overcome our fear. It is to be taken up in the transcendent mystery of a covenant of love.

MINOR THEME VII

STARTING AGAIN AS SERVANTS OF THE LORD

When we move away from the well of refreshment into the mainstream of action, we do so not to build up personal fame and fortune as such, but to be servants of the Lord. Living a life of self-forgotten service for God's sake is not easy. We are tempted to bargain for the attention of others. We want to make sure our good deeds are seen, to seek praise for our achievements, to push ourselves to the forefront of action when God may ask us only to be silent witnesses to the way, the truth, the life. In our drive to be leaders, we forget to prepare ourselves by being followers. In our rush to become masters, we forget that we must first be disciples. The Lord does not want pious robots to serve him but unique persons ready to become creative partners in the mystery of redemption. In our relationship with God, we must remain mindful of the distance between his divinity and our humanity. We are aware that without God we can do nothing. We welcome the opportunity to live in hidden adoring presence to his majesty, going forth into the world as messengers when and where God calls. At the same time we delight in the nearness between the Divine Persons and our personhood. God has come to us in a relationship of intimacy that manifests the highest trust and faith in our humanity. He has signified his need for us to be full participants in the unfolding of his reign on earth. This relationship between Jesus as loving master and ourselves as faithful disciples encourages us to start again. Our model for such service and intimacy can be the mother of God. When the angel told Mary she was to bear God's son, she gave her consent, though she did not fully understand what was about to happen. She responded to this call as a humble servant. Through her was accomplished the fulfillment of God's promise to be with his people forever. By identifying with Mary in her service to God, we can seal our covenant relationship and fulfill the purpose for which we have been made.

READINGS FROM HOLY SCRIPTURE

Old Testament

Nb. 6:1-21—The nazirite is a consecrated servant of the Lord.

Jg. 13:1-35—Samson shall be God's nazirite from his mother's womb to his dying day.

Jg. 14:1-20; 15:1-20; 16:1-31—The story of how Samson serves Yahweh.

1 S. 3:1-21—When God calls Samuel, he responds, "Speak, Yahweh, your servant is listening."

1 S. 16:1-23—David, Yahweh's anointed servant, in turn offers his service to Saul.

2 S. 7:1-29—The Lord said to Nathan the prophet: "Go and tell my servant David, 'Thus Yahweh speaks: Are you the man to build me a house to dwell in?...' "

1 K. 8:1-66—Solomon, David's son, serves God well. When he completes the building of the Temple, Yahweh takes possession of it. He hears the prayer of his servant for himself and for his people.

1 Ch. 17:1-27—The prophecy of Nathan and David's prayer. "Yet in your eyes, O God, this is still not far enough, and you make your promises extend to your servant's House into the distant future."

2 Ch. 5:1-14; 1-42—Solomon's prayer, when the Lord takes possession of his Temple. "Listen to the prayer and entreaty of your servant, Yahweh my God; listen to the cry and to the prayer your servant makes to you."

Ps. 18—The King's servant relies on him for support.

Ps. 26—The servant of Yahweh tries to live his life in innocence.

Ps. 31—Yahweh protects his trusting servant.

Ps. 68—God rains a downpour of blessings on those who serve him.

Ps. 91—"I rescue all who cling to me, I protect whoever knows my name."

Ps. 134—"Come bless Yahweh, all you who serve Yahweh, serving in the house of Yahweh..."

Si. 44:1-25; 45:1-26; 46:1-20; 47:1-25; 48:1-25; 49:1-16; 50:1-29—This eulogy of the ancestors praises the outstanding servants of God from Enoch to Simon, the high priest.

Is. 42:1-25—First song of the servant of Yahweh.

Is. 49:1-26—Second song of the servant of Yahweh.

Is. 50:4-11—Third song of the servant of Yahweh.

Is. 52:13-15; 53:1-12—Fourth song of the servant of Yahweh.

Jr. 15:1-21—"If you come back, I will take you back into my service, and if you utter noble, not despicable thoughts, you shall be as my own mouth."

Ezk. 34:1-31—Yahweh means to raise up one shepherd, his servant David, to put him in charge of his flock. "I, Yahweh, will be their God, and my servant David shall be their ruler."

Dn. 6:2-29—Daniel is thrown into the lion pit and King Darius says to him, "Your God himself, whom you have served so faithfully, will have to save you."

New Testament

Lk. 1:26-38—At the time of the annunciation, Mary is a model of docile service. "...let what you have said be done to me."

Lk. 1:46-56—The song of the Lord's lowly handmaid, Mary. "My soul proclaims the greatness of the Lord..."

Lk. 2:22-35—When Jesus is presented in the Temple, Simeon says, "Now, Master, you can let your servant go in peace..."

Lk. 2:41-50—When Jesus is found among the doctors of the Law, he is already serving his Father.

Mt. 11:2-19; Lk. 7:18-35—Jesus commends John the Baptist, God's true servant, but he condemns his contemporaries.

Lk. 17:7-10—The meaning of humble service.

Mt. 12:15-21—Jesus is the "servant of Yahweh."

Mt. 20:20-23; Mk. 10:35-40—Can the servants of the Lord drink the cup he is going to drink?

Mt. 20:24-28; Mk. 10:41-45—Leadership with service. "...the Son of Man came not to be served but to serve..."

Jn. 13:1-20—As an example of the kind of service he is talking about, Jesus washes his disciples' feet.

Jn. 15:1-27—"A servant is not greater than his master."

Mt. 22:41-46—Christ is not only son but Lord of David.

Mt. 23:1-12—"The greatest among you must be your servant."

Mt. 24:45-51—Parable of the conscientious steward.

Mt. 25:14-30; Lk. 19:11-27—The wicked and lazy servant buries his talents and is thrown by his master out into the dark.

Ac. 4:23-31—The apostles' prayer under persecution. "And now, Lord,...help your servants to proclaim your message with all boldness..."

Rm. 1:1-15—Paul addresses the Church in Rome as a servant of Christ Jesus.

1 Co. 4:1-21—"People must think of us as Christ's servants, stewards entrusted with the mysteries of God."

2 Co. 5:11-21; 6:1-10—"...we prove we are servants of God by great fortitude in times of suffering..."

Ga. 1:1-10—"Would you say it is men's approval I am looking for? If I still wanted that, I should not be what I am—a servant of Christ."

Ep. 3:1-21—Paul refers to himself as a servant of the mystery.

Col. 1:21-29; 2:1-5—Paul reflects on his labors in the service of the pagans.

Col. 3:5-17—When serving his brothers and sisters, the Christian "...should be clothed in sincere compassion, in kindness and humility, gentleness and patience."

1 Th. 5:12-28—The brothers are to be considerate to those who are serving among them and are above them in the Lord as their teachers. They are to have the greatest respect and affection for them because of their work.

2 Tm. 2:1-26—A servant of the Lord has to be as gentle as Jesus was.

* * * * *

To be God's servant at the same time humbles us and makes us deeply grateful. We feel humble because he has chosen us as his own servants despite our limitations and lack of strength; we feel thankful because the Almighty has reached out and touched us in a bond of intimate love. It becomes our joy to serve such a master and do whatever he wills. No burden is too great to bear when we experience his nearness and receive the tender care his love brings.

READINGS FROM THE LITERATURE OF SPIRITUALITY

He Leadeth Me, (Chapters 10 and 12)—"In all the years I served in the Siberian camps, with few exceptions, I was assigned to the lowest work and the roughest brigades. That was my lot because of the charges I had been convicted on.... I came during all those years, to know work at its worst—at its most brutal, its most degrading, its most dehumanizing worst...and yet I did take pride in it. I did each job as best I could. I worked to the limit of my strength each day and did as much as my health and endurance under the circumstances made possible. Why? Because I saw this work as the will of God for me."

Introduction to the Devout Life, (Part III, Chapters 1, 2 and 10; Part V, Chapters 9-18)—The servant of the Lord is characterized by his practice of the "virtues of excellence." He manages his affairs with care and does not fall prey to worry, over-eagerness, and anxiety. He regularly places himself in the presence of God and prays for the grace to establish himself firmly in his love and service.

The Climate of Monastic Prayer, (Chapters VII, VIII and X)—St. Gregory typifies many monks in that he finds himself torn between the desire of his heart for solitary contemplation and his duty to devote his time and energy to active charity as "servant of the servants of God."

The Book of Her Life, (Chapters 24 and 34)—St. Teresa maintains firm friendship with people who love God and try to serve him. Once she was asked to comfort a great lady who was in "sore distress." She describes what happened to her there, how the Lord granted her the great favor of being the means whereby his Majesty aroused a great person to serve him in earnest. and how later she obtained help and protection from him.

Story of a Soul, (Chapter VIII of Manuscript "A")—St. Thérèse becomes God's servant in the fullest sense of this word at the ceremony of her reception into Carmel.

The Vowed Life, (Part Six)—Religious life is a life of service, not mere service but cultural participation. "When I participate culturally in my service, I am not merely preoccupied with the flawless execution of the operations that constitute a specific type of service. I want also to participate in the very humane movement of the culture that gave rise to this kind of service. I see this service as a set or series of motions which express, embody and carry on this human concern.... Moreover, in cultural participation, I not only participate in the one human concern that gave rise directly to my specific service, such as care for children in education; I participate also in other cultural constellations of value and meaning which indirectly inspire and animate this specific service."

The Participant Self, (Book II, Preface)—The servant strives to be a cultural participant. "Absence of participation leaves man restless and forlorn. Restoration to a life of sharing may only happen when he returns to an appreciation of self and others and learns anew how to serve others in ways meaningful to him."

SUPPLEMENTARY READING

The Vowed Life, (Part Four)—The master-disciple relationship, so essential to the life of service, is lived with special intensity during the time of initiation to the vowed life.

Thomas Merton on Prayer, (Chapter 4)—Two essential qualities of the life of Christian service are asceticism—in which man becomes detached from all illusions about himself—and contemplative prayer—in which he meets God as God.

* * * * *

When we leave our spiritual oasis, our intention to be servants of the Lord takes on a new depth of meaning. What we do is not merely another duty to be met in a long string of tiring projects. It becomes a way of participating in God's providential care for the world. Whether we are buying gifts or baking bread, writing books or painting walls, we sense the deeper meaning behind what we are doing when every action becomes a symbol of service to the Trinity.

MINOR THEME VIII

STARTING AGAIN IN OBEDIENCE TO GOD'S WILL

Just as stopping in a little cafe refreshes your body and renews your mind, so the stepping aside experience nourishes our spiritual life and leads naturally toward some resolution. To start living the life of the spirit at a depth previously unknown, we have to become more finely attuned to the challenges and appeals of God's will in the events of everyday life. Whether walking with the crowd or away from them, we have to listen with alert inner ears to God's voice. There is no better aid to listening than uniting ourselves intimately to the Lord. Jesus is the model of perfect obedience. He responded in full to the Father, even when, as in the garden of Gethsemane, all that was human in him would have wanted the cup of suffering to pass him by. The will of the Father came first for Jesus. He knew he would accept the purpose for which he had come to earth. The distinctive feature of his life was surrender to the Father. It should be the main mark of our lives, too, for we are his servants. Thus, guided by Christ and his church, our spiritual life begins anew in joyful obedience to the Father's will.

READINGS FROM HOLY SCRIPTURE

Old Testament

Gn. 22:1-19—Abraham obeys Yahweh's command, even though it means sacrificing his own son. Yahweh replies, "...because you have done this, because you have not refused me your son, your only son, I will shower blessings on you..."

Ex. 40:1-33—Moses completes his work and Yahweh takes possession of the sanctuary. "Moses did this; he did exactly as Yahweh directed him."

Dt. 5:1-22—Moses asks Israel to listen to the laws and customs he proclaims to learn these commandments and take care to observe them.

Dt. 5:23-33; 6:1-2—Moses explains that to love Yahweh is the essence of the Law. "For us right living will mean this: to keep and observe all these commandments before Yahweh our God as he has directed us."

Dt. 11:1-32—Moses tells the people that they must love Yahweh and always keep his injunctions. "Let these words of mine remain in your heart and in your soul...a blessing, if you obey the commandments of Yahweh...a curse, if you disobey..."

Dt. 26:16-19; 27:1-26; 28:1-69—What will happen if the people obey the voice of Yahweh; what will happen if they disobey.

Ps. 40—"My God, I have always loved your Law from the depths of my being."

Ps. 50—"Listen, my people, I am speaking..."

Ps. 95—"If only you would listen to him today..."

Ps. 103—Yahweh's love lasts forever as long as his children remember to obey his precepts and be attentive to his word of command.

Ps. 119—"Ah, how happy those of blameless life who walk in the Law of Yahweh!"

Ps. 143—A humble entreaty. "...teach me to obey you..."

Is. 1:1-2—Yahweh detests religious hypocrisy. Those willing to obey shall eat the good things of the earth. Those who persist in rebellion shall be eaten by the sword instead.

Is. 28:1-2—"Listen to the word of Yahweh, you scoffers...or your bonds will be tightened further.... Listen closely to my words, be attentive and understand what I am saying."

Is. 48:1-22—"If only you had been alert to my commandments, your happiness would have been like a river, your integrity like the waves of the sea."

New Testament

Jn. 5:1-47—"I can do nothing by myself; I can only judge as I am told to judge, and my judging is just, because my aim is to do not my own will, but the will of him who sent me."

Jn. 6:22-71—"...I have come from heaven, not to do my own will, but to do the will of the one who sent me."

Jn. 7:1-52—"My teaching is not from myself: it comes from the one who sent me; and if anyone is prepared to do his will, he will know whether my teaching is from God or whether my doctrine is my own."

Mt. 6:7-15; Lk. 11:1-4—How to pray: "...your will be done..."

Mt. 10:37-39—Renouncing self to follow Jesus.

Mt. 12:46-50; Mk. 3:31-35; Lk. 8:19-21—The true kinsmen of Jesus. "Anyone who does the will of my Father in heaven, he is my brother and sister and mother."

Mt. 16:24-28; Mk. 8:34-38; Lk. 9:23-36—The condition of following Christ.

Jn. 14:1-21—"If you ask for anything in my name, I will do it. If you love me you will keep my commandments."

Jn. 14:23-31—"If anyone loves me he will keep my word, and my Father will love him and we shall come to him and make our home with him."

Mt. 26:36-46; Mk. 14:32-42; Lk. 22:39-46—The Mount of Olives. "...let it be as you, not I, would have it."

Rm. 5:12-21; 6:1-23—"As by one man's disobedience many were made sinners, so by one man's obedience many will be made righteous."

Rm. 7:1-25—The inward struggle. "...for though the will to do what is good is in me, the performance is not, with the result that instead of doing the good things I want to do, I carry out the sinful things I do not want."

2 Co. 1:12-24; 2:1-17; 3:1-18—Paul reviews some recent events and explains, "What I really wrote for, after all, was to test you and see whether you are completely obedient. "

Ep. 5:21-33; 6:1-20—The morals of the home. "Give way to one another in obedience to Christ."

Heb. 13:7-19—Obedience to religious leaders.

* * * * *

Doing the will of the Father is for Jesus the essence of holiness. Obedience is not reducible to conformity to an external code. True listening has to emerge from an inner attitude of surrender. Neither is obedience a state of passivity; rather it is an alert openness to the persons, events, and things the Father sends into our lives as messengers of his will. Christ invites us freely to choose his way. He sends the Holy Spirit to be our Comforter and Guide. If we are truly open, we can trust the Lord to lead us in the direction that guarantees our happiness.

READINGS FROM THE LITERATURE OF SPIRITUALITY

He Leadeth Me, (Chapters 16 and 17)—"I could testify from my own experiences, especially from my darkest hours in Lubianka, that the greatest sense of freedom, along with peace of soul and an abiding sense of security, comes when a man totally abandons his own will in order to follow the will of God...true freedom meant nothing else than letting God operate within my soul without interference, giving preference to God's will as manifested in the promptings, inspirations, and other means he chose to communicate, rather than in acting on my own initiatives...the fullest freedom I had ever known, the greatest sense of security, came from abandoning my will to do only the will of God. What was there to fear so long as I did his will? Not death. Not failure, except the failure to do his will."

Introduction to the Devout Life, (Part III, Chapters 3 and 11)—"Obey meekly without answering back; readily and without delay; cheerfully without grumbling; but above all lovingly, for love of him who for love of us accepted an obedience which brought him to death, death on a cross, and who, in the words of St. Bernard, 'preferred obedience to life.' "

The Climate of Monastic Prayer, (Chapter XVI)—"This is the genuine climate of serious meditation, in which, without light and apparently without strength, even seemingly without hope, we commit ourselves to an entire surrender to God. We drop our arrogance, we submit to the incomprehensible reality of our situation and we are content with it because, senseless though it may seem, it makes more sense than anything else.... Here then we make not the confident and conspicuously generous resolutions of our moments of light, but we abandon ourselves in submission colorlessness, hiddenness, humility and distress to the will of God."

The Book of Her Life, (Chapters 37 and 38)—In obedience to her superiors, St. Teresa writes of some of the favors the Lord granted to her. For no trial must we renounce blessings which are everlasting. She describes also some of the heavenly secrets, visions, and revelations his Majesty was pleased that she should experience.

Story of a Soul, (Chapter X of Manuscript "C")—St. Thérèse writes under obedience of her resolution to refer to God whatever good there is in her since he has willed it in the first place and to accept everything out of love for him—"...to suffer even to the point of dying of grief."

The Vowed Life, (Parts One, Three, Four and Five)—Man's biological survival and development as well as his human and spiritual unfolding demand a threefold openness to reality that includes an instinctive obedience to biologically relevant events; an instinctive, periodical, and purely nurturing exchange between higher mammals of the same species; and a well-modulated biologically relevant use of surrounding nature. These attitudes are three prepersonal foreshadowings or pointers to the threefold path to religious presence of which obedience is a first step, for in the widest sense it is the listening openness of the whole person to the meaning of all events in any given life situation.

SUPPLEMENTARY READING

The Book of Her Life, (Chapters 25-29)—St. Teresa describes authentic and inauthentic locutions and visions in the spiritual life. This information might be helpful to some in regard to the discernment of God's will and the direction of souls.

* * * * *

Through the hidden, humble lives of those who try always to do the will of the Father, the reign of God renews the face of the earth. Picture yourself in a plane on a clear day. You look down at the houses and cars dotting the landscape and imagine not only the troubles every family incurs but the thousands of good things that happen when they listen to one another's needs and respond out of love—when they live in their own way in obedience to God's will. All of these hearts raised to the Lord represent a vast tapestry of sin and forgiveness. Amidst the pressures of daily life, these many good deeds may be missed. God sees and knows his servants. Pleased by their silent struggles, God pours out his graces on all who strive to obey his holy will.

MINOR THEME IX

STARTING AGAIN IN RESPECTFUL LOVE

The impetus to start again on the path of transcendence comes with the knowledge that God has destined us for himself. Because he loved us first and called us to himself by countless merciful acts, we desire above all to love him. We discover in that love not only the inner meaning of truths we would otherwise never be able to understand; we also find our true selves. Loving God and expressing the overflow of this love in relation to our neighbor arouses in our hearts a desire to identify more fully with the spirit of Christ. Moved by his grace, it is possible to live in an attitude of respectful love for self and others. Rather than trying to force our lives into a preconceived mold, we give ourselves and those for whom we care room to grow into the delicate designs of Christ. To each person we show the respect that ought to be accorded to one who is another Christ. We look again at all the beautiful attributes that bubble below the sometimes marred surface of the human condition. We manifest a love that goes beyond mere liking or fickle affinity to the heart and soul of the person. As long as we walk the spiritual road, we must try to see the face of Christ in our brothers and sisters, and offer each one the respect they deserve.

READINGS FROM HOLY SCRIPTURE

Old Testament

Ex. 23:1-9—Duties toward enemies. "You must not oppress the stranger; you know how a stranger feels, for you lived as strangers in the land of Egypt."

Rt. 1:1-22; 2:1-23—Ruth loves Naomi too much to leave her.

1 S. 24:1-23—David spares Saul out of love and respect for him as the anointed of Yahweh.

1 S. 26:1-2—David spares Saul once again and this time the king recognizes his error.

Ps. 36—"Yahweh, protector of man and beast, how precious, God, your love!"

Ps. 51—"God, create a clean heart in me, put into me a new and constant spirit..."

Ps. 69—"In your loving kindness, answer me, Yahweh, in your great tenderness turn to me..."

Ps. 78—We are to imitate God's love for us in the way we treat others. "Compassionate, however, he forgave their guilt instead of killing them, repeatedly repressing his anger instead of rousing his full wrath..."

Ps. 116—"Yahweh is righteous and merciful, our God is tenderhearted..."

Ps. 118—"His love is everlasting!"

Ps. 133—Brotherly love. "How good, how delightful it is for all to live like brothers."

Ps. 145—"He, Yahweh, is merciful, tenderhearted, slow to anger, very loving, and universally kind; Yahweh's tenderness embraces all his creatures."

Pr. 5:1-23—Where the wise man's love should be.

Sg. 1:1-17; 2:1-17; 3:1-11; 4:1-16; 5:1-16; 6:1-12; 7:1-14; 8:1-14—The Song of Songs. "I will seek him whom my heart loves."

Si. 3:30-31; 4:1-10—Charity to the poor.

Mi. 7:8-20—God's love ought to guide our own. "What god can compare with you: taking fault away, pardoning crime, not cherishing anger for ever but delighting in showing mercy?"

New Testament

Mt. 5:20-48—According to the new standard Christ brings, we are to love our enemies and pray for those who persecute us.

Lk. 6:27-42—Love of enemies.

Mt. 7:1-5—"Do not judge, and you will not be judged..."

Mt. 7:12—The golden rule means treating others as we would want them to treat us.

Mt. 18:15-18—Fraternal admonition.

Mt. 18:21-22—Forgiveness of injuries.

Mk. 9:41—Charity shown to Christ's disciples.

Lk. 7:36-50—The woman who was a sinner, in a gesture of infinite respect, covered Jesus' feet with kisses and anointed them with ointment.

Mt. 22:34-40; Mk. 12:28-34; Lk. 10:25-28—The greatest commandment of all.

Lk. 10:29-37—Parable of the good Samaritan.

Mt. 25:31-46—The Last Judgment. "I tell you solemnly, in so far as you did this to one of the least of these brothers of mine, you did it to me."

Mt. 26:6-13; Mk. 14:3-9—The anointing at Bethany. Jesus says to leave the woman alone for what she has done for him will also be told in remembrance of her.

Rm. 8:31-39—A hymn to God's love. "With God on our side who can be against us?"

Rm. 12:3-21—Humility and charity. "Bless those who persecute you: never curse them, bless them."

Rm. 13:8-10—Love and law. "Love is the one thing that cannot hurt your neighbor; that is why it is the answer to every one of the commandments."

1 Co. 12:1-31; 13:1-13—In the order of importance of spiritual gifts, love is first.

Ga. 5:1-26; 6:1-10—Christian liberty and charity, kindness and perseverance.

1 Th. 4:1-12—Live in holiness and charity.

Heb. 13:1-6—"Continue to love each other...and remember always to welcome strangers."

1 P. 1:22-25—Love in sincerity. "...Let your love for each other be real and from the heart..."

1 Jn. 2:3-11 and 3:10-24—Keep the commandments, especially the law of love.

1 Jn. 4:7-21; 5:1-21—Love and faith. "We can be sure that we love God's children if we love God himself and do what he has commanded us..."

* * * * *

Though we try to be self-giving and respectful of others, we know from experience that self-centeredness often takes precedence over other-centeredness. Before we know it, we are thinking first about ourselves and secondly, if at all, about God and others. On our own we would never be able to reverse this egocentric tendency; we would never be able to purify our love and reach out in compassion and respect to others. That is why we depend so much upon Christ living in us. It is his spirit that works to purify our love of selfish one-sidedness. Without his grace, our "What's-in-it-for-me" attitude would easily take over. With his grace, we come not only to love him as the source and center of our life; we come also to love our brothers and sisters in respectful care. We try to treat them—even the least of them—as we would want them to treat us.

READINGS FROM THE LITERATURE OF SPIRITUALITY

He Leadeth Me, (Chapters 19, 20 and Epilogue)—"A man of faith is always conscious of God, not only in his own life but in the lives of others. This is the basis of true charity, of that great commandment by which we are instructed to 'love God with our whole mind and our whole heart and our whole soul, and our neighbor as ourselves.' Faith, then is the basis for love; it is in the insight of faith that we understand the fatherhood of God and the brotherhood of all men."

Introduction to the Devout Life, (Part III, Chapters 12-13, 17-22, 26-30 and 36)—The chastening of love is especially necessary where friendship is concerned. St. Francis helps Philothea distinguish between true and false friendship, cautions her against rash judgment, and stresses continual examination of heart to see if she is treating her neighbor as she would wish him to treat her.

The Climate of Monastic Prayer, (Chapter XIX)—"There is no contradiction between action and contemplation when Christian apostolic activity is raised to the level of pure charity. On that level, action and contemplation are fused into one entity by the love of God and of our brother in Christ."

The Book of Her Life, (Chapters 39 and 40)—St. Teresa describes the promises God made to her on behalf of persons for whom she prayed. Prayer was for her the best expression of Christ-centered love and concern.

Story of a Soul, (Chapter IX of Manuscript "B")—"*Charity* gave me the key to my *vocation*. I understood that if the Church had a body composed of different members, the most necessary and most noble of all could not be lacking to it, and so I understood that the Church *had a Heart and that this Heart was BURNING WITH LOVE. I understood it was Love alone* that made the Church's members act, that if *Love* ever became extinct, apostles would not preach the Gospel and martyrs would not shed their blood. I understood that LOVE COMPRISED ALL VOCATIONS, THAT LOVE WAS EVERYTHING, THAT IT EMBRACED ALL TIMES AND PLACES...IN A WORD, THAT IT WAS ETERNAL! Then, in the excess of my delirious joy, I cried out: O Jesus my Love...my *vocation*, at last I have found it.... MY VOCATION IS LOVE!"

Beginning to Pray, (Chapter VI)—In icons of the Virgin and child, the Incarnate Son, being true man and true God, expresses to Mary all the love and tenderness of man and God. This love of the Divine Word for his creatures is what binds man to man. Archbishop Bloom witnesses such selfless love in the person of Staretz Silouan.

Gift from the Sea, (Chapter V)—The growth of marital love moves through many stages, one essential move being that from romance to respect.

The Vowed Life, (Parts Three, Four and Five)—Chaste or respectful love is a lifelong effort to be respectfully present "...to the other in marriage or outside marriage with a love that in no way violates his integrity, that in no way ravishes his dignity, his right to privacy, and his unique personal and spiritual calling."

The Participant Self, (Book II, Chapters I-IV)—"Interest in the other is not only response to need but communication of respect. Respectful interest arises from my faith in you as an origin of meaning, unique and irreplaceable."

SUPPLEMENTARY READING

Thomas Merton on Prayer, (Chapters 5 and 6)—The meaning of contemplative prayer for Merton is not merely a mental exercise, but a gradual result of man's total submission of his being to God. "As such it involves a twofold movement: man entering into the deepest center of himself where he discovers his complete emptiness, and then passing through that center to his true self where he discovers the freedom that is his as a son of God who is seeking to recover his perfect likeness to God in Christ and by the Spirit of Christ...for man to achieve this transcendent self, there is need for renunciation and sacrifice in his life of prayer. For it is such ascetical discipline that will give him the detachment he needs, not only to recognize his own freedom as a son of God, but also to become aware of all others who share that sonship in Christ."

* * * * *

The worst deprivation any human being can experience is that of being unwanted. Christ redeemed this lack of love by accepting those others did not want: prostitutes, adultresses, publicans. All found in him the response of acceptance, gentleness and concern. He did not break the crushed reed nor did he quench the quivering flame. To live in the spirit of Christ is thus to live in respectful presence to others.

MINOR THEME X

STARTING AGAIN IN POVERTY OF SPIRIT

Christ sent his Holy Spirit to guide every pilgrim on the path to salvation We cannot be thus led if we are too blind to see the light. To follow the Spirit's guidance, we ourselves must be poor in spirit. We must, in other words, be detached inwardly from the clinging tendrils of pride and possessiveness, of avarice and envy, of willfulness and needless worry—all of which cloud our inner vision like smudges on a window pane and mar our possibility to trust the Holy Spirit's direction of our lives. God uses grace to purify us of these dark spots so we can see ourselves and others in his likeness as we strive to regain the spirit of poverty lost by sin. Dispossessing ourselves of such inner obstacles to poverty as clinging to minor things, excessive desires that are self-centered, anger and lust, is much more difficult than merely putting aside material possessions or withdrawing from contact with others. That is why God has to be the principal agent in the work of self-emptying. Without his help we could not even start on this road. Without the example of

Jesus' own self-emptying, we would lose courage. Despite the many imperfections we have yet to face and forego, he remains at our side. He offers the fullness of his love to those who are poor in spirit. He gives us the courage to begin again. He assures us that we shall reach our goal if we keep his word, if we become each day more like the blessed poor of Yahweh, who see God.

READINGS FROM HOLY SCRIPTURE

Old Testament

1 S. 2:1-11—The song of Hannah. "He raises the poor from the dust, he lifts the needy from the dunghill to give them a place with princes..."

2 K. 18:1-37; 19:1-37; 20:1-21 and Is. 36:1-22; 37:1-38; 38:1-20—During his reign, King Hezekiah relies on Yahweh to give him strength to combat the Assyrian invasion. In consulting the prophet Isaiah, he receives this sign. "The surviving remnant of the House of Judah shall bring forth new roots below and fruits above; for a remnant shall go out from Jerusalem, and survivors from Mount Zion."

Ps. 12—"For the plundered poor, for the needy who groan, now will I act," says Yahweh.

Ps. 22—"For he has not despised or disdained the poor man in his poverty..."

Ps. 37—"Yahweh who can compare with you in rescuing the poor man from the stranger, the needy from the man who exploits him?"

Ps. 37—Do not worry about men who scheme to bring the poor and needy down. Yahweh will take care of his own.

Ps. 49—The futility of riches.

Ps. 70—"To me, poor wretch, come quickly, God!"

Ps. 86—"Listen to me, Yahweh, and answer me, poor and needy as I am..."

Ps. 109—"Reduced to weakness and poverty, my heart is sorely tormented..."

Ps. 118—"It was the stone rejected by the builders that proved to be the keystone..."

Ps. 132—"I will bless her virtuous with riches, provide her poor with food..."

Si. 7:32-36—The poor and afflicted.

Is. 4:2-6—The remnant of Jerusalem.

Mi. 5:6-7—"...the remnant of Jacob will be like a dew from Yahweh..."

Zp. 3:11-13—The humble remnant of Israel.

New Testament

Mt. 5:1-12; Lk. 6:20-26—"How happy are the poor in spirit; theirs is the kingdom of heaven."

Lk. 12:13-21—On hoarding possessions. "...a man's life is not made secure by what he owns "

Lk. 14:1-24—On choosing places at table and guests to be invited. "For everyone who exalts himself will be humbled, and the man who humbles himself will be exalted."

Lk. 14:25-33—"...none of you can be my disciple unless he gives up all his possessions."

Lk. 16:9-13—The right use of money.

Lk. 16:19-31—The rich man and Lazarus.

Lk. 18:9-14—The prayer of the publican is beheld with great favor by God.

Mt. 19:16-30; Mk. 10:17-31; Lk. 18:18-30—Jesus tells the story of the rich young man and describes the reward of renunciation.

Mk. 12:41-44; Lk. 21:1-4—The widow's mite. "...she from the little she had has put in everything she possessed..."

Mt. 21:33-46; Mk. 12:1-12; Lk. 20:9-19—Parable of the wicked husbandmen. Jesus is the stone rejected by the builders that became the keystone.

Mt. 22:1-14—Parable of the wedding feast. "For many are called, but few are chosen."

Mt. 22:15-22; Mk. 12:13-17; Lk. 20:20-26—"Give back to Caesar what belongs to Caesar—and to God what belongs to God."

Mt. 27:45-55; Mk. 15:33-39; Lk. 23:44-46; Jn. 19:28-30—The death of Jesus marks his moment of utmost poverty.

Ac. 4:1-22—When the elders and scribes interrogate Peter and John, the disciples, poor and under persecution, remind them that the stone rejected by the builders has become the keystone.

Rm. 11:1-24—The remnant of Israel. "It was not Israel as a whole that found what it was seeking but only a chosen few."

Ph. 2:1-11—"...he did not cling to his equality with God but emptied himself to assume the condition of a slave..."

Jm. 2:1-13—The brothers must have respect for the poor.

1 P. 2:1-10—Peter testifies that Christ "...is the living stone, rejected by men but chosen by God and precious to him..."

Rv. 7:1-17—When that day comes, the Lamb will reward the poor who have served him through the great persecution leading them to springs of living water and wiping all tears from their eyes.

* * * * *

Like the *anawim* of the Old Testament who kept the covenant when many among the chosen people were caught in possessiveness and pride, so must we renounce our self-centeredness and follow Christ in a spirit of poverty. We must learn to distinguish what is lasting from what is relative, what is functional and passing from what is transcendent and permanent. An attitude of inner poverty helps us to recover a sense of value and order; to meet people in their own right, freed from possessive tendencies; and, most of all, to accept our poor self, weak and limited as it is, as God's own gift.

READINGS FROM THE LITERATURE OF SPIRITUALITY

He Leadeth Me, (Chapters 9, 15 and 18)—Father Ciszek learns to accept his inner poverty in prison. "That God could use someone like myself, stubborn and sometimes stupid and full of failings, was the one thing I had learned through trial and error, through suffering and defeat, and now was no time to start backsliding."

Introduction to the Devout Life, (Part III, Chapters 4-9, 14-16, 23 and 37-41) —"A proud and self-reliant man rightly fears to undertake anything, but a humble man becomes all the braver as he realizes his own powerlessness; all the bolder as he sees his own weakness, for all his confidence is in God, who delights to reveal his almighty power in our infirmity and his mercy in our misery."

The Climate of Monastic Prayer, (Chapters VI and XI-XV)—In the language of the monastic fathers, all prayer, reading, meditation and all the activities of the monastic life are aimed at purity of heart, an unconditional and totally humble surrender to God, a total acceptance of ourselves and of our situation as willed by him. It means the renunciation of all deluded images of ourselves, all exaggerated estimates of our own capacities, in order to obey God's will as it comes to us in the difficult demands of life in its exacting truth. Purity of heart is then correlative to a new spiritual identity—the "self" as recognized in the context of realities willed by God. Purity of heart is the enlightened awareness of the new man, as opposed to the complex and perhaps rather disreputable fantasies of the "old man."

The Book of Her Life, (Chapters 30-33, 35 and 36)—St. Teresa takes up again the story of her life to discuss the severe temptations and purifying inner trials she suffered while walking the road to perfection. The Lord also tells her that the main virtue to be observed in the convent of Saint Joseph she is founding is holy poverty.

Story of a Soul, (Chapter XI of Manuscript "C," Epilogue)—St. Thérèse's care to purify earthly friendship lest it predominate over divine, her acceptance of weakness as a sign of her total dependence on God, her willingness to empty herself totally for his sake—these signs and many more show the depth of her poverty of spirit and purity of heart.

Beginning to Pray, (Chapter II)—"We must rejoice that, poor as we are, we are so rich; yet we must long for the true riches of the kingdom, being careful not to be beguiled by what we already possess so that we turn away from what is ahead of us. We must remember that all we possess is a gift. The first Beatitude is one of poverty, and only if we live according to this Beatitude can we enter into the Kingdom of God."

Gift from the Sea, (Chapter II)—"...I want first of all—in fact, as an end to these other desires [to give and take from my children and husband, to share with friends and community, to carry out my obligations to man and to the world, as a woman, as an artist, as a citizen]—to be at peace with myself. I want a singleness of eye, a purity of intention, a central core to my life that will enable me to carry out these obligations and activities as well as I can."

SUPPLEMENTARY READING

The Vowed Life, (Parts Three, Four and Five)—"Poverty in the deepest sense signifies the wise use and celebration of things. It aids my openness to all dimensions of their meaning. Poverty of spirit prevents the human person from being overwhelmed by possessing things, from being tied permanently to them, and from being fixated on only one dimension of their potentially infinite significance."

* * * * *

To live in poverty of spirit is to enjoy a life centered in God. Empty of possessiveness, egoism, and pride through God's progressive action of purification, we find a new sense of freedom. The paradox of renunciation is that it grants us inner liberation. Rather than clinging to what we own as if it were ours, we celebrate life as God's gift. As the saints say, we possess everything because we know we possess nothing. We believe that all belongs to God and all is to be returned to him. We keep nothing for ourselves but, while on earth, we use God's gifts wisely and with gratitude. Our life becomes a combination of adoration and thanksgiving. In our poverty, we adore God and thank him for all the good he gives. In the lowliness of our heart, we worship him alone and gratefully acknowledge that he is the source of every good and perfect gift.

CONCLUSION

As sleep is essential to restore the body, so stepping aside is necessary to revive our spirits. When life becomes too much, we have to recollect ourselves and regain the energy to start again. If we neglect this need for a quiet corner and press ourselves to continue, we may have to pay the price of loss of inspiration and a mounting sense of meaninglessness. Only when we maintain the intimate bond between ourselves and the Sacred does life reach its fullest potential. As these readings have shown, we must find our special place, wherever that may be. We need to drink from a nourishing source. Thus refreshed, we can begin our journey anew, moving toward the final goal faith already sees.

PART THREE

SAMPLE BIBLIOGRAPHY

Introduction

What follows is a selected, annotated bibliography of all the sources in the literature of spirituality referred to in the preceding chapters in accordance with their proper classification—essential, secondary, edifying, recreative—as well as a sampling of additional sources that may enable interested persons to plan reading programs for themselves or those under their care in line with the models presented in Part Two.

It goes without saying that this bibliography is in no way to be considered exhaustive. It is only a sampling of the vast amount of spiritual literature available, from which the author has made an attempt at judicious selection for the average reader. Additional references can be found by following the guidelines established in Part One. Annotations are also given for all the texts that appear in Part Two.

Please note: Books with an asterisk (*) in front of them are, to my knowledge, *Not in Print* but ought still to be available in a good library or possibly in a specialty bookstore or catalog. I have retained these references in this revised edition of my book because of their importance in the field of literature and spirituality. Last, but not least, books written by myself and Fr. Adrian van Kaam, formerly published by Dimension Books, can be obtained for the most part from the Epiphany Association, 1145 Beechwood Blvd., Pittsburgh, PA 15206-4517 or by calling (412) 661-5678.

HOLY SCRIPTURE

The Jerusalem Bible. Reader's Edition. Alexander Jones, General Editor. New York: Doubleday, 1985.
See Reading Programs I, II, III for selected readings from this edition.

The New American Bible. Wichita: Catholic Bible, 1992-93.
This edition, translated from the original languages with critical use of all the ancient sources, is sponsored by the Bishops' Committee of the Confraternity of Christian Doctrine. A revised edition of the New Testament is now available.

I
ESSENTIAL

à Kempis, Thomas. *The Imitation of Christ.* Ed. Harold C. Gardiner. Ann Arbor, MI: Servant, 1992. See also Thomas à Kempis, *The Imitation of Christ.* Trans. William C. Creasy. Notre Dame, IN: Ave Maria, 1989.
This immortal classic offers a series of inspiring meditations to deepen the reader's interior life, sense of discipleship, and awe for eucharistic oneness with the Lord.

Aelred of Rievaulx. *Spiritual Friendship.* Trans. Mary Eugenia Laker. Kalamazoo, MI: Cistercian Publications, 1974.
A humanist and a Christian monk, Aelred advocated friendship on both the natural and supernatural planes. Frankness and not flattery, generosity and not gain, patience in correction and constancy in affection he saw as the marks of a true friendship. If a friend prays for another, the friendship will be extended to include Christ. "Thus ascending from that holy love with which he embraces a friend to that with which he embraces Christ, he will joyfully partake in abundance of the spiritual fruit of friendship, awaiting the fullness of all things in the life to come."

Albert and Thomas: Selected Writings. Trans. and ed. Simon Tugwell. *Classics of Western Spirituality.* New York: Paulist, 1988.
This volume contains writings by two thirteenth-century Dominicans, both canonized saints, both Doctors of the Church—St. Albert the Great, patron saint of natural scientists, and the "Common Doctor," St. Thomas Aquinas. Both are famous for their contributions to philosophy and theology, but they are also, in different ways, both important in the history of spirituality. In particular, St. Thomas' huge common sense gives his message an abiding value which can be appreciated by ordinary Christians trying to practice their faith as well as by people who are concerned with more sophisticated attempts to articulate and understand their religion.

Anonymous. *The Cloud of Unknowing.* Ed. William Johnston. Garden City, NY: Doubleday, 1973. See also Anonymous, *The Cloud of Unknowing.* Ed. James Walsh. *Classics of Western Spirituality.* New York: Paulist, 1981.
This fourteenth-century spiritual classic, written in Middle English by an unknown monk and mystic, offers the reader a literary work of great beauty as well as a practical guide to a life of contemplation. (See Reading Program II)

Anonymous. *The Way of a Pilgrim.* Trans. R.M. French. San Francisco: Harper, 1991.
This text offers an extraordinary account of the life of a pilgrim, a wanderer-in-Christ, who takes us to the heart of Eastern Christianity and the hesychast method of prayer. (See Reading Program III)

**The Art of Prayer: An Orthodox Anthology.* Compiled by Igumen Chariton of Valamo. Trans. E. Kadloubovsky and E.M. Palmer. London: Faber and Faber, 1966.
This collection of texts on prayer, drawn from Greek and Russian sources, presents the spiritual teaching of the Orthodox Church in its classic and traditional form. It pre-

sents a picture of prayer in its various degrees, from ordinary oral prayer to unceasing prayer of the heart. Above all, it is concerned with the Jesus Prayer ("Lord Jesus Christ, Son of God, have mercy on me, a sinner") around which many Orthodox Christians over the centuries have built their spiritual life. Through this one prayer, persons may enter with the help of grace into the deepest mysteries of Christian knowledge.

Augustine, St. *City of God.* Ed. David Knowles. New York: Viking Penguin, 1984.
A great Christian classic, considered St. Augustine's masterpiece, this book is a vast synthesis of religious and secular knowledge. It progresses from Augustine's contention that paganism bore within itself the seeds of its own destruction to his cosmic interpretation of history in terms of the struggle between good and evil: the City of God in conflict with the Earthly City or the City of the Devil.

Augustine, St. *The Confessions of St. Augustine.* Trans. John K. Ryan. Grand Rapids, MI: Baker House, 1977. See also the edition by John K. Ryan (trans.), New York: Doubleday, 1960.
This spiritual journal offers the reader, as no other book of Augustine's does, not only a penetrating look into his character and deeds but also a unique guide to understanding and living the Christian spiritual life.

Bernard of Clairvaux, St. *On The Song of Songs.* Trans. Kilian Walsh. Kalamazoo, MI: Cistercian Publications, 1971.
In the first twenty of St. Bernard's eighty-six Sermons on the Song of Songs, the reader discovers the depth, vitality, and spontaneity of his spiritual doctrine and experience. The saint's main purpose is to direct our love to God and to restore the soul with the help of grace to the dignity of its divine origin.

Bernard of Clairvaux, St. *The Steps of Humility and Pride* and *On Loving God.* In *Treatises II.* Trans. M. Ambrose Conway and Robert Walton. Kalamazoo, MI: Cistercian Publications, 1974.
These two treatises, in addition to being among the best known and perennially popular of Bernard's works, offer the reader some of the finest examples of medieval monastic literature, incorporating both practical suggestions and mystical vision. *The Steps of Humility and Pride* graphically depicts the soul's journey from self-knowledge to the experience of the Transcendent God and the obstacles rooted in pride the soul encounters along the way. *On Loving God* is a fine example of the spirituality developed in the Church since the time of the Fathers, affirming as it does that God is to be loved without any limit because he has loved us first.

Bernard of Clairvaux: Selected Works. Trans. G.R. Evans. *Classics of Western Spirituality*. New York: Paulist, 1987.
By age twenty-five, Bernard was abbot of the Cistercian monastery he founded at Clairvaux. There he became the spokesman for a revival of monastic life centered on the strict observance of the Rule of St. Benedict. His lived understanding of the Rule was mingled not with the abrasive, shrill style of the prophet but with a sweetness and

purity of vision that earned him the title *Doctor mellifluus.* His sense of the love of God, the importance of humility, and the sheer beauty of holiness made his writings favorites of scholars and laymen alike throughout the ages.

Bonaventure: The Soul's Journey into God; The Tree of Life; The Life of St. Francis. Trans. Ewert Cousins. *Classics of Western Spirituality.* New York: Paulist, 1978.

Called "Prince of Mystics," "Seraphic Doctor," "Devout Teacher," Bonaventure holds a central position in the history of Christian spirituality. His work, in faithfulness to his Franciscan heritage, is grounded in the doctrine of the Trinity and devotion to the humanity of Christ. Within Christianity he achieved a striking integration of Eastern and Western elements. The three works contained in this volume offer the core of his vision. *The Soul's Journey into God,* considered Bonaventure's masterpiece, takes the six-winged Seraph as the symbol for the six stages of contemplation in which the created world is seen as a reflection of God. *The Tree of Life* is a simple meditation on the life of Jesus, and *The Life of St. Francis* was the official biography commissioned by the Franciscan Order in 1260.

Boylan, Dom Eugene. *This Tremendous Lover.* Westminster, MD: Christian Classics, 1987.

This book relates individual sanctity to the holiness of Christ, conjoining for the reader two great streams of concern: holiness for the ordinary person and the doctrine of the Mystical Body. (See Reading Program II)

Carretto, Carlo. *The God Who Comes.* Trans. Rose Mary Hancock. Maryknoll, NY: Orbis Books, 1974.

This is a book of prayerful reflections on Holy Scripture that both consoles and challenges. It is consoling because of the author's conviction that whirlwind changes in the Church have blown away pseudo-traditions, attitudes, and devotions that fostered spiritual immaturity; it is challenging because of his insistence that each Christian meet the test of faith by finding that "the God who comes" is already here—in events, in other persons and within oneself. (See Reading Program I)

Carretto, Carlo. *Letters from the Desert.* Trans. Rose Mary Hancock. Maryknoll, NY: Orbis Books, 1982.

Born of the author's solitude and contemplation as a Little Brother of Jesus in the desert country of North Africa, these reflections stand well within the ancient Christian tradition of desert experience, allowing the thoughtful reader an opportunity for encounter with self, God, and others in silence. (See Reading Program I)

Catherine of Siena, St. *The Dialogue of Catherine of Siena.* Trans. Algar Thorold. Rockford, IL: Tan Books, 1976. See also Catherine of Siena, *The Dialogue.* Trans. Suzanne Noffke. *Classics of Western Spirituality.* New York: Paulist, 1980.

This work, dictated by St. Catherine while in a state of ecstasy to her secretaries, was completed in 1370. It is considered a unique example of "ecclesiastical" mysticism, for its special value lies in the fact that from first to last it is an authentic mystical exposition of the creeds taught to every child and a colloquial description of the elements that comprise practical Christianity.

Chautard, Dom Jean-Baptiste. *The Soul of the Apostolate.* Trans. A Monk of Our Lady of Gethsemani. Rockford, IL: Tan Books, 1977.
The author's continual plea for combining the contemplative with the active life is developed with clarity, industry, and eloquence in this enduring treasure of spiritual meditation and practical suggestions, directed especially to readers who desire to elevate their daily work to a supernatural level by the enrichment of their interior lives. (See Reading Program II)

Ciszek, Walter J. with Daniel L. Flaherty. *He Leadeth Me.* New York: Doubleday, 1975.
The author of *With God in Russia* tells the inside story of his years of hard labor in the prison camps of Siberia, helping readers understand how, through long years of isolation and suffering, stripped of external physical and religious consolations, God led him to a new depth of trust and true spiritual surrender. (See Reading Program III)

de Caussade, Jean-Pierre. *Abandonment to Divine Providence.* Trans. John Beevers. New York: Doubleday, 1993.
One of the great Christian classics of all time, this book is for those who truly seek God. In it the author outlines the means to attain holiness through total surrender of the soul to God and cooperation with his will in all things, emphasizing acceptance of the present moment as "an ever-flowing source of holiness." (See Reading Program I)

de Sales, Francis, St. *Introduction to the Devout Life.* Trans. Michael Day. New York: E.P. Dutton, 1961. See also the edition by John K. Ryan (trans.). New York: Doubleday, 1972.
This is an outstanding example of Christian mystical and devotional literature, written for readers who, to all outward appearances lead an ordinary life, and who, within their limits, long for a life of Christian piety while participating in the affairs of the world. The text is addressed to *Philothea*, that is, to the soul who aspires to devotion out of love for God. (See Reading Program III)

*de Sales, Francis, St. *Treatise on the Love of God.* In *Library of St. Francis de Sales.* Volume Two. Trans. Henry Benedict Mackey. London: Burns, Oates & Washbourne, 1884.
In this monumental work, the saint treats in general the will and its affections, in particular, its chief affection, love, and the will's natural inclination toward a sovereign love of God. He discusses the virtues in detail, not only the virtue of charity in all its parts but also faith, hope, and fear; zeal, obedience, and resignation, together with practical principles and rules regarding the manner of loving and serving God. The text is addressed to *Theotimus*, that is, to the human spirit desirous of making progress in holy love.

*Delp, Alfred. *The Prison Meditations of Father Alfred Delp.* New York: Macmillan, 1963.

These meditations were written by a man condemned to be executed as a traitor to his country in a time of war, yet they sound to the reader like the "voice of one crying in the wilderness" of a faithless society. Delp says we must turn to ourselves and recover something of our lost humanity as a necessary preparation for our ultimate return to God.

**Early Fathers from the Philokalia.* Trans. E. Kadloubovsky and G.E.H. Palmer. London: Faber and Faber, 1954.

This is a collection by Fathers of the Orthodox Church (including St. Isaac of Syria and St. Gregory Palamas) from between the third and seventh centuries. It embraces the immense scope of the doctrines, counsels and practices of saints who reached the highest levels of contemplation and Christian action.

Eckhart, Meister. *Meister Eckhart: A Modern Translation.* Trans. Raymond Bernard Blakney. New York: Harper, 1957.

This text includes Meister Eckhart's *Talks of Instruction, The Book of Divine Comfort, The Aristocrats, About Disinterest*, and selections from sermons, fragments, and legends. The introduction outlines the philosophical and mystical background of Eckhart's life and work, traces his influence on his time and today, and discusses the questions and controversies raised by his writings.

Enzler, Clarence J. *My Other Self.* Denville, NJ: Dimension Books, n.d.

The author adopts the mode of presentation followed by Thomas à Kempis in the *Imitation of Christ.* The reader will, therefore, find Christ speaking to him in intimate conversations, seeking to make him fully aware of what it means to be a Christian "another Christ," Christ's "other self." The *present* moment is Christ's moment: the time for each individual to identify him- or herself with the Lord and to act as Christ wants us to act is *now*.

Francis of Assisi, St. *The Little Flowers of St. Francis.* Ed. Roger Huddleston. Springfield, IL: Templegate, 1988.

In this Christian classic, there lives and breathes the spirit of St. Francis. His warmth and gaiety radiate in the best-loved stories of the Poverello and his followers: Francis' sermon to the birds, the stigmata, the wolf of Gubbio, the soaring "Canticle of Brother Sun," the lives and sayings of Brother Juniper and Brother Giles. Above all, this is the story of how the Little Poor Man taught the world about the love of Christ and how this love can be lived and enjoyed by everyone.

Francis and Clare: The Complete Works. Trans. Regis J. Armstrong and Ignatius Brady. *Classics of Western Spirituality*. New York: Paulist, 1982.

"The Little Poor Man" of Assisi, and Clare, "The Clear One," together shaped the spirituality of early thirteenth-century Europe. Each gathered around them communities of like-minded persons to live out a radical commitment to the Gospel message of poverty. In the process, they left a legacy that has captured the imagination of both believers and non-believers throughout the ages. This edition highlights their love for Lady Poverty and their commitment to radical discipleship in imitation of Christ. Their rules for living in community are unsurpassed in depth and clarity of vision.

Francis de Sales and Jane de Chantal: Letters of Spiritual Direction. Trans. Péronne Marie Thibert. *Classics of Western Spirituality.* New York: Paulist, 1988.
These letters of spiritual direction exchanged between two seventeenth-century mystical writers and friends in Jesus depict the daily struggles of laity, clergy, cloistered religious, bishops, and widows to live the Spirit-filled life. Many of the letters, translated here for the first time into English, offer serious seekers counsels and directives that guide one to a Christ-centered, Gospel-oriented life in church and society.

Gregory of Nyssa, St. *Ascetical Works.* In *The Fathers of the Church,* vol. 58. Trans. Virginia W. Callahan. Washington, DC: Catholic University of America, 1967.
Numbered among the three Cappadocian Fathers of the Church (the other two are St. Basil the Great and St. Gregory of Nazianzus), St. Gregory of Nyssa (brother of St. Basil) who, as a speculative theologian and mystic, is considered the most gifted of the three. The two most influential persons in the formation of St. Gregory's character were St. Macrina his sister, and St. Basil. In his earliest ascetical treatise, *On Virginity,* he draws for the monks a portrait of St. Basil to set before them a model for the ascetic life. Each of his later ascetical writings is a return to the task of giving depth and added substance to his brother's concept of the ascetic ideal. The contents of this volume are splendid proof of St. Gregory's desire to cooperate with his brother in his efforts to promote monasticism. Where St. Basil sought to systematize the ascetic life, St. Gregory undertook to interpret the philosophical, theological, and mystical implications of this life. The second and third treatises included here (*On What It Means to Call Oneself a Christian* and *On Perfection)* respond to the question, What is the nature of the true Christian? St. Gregory stresses the need for persons who call themselves Christians to reflect in their lives the nature of Christ whose name they have assumed. He then lists ten expressions which, applied to Christ, reveal his nature to us. He continues to maintain that the true Christian is one whose life is Christ-like. Three other treatises comprise this volume: *On the Christian Mode of Life,* an expressive self-portrait; *The Life of Saint Macrina,* the biography of his sister; and *On the Soul and the Resurrection,* a dogmatic treatise that completes the portrait of St. Macrina as the embodiment of asceticism.

*Gregory of Nyssa, St. *The Lord's Prayer. The Beatitudes.* In *Ancient Christian Writers,* No. 18. Trans. Hilda C. Graef. Westminster, MD: Christian Classics, 1954.
In this justifiably famous treatise on prayer and the ideals of Christian living, St. Gregory writes of prayer as a necessity not to be neglected in the face of worldly diversions. The Lord's Prayer makes us deeply aware of our presumption in addressing God as Father and of our responsibility to imitate the Father's mercy in extending forgiveness. Consequently, prayer becomes an indictment of oneself unless the petitioner vows service to God, flees worldly vanities, and strives for complete virtue. Living the Beatitudes is a sure way to attain the latter ideal.

Gregory of Nyssa: The Life of Moses. Trans. Abraham J. Malherbe and Everett Ferguson. *Classics of Western Spirituality.* New York: Paulist, 1978.
This text justifies the regard accorded to St. Gregory as a brilliant and subtle thinker, as a profound mystical teacher, and indeed as the founder of mystical theology in the church. This work has special significance because it reflects his "spiritual sense" of the scriptures. He maintained that the ultimate purpose of the Bible was not its historical teachings but its capacity for elevating the soul to God. He sees communion with God as a constant ascent from glory to glory. Thus in meeting God, there is never frustration or satiety, but only the discovery of true love. Thus Gregory, while being Greek, transcends the Greek mind itself and indicates to his contemporaries and to future generations the path to the living God.

*Grou, Jean Nicholas. *How to Pray.* Trans. Joseph Dalby. Nashville, TN: Upper Room, 1973.
In this edition of one of the recognized masterpieces of literature on prayer, the reader learns that the heart of prayer is silence, since it is not we who pray but God who prays in us.

Hadewijch: The Complete Works. Trans. Mother Columba Hart. *Classics of Western Spirituality.* New York: Paulist, 1980.
Hadewijch, a Beguine of the thirteenth century, was endowed in no less a degree than St. Teresa of Avila with the gifts of visionary mysticism and literary genius. Dedicating herself to a life of true spirituality, without taking the veil, she understood that she was called to communicate to others the profound knowledge of the things of God granted to her in her mystical life. Nearly all her writings, both prose and poetry, were intended for younger Beguines. Her experiences and her message were lost to sight until the late nineteenth century. However, since the rediscovery of Hadewijch, her importance has been progressively appreciated. The hidden dimension of her life is now open so that we may share it according to the particular needs of our own day. Through her strong prose, her poetic paradox, and her visionary allegory and analogy, we gradually learn the meaning she sees for all believers in the humanity and divinity of Christ, the trinity and unity of God, and the wonderful interplay—in our personal lives—of Divine Love, our own deepest sufferings, and our power to love and help those around us.

Hilton, Walter. *The Ladder of Perfection.* Trans. Leo Sherley-Price. New York: Viking Penguin, 1988.
This book is numbered among the spiritual classics in that unique flowering of mystical writing that took place in England in the fourteenth century along with the works of Dame Julian of Norwich, Richard Rolle, and the anonymous author of *The Cloud of Unknowing.* This abridged version is of practical value not only for Christians but for anyone for whom religion has become an urgent personal question. If one is prepared to take the necessary steps, there is no reason to doubt that God will lead one to a "state of perfection."

Ignatius Loyola, St. *The Spiritual Exercises of Saint Ignatius Loyola.* Trans. Thomas Corbishley. Trabuco Canyon, CA: Source, 1991.

The *Exercises* are intended for use by retreatants under guidance of a master as well as for the general reader who wishes to share in the riches of a spiritual text that fosters growth in the Christian life and commitment to one's God-given mission in the world.

Jeremy Taylor: Selected Works. Ed. Thomas K. Carroll. *Classics of Western Spirituality.* New York: Paulist, 1990.

Jeremy Taylor has been called the "Shakespeare of Divines." Like his contemporary, Lancelot Andrewes, he drew on the spirit of the Renaissance. Rich classical allusions, ornate symbolism, and flowing cadences enhance his presentation of the sacred truths of holy writ. His own experience of life made him no stranger to suffering, having buried his first wife and his five sons. In his best-known work, *Holy Dying*, we have not only a fine example of a genre of spiritual literature common to the late Middle Ages, but one of the most moving meditations on death ever written. In it we see a man proclaiming the truths of Christianity, not with the bold speculative originality of mystics like Eckhart or the systematic precision of Albert the Great, but with a sheer literary brilliance that enabled him to craft words that stood like windows to the unseen world of which they spoke: words that could awaken and stir, that could define and articulate the myriad sentiments and subtleties of the holy life. Taylor blended the insights of the Fathers with the forces of his own time into brilliant new forms of expression.

Johann Arndt: True Christianity. Trans. Peter C. Erb. *Classics of Western Spirituality.* New York: Paulist, 1979.

Albert Schweitzer called Arndt the "prophet of interior Protestantism." This great German Lutheran mystic aroused Calvinist hostility by his spirituality of Christ in the heart of man. Inspired by St. Bernard, Angela of Foligno, Johannes Tauler and Thomas à Kempis, Arndt and his masterpiece later came to be venerated by the entire pietist tradition. In Arndt's words, "Everything which is born of God is no shadowy work but a true life work. God will not bring forth a dead fruit, a lifeless and powerless work, but a living God. Our faith is the victory which conquers the world." This is his principal mystical work and one of the most important in the Protestant tradition.

Johannes Tauler: Sermons. Trans. Marie Shrady. *Classics of Western Spirituality.* New York: Paulist, 1985.

Along with Meister Eckhart and Henry Suso, Johannes Tauler was one of the most influential German mystical writers of the fourteenth century. Working as a mendicant preacher in the Order of Preachers, Tauler attempted to address the concerns of the newly ascendant merchant class for a practical, active spirituality while being true to the apophatic tradition that he saw in Eckhart. If Eckhart can be called the greatest theoretician of the spiritual life in fourteenth-century Europe, then Tauler was certainly the one who most effectively interpreted Eckhart's message to a broader audience, adding a measure of balance and clarity lacking in his master. Tauler's sermons were among the most influential spiritual writings of the late Middle Ages, esteemed in their own day by their hearers and later by both Catholics and Protestants. Preaching in the context of an everyday medieval reality, Tauler tried to make translucent to all people of good will what he perceived to be the ultimate union, our return to God.

John Cassian: Conferences. Trans. Colm Luibheid. *Classics of Western Spirituality*. New York: Paulist, 1985.

At the turn of the sixth century, there arose in the deserts of Egypt and Syria monastic movements that offered men and women a radical God-centered alternative to the present society. Among the most eloquent interpreters of this new movement to western Europe was John Cassian. Drawing on his own early experience as a monk in Bethlehem and Egypt, he journeyed to the West to found monasteries in Marseilles and the region of Provence. This volume presents Cassian's masterpiece. The *Conferences* is a study of the Egyptian ideal of the monk. Like the Rule of St. Benedict, Cassian's work offers a protection against excess and a constant recall to the primitive simplicity where eastern spirituality meets western community life.

John of the Cross, St. *The Collected Works of St. John of the Cross*. Trans. Kieran Kavanaugh and Otilio Rodriguez. Washington, DC: Institute of Carmelite Studies, ICS Publications, 1991.

This one-volume edition offers readers a superb translation of *The Ascent of Mount Carmel, The Dark Night, The Spiritual Canticle, The Living Flame of Love, The Minor Works,* and St. John's poetry. Each text unfolds with accuracy and grace St. John's intention to teach souls the dynamics of growth in union with God. He charted the course they must follow to achieve divine intimacy, beginning with the first feeble steps and eventually reaching perfect union. Interest in St. John's writings has never been greater than in our day. In every age the classics are translated anew, for our idiom is constantly evolving; but the spiritual needs to which St. John so vibrantly responds are always basically the same. (See Part One, III, of this book for a reflection on his *Counsels To a Religious on How To Reach Perfection.)*

John Ruusbroec: The Spiritual Espousals and Other Works. Trans. James A. Wiseman. *Classics of Western Spirituality*. New York: Paulist, 1985.

John Ruusbroec lived as a monk in a time when medieval society was racked by the Hundred Years' War, the Black Death, and peasant insurrections. The Church, which was by no means spared the turmoil of the age, saw the decline of its mendicant orders, the "Babylonian Captivity" of the papacy in Avignon, and the rise of wide-ranging heretical movements such as the Free Spirit heresy that disparaged the Church and its sacraments in favor of an immediate experience of God. Yet John produced a corpus of works on the spiritual life that has made him the most important Flemish mystic in an age of such greats as Johannes Tauler and Julian of Norwich. Four of Ruusbroec's most influential writings are collected in this one volume: *The Spiritual Espousals, A Mirror of Eternal Blessedness, The Little Book of Clarification,* and *The Sparkling Stone*, masterpieces of a great contemplative and a superb mystical writer.

John Wesley and Charles Wesley: Selected Writings and Hymns. Ed. Frank Whalin. *Classics of Western Spirituality*. New York: Paulist, 1981.

John and Charles Wesley were the leaders of the Methodist revival that swept early eighteenth-century England and resulted in the founding of what was destined to become a major force in the history of Christianity. In this volume, the works of the two men who shared a spiritual as well as a natural brotherhood are considered. From John's early period are taken his *Forms of Prayer, Scheme of Self-Examination*, and translations of German hymns. His mature spirituality is revealed in selections from his *Journal, Rules of Methodist Societies,* and *The Plain Account of Genuine Christianity*. Together with a selection of Charles' hymns, these works reveal a spirituality that synthesized into a unique "Wesleyan" blend elements from the Church Fathers, the Catholic mystics, and the Protestant Reformers.

Julian of Norwich. *The Revelations of Divine Love*. Ed. Roger L. Roberts. Ridgefield, CT: Morehouse, 1982. See also Julian of Norwich, *Showings*. Trans. Edmund Colledge and James Walsh. *Classics of Western Spirituality*. New York: Paulist, 1978.

Here is a classic of the golden age of English spiritual writing that reveals Dame Julian's capacity to wrestle with the deepest mysteries of theology and life while at the same time showing herself to be a generous and loving woman with an extraordinary delicacy of feeling. She is able to express these revelations of high divinity in a language at once humorous and profound that goes directly to the heart. Though the idiom in which she writes and the details she gives may appear strange to the modern reader, the perennial truth of her message shines forth, for her own moments of truth are but an explicit showing of the deposit of revealed truth available to all Christians.

Lawrence of the Resurrection, Brother. *The Practice of the Presence of God*. Trans. Donald Attwater. Springfield, IL: Templegate, 1974. See also the edition by Hal H. Helms (ed.). Orleans, MA: Paraclete, 1984.

A spiritual classic for Christians of every denomination, this text tells of a spirituality within reach of all because it is based on the practice of ceaseless prayer, cultivated by a sense of the presence of God alive in each loving and longing soul. (See Reading Program II)

*Libermann, Francis. *Spiritual Letters to Clergy and Religious*. Three Volumes. Trans. Walter van de Putte. Pittsburgh: Duquesne University, 1963, 1964, and 1966.

The Venerable Francis Libermann is generally considered one of the Church's outstanding directors of souls. In his relatively short life, he wrote thousands of letters to priests, religious, and lay persons, filled with sound advice for their growth in the love of God and neighbor. As a result, his spiritual message has become an accepted path to holiness for all. These volumes offer the reader a selection from the letters he addressed to clergy and religious. Their profound insight into human nature, their practical advice and stress on the common life, their prayerful promise of perfect contentment for those who live in Jesus and Mary, will appeal to every sincere seeker.

Maritain, Raissa. *Raissa's Journal.* Albany, NY: Magi Books, 1974.
Shortly after Raissa's death in 1960, her husband, Jacques, began to go through her papers. Among them he found a set of journals Raissa had kept over the fifty-four years of their life together. Only after her death did her husband read them. They so overwhelmed him that he had a selection published for their friends, asking whether or not they thought the journals should be made public. Though at first hesitant, almost all agreed that a regular edition should be made available. This present edition of the journal was approved by Jacques before his death in 1973. Few people have written more starkly and vividly of the spiritual life; few have had the perceptions that come from a life of utter and absolute abandonment to the will of God—perceptions supplemented in the author's case by the highest poetic gifts and philosophical learning.

*Marmion, Dom Columba. *Christ in His Mysteries.* Trans. by Mother M. St. Thomas of Tyburn Convent. St. Louis: Herder, 1939.
These conferences rank among the classics of Christian spirituality because they combine dogmatic depth with psychological understanding. Christ, the transcendent yet accessible exemplar of Christian life, is manifested to us by the states and mysteries, the virtues and actions of his sacred humanity. Thus the mysteries of the God-Man are not only models we must consider; they contain within themselves treasures of merit and grace. In preliminary conferences, the author shows how much Christ's mysteries are ours and how, in a general manner, we can come in contact with them and assimilate their fruits. The first part of the book attempts to sketch in outline form the essential traits of the *Person* of Jesus, the Eternal Word made Flesh; the second part is devoted to the contemplation of the *mysteries* of the God-Man.

*Marmion, Dom Columbia. *Christ, the Life of the Soul.* Trans. by a Nun of Tyburn Convent. St. Louis: Herder, 1925.
These conferences comprise instructions and meditations given during retreats; they are the fruit of reflection and prayer more than of study. The author's aim is to fix the hearts of his readers on Jesus Christ and on his word. He is the Alpha and Omega of all sanctity and his word is the divine seed from which all sanctity springs. Little by little, however, people not content with the simplicity of the divine message mingled their own conceptions with those of God. To counteract this tendency, the author tries to deliver God's message in his own words, according to the divine simplicity of his plan, hoping thereby to free souls from self-bondage and to facilitate for them, by rendering it more attractive, their ascent to God. The first part of the book shows Holy Providence by turns enveloping in the same design of divine economy Christ, the Word made flesh, and ourselves. The second part is devoted to showing forth the work of the soul that wills to receive abundantly the divine life of which Christ is the source. The third part describes in detail how we die to sin and live for God.

Merton, Thomas. *The Climate of Monastic Prayer.* Kalamazoo: Cistercian, 1973.
This practical, non-academic study of monastic prayer offers direction to all interested Christians, since all of us share the call to be women and men of prayer. (See Reading Program III)

Merton, Thomas. *Life and Holiness.* New York: Doubleday, 1969.
This powerful, simple, and beautiful exposition of the essentials of the spiritual life combines authoritative explication, rooted in experience, and mystical motivation, originating in the sense of mystery.

Merton, Thomas. *New Seeds of Contemplation.* New York: New Directions, 1972.
An enlarged and revised version of *Seeds of Contemplation,* these meditative reflections seek to awaken the dormant inner depths of the spirit so long neglected in the West and to nurture the contemplative dimension of our spiritual lives. (See Reading Program I)

Merton, Thomas. *No Man Is An Island.* New York: Walker, 1986.
This is a book of meditations on such basic truths of the spiritual life as love, hope, mercy, recollection and inward solitude. (See Reading Program I)

Merton, Thomas. *The Sign of Jonas.* New York: Hippocrene, 1983.
In this journal of a young monk, the author records his day-to-day experiences and meditations, his doubts and uncertainties, his difficulties and joys as he approaches solemn vows and ordination. Merton gives us a record not only of one man but of everyone struggling to effect the closest possible union with God. Merton's message is not confined to the cloister; it reaches out to all Christians who sincerely seek the "sign of Jonas,"—the sign of Christ's resurrection. (See Reading Program I)

Merton, Thomas. *Thoughts in Solitude.* Boston: Shambhala, 1993.
These reflections on the spiritual journey and the love of solitude are not simply a formula for the eremitical life; they have a bearing on the whole future of humanity and the world, endangered exactly because we have lost touch with the living God. (See Reading Program II)

Newman, Cardinal John Henry. *Apologia Pro Vita Sua.* New York: Doubleday, 1989.
One of the great literary and spiritual classics of all times, Cardinal Newman's *Apologia* tells of his change of religious opinions from his first childhood experiences until finally, after years of study and deliberation, all doubts resolved "in perfect peace and contentment," he entered "the one Fold of Christ." This dynamic account of spiritual conversion is unsurpassed in its sheer power of style, its remarkable absence of pose, its simple dignity. It reveals the intimate self of a sensitive and reserved man, led by grace from doubt to surrender.

*Nicholas of Cusa. *The Vision of God.* New York: Frederick Ungar, 1960.
A classic work of mysticism by one of the great figures of the fifteenth century—a scholar, churchman, and reformer who in his actions and his writings "lived toward God"—Nicholas of Cusa holds a place as one of the most notable teachers of the contemplative life. Man, he believed, can apprehend God's inner being (which he characterized as a coincidence of opposites) only by a "learned ignorance" transcending rational understanding. The device by which the author brings his readers to a certain

vision of God is by showing them—first from one angle and then from another—the gaze of the Eternal ever bent upon each contemplating soul.

*Pope John XXIII. *Journal of a Soul.* Trans. Dorothy White. New York: McGraw-Hill, 1965.

This journal, of which Pope John says, "My soul is in these pages," was begun at the age of fourteen. One of Angelo Giuseppe Roncalli's early aspirations was to find a way of becoming like the saints. The diaries were continued almost without break across sixty-seven years, the last entry being written about six months before his death in 1963. Humility and love were his constant strivings, obedience and peace his motto. His journal helps readers to understand how the simple peasant boy achieved the greatness, the love of humanity, and the interior spiritual strength that invigorated his pontificate and inaugurated an era of reform and renewal within the Church. It gives an overwhelming example of the fruits of a life dedicated to spiritual perfection and to the thesis, "God is everything; I am nothing."

Pseudo-Dionysius: The Complete Works. Trans. Colm Luibheid. *Classics of Western Spirituality.* New York: Paulist, 1987.

There are few figures in the history of western spirituality who are more enigmatic than the fifth- or sixth-century writer known as Pseudo-Dionysius. The real identity of the person who chose to write under the pseudonym of Dionysius the Areopagite is unknown. Even the exact dates of his writings have never been determined. Moreover the texts themselves, though relatively short, are at points seemingly impenetrable and have mystified readers over the centuries. Yet the influence of this shadowy figure on a broad range of mystical writers from the early Middle Ages on is readily discernible. His formulation of a method of negative theology that stresses the impotence of human attempts to penetrate the "cloud of unknowing" is famous as is his meditation on the divine names. This lucid translation presents the reader with a rich and varied examination of the main themes of Dionysian spirituality and a comprehensive tracing of Dionysius' influence on medieval authors and the mystical tradition as a whole.

Quaker Spirituality: Selected Writings. Ed. Douglas V. Steere. *Classics of Western Spirituality.* New York: Paulist, 1984.

Simplicity in forms of worship, opposition to violence, concern for social injustice, and, above all, a faith in the personal and corporate guidance of the Holy Spirit are characteristics of the spirituality of the people called Quakers. From their beginnings in seventeenth-century England until today, the Quakers have attempted to radically live out their belief in the presence of God's Spirit within their hearts. In this book, Douglas V. Steere has assembled a comprehensive collection of Quaker writings. Included are selections from the journals of George Fox and John Woolman, Thomas Kelly's *Testament of Devotion*, and the works of Caroline Stephen and Rufus Jones.

Quoist, Michel. *Prayers.* Trans. Agnes M. Forsyth and Anne Marie de Commaille. Kansas City: Sheed & Ward, 1985.

This inspirational classic speaks directly to millions of Christians who have been searching for a book of prayers as relevant as everyday life itself. Our prayers, of course, should be the most personal of utterances, yet our private moments with God usually find us mute, our heads filled with the trivia of our days. For those many moments when we truly wish to communicate with God—but need someone else's prayers to "get us started"—this collection speaks with eloquent simplicity of the world we often take for granted. More than a collection of intimate dialogues with God, this text offers a compelling introduction to a life of prayer, setting before us the full range of Christian spirituality and helping us to know ourselves and our God.

*Richard of St-Victor. *Selected Writings on Contemplation.* Trans. Clare Kirchberger. New York: Harper, 1957.

The texts selected here are mainly from *Benjamin Minor* and *Benjamin Major* and are illustrative of Richard's theories on mystical theology. *Benjamin Minor,* the exposition of the story of Jacob and his clan, is the basis of a treatise on the psychology of the vices and virtues. In his greatest work, *Benjamin Major,* the expounding of the teaching on mystical theology occupies the main part of every chapter. For the general reader both the argument and method of this twelfth-century theologian may seem unfamiliar and present difficulties. Therefore, a general explanation of the main points of his thinking is given in the Introduction. The major influences on his work include St. Augustine, St. Gregory the Great, Venerable Bede, St. Jerome, and Dionysius the Areopagite. From first to last he is a psychologist who turns the theological problems he finds in St. Augustine and Pseudo-Dionysius in the direction of the humanist solutions of the twelfth century. The knowledge of what goes on in the human mind becomes an all-absorbing preoccupation. It leads to the evolution of his conception of contemplation and particularly to the systematization of the hitherto unexplored field of supernatural phenomena in prayer. Even when he describes the last heights of contemplation, where all action is from God and man remains passive in the ecstasy of the darkness of contemplation, Richard's writings show that at no point are we free from the natural laws, experiences, and habits which govern our being. Richard's influence was especially great on the English mystics of the fourteenth century.

Richard of St Victor: The Twelve Patriarchs; The Mystical Ark; Book Three of the Trinity. Trans. Grover A. Zinn. *Classics of Western Spirituality.* New York: Paulist, 1979.

One of the great mystics of the Christian tradition, Richard is the link between the early influence of Pseudo-Dionysius and the great mystical awakening in medieval Europe. For his genius in bringing together both the Latin and Greek traditions, all contemplatives owe him a great debt. Born in twelfth-century Scotland, he joined he Abbey of St-Victor in Paris where he became Superior and Prior. *The Twelve Patriarchs* (or *Benjamin Minor*) is a scriptural allegory based on the story of Jacob that illustrates a unified view of the person and the relationship between contemplation and action. *The Mystical Ark* (or *Benjamin Major*) completes this study. *In Book Three of the Trinity,* Richard teaches us about the disciplines and dangers of the mystical quest.

Rolle, Richard. *The Fire of Love.* Trans. Clifton Wolters. Baltimore: Penguin, 1972.

A book of medieval devotion written by a hermit who had, and was still having, profound mystical experiences, Rolle's intention was to inflame in others the love and joy he felt in the unutterable knowledge of his Creator. Partly autobiographical and partly a practical manual of the devout life, erratic and even turbulent at times, *The Fire of Love* explores the shadowland beyond the realm of common Christian experience, the ineffable sweetness of the divine presence, and God's action in drawing the soul into profound union with him.

The Rule of St. Benedict. Trans. Luke Dysinger. Trabuco Canyon, CA: Source, 1993.
It is through St. Benedict and his order that the essentials of western civilization were preserved amid the chaos and confusion of the Dark Ages. The Rule which he established for his monks, and which for centuries has been a source of spiritual reading, has had an influence extending far beyond the cloisters of his own community. It should be of service and interest to monks and to general readers alike for it is addressed to persons who choose to renounce their own will and to follow Christ's way of loving obedience to the Father.

The Sayings of the Desert Fathers: The Alphabetical Collection. Trans. Benedicta Ward. Kalamazoo, MI: Cistercian Publications, 1975.
This collection makes accessible in English the sayings of the Desert Fathers, previously available only in fragments. The wisdom of the desert speaks directly to all who understand that in one way or another the time for rendering accounts is upon us. To meditate on that wisdom is to enter an eternal dimension. From their unrelenting courage, from their vision of God, the Desert Fathers possessed such a love that nothing less than their whole being could respond to it. If we wish to understand their sayings, we must approach them with veneration, silence our judgments and thoughts, and meet them on their own ground. Only then can we hope to emulate the earnestness, determination, and infinite compassion of their silent communion with God.

Symeon The New Theologian, The Discourses. Trans. C. J. de Catanzaro. *Classics of Western Spirituality.* New York: Paulist, 1980.
This great spiritual master of Eastern Christianity was an abbot, a spiritual director of renown, a theologian and an important church reformer. These *Discourses,* which form the central work of his life, were preached by St. Symeon to his monks during their morning Matins ritual. They treat such basic spiritual themes as repentance, detachment, renunciation, the works of charity, impassibility, remembrance of death, sorrow for sins, the practice of God's commandments, mystical union with the indwelling Trinity, faith, and contemplation.

Teresa of Avila, St. *The Book of Her Life* in *The Collected Works of St. Teresa of Avila.* Volume One. Trans. Kieran Kavanaugh and Otilio Rodriguez. Washington, DC: Institute of Carmelite Studies, ICS Publications, 1976.
Written at the express command of her confessors, this autobiography gives an accurate and detailed account of St. Teresa's spiritual progress, describing the interior conflicts she experienced and the crisis which ended in her resolve to seek perfection and walk in the way of prayer. In this first volume of a newly translated edition of St. Teresa's writings, the reader will also find *Spiritual Testimonies,* and *Soliloquies.* (See Reading Program III)

Teresa of Avila, St. *Interior Castle.* Trans. E. Allison Peers. New York: Doubleday, 1972. See also Teresa of Avila, *The Interior Castle.* Trans. Kieran Kavanaugh and Otilio Rodriguez. *Classics of Western Spirituality.* New York: Paulist, 1979.

This, the most sublime and mature of St. Teresa's mystical writings, expresses the full flowering of her deep experience in guiding souls toward spiritual perfection. In its image, language, and style, the book is extremely simple. St. Teresa envisioned the soul as a castle made of a single diamond in which there are many rooms, just as in heaven there are many mansions. She describes the various mansions of this castle—the degrees of purgation and continual strife—through which the soul in its quest for perfection must pass before reaching the innermost chamber, the place of complete transfiguration and communion with God.

Teresa of Avila, St. *The Way of Perfection.* Trans. E. Allison Peers. New York: Doubleday, 1991. See also Teresa of Avila, *The Way of Perfection* in *The Collected Works of St. Teresa of Avila.* Volume Two. Trans. Kieran Kavanaugh and Otilio Rodriguez. Washington, DC: Institute of Carmelite Studies, ICS, 1980.

St. Teresa's superb classic on the practice of prayer for all who are seeking a more perfect way of life, beings with a treatment of the three essentials of the prayer-filled life—fraternal love, detachment from created things, and true humility—and culminates in a detailed and inspiring commentary on the Lord's Prayer. In the second volume of ICS's newly translated edition of St. Teresa's writings, the reader will also find her *Meditations on the Song of Songs* and *The Interior Castle.* In Volume Three of *The Collected Works* (1985), the reader will find *The Book of Her Foundations* and *Minor Works.* (See Reading Program I)

Thérèse of Lisieux, St. *Collected Letters of St. Thérèse of Lisieux.* Trans. F.J. Sheed. Westminster, MD: Christian Classics, 1974. See also *Letters of St. Thérèse of Lisieux.* Vols. I and II. Trans. John Clarke. Washington, DC: Institute of Carmelite Studies, ICS, 1982, 1988.

The 1974 edition is a collection of two hundred and forty-six letters, exactly as the saint wrote them and in the order of her writing—from the notes she wrote as a child, with a big sister guiding her hand, to the inscription she penned on the back of a picture of Our Lady when death was upon her. Autobiographically, the letters may be even more revealing than the *Story of a Soul* itself. Precisely because she wrote them without any notion that others besides her correspondents would read them, many of them were "scribbled in haste." Certainly they document her story in remarkable detail and enable readers to watch the "Little Flower" grow to Christian maturity. The definitive collection of the letters has now been published by the Institute of Carmelite Studies.

Thérèse of Lisieux, St. *Story of a Soul: The Autobiography of St. Thérèse of Lisieux.* Trans. John Clarke. Washington, DC: Institute of Carmelite Studies, ICS, 1976.

Based on her original manuscripts, this spiritual classic describes in simplicity and purity of heart St. Thérèse's mission, despite innumerable physical, emotional, and spiritual obstacles, to make God loved as she loved him and to teach souls her little way. (See Reading Program III)

van Kaam, Adrian. *On Being Involved: The Rhythm of Involvement and Detachment in Daily Life*. Denville, NJ: Dimension Books, 1970.
The reader learns in these profound reflections on a basic rhythm of the spiritual life that beyond our inner divisions and distractions, there is a unity and peace to which we can aspire and where we will encounter the sacred dimension of all that is. (See Reading Program I)

van Kaam, Adrian. *On Being Yourself: Reflections on Spirituality and Originality*. Denville, NJ: Dimension Books, 1972.
This is an experiential description of personality growth and its obstacles, enabling readers to discover their true selves, to relate in an authentic way to life and community, and to rise day by day with God's grace to the fullness of Christian presence.

van Kaam, Adrian. *Spirituality and the Gentle Life*. Denville, NJ: Dimension Books, 1974. Rpt. Pittsburgh: Epiphany Books, 1994.
This is a collection of meditative reflections on the experiential meaning of human gentleness and its role in our spiritual emergence. The text unfolds in three main parts: the gentle lifestyle, gentleness and aggression, and gentle communion with Divine Mystery. (See Reading Program II)

*Vincent de Paul, St. *The Conferences of St. Vincent de Paul to the Sisters of Charity*. 4 Vols. Trans. Joseph Leonard. Westminster, MD: Christian Classics, 1968.
These conferences contain the prayers, counsels, and discourses St. Vincent addressed both to the Daughters of Charity and to members of the Congregation of the Mission. The external labors of this great saint are universally known and admired: these conferences reveal the profound inner life which nourished his apostolic activity. Devout persons, religious or lay, will find in them ample food for greater sanctification and elevation of their spiritual life. They will discover that the condition of a life of outward action is precisely the intensity of the inner life, if they take as their master and model our Lord, Jesus Christ.

William Law: A Serious Call to a Devout and Holy Life. The Spirit of Love. Ed. Paul G. Stanwood. *Classics of Western Spirituality*. New York: Paulist, 1978.
Often called the greatest of the post-Reformation English mystics, William Law became a Fellow of Emmanuel College, Cambridge and was ordained a priest in the Anglican Church. After losing his position at Cambridge for refusing to take the Oath of Allegiance to George I, he became the center of a small spiritual community. Included among his disciples were John and Charles Wesley. Law's practical work as a spiritual director, as expressed in this, his best-known piece, deeply influenced the English Evangelical Revival. The simplicity of its teaching and its vigorous style soon established the work as a classic, more influential than any other post-Reformation spiritual book except *Pilgrim's Progress*. In his later years, Law became an intense admirer of the teaching of Jacob Boehme on the coincidence of opposites. He gave this

doctrine an original turn in his little-known but exquisite mystical treatises—the most important being *The Spirit of Love*, which amply demonstrates the range of Law's thought and his development as a genius of style and devotion.

William of St. Thierry. *The Golden Epistle: A Letter to the Brethren at Mont Dieu.* Trans. Theodore Berkeley. Kalamazoo, MI: Cistercian Publications, 1971.
An apology for a transcendent way of life, a practical guide to transcendence, time-proven ascesis, and deep spiritual insight—warm, personal, practical, lofty, sublime, mystical—all of these attributes make of this work written to a novice when William was a mature monk, truly a "golden" epistle. His letter, which first appeared in 1145, speaks to people of every age of what is deepest in them—the unquenchable desire to transcend self and find the fullest meaning of being in personal union with the Divine. This is the penultimate work of a great spiritual master whose power of thought and poetical lyricism draws out the reader's ardent love and desire for God.

William of St. Thierry. *On Contemplating God, Prayer, Meditations.* Trans. Sister Penelope. Kalamazoo, MI: Cistercian Publications, 1971.
Friend of Bernard of Clairvaux and fellow abbot, William of St. Thierry is also a profound spiritual writer, who takes into account the practical realities of monastic and Christian life. In his first treatise, *On Contemplating God,* he sets forth the principles of spiritual living that lead the soul to the plenitude of love. The first part is more personal and intimate, for in it William describes the desire that urged him to the contemplation of God. The second part is more didactic, for it reflects on the way in which God brings to realization the desire of his creatures. This volume also contains William's prayers and several meditations on happiness as the contemplation of God.

Writings from the Philokalia on Prayer of the Heart. Trans. E. Kadloubovsky. London: Faber and Faber, 1992.
This is a collection of writings by Fathers of the Eastern Church from the fourth to the fourteenth century, who attained the summit of perfection through practice of the Prayer of Jesus. It offers readers a means of entering further into the Orthodox mind and contains much practical counsel for persons who would follow the injunction to "pray always."

II
SECONDARY

Athanasius, St. *Life of St. Anthony.* Trans. Sister Mary Emily Keenan. In *The Fathers of the Church,* Vol. 15, *Early Christian Biographies.* Ed. Roy J. Deferrari. Washington, DC: Catholic University of America, n.d. See also Athanasius, *The Life of Antony and the Letter to Marcellinus.* Trans. Robert C. Gregg. *Classics of Western Spirituality.* New York: Paulist, 1980.
The *Life* was written between 356 and 357, not long after the death of St. Anthony, while St. Athanasius was in hiding during the Arian persecution. It is of major importance in the history of monasticism, for St. Anthony is looked upon as the father of

Christian monastic and religious life. As a matter of fact, the long ascetical sermon in this account is considered the first monastic rule. Moreover, this work has been the pattern of countless "lives" of holy persons from the time of its publication to our own day. It offers continuing inspiration for conversion and complete surrender to the call of Christ, notably exemplified in St. Augustine's *Confessions.*

Aulén, Gustaf. *Dag Hammarskjöld's White Book: An Analysis of Markings*. Philadelphia: Fortress, n.d.
A thorough analysis of Dag Hammarskjöld's faith as it develops and is disclosed in *Markings*, this is a book that, from beginning to end, presents a true picture of the author's spiritual life.

*Bouyer, Louis. *Introduction to Spirituality*. Trans. Mary Perkins Ryan. Collegeville, MN: Liturgical Press, 1961.
This book is a manual for practical use by seminarians, priests, novices, religious, and all the faithful who wish to deepen their spiritual life by going to the sources of Holy Scripture, illuminated by Catholic tradition. It is meant to serve the reader as an initiation into the fundamental problems of every spiritual life and into the perennial principles governing the solution to these problems.

*Bouyer, Louis. *The Spirituality of the New Testament and the Fathers*. In *A History of Christian Spirituality*, Volume I. Trans. Mary Perkins Ryan. New York: Desclée, 1963.
The first of three volumes covering the history of Christian spirituality from its Jewish origins to modern times, this is both a readable guide for the non-specialist and a comprehensive manual and reference book for students and teachers. In this volume, the author surveys the spirituality of the New Testament and the Fathers of the Church, paying special attention in Part One to the Jewish foundations of Christianity before examining in detail the teaching and influence of Jesus, the Primitive Church and St. Paul, the Synoptic Gospels, the Johannine writings, the Epistle to the Hebrews, and the epistles linked with the names of Peter, James, and Jude. Part Two describes and discusses the spirituality of the first Christian generations, the martyrs, the problem of gnosis in its different manifestations, the different schools of monasticism and mysticism in eastern and western Christianity, and the writings and teachings of the Fathers concluding with St. Benedict.

*Bouyer, Louis. *The Spirituality of the Middle Ages*. In A *History of Christian Spirituality*, Volume II. Trans. The Benedictines of Holme Eden Abbey. New York: Desclée, 1968.
This second of a three-volume series recounts the history of spirituality in two important periods: from the sixth century to the beginning of the thirteenth (a continuation of the Age of the Fathers) and from the twelfth to the dawn of the sixteenth, focusing on, among other developments, the "Franciscan Spring," Dominican spirituality, German spirituality in the fourteenth century (Meister Eckhart, Johannes Tauler, Henry Suso, the Rhineland School, John Ruusbroec), lay spirituality from the fourteenth to the sixteenth century, and the movements toward Reformation and the subsequent

Counter-Reformation. Found here also is a noteworthy appendix on Byzantine spirituality.

*Bouyer, Louis. *Orthodox Spirituality and Protestant and Anglican Spirituality*. In *A History of Christian Spirituality*, Volume III. Trans. Barbara Wall. New York: Desclée, 1969.
In this last of three volumes covering the history of Christian spirituality from its Jewish origins to recent times, the author surveys Orthodox spirituality, the rebirth of Greek spirituality, and the development of Protestant and Anglican spirituality. The development of spirituality in the Christian East, then in Russia and again in Greece in the second half of the eighteenth century, and back to the Slav world, is the story the author traces in the first half of this book. In the second half, in three detailed sections, he offers an exhaustive and critical analysis of the Anglican and Protestant spiritual idioms, paying particular attention to the consequences of Luther's clash with the Catholic Church and the growth, fathered by Richard Hooker and others, of the specific Anglican reaction to what was seen as the shortcomings of Lutheran spirituality. This volume together with two earlier ones (*The Spirituality of the New Testament and the Fathers* and *The Spirituality of the Middle Ages*), ranks as one of the standard works on the history of Christian spirituality and provides invaluable background information for the spiritual reader.

Bouyer, Louis. *Women Mystics*. Trans. Anne E. Nash. San Francisco: Ignatius, 1993.
The author focuses on the lives and writings of five women mystics. He shows that, contrary to the modern idea of the supposed inferiority of women, there is an inheritance from Christianity proving women have played a fundamental role in the Church. He establishes this point by studying those whose influence and sustained tradition, continually renewed, have been decisive in initiating an interior renaissance the Church needs as much today as yesterday. He concentrates on Hadewijch of Antwerp, Teresa of Avila, Thérèse of Lisieux, Elizabeth of the Trinity, and Edith Stein, revealing a striking, creative continuity from one to the other. This book portrays how the prayer and interior life of each of these women has led modern Christians from idle speculations to the reality of the Christian experience in its purity and fecundity.

*Braso, Gabriel M. *Liturgy and Spirituality*. Trans. Leonard J. Doyle. Collegeville, MN: Liturgical Press, 1960.
In this exhaustive explanation of the principles of the spiritual life as practiced and taught by the Church in her liturgy, the author rediscovers, along with the reader, that the Church's public worship is the basic food and rule of the spiritual life of the Christian. He discusses at length three obstacles that tend to disfigure it—individualism, superficiality, and utilitarianism—and shows by contrast what true liturgy does and means. In addition, Braso describes the doctrinal foundations on which the liturgy rests; the elements that make up the structure of the liturgical action and its essential characteristics; the relations of the individual to the liturgy; and the direction of the liturgy toward a strong parochial, ritual, communitarian, and hierarchical life. The author's overall aim is to bring out the organic unity of the Christian life, centered in

the priestly liturgy of Christ, and to facilitate the rediscovery by all Christians of the liturgy as a pure and abundant source of human and Christian living.

Brenan, Gerald. *St. John of the Cross: His Life and Poetry.* Cambridge, MA: Cambridge University, 1976.
The author offers a modern interpretation of St. John's life together with a new translation of his poetry. He identifies St. John not only as one of the greatest and most uncompromising of the Catholic mystics, but also as one of the supreme poets of any age or country.

Brown, Raymond E., Joseph A. Fitzmyer, and Roland E. Murphy (Eds.) *The Jerome Biblical Commentary*. Englewood Cliffs, NJ: Prentice-Hall, 1986.
This highly lauded commentary on the whole Bible is not only *about* the Bible; it also brings the reader to the Word of God itself—to read it, to study it, and to meditate on it. The editors follow the advice of Pius XII, who said: "The Word of God...needs no artificial devices nor human adaptations to move hearts and arouse souls. For the sacred pages inspired by God are in themselves rich in original meaning; endowed with a divine power, they have their own value; adorned with heavenly beauty, of themselves they radiate light and splendor, provided only that they are so fully and accurately explained by the interpreter that all the treasures of wisdom and prudence contained therein are brought to light." The present commentary makes it possible for the Word of God to act on us in this spiritual way, since it is concerned principally with expounding the theological doctrine of the individual books and texts in relation to faith and morals. The exegesis found in the commentary will not only be of use to professors of theology but will also be of assistance to persons charged with the presentation of Christian doctrine to the people.

Buber, Martin. *I and Thou.* Trans. Walter Kaufmann. New York: Macmillan, 1978.
The author, a scholar in the fields of philosophy and art, is best known for his revival of Hasidism, a mystical movement that swept East European Jewry in the eighteenth and nineteenth centuries. Out of this interest evolved his dialogical, or "I-Thou" philosophy, stressing the mutuality between God and man.

Buber, Martin. *Between Man and Man.* Trans. Ronald Gregor Smith. New York: Macmillan, 1985.
The author takes the dialogical principles he developed in *I and Thou* and applies them in five related essays to such critical problems of modern life as politics and education.

*Buber, Martin. *Tales of the Hasidim: The Early Masters* (Volume I) and *The Later Masters* (Volume II). Trans. Olga Marx. New York: Schocken, 1947.
The purpose of this book is to introduce readers of legendary tales to the real story of the experience of the "zaddikim," a term usually translated by "the righteous." These are the leaders of the hasidic communities, whose tales constitute the body of transmitted legend. The "hasidim," the devout, or more accurately those who keep faith with the covenant, are members of such communities. This book intends to express and document the association between the zaddikim and the hasidim. It treats the first

six generations of this movement—three in each volume. The hasidic movement did not weaken hope in a Messiah. Rather, it kindled its followers to rejoice in the world and in life as it is. It broke down the barriers separating the sacred and the profane by teaching that every profane act can be rendered sacred by the manner in which it is performed.

Bucke, Richard Maurice. *Cosmic Consciousness.* New York: Viking Penguin, 1991.
This is a classic study of the mental and spiritual activity of the human race where, at intervals, certain individuals have appeared who are gifted with the power of transcendent realization or illumination. Their lived knowledge constitutes a definite advance in humankind's relationship with the Infinite. The author shows from available records that this transfiguring gift of illumination is on the increase. He gives full details of cases that verify the experience of "cosmic consciousness."

Burrell, David. *Exercises in Religious Understanding.* Ann Arbor, MI: Books on Demand, n.d.
To point out the ways whereby reflective religious thinkers work and to suggest how these skills can be acquired is the dual purpose of this book. It is a manual of apprenticeship in acquiring religious understanding. The thought of Augustine, Anselm, Aquinas, Kierkegaard, and Jung on selected religious topics is developed expressly to show how each handled these issues and to provide living examples of religious understanding.

Burrows, Ruth. *Ascent to Love: The Spiritual Teaching of St. John of the Cross.* Denville, NJ: Dimension, 1987.
According to the author, John of the Cross is an utterly safe guide for beginners. She strips away the mistaken belief that St. John is a director only for the most advanced. She reveals him as an excellent guide for the ordinary Christian who longs to come close to God but does not find sufficient help and nourishment in conventional congregational or community life. While the saint is probably best known for his sublime poetry, his writings also reveal a practical understanding of the fact that everyone begins their spiritual life at the bottom of the ladder of love. The surest sign of progress is the conviction that no progress is being made. While St. John's writings must be interpreted in the light of twentieth-century insights, his basic principles remain unchallenged and are of immense significance today. He wants to show beginners, as well as those who have made some progress, how to surrender themselves into God's hands when it is God's good pleasure to take control. In this book, we also find St. John's descriptions of the absolutes of the spiritual life, the bedrock principles, the "musts" deriving from who and what God is and we are.

*Butler, Dom Cuthbert. *Western Mysticism: The Teachings of Augustine, Gregory and Bernard on Contemplation and the Contemplative Life.* New York: Harper, 1966.
The Fathers and Doctors of the Church whose teaching the author reviews, embody the rise of mysticism in the western Church. How it took root, spread, and permeated the whole of Latin Christendom for more than 700 years is shown in a methodical and

scientific manner based primarily on the words of three of the great religious geniuses of western Christianity.

Carrington, Patricia. *Freedom in Meditation*. Garden City, NY: Anchor/Doubleday, 1978.

The author, a regular meditator, professionally uses meditation with her patients and conducts research in this area according to her own method, namely, Clinically Standardized Meditation, used successfully in a number of organizations and by individuals interested in learning a simple, westernized technique. Her research on the use of meditation as an adjunct to psychotherapy is a landmark in this area. One of the purposes of this book is to separate useful instructions from useless ones, the methods of handling meditation that may prove appropriate for our modern world from those that are suitable only for small numbers of people under special conditions—or those which may not be useful at all. The author insightfully treats such problems as how difficulties arising from the practice of any form of popular meditation can best be handled; how blocks to meditation can be overcome; and whether certain forms of meditation suit certain types of people better than they do others. In the course of the book, she searches for answers to some of the more puzzling aspects of meditation and views it in a different light in relation to psychotherapy—not as a replacement but as a promising partner. This claim is substantiated by impressive psychological case materials, illustrating the effects of meditation on the lives and emotions of average people and encouraging individuals to find the technique that is congenial to their personality.

*Chesterton, G.K. *Saint Thomas Aquinas—"The Dumb Ox."* New York: Doubleday, 1956.

Though no formal biography, this book manages to capture the spirit of St. Thomas, to elucidate his philosophy, and to reveal the inner life of this holy friar, dubbed as a "dumb ox" by his fellow students but today universally recognized as perhaps the greatest Catholic theologian of all time.

The Collegeville Bible Commentary. Eds. Dianne Bergant and Robert J. Karis. Collegeville, MN: Liturgical, 1989.

This book fills the need for a one-volume text that incorporates the best of historical-critical scholarship with a concern for the literary and theological dimensions of the Bible. The focus is on units of material rather than on isolated verses; the style is readable and engaging without being superficial. As a basic handbook in introductory Scripture classes, it allows instructors to build upon the vital data and sound insights it presents from a variety of authors in a format that will appeal to the multitudes now devoting themselves to a serious study of Holy Scripture. Each article sets out the scholarly approach utilized (historical, literary, cultural, social, etc.), explains clearly why the text is examined in this way, and shows what readers stand to gain from such an investigation. With the Bible at hand, this book serves as an excellent tool for study while meeting one of the most urgent pastoral needs of our time. While sensitive to the Bible's background, it reveals the Word in its timeless quality and shows how it speaks to us today. Both from the point of view of general editorship and specific contributions, this collection of commentaries succeeds in its aim to offer the kind of erudite yet accessible overview many are seeking.

de Nicolas, Antonio T. *St. John of the Cross: Alchemist of the Soul.* New York: Paragon House, 1989.

Modern American readers remain unaware for the most part of the role of poetry in the Spanish language, which alone, among major European languages, has preserved to this day something of the traditional sense and significance of poetry—thanks most of all to the figure to whom this volume is devoted, St. John of the Cross. He is at once one of Spain's greatest saints as well as the supreme poet of the Spanish language, whose poetry represents the deepest yearning of the soul for God. In it is to be found the techniques of spiritual realization associated with the way and method of St. John as seer and mystic. Both poetry and prose remind us that human love is but a reflection of the love of God, which is rooted in the substance of the soul. While the writings of St. John are, of course, Christian, the author shows that there are a number of symbols of Sufi origin that can be seen in his work and that bear testimony to the presence of certain elements of Islamic literary culture—both Arabic and Persian—in the Spain in which the saint flourished. For example, the symbol of the "dark night," so prominent in St. John's poetry, is used by many Sufi authors, including the Persian poet Shabistari and the Sufi saint of Ronda, Ibn'Abbad. While St. John of the Cross' writings have been translated several times into English, no previous rendering makes them appear with such vividness and significance to contemporary readers as does this translation.

de Unamuno, Miguel, *Tragic Sense of Life.* Trans. J.E. Crawford Flitch. New York: Dover, 1954.

This volume is the acknowledged masterpiece of one of Spain's most influential philosophers. He builds up his theory of life from an inner deadlock involving faith and reason and finds the basis for his belief—or rather for his effort to believe in the survival of a will to live.

Egan, Harvey D. *Christian Mysticism: The Future of a Tradition.* New York: Pueblo, 1984.

Christian mysticism is unique in its view of Jesus' death and resurrection as the cause and exemplar of the mystical life in all its purity. Jesus' saving death on the cross exemplifies the mystical letting-go of everything consoling, tangible, and finite in order to surrender totally to the mystery of the Father's unconditional love. In this introduction to Christian mysticism, the author presents four mystics as paradigms of the classical tradition: St. Ignatius of Loyola, St. Teresa of Avila, St. John of the Cross, and the unknown author of *The Cloud of Unknowing.* From this foundation he moves to two contemporary figures, Thomas Merton and Pierre Teilhard de Chardin, each of whom reflects a contemporary transposition of the two mystical traditions, the *apophatic*, which emphasizes the radical difference between God and creatures, and the *kataphatic*, which emphasizes the similarity between God and creatures. Throughout these writings, the author aims to help us listen to the ultimate Guide, the indwelling Holy Spirit. This book is of great value not only to academics interested in mystical theology, but also to Christians who look for guidance in prayer and who aspire to mysticism. It emphasizes Christian mysticism as the fullness of both Christian religious existence and of authentic human living. It centers on the Christian mystics as pioneers of a new, transformed, fully genuine humanity, for they amplify and make visible what human life ultimately means: being loved by a God of unconditional love and being called to serve others with compassion and practical concern.

Eliade, Mircea. *The Sacred and the Profane: The Nature of Religion.* Trans. Willard R. Trask. Magnolia, MA: Peter Smith, 1983.
Using examples drawn from India, China and the Near East, from primitive religions as well as from Christianity, the author treats the significance of religious myth, symbolism, and ritual within life and culture. This book introduces the reader to life in a sacralized world charged with religious values versus a desacralized one devoid of transcendent sensitivity.

*Fedotov, G.P. *The Russian Religious Mind.* Two Vols. Ed. John Meyendorff. Cambridge, MA: Harvard University, 1966.
An illuminating study of Russian religious thought and feeling from its earliest sources in pre-Christian paganism to the rise of the monarchy, this book is both a work of religious psychology and a historical survey of the faith-filled persons, social developments, and spiritual movements of the time.

Foster, Richard J. *Celebration of Discipline: The Path to Spiritual Growth.* San Francisco: Harper & Row, 1978.
One of the pinnacles of the Christian life is the moment in which Christ brings us to know him in a deep and radically renewing way. But what follows this awakening? How can the Christian develop this incomparably fertile experience into a lifestyle that will bear abundant spiritual fruit? The author locates this path in such classical spiritual disciplines as meditation, prayer, fasting, study, simplicity, solitude, submission, service, confession, worship, guidance, and celebration. Each of these disciplines breaks us free of superficial habits that distance us from God. All have traditionally played a vital part in the Christian meditative life. This laudable book recovers them for us today. Featuring the best ideas of such key Christian thinkers as George Fox, Francis of Assisi, Evelyn Underhill, and Thomas Kelly, the author shows that discipline does not mean dreary, dutiful pacing in a lonely garden but being filled with joy and gratitude as we become ever more open to the presence of God.

Frankl, Viktor E. *Man's Search for Meaning: An Introduction to Logotherapy.* Boston: Beacon, 1992.
After three grim years at Auschwitz and other Nazi prisons, the author gained his freedom only to learn that almost his entire family had been wiped out. During, and indeed partly because of, the incredible suffering and degradation of those years, he developed his theory of logotherapy which, in his own words, "...makes the concept of man into a whole...and focuses its attention upon mankind's groping for a higher meaning in life."

Fremantle, Anne. *The Age of Belief: The Medieval Philosophers.* New York: New American Library, 1955.
Gathered in one volume is the wisdom of the most spiritually harmonious age western man has known—the period from the fifth to the fifteen century when religious and social institutions were closely related and found guidance in the writings of such dominant philosophers as Augustine, Aquinas, Boetheius, Erigena, Anselm, Abelard, Bonaventure, and Averroes. Selections from their work are presented here, together with an interpretation by the author that is woven throughout the texts.

Gilson, Etienne. *The Mystical Theology of Saint Bernard.* Trans. A.H.C. Downes. Kalamazoo, MI: Cistercian Publications, n.d.
This is a study of St. Bernard's theology on which his mysticism rests. Though not a metaphysician in the strict sense, he is a theologian whose speculative vigor and power of synthesis puts him among the likes of an Anselm or a Thomas Aquinas.

Greene, Dana. *Evelyn Underhill: Artist of the Infinite Life.* New York: Crossroad, 1990.
Through her profound spiritual commitment and brilliant discernment, Evelyn Underhill (1875-1941) defined the most important religious issues of this century. Now almost fifty years after her death, this legacy endures. Underhill's contribution to Christian mysticism is enormous. Two of her books, *Mysticism* and *Worship*, continue to be read as classics in the field. This new biography focuses on the connections between Underhill's life and work. Using new archival material, the author shows that Underhill's greatest interest and the focus of her writings was the spiritual life. The challenges and questions she dealt with in her collected works have only grown in significance in the intervening years. This authoritative biography introduces us to and enhances our appreciation of her world and ours. The persistence of Underhill's vision and the passion and single-mindedness with which she searched for the transcendent meet in her works, for she used her craft in the service of one major theme—the human experience of sensing and responding to the Infinite.

Heidegger, Martin. *Discourse on Thinking.* Trans. John M. Anderson and E. Hans Freund. San Bernardino, CA: Borgo, 1991.
This discourse formulates Heidegger's concern for meditative (vs. calculative) thinking and makes clear his understanding of the relation of meditative thinking to contemporary life.

Heschel, Abraham J. *Who Is Man?* Stanford, CA: Stanford University, 1965.
The lectures published in this volume are a prolegomena to the comprehensive study of man that has long intrigued the author. Some related spiritual topics that interest him are solitude, solidarity, reciprocity, sanctity, transcendent meaning, the sense of the ineffable, requiredness, indebtedness, and celebration.

Higgins, John J. *Thomas Merton on Prayer.* New York: Doubleday, 1975.
A comprehensive study of Merton's thoughts on prayer, this book reflects the full scope of his contemplative life and writings and explores the two central forces of his

spirituality: man's search for God and his discovery of God through love shared with others in their quest for a personal awareness of Christ. (See Reading Program III)

*Jamart, François. *Complete Spiritual Doctrine of St. Thérèse of Lisieux.* Trans. Walter van de Putte. Staten Island, NY: Alba House, 1961.
Deploring the many works which present only a partial or a distorted version of the spirituality of St. Thérèse, the author spent many years of research and study to prepare this work. In it he cuts away the sensational, the pietistic, the emotional and comes to an accurate, unaltered presentation of the saint's "little way." Bearing in mind the universality of St. Thérèse's doctrine, the author proceeds with simplicity of style and orderly progression of thought to create a work not for the initiated few but for all Christians seriously interested in finding a sure and simple way to Christ.

James, William. *The Varieties of Religious Experience.* Ed. Martin E. Marty. New York: Viking Penguin, 1982.
This is a monumental book on religious experience for everyone interested in seeing the connections between religion and psychology and philosophy. In it the author defines faith as the sense of life by virtue of which we do not destroy ourselves. Faith, in other words, is the force by which we live.

Johnston, William. *Mysticism of the Cloud of Unknowing.* Trabuco Canyon, CA: Source Books, 1992.
This is the first extended and coherent theological treatment of all the works by the anonymous author of *The Cloud of Unknowing*, seen in the light of a conscious comparison with Oriental ways of contemplation.

Johnston, William. *Silent Music: The Science of Meditation.* New York: Harper, 1974.
Beginning with a survey of the latest scientific research into altered states of consciousness, whether one is involved with TM or biofeedback, the author draws out their implications for the practice of meditation. He then outlines the ways, common to many religious traditions, eastern and western, by which one enters the deeper states of consciousness. In addition, Johnston shows how meditation can be therapeutic in regard to the physiological and psychological benefits gained and how it has a remarkable impact upon relations between people and the search for friendship and intimacy. The "non-attachment" and "knowledge of empathy" required in meditation can help people meet the mystery at the core of their being.

Johnston, William. *The Still Point: Reflections on Zen and Christian Mysticism.* New York: Fordham University, 1986.
The western world, at a time when human values, principles, and ideals are being questioned and rejected, has turned to an interest in the age-old practice of the East—the quest for inner peace and tranquillity as found in the experience of contemplation of Zen Buddhism. In this sympathetic study, the author, a professor of literature and religion at Sophia University in Tokyo, compares the principles and practice of Zen with the traditional concepts, aims, and results of Christian mysticism. The former seeks to *begin* by emptying the mind of thought; the latter *culminates* in the abandon-

ment of images and thoughts so that the flame of contemplative love may rise in the heart.

Jones, Rufus M. *Spiritual Reformers in the 16th and 17th Centuries.* Magnolia, MA: Peter Smith, 1959.
This study introduces us to many prominent spiritual leaders of the Reformation and presents a history of the beginnings of the Quaker movement.

Jörgensen, Johannes. *St. Francis of Assisi* Trans. T. O'Conor Sloane. Garden City, NY: Doubleday, 1955.
Every phase in this biography of the life and work of St. Francis has been examined reverently but at the same time with intelligence and understanding. The character of Francis is one of great strength and sweetness. Rigorous and austere in his own life, his austerity had in it nothing of blind fanaticism. His ideal was poverty, yet he neither condemned nor despised the wealth he had renounced. By nature a joyful spirit, the saint's whole life was lived in praise of the Risen Christ. His appeal is timeless and to all.

Keating, Thomas. *The Mystery of Christ: The Liturgy as Spiritual Experience.* Rockport, MA: Element, 1987.
This book contains original and evocative reflections on the experience of Christ in the liturgy. It demonstrates the contemplative dimension of Christian worship and helps us to recover the deeper meaning of the liturgical year. According to the author, the liturgy enshrines and manifests the vital unity between Christian spirituality and theology. It is designed above all to transmit the mind of Christ, the consciousness that Jesus manifested of the Ultimate Reality as "Abba," the God of infinite compassion. The author also contends that contemplative prayer is the ideal preparation for liturgy. Liturgy, in turn, when properly executed, fosters contemplative prayer. Together they further the ongoing process of conversion to which the Gospel calls us. When we really participate in the liturgy with adequate preparation and understanding, we receive the experience of God in ever increasing degrees. In whatever way the transmission of the Mystery of Christ takes place, it is always recognized as a gift or grace. In the context of this Mystery and our participation in it, grace is the presence and action of Christ not only in the sacraments of the church and in prayer, but also in everyday life.

Keating, Thomas. *Open Mind, Open Heart: The Contemplative Dimension of the Gospel.* Rockport, MA: Element, 1986.
This book is designed to initiate the reader into a warm, living relationship with God and to the art and discipline of centering prayer. Written by an acknowledged modern master, the book moves one beyond discursive meditation and particular acts to the intuitive level of contemplation. Keating gives an overview of the history of contemplative prayer in the Christian tradition, and step-by-step guidance in the method of centering prayer. According to the author, contemplative prayer is a process of interior transformation, a conversation initiated by God and leading, if we consent, to divine union. One's way of seeing reality changes in this process. A restructuring of con-

sciousness takes place which empowers one to perceive, relate, and respond with increasing sensitivity to the divine presence in, through, and beyond everything that exists. Special attention is paid to the role of the Sacred Word, to Christian growth and transformation, and to the exploration in daily life of the contemplative dimension of the Gospel. The author takes us into a realm of the greatest adventure, where one is open to the Infinite and hence to infinite possibilities.

*Knox, Ronald A. *Enthusiasm: A Chapter in the History of Religion with Special Reference to the Seventeenth and Eighteenth Centuries.* New York: Oxford University, 1961.
Who were the religious enthusiasts who believed themselves the direct recipients of special divine inspiration? Were their leaders heretics or saints? What were the perilous currents of religious belief that left the mainstream of early Christian doctrinal religion? The author addresses himself to these questions and presents in the course of his research the personalities and religious philosophies of various "enthusiasts" and enthusiastic movements of the seventeenth and eighteenth centuries, such as Jansenism and Quakerism, and such magnetic and forceful leaders as George Fox and John Wesley.

Leclercq, Jean. *The Love of Learning and the Desire for God: A Study of Monastic Culture.* Trans. Catharine Misrahi. New York: Fordham University, 1985.
This is a splendid synthesis of monastic civilization in which the author pours out the riches of his vast knowledge with a freshness of approach that brings to life the spirit of the Benedictine centuries. He points to the two central currents that vivify monastic civilization in the West: the literary heritage of Greco-Roman antiquity and the eschatological longing for God which motivates the religious experience of the monk. It is the conflict between the "City" and the "Desert" which stimulates the historical development of medieval monasticism. Both "City" and "Desert" find their harmony in the liturgy, where the spiritual enthusiasm of the monk draws all the arts into the service of the Triune God.

Lewis, C.S. *Miracles.* New York: Macmillan, 1978.
For the reader who has difficulty in finding use for miracles, the author restores them to their reasonable place as part of God's way with us, as the possibility of God's intervention in nature and human affairs. This book is intended as a prologue to historical inquiry. Since the author is not a trained historian, he does not examine such evidence for Christian miracles. His aim is to put readers, if they wish, in a position to do so. It is no use going to the texts until we have some idea about the possibility or probability of the miraculous—for, if miracles do occur, then we may be sure that *not* to have known them would be the real inconsistency.

A Little Brother of Jesus. *Silent Pilgrimage to God: The Spirituality of Charles de Foucauld.* Trans. Jeremy Moiser. Ann Arbor, MI: Books on Demand, n.d.
This book describes the main themes of Foucauld's spirituality and presents a brief anthology of one of the major spiritual writers and mystics of our time. His early youth, his conversion, his service, prayer and asceticism culminate in his joining the Trappists and his later establishment of a hermitage in the Sahara, where he hoped to

witness to Christianity by being for the Moslem tribes a "brother to all." He was murdered on December 1, 1916, by a band of marauders belonging to a fanatical Moslem sect. He had no disciples in his lifetime, but the publication of his personal papers inspired the founding of the Little Brothers of Jesus in 1933 and the Little Sisters of Jesus in 1936. They are now present in almost every corner of the earth, dedicated to the poor and the oppressed and sharing their life when possible.

The Living Testament: The Essential Writings of Christianity Since the Bible. Eds. M. Basil Pennington, Alan Jones, and Mark Booth. San Francisco: Harper and Row, 1985.

This is a comprehensive collection of the major writings composed after the New Testament that have influenced the development of Christianity and that continue to speak powerfully to the needs of Christians today. This volume helps us to understand how a personal faith evolves while opening us to the insights and outpourings that have come from the church's most inspired writers, leaders, and exemplars. In the text we find a treasurehouse of the actual words of such teachers as Origen, Athanasius, St. Anthony the Great, St. Jerome, St. John Chrysostom, St. Ambrose, St. Augustine, St. Leo the Great, St. Patrick, Dionysius the Areopagite, St. Anselm, St. Bernard of Clairvaux, St. Francis of Assisi, St. Bonaventure, Thomas Aquinas, Thomas à Kempis, Martin Luther, St. Ignatius, St. John of the Cross, Thomas Cranmer, John Donne, Blaise Pascal, John Wesley, Johnathan Edwards, Charles Finney, John Henry Newman, Thérèse of Lisieux, Karl Barth, C.S. Lewis, Martin Luther King, Jr., Mother Teresa, Billy Graham and others. The entire collection of seminal writings is a source of spiritual wisdom, comfort, guidance, and inspiration. The intention of the editors is to make accessible in one volume a vast body of Christian writings by concentrating on the best and most readable texts of our faith and formation tradition.

*Maloney, George A. *The Mystic of Fire and Light: St. Symeon, the New Theologian.* Denville, NJ: Dimension Books, 1975.

This is a lively presentation of the life and teaching of St. Symeon, an eleventh-century Byzantine mystic, who has much to offer modern people looking for an adequate religious experience to fill their inner hunger for union with God. St. Symeon's openness to the presence and power of the Holy Spirit made him one of the leading mystics of the church; he announces that we are destined by God's plan of salvation to enter into an ever-increasing consciousness of being immersed in the divine fire and light, the living, loving presence of Jesus Christ and his Spirit of Love, without being annihilated, but rather by attaining, in an unending process of assimilation into God, the goal for which we were created.

Marcel, Gabriel. *Homo Viator: Introduction to a Metaphysics of Hope.* Trans. Emma Craufurd. Magnolia, MA: Peter Smith, n.d.

Homo viator (or, as Marcel calls him, "itinerant man") is an outstanding example of a philosophy that is concerned not merely with conceptual and linguistic issues but with the urgent questions we ask, and especially with our need to hope. Marcel excels in his concrete analyses of the attitude of hope. He describes the family community in its temporal and supratemporal aspects and the forgotten virtue of personal fidelity. His essay on Rilke as a witness to the spiritual is especially enlightening.

Maritain, Jacques. *Approaches to God.* Trans. Peter O'Reilly. Westport, CT: Greenwood, 1978.
For humans there are as many ways to approach God as there are wanderings on the earth or paths to the heart. The author tries in this book to mark out some of these ways which, from the point of view of philosophical reflection, seem to be the principal ones, starting with the natural or pre-philosophic knowledge of God, proceeding through the five ways of St. Thomas, and moving toward the use of the practical intellect and the desire to see God.

Marshall, Michael. *Restless Heart: The Life and Influence of St. Augustine.* Grand Rapids: Eerdmans, 1987.
It is ironic, says the author, that while the world of Islam still recognizes Augustine, the great saint of late antiquity (354-430), as "Rumi Kabir," the "Great Christian," many Christians today know scarcely anything about him. St. Augustine has been for too long buried beneath the dust and debris of much brilliant scholarship but kept from speaking, as he always did in life, to the man and woman in the pew. This book grew out of the author's long-standing enthusiasm for the life and work of Augustine—an enthusiasm that was sparked by making a long-awaited pilgrimage to the streets Augustine trod, the cities in which he lived and in a sense continues to live: Hippo, Thagaste, Djemila, Rome, Milan, and Florence. He was accompanied on his trips by the Rev. Charles Bewick, a gifted photographer,. Nearly sixty of his photographs—most in full color—illustrate the text, providing also a pictorial record of the journey. What results is not a picture of an other-worldly saint but of a colorful human being, who was also a decisive figure in the history of the church. This biography releases Augustine, the scholar, from the eclectic environment of scholarship and gives him back to the laity so that we can see him at his best—speaking in church and inspiring the faithful.

McKenzie, John L. *Dictionary of the Bible.* Ann Arbor, MI: Servant, 1992.
This is a one-volume dictionary of the Bible for general use—not necessarily for advanced scholarship. In it readers can find a synthesis of insights that open them to a basic understanding of the scriptures.

Merton, Thomas. *The Ascent to Truth.* San Diego, CA: Harcourt, Brace, 1981.
The ascent to truth is a journey toward the highest summit of knowledge. By showing that this truth is reached in contemplation, Merton presents a brilliant exposition of the doctrine of St. John of the Cross symbolized as the "dark night of the soul."

Merton, Thomas. *Contemplative Prayer.* New York: Doubleday, 1989.
In Merton's words, this book is a practical nonacademic study of prayer—the fruit of several decades of reflection and experience. In his familiar, conversational style, the author illumines the hard realities and upheavals of authentic prayer life as well as the joy, reverence, and expectation that inform it. He is as present to the living traditions

of prayer in the Church as he is to the spiritual inertia and lack of confidence that mark the contemporary Christian's disregard and fear of prayer. It is this combination of personal experience, traditional knowledge, and contemporary sensitivity that makes this study so valuable for spiritual readers.

Merton, Thomas. *Disputed Questions*. San Diego, CA: Harcourt, Brace, 1965.
These essays on the spiritual and social life in today's society range from the absurd in sacred art to a philosophy of solitude. The author focuses on such figures as Boris Pasternak, St. John of the Cross, and the "sixth-century desert Hemingway," St. John Climacus. From their example, the "new mass-man" must reconstruct his own solitude, a solitude in which one will gain the perception and love that is necessary for a valid encounter with others.

Merton, Thomas. *Mystics and Zen Masters*. New York: Farrar, Straus & Giroux, 1986.
In this study of the way of meditation or contemplation in both eastern and western religions, the author attempts to approach Zen as a concrete and lived ontology which explains itself not in theoretical propositions but in acts emerging out of a certain quality of consciousness and awareness. Aspects of the Christian tradition itself are not neglected. The Patristic Age, early monasticism, the English and seventeenth-century mystics, Russian Orthodox spirituality, the Shakers, and Protestant monastic communities are treated either in detail or in passing. The central concern uniting all these essays is to understand various ways in which different traditions have conceived the meaning and method of the way that leads to the highest levels of religious or metaphysical awareness.

Merton, Thomas. *Spiritual Direction and Meditation*. Collegeville, MN: Liturgical Press, 1960.
The first part of this book is addressed to Christian laity and religious, who seek a director or who desire to take full advantage of a guide's wisdom and experience. The director is not to be seen as a problem-solver or as one declaring the holy will of God beyond all hope of appeal, but as a trusted friend who, in an atmosphere of sympathetic understanding, helps and strengthens us in our groping efforts to correspond with the grace of the Holy Spirit, who alone is our Director in the fullest sense of this word. The second part of the book comprises notes on meditation for those who would like to practice it every day.

Merton, Thomas. *The Wisdom of the Desert: Sayings from the Desert Fathers of the Fourth Century*. Boston: Shambhala, 1994.
These sayings have been selected and edited in such a way that their perennial freshness becomes apparent, for the maxims of the first Christian hermits, as Merton explains, have a simple, unassuming wisdom born of a lifetime's striving after God in solitude, poverty, fasting, and prayer. (See Reading Program I)

Merton, Thomas. *Zen and the Birds of Appetite*. Boston: Shambhala, 1993.
This collection of essays about complex Asian concepts shows that there must be a little of Zen in all authentic creative and spiritual experience. The study of Zen is, there-

fore, not a study of a doctrine, still less a polemic about ultimate religious principles; it is simply an attempt to reach the ground of pure, direct experience which underlies all creative thought and activity.

A Monk of the Eastern Church. *Orthodox Spirituality: An Outline of the Orthodox Ascetical and Mystical Tradition.* Crestwood, NY: St. Vladimir's Seminary, 1978.

This book is neither a scholarly history of Orthodox spirituality, nor a far-searching theological treatise on the ascetical and mystical life, nor a description of the psychology of Orthodox mystics, but a short and simple introduction to the first principles of the spirituality of the Eastern Orthodox Church and its great masters, including St. John Chrysostom, St. Basil the Great, and St. Gregory Nazianzen—masters common to East and West. An excellent bibliography is included for further study.

Muggeridge, Malcolm. *Jesus.* San Francisco: Harper, 1976.

Though now a fervent believer in the unique truth and continuing relevance of Jesus, as revealed in the Gospels, in the stupendous drama of the Incarnation, Passion, and Resurrection, the author accepts no sectarian rules and is sceptical about current attempts to make Christianity conform to today's materialist outlook and values. His concern is with the essential significance of Jesus' birth, life, ministry, death, and continuing presence in the world—handed down via traditional Christianity and lived out in its ministers from the simplest to the most sophisticated, from the Apostle Paul and St. Augustine to people like Dietrich Bonhoeffer and Mother Teresa.

Muggeridge, Malcolm. *Something Beautiful for God: Mother Teresa of Calcutta.* San Francisco: Harper, 1986.

The story of Mother Teresa and her religious order emerges from a film the author and his colleagues made in Calcutta. It includes, along with other writings about and by her, the transcript of the author's conversations with this exemplary Christian whose words carry a message to a world hungering for faith, hope, and love.

Mulholland, M. Robert, Jr. *Invitation to a Journey: A Road Map for Spiritual Formation.* Downers Grove, IL: InterVarsity, 1993.

The process of being conformed to the image of Christ for the sake of others is the author's definition of spiritual formation. He thus counters our culture's tendency to make spirituality trivial or merely a private affair between "Jesus and me." His book helps Christians to understand that we become like Christ gradually, not instantly. To encourage the hesitant, he shows how different personalities call for different forms of piety. (Not everyone may be made especially for early morning quiet times!) Finally he reviews the classical spiritual disciples and demonstrates why it is so important for us to undertake our spiritual journey with (and for the sake of) others. All along the way, this spiritual road map is profoundly biblical and down to earth. It is, in the finest tradition of spiritual literature, a vital help to Christians at any state of their journey. In other words, holistic spirituality is a pilgrimage of deepening responsiveness to God's control of our life and being.

Muto, Susan. *John of the Cross for Today: The Ascent*. Notre Dame, IN: Ave Maria, 1991.

This book offers a reliable formative and informative approach to the great mystic's teachings as well as sound, practical wisdom for spiritual living. It guides readers along the way of purgation and illumination to the mountaintop of divine union revealed in *The Ascent*, the primer for all of St. John's writings.

Muto, Susan. *John of the Cross for Today: The Dark Night*. Notre Dame, IN: Ave Maria, 1994.

This book, a sequel to the author's companion text to *The Ascent of Mount Carmel*, gives readers a chance to walk with the saint through the passive nights of sense and spirit, from the caverns of purgation to the dawning of new light and the inner liberation only union with God can bring. It offers, under the watchful eye of St. John, reliable guidelines to contemplative prayer and the startling insight that this way of life is for everyone.

Muto, Susan. *Pathways of Spiritual Living*. New York: Doubleday, 1984; rpt. Petersham, MA: St. Bede's, 1988.

This text integrates original reflections on silence, formative reading, meditation, journal-keeping, contemplative prayer, and action. The author presents in a fresh manner the basic path Christians must follow to find their destiny in life, their peace and joy.

The New Dictionary of Catholic Spirituality. Ed. Michael Downey. Collegeville, MN: Liturgical, 1993.

This volume represents a collaborative attempt in English to take stock of the remarkable developments in church and world since Vatican Council II, but with a specific focus on the reform and renewal of Catholic spirituality that the Council set in motion. Contributors have been collected from various parts of the English-speaking world to produce a reliable theological and pastoral resource that takes into account the importance of ecumenical and interreligious dialogues. The specific concern of the discipline of spirituality is to focus upon the relational and personal (inclusive of the social and political) dimensions of the human person's relationship to the Divine. Also stressed is the relationship between spirituality and biblical theology, systematic theology, moral theology, pastoral theology, and liturgical studies. In planning and organizing the *Dictionary*, each entry of whatever length, stands alone, though cross-references and bibliographies are provided and are listed alphabetically at the end.

Nouwen, Henri J.M. *Pray to Live: Thomas Merton: A Contemplative Critic*. Ligouri, MO: Ligouri Publications, 1991.

An introduction to the life and thought of Thomas Merton, this book aims to uncover the main trends in his richly diverse and productive life in order to help us to understand his commitment to a contemplative critique of self and world. The author hopes that this understanding will lead readers to an attentive meditation on Merton's writings and a continuing search for the contemplative foundation of our own fragmented, restless lives.

Otto, Rudolf. *The Idea of the Holy.* Trans. John W. Haney. London: Oxford University, 1958.
The author claims that religion, before it became "morality touched with emotions," was the emotion itself, or a group of emotions, and it still is. Those emotions, according to Otto, include: the feeling of the uncanny; the thrill of awe or reverence; the sense of dependence, of impotence, or of nothingness; the feelings of religious rapture and exaltation. The author calls these non-rational feelings—the sense of the tremendous, the awful, the mysterious, in short, the "numinous." Religion clearly must accommodate both factors: the numinous and the ethical.

The Oxford Illustrated History of Christianity. Ed. John McManners. New York: Oxford University, 1990.
This richly illustrated book tells the story of Christianity from its origins to the present day. Every aspect of the faith is explored, ranging from Christian interpretations of the historical process to the relations between religious and artistic inspiration. The first section runs chronologically from the earliest Christian communities to 1800. There are chapters on Western Europe in the Middle Ages and on Eastern Christendom, on Christianity and Islam, the Reformation, the Enlightenment, and the expansions of Christianity. The second section is divided by geographical area and covers the period from 1800 to the present day. There are special studies of Britain and Europe, North America, South America, Africa, India and the Far East, and the Orthodox Churches of Eastern Europe. The final section, "Christianity Today and Tomorrow," considers questions of Christian conscience and belief and explores new images of the Christian community, ending with a glimpse of the future of Christianity. The book includes ten maps, a chronology, annotated guides to further reading, and a full index.

Pieper, Josef. *Leisure, The Basis of Culture.* Trans. Alexander Dru. New York: New American Library, 1963.
Leisure is an attitude of mind and a condition of soul that fosters a capacity to perceive the reality of the world. With a series of philosophical, religious, and historical examples, the author shows that the Greeks understood and valued leisure, as did the medieval Europeans. He points out that religion can be born only in leisure—a leisure that allows time for contemplation of the nature of God, a leisure that has been, and always will be, the first foundation of any culture. (See Reading Program II)

Rohrback, Peter-Thomas. *Conversation with Christ: An Introduction to Mental Prayer.* Rockford, IL: Tan Books, 1982.
The present volume is a response to the question, "How can I meditate?" Rather than present a host of "mental gymnastics" that may leave people with the feeling that meditation is only for specialists in religion, the author offers all who wish to deepen their spiritual life the concept of meditation popularized by St. Teresa of Avila, for whom meditation is merely the framework in which one carries on a heart-to-heart conversation with Christ. In her concept of mental prayer, a few simple interior acts are required to stimulate this conversation and sustain it when it starts to lag.

Scholem, Gershom G. *Major Trends in Jewish Mysticism.* New York: Schocken, 1961.
The first solid foundation for the study of Jewish mysticism is laid in this book as the author outlines the movement from its beginnings in antiquity to its latest phase in Hasidism.

Sertillanges, A.D. *The Intellectual Life: Its Spirit, Conditions, Methods.* Trans. Mary Ryan. Washington, DC: Catholic University Press of America, 1987.
This is a discriminating account of the nature and dignity of the vocation of the intellectual life, discussing with a wealth of illustrations and insights such subjects as the virtues of a Catholic intellectual, the organization of life to support creative output, and the spirit of work that aims to preserve the sense of Divine Mystery. (See Reading Program II)

Simmons, Henry C. *In the Footsteps of the Mystics: A Guide to the Spiritual Classics.* New York: Paulist, 1992.
The purpose of this book is to introduce readers to a wide variety of authors whose writings are known collectively as the *Classics of Western Spirituality* because devotional writings of the present day are not enough to nourish the spirit adequately. The author does not intend this book to be used passively. It is not a matter simply of reading what other people have said about these things but of coming to know the spiritual mentors of the ages. Convinced that one's personality type impacts the way one prays, the author also offers a simple personality profile of four "ways" of spirituality. The various authors quoted are then grouped according to these "types" to allow readers to sample both those of kindred spirit as well as those whose approach may seem a bit alien. He also gathers together short, bite-size excerpts from a variety of classical writers, grouping them around timeless human concerns—one's approach to God; the call to love both God and neighbor simultaneously; prayer styles; the meaning of sin and forgiveness; the relationship of body and spirit; and how community fits into all these concerns.

The Study of Spirituality. Eds. Cheslyn Jones, Geoffrey Wainwright and Edward Yarnold. New York: Oxford University, 1986.
This text focuses on the individual devotion of Christians. Spirituality is here defined as a combination of praying and living as practiced both by ordinary believers and by those whose special gifts have led to their recognition as saints. The scope of the current work is enormous—over sixty writers, representing the Anglican, Roman Catholic, Free Church and Orthodox traditions, study the nature and form of individual reverence. The myriad patterns of Christian discipleship that have evolved through centuries in varying cultures are descriptively and analytically discussed. Careful attention is given to the biblical witness; the Greek, Syrian, Russian, Latin and Protestant traditions receive detailed treatment; notice is also taken of the contemporary charismatic and ecumenical movements and the interaction between Christianity and other religions. This exhaustive survey of the history of spirituality is preceded by a theological introduction and concludes with a consideration of some contemporary pastoral issues. Special sections are devoted to spirituality in non-Christian religions and

to present-day spirituality—all providing an invaluable resource for scholars and students of religion and theology, for spiritual counselors, and for anyone who seeks to bring the ephemeral dimension of Christian faith into vivid focus.

Suzuki, D.T. *Mysticism, Christian and Buddhist: The Eastern and Western Way.* New York: Routledge, Chapman & Hall, 1982.

In this comparative study, the author tries to present arguments for his opinion that the Zen Buddhism of the East and the Christian mysticism of Meister Eckhart meet on common ground. He argues that the differences between these faiths are less significant than their similarities. The last section of the book offers a remarkable selection of writings from Japanese mystics.

*Tanquerey, Adolphe. *The Spiritual Life: A Treatise on Ascetical and Mystical Theology.* Trans. Herman Branderis. Westminster, MD: Christian Classics, 1930.

This is an orderly summary of the main questions of the spiritual life presented in manual form and an invaluable sourcebook for spiritual reading. Nearly one fourth of the work is devoted to the fundamental doctrines of the elevation and the fall of man and his redemption through the grace merited by Christ. These pages, together with the remainder of the text, form a practical, devotional point of view and lay a foundation for the study of Christian perfection. The essential characteristics of the "three ways" (purgative, illuminative, and unitive) are stressed in the second part of the treatise. Since dogma is the foundation of ascetical and mystical theology, care has been taken to recall briefly the truths of faith on which the spiritual life rests. The reader will find an excellent bibliography outlining the writings of all major spiritual authors from the Patristic Age, the Middle Ages, and modern times, together with an outline of authors from the main schools of spirituality (Carmelite, Salesian, the French school of the seventeenth century), and related bibliographical information.

Underhill, Evelyn. *Mysticism: A Study of the Nature and Development of Man's Spiritual Consciousness.* New York: Doubleday, 1990.

In this classic study, there are two main divisions: the first, called "The Mystic Fact," explains the relation of mysticism to vitalism, psychology, theology, symbolism, and magic; the second part, "The Mystic Way," describes the awakening, purification, and training of the self in its ascent to the path which leads to the blessedness of the unitive life. The appendix is equally excellent, offering a historical sketch of European mysticism from the beginning of the Christian era to the death of Blake. The bibliography is in four parts, including original works and writings on the lives of the mystics; general works on mysticism; supportive studies from philosophy, psychology, and theology; and texts from the related fields of alchemy and magic.

Underhill, Evelyn. *The Mystics of the Church.* Ridgefield, CT: Morehouse, 1988.

Some of the most creative figures in Christian history are examined in this book which demonstrates that the mystics—those who in some degree experience God directly—are not by nature rebels to authority but its constructive friends who throughout church history have been revitalizers of faith. A portrait of Paul opens the book, not Paul, the theologian and organizer, but Paul, the mystic, upon whose teaching the Church was founded. There follow chapters on every great period of mysticism in the Church, vividly presenting such figures as Cassian, St. Augustine, St. Francis and his disciples, the English medieval mystics, Eckhart and other North Europeans, the two Catherines (of Siena and of Genoa), St. Teresa and St. John of the Cross. Protestant mystics and lesser known figures are shown in historical perspective. For each, the author presents biographical material, emphasizing their beliefs and spiritual struggles and their subsequent efforts to raise the religious consciousness of both churchmen and the laity.

van Kaam, Adrian. *The Dynamics of Spiritual Self-Direction.* Pittsburgh: Epiphany Books, 1993.
This book describes in detail how we can discover the unique self-direction God wants for our lives. The author considers in a richly exemplified text such interrelated topics as self-alienation and call-appreciation; the developmental history of the discovery of the divine direction of one's life; examination of conscience and guilt; self-emergence; and the dynamics of spiritual direction, both in-private and in-common, as practiced in the Church.

van Kaam, Adrian. *In Search of Spiritual Identity.* Denville, NJ: Dimension, 1975.
This book researches the foundations of the spiritual life and deals with the attitudes enabling us to hear the call of our deepest self in Christ. The author develops in an original way the relation between fundamental spirituality and special spiritualities. He describes the science and language of spirituality, the spiritual reading of Holy Scripture, and what he calls the "psychodynamics of spiritual presence." His description of the difference between introspection and transcendent self-presence is especially helpful for spiritual readers. In the concluding chapters of the book, he outlines in detail his project of study and research in formative spirituality.

van Kaam, Adrian. *A Light to the Gentiles: The Life Story of the Venerable Francis Libermann.* Washington, DC: University Press of America, 1985.
This is a fully-documented, universally relevant "psycho-biography" of the Venerable Francis Libermann, founder of the Holy Ghost Fathers and one of the great spiritual leaders of modern times.

van Kaam, Adrian. *Religion and Personality.* Pittsburgh: Epiphany Books, 1991.
This book presents a clear and forceful analysis of all aspects of the religious personality, which has as its basic approach the reconciliation of spiritual and psychological factors as the means of achieving true sanctity. The author first looks at the structure of the religious personality, followed by a straightforward discussion of the necessary components of the religiously-oriented life. He then outlines the development of the personality in a section highlighted by its firm grasp of the difficulties and discouragements encountered in the quest for spiritual perfection. He concludes with a consideration of deviations in the religious personality and those neurotic tendencies that obstruct the development of the religious mode of existence.

van Kaam, Adrian. *The Transcendent Self: The Formative Spirituality of the Middle, Early and Later Years of Life*. Pittsburgh: Epiphany Books, 1991.
This book shows us how to set up a dialogue between our transcendent self and the conflicts experienced in the process of facing mid-life as a formation opportunity. The author makes many practical suggestions for creatively resolving the problems associated with family life and the demands of daily functioning.

van Kaam, Adrian and Susan Muto. *Commitment: Key to Christian Maturity*. Mahwah, NJ: Paulist, 1989.
This book explores what it means to experience in-depth commitment as lay persons in the world. It includes formative teachings on fidelity and daily examples of how to live the threefold path of spiritual deepening. Forming family and community in the Spirit; fostering Christian living in the workplace; and practicing the prayer of presence and other spiritual disciplines as avenues to service and inner fulfillment are some of the themes covered in this rich text.

van Kaam, Adrian and Susan Muto. *Commitment: Key to Christian Maturity, a Workbook and Study Guide*. Mahwah, NJ: Paulist, 1991.
This is a comprehensive presentation of every significant insight in the original text along with guidelines for facilitating individual study and small group discussions. It encourages participation in the light of five working directives: Return to the Message; Reflect upon the Meaning; Relate to Scripture; Record your Dialogue; and Reclaim the Classics.

van Kaam, Adrian and Susan Muto. *The Power of Appreciation: A New Approach to Personal and Relational Healing*. New York: Crossroad, 1993.
The authors share their own and other stories of the difference appreciative living makes in an attempt to alter the painful dissonance we may feel between who we are and the time and place in which we have to live our everyday existence. They offer a new approach to personal and relational healing to anyone who wants to move from dissonant depreciation to consonant appreciation of life and world.

van Kaam, Adrian and Susan Muto. *Practicing the Prayer of Presence*. Mineola, NY: Resurrection Press, 1993.
In explaining this classic way of prayer, the authors' aim is to help us to deepen our personal awareness of God's presence. They bring out the significance of the "sacrament of everydayness" for work, study, and prayer—for the rhythms of action and contemplation that comprise our daily life in the world.

von Balthasar, Hans Urs. *Two Sisters in the Spirit: Thérèse of Lisieux and Elizabeth of the Trinity*. San Francisco: Ignatius, 1992.
Thérèse of Lisieux and Elizabeth of the Trinity, who died at the age of twenty-four and twenty-six, respectively, understood the act of total surrender to the Triune God as the highest possible form of engagement on behalf of the world's salvation. They knew that this calling has to burrow itself into hiddenness even as roots disappear into the ground. Fully agreed on this basic point, Thérèse and Elizabeth engage in an odd

yet fruitful opposition to one another within this common concern. Both devote their lives entirely to the fullness of the faith. The two works that make up the present book reveal that the center of their own and every Christian vocation is to hear and embody the Divine Word in the eucharist of everydayness.

von Hildebrand, Dietrich. *Liturgy and Personality: The Healing Power of Formal Prayer.* Manchester, NH: Sophia Institute, 1992.
The author reflects on the richness of liturgical tradition in the Catholic Church and uncovers the relationship of liturgy and ritual to personality development.

von Hildebrand, Dietrich. *Transformation in Christ.* Manchester, NH: Sophia Institute, 1990.
The path that leads to true holiness, transformation in Christ, is penetratingly analyzed and made eminently applicable for the true follower of Christ in chapters on the desire to change as the beginning of all spiritual growth and on the successive attitudes (Beatitudes) that must be developed by those who strive for Christian perfection. (See Reading Program I)

Waddell, Helen, trans. *The Desert Fathers.* Ann Arbor, MI: University of Michigan, 1957.
The desert has bred fanaticism, frenzy, and fear, but it has also bred heroic gentleness and a transformed life of prayer. The words of those quiet men who in the fourth century founded the desert rule are here translated and introduced with a vivid description of the rich solitude of the desert. (See Reading Program I)

Watts, Alan W. *The Way of Zen.* New York: Random House, 1989.
This book is intended for general readers as well as for more serious students of Zen. It is divided into two parts. The first deals with the background and history of Zen, the second with its principles and practices. The author draws upon, as source material, almost all the studies of Zen in European languages, using both early Chinese records and a number of personal encounters with teachers and students of Zen over more than twenty years. The result is a lucid explanation in western language of Zen in the context of oriental religious history.

III
EDIFYING

Achterhoff, Mary. *Grace in Every Season: Through the Year with Catherine Doherty.* Ann Arbor, MI: Servant, 1992.
This rich seasonal devotional reads like a sampler of the everyday spirituality of Catherine Doherty—a spiritual giant of the twentieth century, who counted Thomas Merton and Dorothy Day among her friends, founded the Madonna House apostolate with her husband, Eddie, and left extensive writings to her spiritual sons and daughters. One enjoys deep insights on prayer and spiritual growth as well as homespun

words of advice on work and family life. Nostalgic entries recall Christmas and Easter customs from Catherine's childhood in the Old Russia of the czars. Whenever Catherine spoke, on whatever topic, her words ultimately reflected one thing: her passionate love affair with God. It was a love affair Catherine lived to the hilt, never counting the cost, one into which she dove head-first every day, on good days and bad, in all the seasons of the year.

Bloom, Anthony. *Beginning to Pray.* Ann Arbor, MI: Servant, 1993.
This is a book for anyone who wishes to speak to God. It is based on talks given by the author to people who had never really prayed. Bloom says we must simply enter into the realm of God and not seek information about prayer. The day when God is absent, when he is silent—that day often marks the beginning of "living prayer." (See Reading Program III)

Bloom, Anthony and Georges Lefebvre. *Courage to Pray.* Third Edition. Crestwood, NY: St. Vladimir's Seminary, 1984.
This is an exploration of prayer as encounter, inner freedom, and being, by two men of prayer: as encounter, because through it we meet God, neighbor, and ourselves shorn of pride and pretext; as inner freedom, for it must be approached without prejudice, humbly, sometimes cautiously but always with courage; as being, for it is not something added on but a being aware of who we are. "It is and remains our deepest truth, even when we walk in darkness."

Bloom, Anthony. *Living Prayer.* Springfield, IL: Templegate, 1975.
The author, whose personal spirituality is rooted in the eastern Orthodox tradition, presents an inspiring book on prayer in which he holds that unless prayer "lives," unless it is linked realistically to action and behavior, it is not genuine prayer.

Bloom, Anthony. *Meditations: A Spiritual Journey Through the Parables.* Denville, NJ: Dimension Books, 1971.
The author follows a path traced by centuries of Christian pilgrims, taking as landmarks for meditation certain passages of the Gospel, notably the parables of the Pharisee and the Publican, the parable of the Prodigal Son, and the parables of the Last Judgment. "At the close of our journey," he says, "we ought to be able to forget ourselves so that we can enter into a vision which transcends us, and at the same time leads us to the complete trust that alone can bring us to a true conversion, to a return to the Lord, to the beginning of a new relationship with him, to our coming home."

Bodo, Murray. *Francis: The Journey and the Dream.* Cincinnati: St. Anthony Messenger, 1988.
This is not so much a biography of St. Francis as a meditation on the life of one who found peace and joy through perfect detachment. This book is the author's own version of pursuing a dream and a journey with the poor man of Assisi. It is a commentary on events of his life, complemented by reflections addressed to anyone who wants to set out on a journey to that peace and joy that surpasses all understanding.

Bodo, Murray. *Tales of St. Francis*. Cincinnati: St. Anthony Messenger, 1988.
This book is the result of the author's fascination with stories. It was through story that he first came to know St. Francis and his early companions. He fell under their spell, their charm and folk-like quality, their multiplicity of styles and viewpoints; and he began to wonder what would be revealed in retelling the stories that have shaped and formed his own life as a twentieth-century Franciscan. Thus began this book, a work of joy, to be sure, yet something more, for storytelling became an act of humility before his spiritual ancestors. The resultant connectedness, the communion with them that he began to experience, became the underlying justification for this book that speaks to something profound within us, some deep desire of the human heart.

Bonhoeffer, Dietrich. *Letters and Papers from Prison*. New York: Macmillan, 1981.
Bonhoeffer's letters show his daily concerns and the enormous warmth and humanity of the young German pastor, who was executed by the Nazis in 1945 for his part in the "officers' plot." References to Bonhoeffer's fiancée and their plans for marriage are included from Bonhoeffer's parents, brothers, sisters, and other relatives. The book also contains hitherto inaccessible letters and legal papers referring to Bonhoeffer's trial and a reminiscence by Karl-Friedrich Bonhoeffer of the time spent in prison by members of his family. These and other pieces—when combined with the historical and theological passages—give aspects of Bonhoeffer's experience a new setting in the context of the war years. Here is an account of the life lived by some conscientious Christians and others at a greater remove from belief, when the dilemma of both an external and an internal destruction came upon them. It was at precisely that point that Bonhoeffer's visions of a future Christianity took shape.

Browne, Sir Thomas. *Religio Medici: Letter to a Friend and Christian Morals*. Ed. Jean-Jacques Denonain. Peru, IL: Sugden, Sherwood, 1990.
This reflection on science and religion by a seventeenth-century physician is not a mere introspective "anatomy" in which the thinker seeks to analyze himself; it is rather a "memorial" intended to record for the author's lifelong use a sum of personal views resulting from temperament and experience. Written at the sober age of thirty by a man who settles down to a grave calling in his native country after years of browsing among books and roaming foreign lands, the text is to some extent the philosophical and spiritual treatment of a thinker who has taken his bearings, grappled with and solved a number of important questions, and who has, on the whole, reached his own final truth, for in front of the failures of human reason, he willingly surrenders himself to the humblest form of faith.

Burrows, Ruth. *Guidelines for Mystical Prayer*. London: Sheed and Ward, 1976.
How could mystical union with God be possible for us! We are far too mediocre and unimportant. Yet it is exactly this weakness of ours that God can use. Anything else would get in the way and hinder him. Here the author clearly speaks from within the great Carmelite mystical tradition, but she develops it in a fresh way. For while we easily imagine that much more natural virtue is necessary before God starts to draw us to union with himself, it is also easy to underestimate the creatively new changes his power then effects in us. The usual images, the ladder, the castle, the mountain, imply

a smooth progress that is false to reality. Here instead we are presented with a pattern of islands, separated from one another by two stretches of barren water, over which no passage can be seen. Each island is a whole world of the spirit, radically distinct from the others. This book should be taken as a starting-point for thought and as a vehicle of the Gospel invitation: Follow me. For, as the author says, "The heart of mysticism is Jesus."

Chesterton, G.K. *Orthodoxy.* New York: Doubleday, 1973.
In these pages the author attempts, through a set of mental pictures rather than in a series of deductions, to state the philosophy in which he has come to believe. He does not call it his philosophy, for he did not make it. God and humanity made it and it made him. He calls this book, "a sort of slovenly autobiography"—one that contains the history of a great mind.

Chesterton, G.K. *St. Francis of Assisi.* New York: Doubleday, 1987.
Rather than treat St. Francis as a figure of secular or religious history, the author has chosen to put himself in the position of an ordinary modern outsider and inquirer who wants to explore what in the life of this poet and lover of God people of all ages have found so admirable and edifying. The saint becomes as real in his eyes as a guest at table; he portrays Francis living and ardent, gracious and bubbling over with joy—the joy that comes of abnegation and perfect love. He believes that the full and final spirit in which we should turn to St. Francis is a spirit of gratitude for what he has done. He understood to its very depths the theory of thanks; he knew that we can best measure the towering miracle of the mere fact of existence if we realize that but for some strange mercy we should not even be here.

*de Chardin, Pierre Teilhard. *Le Milieu Divin: An Essay on the Interior Life.* London: William Collins, Fontana Books, 1964.
If *The Phenomenon of Man* (1959) contained the kernel of Teilhard's scientific thought, this text is the key to the religious meditation that accompanied it. The purpose of this essay on life or on inward vision is to prove that the most traditional Christianity, expressed in Baptism, the Cross, and the Eucharist, can be interpreted so as to embrace all that is best in the aspirations peculiar to our times. The author does not pretend to offer a complete treatise on ascetical theology—only a simple description of a psychological evolution observed over a specified interval of time and space. To him the divine milieu would lose its grandeur and savor if one did not feel so completely swept away in the divine ocean that no initial point of support were left from which one could act.

*de Unamuno, Miguel. *The Agony of Christianity.* Trans. Kurt F. Reinhardt. New York: Frederick Unger, 1960.
The furious struggle to be a Christian is the essence of Unamuno's "agony," poured out in fierce anguish of soul in this confession of faith that bears the burden of so much doubt. Unamuno was convinced that reason was powerless to penetrate the mysteries of faith, yet he thirsted for immortality of soul and for resurrection. His "agony" is almost synonymous with existential despair, rooted in the dialectic of faith versus

reason in which the only way out of the dilemma appeared to be Tertullian's *"credo quia absurdum"* and Kierkegaard's "leap of faith."

Dent, Barbara. *My Only Friend is Darkness: Living the Night of Faith.* Notre Dame, IN: Ave Maria, 1988.

Fully committed Christians, who have advanced far enough in the love of God to enter the night of faith and feel the need for explanation, guidance, and reassurance, will benefit greatly from the insights in this text. Although dealing with a difficult subject, the author writes clearly and readably, making excellent use of parables and images to clarify those things that defy straightforward explanation. She guides readers through the deep purifications endured by the spirit as it is cleansed by God of its sinful inclinations. She examines the variety and intensity of sufferings, upheavals, turmoils, temptations, setbacks, and workings of grace upon the deepest levels of our being, comparing this experience to depth psychotherapy in the way it examines the hidden levels of our being and works to heal old wounds. Drawing heavily on the writings of St. John of the Cross and her own personal experiences of the dark night of the soul, she has produced a powerful book and made a significant contribution to the edifying literature of spirituality.

Doherty, Catherine de Hueck. *Poustinia: Christian Spirituality of the East for Western Man.* Notre Dame, IN: Ave Maria, 1975.

The author, director general of Madonna House and a native of Russia, has the gift of a great and joyous faith and of making the spiritual life a journey, a pilgrimage, which she carries into the Trinity. She speaks of a silence that is the speech and silence of God, of a prayer welling up from the heart of the poor and hungry who have no words for the gift that sustains them. (See Reading Program I)

Donne, John. *Devotions Upon Emergent Occasions Together with Death's Duel.* Ed. Anthony Raspa. Oxford University, 1987.

In 1623, during a dangerous illness, John Donne, then Dean of St. Paul's and already famous for his poems and sermons, wrote the passionate musings on body and soul which comprise these devotions. They are cast in three forms: meditations on the human condition, which reflect each stage of his sickness; expostulations addressed to God in a spirit of inquiry; and prayers. The theme of the devotions—a record of a journey through the valley of the shadow—brings out all of Donne's special characteristics: his preoccupation with sin and death; his acuteness of psychological analysis; his keen awareness of the tension between his soul and the world ("...never send to know for whom the bell tolls; it tolls for thee"); the originality of his wit; the troubled and sometimes lurid power of his imagination.

Elchaninov, Alexander. *The Diary of a Russian Priest.* Trans. Helen Iswolsky. Second Edition. Crestwood, NY: St. Vladimir's, 1982.

While being deeply rooted in the spiritual and ascetic traditions of the Orthodox church, Father Alexander was at the same time closely in touch with the intellectual movements of his day. He came to the priesthood through the gates of secular culture after experiencing to the full the tensions and difficulties of Russia's tragic destiny. His book is of particular value to people trying to live the Christian life in an increasingly secular and materialistic world. He writes on themes of universal concern: on sin, marriage, the meaning of art, facing illness and death. Prior to his own death from a tragic illness in 1934, he worked for a time as a teacher and in social work. He was ordained comparatively late in life after passing through the harrowing experience of the 1917 revolution.

Evely, Louis. *That Man Is You.* Trans. Edmond Bonin. Westminster, MD: Christian Classics, 1966.
Starting from the basic principle that God's love and revelations are actual, the author views our whole relationship with God as something positive and so devastatingly direct that we wonder why we did not draw these conclusions ourselves. His meditations on scripture reading, love of neighbor, forgiveness, the life of faith, and lay spirituality, among others, are so simple yet so revolutionary that they can alter the course of our entire life.

Farrell, Edward J. *The Father is Very Fond of Me.* Denville, NJ: Dimension Books, n.d.
As its title indicates, this book emphasizes the love of the Father for each person in the concrete circumstances of his or her individual life with all its difficulties and problems, its anguish, frustration and possibly even despair.

Farrell, Edward J. *Prayer Is a Hunger.* Denville, NJ: Dimension Books, n.d.
The author shares with us his experiences of retreat and prayer in the desert and constantly challenges us to see familiar things in a new light. Prayer is a journey, a path, created only by walking it. The journal is a way into prayer while penance and communion are Christ's way of praying in us. (See Reading Program I)

Farrell, Edward J. *Surprised by the Spirit.* Denville, NJ: Dimension Books, n.d.
The author speaks of God and divine things in an immediate, personal way—out of lived experience. He tells of the place which prayer, the beatitudes, and the gifts of the Holy Spirit should occupy in our daily lives and offers a wealth of insights into what constitutes the real challenge of Christian life today: the likelihood of our being surprised by the Spirit.

Foster, Richard J. *Prayer: Finding the Heart's True Home.* San Francisco: Harper, 1992.
This is a warm, compelling, and sensitive primer on prayer helping us to understand, experience, and practice it in its many forms—from the simple prayer of beginning again to unceasing prayer. The author clarifies the prayer process, answers common misconceptions, and shows the way into prayers of contemplation, healing, blessing, forgiveness, and rest. The author comes to see that God is big enough to receive us as we are. We do not have to be bright, or pure, or filled with faith, or anything. That is what grace means, not only that we are saved but that we live by it and pray by it. Prayer can move us inward into personal transformation, upward toward intimacy with God, and outward to minister to others. Thus we are led by the author beyond questions to a deeper understanding. We are brought closer to God, to ourselves, and to one another.

Frank, Anne. *The Diary of a Young Girl.* Trans. B.M. Mooyaart-Doubleday. New York: Bantam, 1993.
From the diary of Anne Frank comes the true story of how she, her sister, and her parents, along with four others, shared a small hiding place in an old building in Amsterdam during the Nazi occupation. Her sensitive account of their experiences and feelings during the two fearful years before their discovery gives to readers of all ages a vivid portrait of the unfolding of a soul that is as attractive as it is intimate and inspiring. (See Reading Program III)

Guardini, Romano. *The Lord.* Trans. Elinor Castendyk Briefs. Washington, DC: Regnery Gateway, 1978.
These meditations do not attempt to recount Jesus' life in any chronological order or logical sequence; rather they reverently pause before this or that word or act, ready to learn, adore, obey. This book is no scientific documentation of history or theology; its chapters are the spiritual commentaries of some four years of Sunday services undertaken with the sole purpose of obeying as well as possible the Lord's command to proclaim him, his message, and his works.

Hammarskjöld, Dag. *Markings.* New York: Ballantine, 1985.
These entries from Hammarskjöld's diary provide what he calls the only true "profile" that can be drawn. Though he wrote for himself and not for the public, the resulting collection can be read, in his words, "...as a sort of *white book* concerning my negotiations with myself—and with God." (See Reading Program II)

Herman, E. *Creative Prayer.* Santa Fe: Sun, 1993.
In these pages the author endeavors with clarity, depth, simplicity, and mystical insight to elucidate the meaning and value of prayer as a creative process whereby people who pray, and their world, are made anew. Written before World War I, this simple and practical book on how to pray has become a devotional classic, addressing the reader on such topics as the ministry of silence, the discipline of meditation, the journey from self to God, and the apostolate of prayer.

Herrigel, Eugen. *Zen in The Art of Archery.* Trans. R.F.C. Hull. New York: Random House, 1989.
This book is the illuminating account of the experience of a German philosopher who came to Japan and took up the practice of archery as an avenue to the understanding of Zen. In the process he discovers that if one really wishes to be master of an art, technical knowledge is not enough. One has to transcend technique so that the art becomes an "artless art" growing out of the unconscious. In the case of archery, the archer and the target are no longer two opposing poles, but one reality. The archer is unconscious of himself as the one who is engaged in hitting the bull's-eye which confronts him. This state of unconsciousness is realized only when, completely empty and rid of ego, he becomes one with the perfection of his technical skill. In this lively experiential account of the author's own struggles with Zen in the art of archery, the western reader may find a more familiar manner of dealing with what often seems a strange and unapproachable eastern experience.

Hillesum, Etty. *An Interrupted Life: The Diaries of Etty Hillesum, 1941-1943.* Trans. Arno Pomerans. New York: Pantheon, 1983.
Etty Hillesum lived in Amsterdam and kept her journals in the dark years from 1941-1943, years of occupation and genocide. Despite all the accounts we have of the Nazi era, the diaries of this startlingly modern young woman—the adult counterpart of Anne Frank's *Diary of a Young Girl*—speak to us of that period in a voice we have never heard before. Etty's diaries are intimate and immediate, full of details about her daily routine, her walks along the city's canals, the smell of jasmine in her yard, the view outside her bedroom window. We come so close to her that we can see through her eyes. The Holocaust enters her diary obliquely, as it must have entered her life. As Etty struggles to keep her humanity intact in the face of an increasingly menacing environment, as she searches in herself for an authentic response to the elemental questions forced upon her by history, we witness her transformation from a worldly, pleasure-loving young woman into a person capable of perceiving the starkest realities of life, confronting the deepest moral questions unflinchingly and with near-mystical intensity and compassion. The diary breaks off in September 1943, on the eve of her deportation to Auschwitz, where she died at the age of twenty-nine.

Holmes, Marjorie. *I've Got to Talk to Somebody, God.* New York: Bantam, 1982.
These prayers for everyday living—for every age—are penned by a woman with a sure, loving touch. She is a wife and mother absorbed in the pains and joys of daily existence: housework, friendship, family, and all the things a woman has to face during the day. Her hope is that this book will lead readers to a renewed discovery of the tremendous release and comfort to be found in our living, loving presence to an always listening God.

Houselander, Caryll. *The Reed of God.* Westminster, MD: Christian Classics, 1987.
In contemplating Our Lady, we find the way to intimacy with God, for Mary is the reed of God who utters infinite music. She reveals the secret of our nearness to Jesus in the ordinary life we all live.

Jesus According to... Contemporary Answers to Jesus' Haunting Question "Who do you say that I am?". Edd Anthony (ed.). Boston: St. Paul Books and Media, 1992.
Jesus once asked his followers, "Who do you say that I am?" A simple question, but throughout the centuries philosophers, theologians, scripture scholars, popular authors, and even enemies of Christ have offered a multitude of answers. All who have walked with the Lord know that Jesus reveals himself in a deeply personal way as our relationship with him grows and matures. This book presents interviews with twenty contemporary disciples who share their personal knowledge and experience of Jesus. Their stories reflect trials and struggles, but they also show how our personal relationship with the Lord can transform our everyday life.

Keller, Phillip. *A Shepherd Looks at Psalm 23.* Grand Rapids, MI: Zondervan, 1988.
From the unique perspective of first-hand knowledge of shepherding, the author presents a true-to-life devotional commentary on one of the best-loved passages in the Bible. Equipped with a shepherd's experience and insight, he leads and prods the reader

to the greenest pastures of discovery and the coolest waters of fulfillment hidden in the "Shepherd Psalm."

Kelly, Thomas R. A *Testament of Devotion.* San Francisco: Harper, 1992.
These devotional essays by a devout Quaker offer perennial wisdom on the light within, holy obedience, the blessed community, the eternal now and social concern, and the simplification of life.

Kierkegaard, Søren. *Purity of Heart Is To Will One Thing: Spiritual Preparation for the Office of Confession.* Trans. Douglas V. Steere. New York: Harper, 1956.
Kierkegaard wrote this edifying discourse for men and women of all ages who seek to be drawn into water that is "70,000 fathoms deep" where life depends not upon half-measures but upon faith. He spoke to "that solitary individual" who, instead of escaping into double-mindedness, chose to come face-to-face in purity of heart with his or her destiny, with his or her vocation, with the eternal God who has singled us out and called us by name.

Kierkegaard, Søren. *Works of Love: Some Christian Reflections in the Form of Discourses.* Trans. Howard and Edna Hong. New York: Harper, 1964.
In this work, we are conducted into the inmost secrets of Christian love. The two parts into which it is divided deal respectively with the great commandment, "Thou shalt love the Lord thy God...and thy neighbor as thyself," and with the so-called love verses in First Corinthians, Chapter 13. In this book, Kierkegaard comes closer than anywhere else to giving an authentic, non-pseudonymous picture of his faith. Christian love is not the same as exotic love and friendship; rather it is an ethico-religious love in which love's immediacy is dethroned and one sees the beloved and the friend as also, and most profoundly, neighbor.

*Lefebvre, Perry D. (ed.). *The Prayers of Kierkegaard.* Chicago: University of Chicago, 1956.
Over 100 of the prayers of Kierkegaard are gathered in this volume from his published works and private prayers, illuminating not only his own life of prayer but also serving as a book of personal devotion for Christian readers today. Following this collection is a reinterpretation by the author of the life and thought of Kierkegaard, who is revealed as fundamentally a religious thinker. In this new perspective, readers discover Kierkegaard's inner sense of vocation and his lifelong concentration on the problem and possibility of becoming a Christian.

Lewis, C.S. *The Four Loves.* New York: Walker, 1986.
Though other authors from Ovid to St. Bernard, from St. Paul to Stendhal, have examined affection, friendship, eros, and charity, few have seen as well as Lewis how each merges into the other, how one can even become another without losing sight of the necessary and real differentiation between them. The author knows the peculiar values of each disposition without supposing any to be all-in-all or self-sufficient. He discerns as well the deceptions and distortions which can render the first three (the natural loves) dangerous without the sweetening grace of charity—the divine love which must

be the sum and goal of all. This anatomy of love is illuminated by the author's gifts of immediacy, lucidity, and aptness of expression and illustration.

Lewis, C.S. *Mere Christianity*. New York: Walker, 1987.
A tone of friendly familiarity pervades these essays, originally given as radio talks. Whatever the reader believes, Lewis makes clear that religion—accepted or rejected—is something extremely serious, demanding the entire energy of one's mind. He uses the term "mere" Christianity to undercut denominational differences and to return to the spirit of Christ. In plain language, one's question should never be, "Do I like that kind of service?" but "Are these doctrines true? Is holiness here? Does my conscience move me toward this? Is my reluctance to knock at this door due to my pride, or my mere taste or my personal dislike of this particular door-keeper?" The main message to remember is this: "Look for yourself, and you will find in the long run only hatred, loneliness, despair, rage, ruin, and decay. But look for Christ and you will find him, and with him everything else thrown in."

Lewis, C.S. *Surprised by Joy: The Shape of My Early Life*. New York: Walker, 1986.
This book tells the story of how the author passed from atheism to Christianity. How far the story matters to anyone but himself depends on the degree to which others (for example, we readers) have experienced what he calls "joy." This experience—so vital in the process of his conversion—is in the end seen as valuable only as a pointer to something other and outer. Since becoming a Christian, the author confesses he is no longer prone to mistake a signpost for the journey's end.

Lindbergh, Anne Morrow. *Bring Me a Unicorn: Diaries and Letters of Anne Morrow Lindbergh, 1922-1928*. New York: Harcourt, Brace, 1993.
This first volume of diaries and letters draws a vivid picture of the author's formative years as a school girl and college student and as a member of a highly gifted, remarkably close-knit family, one that was loving but also constantly challenging her to perform on the highest levels. The volume culminates in the meeting between her and Charles Lindbergh and the development of their extraordinary relationship. The reader watches a self-doubting, shy young girl grow into a clear-sighted and courageous woman of captivating charm, humor, and spirit.

Lindbergh, Anne Morrow. *Hour of Gold. Hour of Lead: Diaries and Letters, 1929-1932*. New York: Harcourt, Brace, 1993.
This second volume of diaries and letters covers the years of Anne's early married life when the shy, sheltered, introspective girl is thrown suddenly into the world of action of her famous husband. Then, in a reversal of terrifying swiftness, the hour of gold turned into the hour of lead with the tragic kidnapping and murder of Charles Lindbergh, Jr. How Anne is able to overcome bitterness and despair and build a new life following the birth of her second son involves the reader in a memorable essay on the nature of grief and the miracle of a new lease on life.

*Lindbergh, Anne Morrow. *Locked Rooms and Open Doors: Diaries and Letters, 1933-1935*. New York: Harcourt, Brace, 1974.
This third volume of diaries and letters finds the Lindberghs faced privately with the problems of readjusting their personal lives while publicly making spectacular strides in pioneering air travel. The diaries give us an immediate sense of the hardships endured by a young woman sharing the exploits of a singularly determined and vigorous man. Her struggles with fear, homesickness for her child, and the varied discomforts of travel touch the reader as much as her description of the rewards of flying, adventure and equal partnership in a demanding task. This volume covers the kidnapping trial and its inevitable tragic re-enactment of the past and ends with a sea voyage from America to England that will change the lives of the Lindberghs once more.

*Lindbergh, Anne Morrow. *The Flower and the Nettle: Diaries and Letters, 1936-1939*. New York: Harcourt, Brace, 1976.
This fourth volume of diaries and letters describes a period of private peace that Anne calls "the happiest years of my life." The Lindberghs move to England, their third son is born, and they find themselves in the stimulating atmosphere of private and governmental circles in the years immediately preceding World War II. The reader receives a volume not only of considerable historical value in the factual sense but also a personal history of two young Americans immersed in the beauty and complexity of Europe.

Lindbergh Anne Morrow. *Gift from the Sea* New York: Random House, 1991.
The setting of this highly acclaimed book is the seashore; the time, a brief vacation that lifted the author from the distractions of everyday existence into the sphere of meditation. As the sea tosses up its gifts—shells rare and perfect—so the mind, left to its ponderings, brings up its own treasures of the deep. The shells (channeled whelk, double-sunrise, argonauta) become symbols for the aspects of life this active woman is contemplating: the restlessness, pressures, and demands we face today; the hunger for leisure and silence; the call to inner peace and integration. (See Reading Program III)

Maloney, George A. *Inward Stillness.* Denville, NJ: Dimension Books, 1976.
This book is an invitation to accept God's call issued in Psalm 46, "Be still and know that I am God." Its main theme is the mystery of deeper communion with God as illumined by insights from eastern Christian writers on the "prayer of the heart." Insights are drawn also from the Far East as well as from modern psychology and the whole area of expanded consciousness to present a form of deep interior prayer that can lead readers into God's mystery and help them to become better human beings. The author presents prayer as a continual process of inner healing that allows us to be attuned to God's "uncreated energies" and to pray unceasingly as we find God in our own human situation.

Merton, Thomas. *The Seven Storey Mountain.* San Diego: Harcourt, Brace, 1990.
Merton's autobiographical account of his conversion to Catholicism and his decision to enter a contemplative order marks the beginning of a lifelong journey to union with God.

Metz, Johannes Baptist. *Poverty of Spirit.* Trans. John Drury. Paramus, NJ: Newman, 1968.

Assent to God starts with a sincere assent to ourselves, to our innate poverty. The poverty of the human condition, freely accepted, is what the author means by poverty of spirit. In prayer we taste the dregs of our poverty, while professing the richness of God. Only then do we become truly rich. (See Reading Program I)

Muto, Susan Annette. *Approaching the Sacred. An Introduction to Spiritual Reading.* Denville, NJ: Dimension Books, 1973.

The author sees spiritual reading as a means to create an inner atmosphere in which God may reveal himself to us as we are and where we are. She discusses common obstacles that prevent us from disposing ourselves to the possible emergence of the Sacred in and through those words of the spiritual writer that happen to touch us here and now as well as facilitating conditions that ready us for this listening. She also offers the reader a series of living and touching examples of her own way of spiritual reading that represent a personal application of the art and discipline to which this book is an introduction.

Muto, Susan. *Blessings that Make Us Be: A Formative Approach to Living the Beatitudes.* New York: Crossroad, 1982; rpt. Petersham, MA: St. Bede's, 1990.

This text takes a fresh look at the spirituality of the Beatitudes as "attitudes of being" that undergird true spiritual living. The author reflects on each saying from the perspective of the purgative, illuminative, and unitive stages of growth and suggests ways to foster Christ-like being and doing in the world.

Muto, Susan. *Celebrating the Single Life: A Spirituality for Single Persons in Today's World.* NewYork: Doubleday, 1982; rpt. New York: Crossroad, 1989.

This breakthrough book suggests concrete ways and means by which single men and women can exist as fully human, fully Christian people. It encourages persons single by choice and by circumstance to participate in a joyful way in the transformation of themselves and the world around them. The author takes a deep, personal look at such topics as solitude vs. loneliness; silence, service, and caring for others as single persons; resisting the workaholic phenomenon; single parenting; and loving family members while living singly.

Muto, Susan Annette. *The Journey Homeward: On the Road of Spiritual Reading.* Denville, NJ: Dimension Books, 1977.

This book is one of the author's seminal publications on formative reading. It incorporates eternal truths of the life of the spirit into the language of today under the inspiration of the *Collected Works of St. John of the Cross.* The author combines reflections on the saint's insights with original prayer-poems that aim to guide laity, religious, and clergy on their journey homeward to God.

Muto, Susan. *Meditation in Motion.* New York: Doubleday, 1986.

This text disproves anyone who thinks "There isn't enough time to pray or meditate as I'd like" by showing that there are many openings in daily life, like those of waiting, that can be used for quiet thinking and reflection. It suggests in an accessible and anecdotal style at the end of each chapter brief spiritual exercises that encourage the art and discipline of "meditation in motion" and at moments of stillness.

Muto, Susan. *Renewed at Each Awakening: The Formative Power of Sacred Words.* Denville, NJ: Dimension Books, 1979.
The author points to the power that resides in sacred words to fashion our personal lives in relation to others and God. She shows how certain key words like peace, emergence, rhythm, suffering, solitude, and silence have the power to make us be and become who we are.

Muto, Susan Annette. *Steps Along the Way: The Path of Spiritual Reading.* Denville, NJ: Dimension Books, 1975.
A sequel to *Approaching the Sacred*, this text offers further insight into the art and discipline of spiritual reading as well as a lively and perceptive study of the ways men and women have struggled to find God in their daily lives, such as the way of unknowing, the way of imitation, the way of spiritual childhood, and the way of ceaseless prayer.

Muto, Susan. *Womanspirit: Reclaiming the Deep Feminine in our Human Spirituality.* New York: Crossroad, 1991.
This autobiographical and narrative text reaffirms the daily, lived spirituality of women—in the workplace, at home, in church, and in society. It highlights the way *womanspirit* holds opposites together with creative energy and offers excellent guidelines to women reflecting on their own faith story.

Nouwen, Henri J.M. *Out of Solitude: Three Meditations on the Christian Life.* New York: Walker, 1986.
These meditations, first given as sermons, take up the themes of our life in action and solitude, community and care, patience and joy. (See Reading Program II)

Nouwen, Henri J.M. *Reaching Out: The Three Movements of the Spiritual Life.* New York: Doubleday, 1986.
This book is written in the conviction that the quest for an authentic Christian spirituality is worth the effort and pain involved, since in the midst of this quest we can find signs of hope, courage, and confidence. The author sees our spiritual ascent occurring in three essential stages: the movement from loneliness to solitude (our relationship to ourselves); the movement from hostility to hospitality (our relationship to others); and the final, most important movement, from illusion to prayer (our relationship to God). (See Reading Program III)

Nouwen, Henri, J.M. *With Open Hands.* New York: Ballantine, 1987.
This is an experiential description of prayer with texts and photos that trace a movement from the resistance of clenched fists to the resilience of open hands. (See Reading Program III)

Nouwen, Henri J.M. *The Wounded Healer: Ministry in Contemporary Society.* Garden City, NY: Doubleday, 1979.
What does it mean to be a minister in contemporary society? This question has been raised during the last few years by many men and women who want to be of service but find the familiar ways crumbling. In this book the author proposes a far-reaching approach to making familiar ways more effective and relevant in our fragmented culture. Noting that modern man is above all suffering man, wounded by a lack of hope, by loneliness, and by the predicament of rootlessness, he suggests that ministers today can only help others deal with these problems if they are willing to go beyond their professional roles and leave themselves open to fellow human beings with their own wounds and suffering. The author then offers concrete methods by which ministers can use this creative, dialectical approach to bring freedom and liberation to those afflicted by the major anxieties of our times. He considers finally how this personal inter-relationship affects the life of ministers themselves, those lonely persons, wounded so they can be of help to others.

Palmer, Parker J. *The Active Life: A Spirituality of Work, Creativity, and Caring.* New York: Harper & Row, 1990.
This book is the result of the author's strange journey toward the knowledge that he is not a monk, that he values spontaneity more than predictability, exuberance more than order, inner freedom more than the authority of tradition, the challenge of dialogue more than the guidance of a role, eccentricity more than staying on dead center. His aim is to show that Christian spirituality ought not to involve a withdrawal from the world and from our own human vitality. The author's own attempts to adapt monastic practices to daily living ultimately failed, in part because he was unable to deny that life is impelled to action and participation. This is the path that sustains for him a spirituality as vital as any other. As a result, this book articulates a bracingly vital, down-to-earth spirituality for persons who live busy active lives—at home or at work, in the arts or politics, when serving others or working for social change. Integrating contemplation with action, he defines a spirituality that "takes us down...into the deep place where self and world and spirit intersect and transformation can begin." This approach teaches us not to fear our activist energies but to embrace, encourage, and channel them.

Pascal, Blaise. *Pensées.* Trans. A.J. Krailsheimer. New York: Viking Penguin, 1966.
Pascal owes his fame as a religious philosopher to his *Pensées,* extraordinary notes for a projected defense of Christianity. These meditations, by a scientific genius in mathematics, display a passionate craving for God in a man who has the mind to conceive and the sensibility to feel the disorder, futility, and meaninglessness of life and suffering unless one can find peace in the Divine Mystery, who alone can satisfy his whole being.

Prather, Hugh. *Notes to Myself: My Struggle to Become a Person.* New York: Bantam, 1990.
Comprising this edifying text are cogent and incisive short paragraphs, personal yet universal, about feelings and experiences, behaviors and relationships. These serve both

as beginnings for exploration of our own religious experiences and as thoughtful, insightful reminders that everyday life is much richer than we might at first think.

The Prayers of John Donne. Ed. Herbert H. Umbach. Albany, NY: NCUP, 1962.
Here, in convenient format, is a selection of Donne's unique prayers edited from the earliest sources. Donne's profound insight into the problems posed by religious belief and his mastery of the language combine to produce works equally remarkable for intellectual power and verbal dignity. His prayers in verse and prose express the ceaseless yearning of our soul for a peace that passes understanding. These words reveal Donne's heart intimately communing with the heart of God.

Puls, Joan. *Every Bush Is Burning: A Spirituality for Our Times.* Mystic, CT: Twenty-Third Publications, 1985.
The Exodus encounter between Moses and Yahweh images the threefold message of this book. All of creation is alive with the presence of God. The earth and all within it are sacred. We are called to respond to God's call to bring ourselves and all people into the kingdom of God. The author develops an incarnational approach to spirituality in the light of such themes as searching, conflict, obedience, freedom, and change. She draws upon contemporary events, personal stories, the world of nature, and the world of contemplation. The book also explores the links between personal spirituality and an ecumenical and global world view. In short, hers is a vision of life that recognizes the centrality of the transcendent desire of humans to discover and name the connections between body and spirit, person and world, the inner life of prayer and the outer life of ministry and relatedness.

Smith, Bradford. *Dear Gift of Life: A Man's Encounter with Death.* Pendle Hill Pamphlet, #142. Lebanon, PA: Sowers Printing, 1965.
Having received confirmation that he has cancer and is going to die, the author knows the months left of his life are final. The message comes home to him, strange and yet familiar, that he is mortal. He prepares himself to live day-by-day in such a way that no joyful secret of existence will be missed. Without a trace of self-pity, he decides to live as if he were already in eternity. In this pamphlet he pours forth, in utterances of piercing simplicity, his sense of what the world is like when time has turned its back to us.

Steere, Douglas V. *On Being Present Where You Are.* Pendle Hill Pamphlet, #151. Lebanon, PA: Sowers Printing, 1967.
The author seeks to discover in a series of interrelated reflections what it means to be present and what genuine presence implies. To be present can, on one level, mean to be located at a given point in space and time but, more than this, it refers to the quality of being "all there"—bodily, mentally, spiritually, not living in "interior emigration." The author relates his remarks to the Quaker emphasis on prayer as an ever available door by which we come into God's presence. (See Reading Program II)

Stein, Edith. *The Hidden Life: Hagiographic Essays, Meditations, Spiritual Texts.* Trans. Waltraut Stein. Washington, DC: ICS, 1992.
This is an inspiring collection of Edith Stein's shorter spiritual writings, many available for the first time in English translation. They were composed during her final years, often at the request of her Carmelite superiors. Here the noted philosopher, Catholic feminist and convert shares her reflections on prayer, liturgy, the lives of holy women, the spirit of Carmel, the mystery of Christian vocation, and the meaning of the cross in our lives. Two basic thoughts direct her thinking, ground her turning to the contemplative life, and support her activities in the service of the church. One of these is the *love of the cross*, which gives our being, unstable because of change and transience, an ultimate security in the constant primal Ground of Eternal Being. The other is *atonement*, which breaks through the disastrous and endless cycle of our own and others' debt of shame in the face of God's goodness and justice and so achieves reconciliation and peace. These essays, poems, and dramatic pieces offer readers a unique glimpse into the hidden inner life of one of this century's most remarkable women. We who are already sufficiently distanced from her in time to listen in on her silence with understanding are permitted to read between the lines of her writings the messages of a soul who had mystical experiences, and probably also a presentiment of the meaning of her life and suffering for posterity.

Storr, Anthony. *Solitude: A Return to the Self.* New York: Ballantine, 1988.
In exploring the connection between solitude and the creative personality, the author offers fascinating and original portraits of such geniuses as Beethoven, Henry James, Goya, Wittgenstein, Kipling and Beatrix Potter, all of whom were alone—either by choice, by circumstance or by enforcement—at crucial periods in their lives. It is not only the great who benefit from solitude. The text also examines the uses that ordinary people make of this sustaining power in times of bereavement and depression, in escaping from the pressures of daily life, in communing with a higher power through prayer, and in finding and expressing their deepest selves. Beautifully and insightfully written, illuminated with superb quotations drawn from world literature, and carefully documented with references to the works of the most important psychologists, this is a book that speaks to a profound and heretofore profoundly neglected human need: the need to be alone.

ten Boom, Corrie, with John and Elizabeth Sherrill. *The Hiding Place.* Great Britain: Hodder and Stoughton, 1971.
Cornelia ("Corrie") ten Boom's worldwide ministry of comfort and counsel began in the concentration camp where she had found, as the prophet Isaiah promised, "a hiding place from the wind, a covert from the tempest...the shadow of a great rock in a weary land." This amazing woman lived the uneventful life of a spinster watchmaker, little dreaming as she cared for her older sister and their elderly father that a world of high adventure lay just around the corner. When Corrie ten Boom stood naked with her sister, Betsie, watching a concentration camp matron beating a prisoner, she realized that it was for the souls of the brutal Nazi guards that she and her sister were to pray. Both women had been sent to the camp for helping Jewish people return to Holland. Christ's spirit and words were their guide; it was his persecuted people they tried to

save—at the risk of their own lives; it was his strength that sustained them through times of profound horror. In and through deep prayer and selfless mortification, Corrie learned and helped others to handle separation; get along with less; stay secure in the midst of insecurity; forgive; deal with difficult people; face death; love one's enemies; and keep the faith even when evil seemed to triumph. As she said, "Every experience God gives us, every person he puts in our lives, is the perfect preparation for the future that only he can see."

ten Boom, Corrie. *Tramp for the Lord.* New York: Pillar Books, 1974.
After her time in prison, the entire world became Corrie ten Boom's classroom. Since Word War II, she traveled around it twice, speaking in more than sixty countries on all continents. During these three decades she became familiar with airports, bus stations, and passport offices. She enjoyed hospitality in a great number of homes and slept in more than a thousand beds. Always in her travels, even in the ninth decade of her life, she carried in her hand and in her heart the Bible—the Word of Life—bursting with Good News. This sequel to *The Hiding Place* reveals that the life of a Christian is an education for higher service. Looking back across the years of her life, Corrie can see the working of a divine pattern, which is the way of God with his children. This book teaches us that faith is like radar which sees through the fog—the reality of things at a distance that the human eye cannot see. Faith enabled this much-loved evangelist to walk the world—a tramp for the Lord—and to learn her lessons in God's great classroom. By sharing her journey, we learn something of the divine pattern in God's plan for us, too.

Thoreau, Henry David. *Walden* and *Civil Disobedience*. Ed. Sherman Paul. Boston: Houghton Mifflin, 1957. See also Henry David Thoreau, *Walden and Other Essays.* New York: Alfred A Knopf, 1993.
Thoreau writes a factual yet imaginative account of his two-year stay at Walden Pond where he went to experience first-hand the glory of nature and the mystery of its Source, to drink deeply of the marrow of life lest he miss the details of its unfolding and, like the rest of us, live and die in quiet desperation. *Civil Disobedience* is an essay on the principles that prompted him not to pay his town tax, even though this act meant imprisonment. Thoreau knew that his refusal to pay the tax was futile, but his purpose in doing so was to undermine expediency by introducing a standard higher than social right and authority—the moral law. (See Reading Program III)

Underhill, Evelyn. *Practical Mysticism.* New York: Ariel, 1986.
The author's purpose in this brief, inspiring text is to introduce the methods, experiences and practices of mysticism to those who have no prior knowledge of the subject. Here we find in clear terms what mysticism is and what it has to offer the average person—how it helps us solve our problems, increase our efficiency, and harmonize prayerful living with the duties and ideals of the active life. Readers who savor this text can learn how the practice of mysticism may enrich their daily living in countless unexpected ways.

van Breemen, Peter G. *As Bread That Is Broken.* Denville, NJ: Dimension Books, 1974.
The author writes in depth with a bold simplicity about the God of love who loves us as he loves his own Son and whose entire will is to save us. The love of God, like the love and acceptance of other persons, makes us into the unique persons we are meant to be. The heart of prayer is thus the realization of God's love for us and our response to God in total surrender. (See Reading Program II)

van Breemen, Peter G. *Called by Name.* Denville, NJ: Dimension Books, 1976.
This book can be read as a living pilgrimage of faith and love, a search for the God who called us into existence, a passageway to total trust in Christ, who has placed us in the actual situation of our daily life with its pain and darkness, its difficulties, its gnawing doubts and troubles. The author centers his attention on prayer rooted in life and treats prayer as an unmasking of all the idols and pretenses of our life that distract us from our basic search for God. Should we ever exclude God from our lives, we would lose our name, our identity; we would no longer be addressed by others because we would no longer abide in that which makes us truly human. These chapters also contain inspiring ideas on the real meaning of contemplation and the vitality of Christian life; on the role of the Blessed Virgin; on the heroism of accepting the ordinary routines of everyday life. Special attention is paid to the restlessness that identifies life today; to the real meaning of celibacy; to the commission given to each Christian to meet the needs of our time.

van Kaam, Adrian. *Personality Fulfillment in the Spiritual Life.* Denville, NJ: Dimension Books, 1966.
The life of the spirit is a life of presence inspired by the sacredness of people, of things, and of events in their deepest reality. On this basis, the author builds his description of self-emergence as a movement from implicit to explicit religious presence. The reader learns to recognize the obstacles to religious presence in contrast to the "threefold path" of obedience, chastity, and poverty of spirit as well as to identity addiction as a counterfeit of religious presence. This text also includes an inspiring reflection on the quality of religious presence that characterizes the Christian. (See Reading Program II)

van Kaam, Adrian. *Personality Fulfillment in the Religious Life.* Denville, NJ: Dimension Books, 1967.
This sequel to *Personality Fulfillment in the Spiritual Life* shows the value of religious life for the individual and for humankind as a whole. Especially valuable for the general reader is the author's description of the dynamics of encounter and its possible distortions and blessings in community life. Helpful also is his stress on the place of religious life in the culture as a center of "value radiation."

van Kaam, Adrian. *The Vowed Life.* Denville, NJ: Dimension Books, 1968.
The author takes up the theme of the "threefold path" of obedience, respectful love, and poverty begun in two previous volumes: *Personality Fulfillment in the Spiritual Life* and *Personality Fulfillment in the Religious Life.* Here he develops the dynamics of the life-call and the meaning of commitment and consecration to a lasting lifestyle. All

readers will benefit from his description of obstacles to religious living in western culture and the contrasting healing power of the vows. (See Reading Program III)

van Kaam, Adrian. *Looking for Jesus*. Denville, NJ: Dimension, 1978.
The author discovers many spiritual insights contained in the first half of the Farewell Discourse of Jesus in St. John's Gospel. His other book, *The Mystery of Transforming Love*, addresses the second half of the same discourse. He approaches both prayerfully and practically spiritual truths that apply concretely to our daily life as Christians.

*van Kaam, Adrian. *The Mystery of Transforming Love*. Denville, NJ: Dimension, 1982.
This book offers a meditative sequel to *Looking for Jesus*. It traces the formative implications of the final part of the Farewell Discourse in St. John's Gospel, with additional original prayer-poems.

van Kaam, Adrian. *The Music of Eternity: Everyday Sounds of Fidelity*. Notre Dame, IN: Ave Maria, 1990.
This book demonstrates that faithfulness to daily events leads to a vibrant life filled with peace and joy, that fidelity to God's "epiphany" or "manifestation" among us allows us to hear the "music of eternity." The author shows in poetry and prose that fidelity, with its rewards and struggles, is a key to living a deeply committed spiritual life in, with, and through the gift of God's grace.

van Kaam, Adrian. *The Roots of Christian Joy*. Denville, NJ: Dimension Books, 1985.
This text presents a series of meditations, on the necessary conditions for fully human, fully spiritual living. It assures us that transcendent joy can flourish even in the midst of pain, suffering, and conflict

van Kaam, Adrian. *The Woman at the Well*. Pittsburgh: Epiphany Books, 1993.
The author uses the Gospel narrative of the meeting of Jesus with the Samaritan woman as a creative and vivid illustration of how Bible reading can be done in an interesting, refreshingly different and spiritually helpful way. He highlights traditional as well as contemporary scriptural insights into one aspect of the event and ends each chapter with an inspiring prayer-poem that summarizes the lesson Jesus wants to teach.

*van Kaam, Adrian, Bert van Croonenburg, and Susan Muto. *The Emergent Self*. Denville, NJ: Dimension Books, 1968.
The authors offer a vibrant and joyful series of short, inspiring meditations on the meaning of human life in relation to the self, the self and others, the self and community, and the self and reality.

van Kaam, Adrian, Bert van Croonenburg, and Susan Muto. *The Participant Self*. Denville, NJ: Dimension Books, 1969.
A sequel to *The Emergent Self*, this text explores one of the most fundamental rhythms of the spiritual life, that of participation and recollection. This is the rhythm of being intimately involved in the communal dimension of experience and yet of being able to

dwell in recollected presence on the meaning of that experience. There are complementary chapters on communion and retreat, labor and leisure, interest and detachment, giving and receiving, and many more aspects of the underlying rhythm of participation and recollection. (See Reading Program III)

van Zeller, Hubert. *The Current of Spirituality.* Springfield, IL: Templegate, 1970.
The world's needs should not be ignored in favor of prayer; rather prayer should be the source of what Christians do in the world. The relation of prayer to success and failure, to happiness and suffering, to work and maturity is the topic of this text. It presents not merely a solid argument for prayer but, more importantly, a practical guide for those who wish to deepen their own Christian life and experience. (See Reading Program II)

von Balthasar, Hans Urs. *Prayer.* Trans. A.V. Littledale. New York: Paulist, 1967. See also Hans Urs von Balthasar, *Prayer.* Trans. Graham Harrison. San Francisco: Ignatius, 1986.
This presentation of prayer enables us at the same time to unlearn the artificial and to relearn the natural ways of prayer. By reminding us of what we are—creative, redeemed and ransomed, adopted sons and daughters of God and co-heirs of Christ —the author makes clear that the whole thrust of our being is toward God. Whether we know it or not, whether we like it or not, we are directed toward the Divine with every bit of life and breath in us. Down to the darkest depths of our being, we yearn for union with God. Prayer is an expression of that yearning; it is most essentially our effort to communicate with God. It, therefore, cuts across the usual divisions of prayer into mental and vocal, meditative and contemplative, individual and public, private and liturgical, to become as real to us as the air we breathe.

*von Dürckheim, Karlfried Graf. *Daily Life as Spiritual Exercise: The Way of Transformation.* Trans. Ruth Lewinneck and P.L. Travers. New York: Harper & Row, 1972.
Daily life seems to be an obstacle to true spiritual growth, but this is only true if one does not know how to use it. More and more people today are looking for new ways to escape the increasing suppression of their essential being by the modern way of life, as evidenced by interest in spiritual exercises such as Yoga and Zen Buddhism. The aim of this book is to show that daily life, especially its routines, can be used as a perpetual opportunity to practice the "Way" and can itself be lived as a spiritual exercise. The author believes that all genuine seekers, regardless of creed or religion, will be helped by the text to open new doors to the freedom of transcendental reality, which manifests itself within our worldly existence.

Weil, Simone, *Waiting for God.* Trans. Emma Craufurd. San Bernardino, CA: Borgo, 1991.
In this collection of letters and essays, we meet one of the truly spiritual writers of this century. She speaks of the problems of belief in the vocabulary of the unbeliever, of the doctrines of the church in the words of the unchurched. Quite suddenly God had taken her as she was—a radical agnostic, contemptuous of religious life and practice as

she observed it. She always clung to her sense of being an "apostle to the Gentiles," planted at the intersection of Christianity and everything that is not Christianity. She refused to become a convert, she would not even be baptized, and it is her unique position, at once in and out of institutional Christianity, that determines her special role and meaning: to remind those to whom religion means comfort and peace that Christ promised not only peace but also the sword and that his own last words were a cry of despair.

Woolman, John. *The Journal of John Woolman and A Plea for the Poor.* Magnolia, MA: Peter Smith, n.d.

The journal or spiritual autobiography was the characteristic literary expression of Quakerism in its first two centuries, and Woolman's journal is one of the finest examples of this genre. He captures the flavor of Quaker culture in which the focus is on ordinary life at home, at meetings, and in community—a life that was an artistic creation as beautiful in its simplicity and proportion as was the architecture of its meeting houses. Its distinguishing marks were not dogmas but practical testimonies for equality, simplicity, and peace. In his quiet way John Woolman reforged these testimonies, tempered them in the stream of love, and converted them once again into instruments of social reform.

IV
RECREATIVE

Alighieri, Dante. *The Divine Comedy.* Trans. Charles H. Sisson. New York: Oxford University, 1993.

Dante's masterpiece combines the qualities of thorough understanding, fidelity, resourcefulness, and poetic feeling. It not only conveys profound and perennial meaning; it resounds with melodic intricacies and passionate yet controlled emotion.

Aucassin and Nicolette and Other Medieval Romances and Legends. Trans. Eugene Mason. New York: AMS, n.d.

The tales brought together in this volume (including, among others, *Aucassin and Nicolette, Our Lady's Tumbler, The Jew Who Took as Surety the Image of Our Lady, The Priest and the Mulberries)* are drawn from the literature of the Middle Ages, and in many cases were written in thirteenth-century France, the work of monks, court poets or professional minstrels. These stories illustrate some of the most important ideas that concerned the medieval mind: devotion to the Blessed Sacrament and the Virgin Mary, the elaborate code of courtly love, and the mystical ceremonies of knighthood.

Benson, Herbert. *The Relaxation Response.* Avenal, NJ: Outlet, 1993.

In this carefully researched book, the author shows how a simple meditative technique evokes the Relaxation Response, which can bring one inner peace and calm in an era when more people than ever are suffering from high blood pressure, heart attacks and strokes. The technique can easily be learned and practiced a few times a day, either at home, in the office, or even on the way to work. Whether one is profoundly religious or a non-believer, the Relaxation Response is congenial, based as it is on age-old wisdom common to the religious and meditative practices of almost all cultures of East and West. In addition to lowering blood pressure and reducing anxiety, laboratory studies have shown that the Relaxation Response helped people to give up smoking, decrease their drinking, and stop taking pills and narcotics. The book also offers an interesting commentary on the popular TM (Transcendental Meditation) movement.

Bolt, Robert. *A Man for All Seasons.* New York: Random House, 1990.
This is a play in two acts about Sir Thomas More, who endured imprisonment and eventual death rather than succumb to the demands of King Henry VIII to place the Church under the jurisdiction of Parliament and the king. Such staunch support infuriated the king who, until More's "betrayal" had regarded him as one of his best friends. More emerges in this excellent drama not only as a Christian saint but also as a hero of true selfhood.

Bernanos, Georges. *The Diary of a Country Priest.* Trans. Pamela Morris. New York: Carroll & Graf, 1984.
In this fictional presentation of priestly attitudes, functions, and tribulations, the reader enters into the life of a small French parish. The phases of the diarist's life recorded here remind us in their simplicity and saintliness of Joan of Arc, symbol of France, for whom the author has a high regard. The diary describes in great detail the impressions and activities of the young priest over a period of one year. His purpose in keeping the diary is to maintain frankness with himself in his relationships with his parishioners and in his service to God. Vowed as he is to foster the human and spiritual advancement of his parish despite his own limitations, he does not waver in his faith, even when he learns that his own life is coming to an end.

Connolly, Myles. *Mr. Blue.* Altamont, NY: Richelieu Court, 1990.
Mr. Blue is the story of a mystic who has visions, dreams up glorious projects, flies kites, squanders a fortune, exults in brass bands, lives in a packing box, preaches God, love, and mercy, and practices charity to the extent of dying to save a friend. Blue is hilariously and outrageously happy, so happy that he is an affront to the "normal person" who allows poverty or discomforting business to make him unhappy. He is a modern St. Francis, a spy for the Eternal, sent here to show us our immense and futile follies.

Craven, Margaret. *I Heard the Owl Call My Name.* Cutchogue, NY: Buccaneer, 1991.
A young minister is sent by his bishop deep into the seacoast wilds of British Columbia to a parish of Kwakiutl Indians called Kingcome. The Indians live in an inlet village and take their sustenance from the sea and from the forest. The bishop had not told him this, but the priest has only two years left to live. Among these vanishing Indians, Mark Brian learns enough of the meaning of life not to fear death. Through his faith and humanity, he becomes part of the village, of the Indian life itself, and a witness to their rituals and beliefs. Then, on a cold winter evening, when he hears the owl in the forest call his name, he understands and accepts what is going to happen.

de Saint Exupéry, Antoine. *Flight to Arras.* Trans. Lewis Galantière. Alexandria, VA: Time-Life, 1991.

The author's flight to German-held Arras in wartime forces him to face possible loss of life, to feel the flow of time, running like sand through his fingers. He finds that the human spirit is not concerned with objects (the business of our analytical faculties) but with the significance that relates objects to one another—with their totality, which only the piercing eye of the spirit can perceive. He learns also that God created us to be responsible for one another and gave us hope as a virtue no hardship can destroy.

de Saint Exupéry, Antoine. *The Little Prince.* Trans. Katherine Woods. New York: Harcourt, Brace, 1993.

This is a wise and enchanting fable, loved alike by children and adults. The little prince lived alone on a tiny planet no larger than a house. He owned three volcanoes, two active and one extinct. He also owned a flower, unlike any flower in the galaxy, one of great beauty in which he took "inordinate pride." It was this pride that ruined the serenity of the little prince's world and started him on the interplanetary travels that brought him to earth, where he learned finally, from a fox, the secret of what is really important in life.

*de Saint Exupéry, Antoine. *Wind, Sand and Stars.* Trans. Lewis Galantière. New York: Harcourt, Brace, 1967.

The author combines the exciting realism of air adventure through the treacherous passes of the Pyrennes, above the Sahara, along the snowy ramparts of the Andes, with the lyrical prose and soaring spirit of a poet who sees in the immediate givens of reality transcendent depths of meaning.

Dillard, Annie. *Pilgrim at Tinker Creek.* New York: HarperCollins, 1988.

This is a mystical excursion into the natural world in which the author, an explorer with a poet's eye, sees the fecundity of nature charged and transfigured with an uncanny flare that can knock the beholder breathless. (See Reading Program I)

Dostoyevsky, Fyodor. *The Brothers Karamazov.* Trans. Constance Garnett. New York: David McKay, 1992.

Dostoyevsky's last novel is at the same time the most mature and complete of his works. Within the framework of a study of heredity, it analyzes the relationships between fathers and sons in all their peculiar outcroppings of hatred, aversion, and consanguinity. It is also a portrayal of different psychological types—from that senile lecher, Karamazov, to his ascetic son, Aloysha; from that other son, Ivan, the intellectual anarchist, to the saintly monk, Zossima. The plot moves on several planes and unfolds as a mystery story. Old Karamazov is murdered, and the circumstances of his death are so strange as to involve all his sons—not only the actual murderer but also those who, though innocents *de facto*, had nevertheless borne murderous intentions at heart and are therefore morally guilty. The Grand Inquisitor, the hero of the legend Ivan narrates to Aloysha, offers the philosophical key to the whole novel, showing how monstrously mixed up good and evil are in us, and that seekers after God may be said to be at their best when they formulate their doubts and conflicts, when they raise the problems of guilt, of our place in the universe, of good and evil. We fail when we want to take the easy way out or settle for an easy consolation.

Egan, Harvey. *An Anthology of Christian Mysticism.* Collegeville, MN: Liturgical, 1991.
A thirty-year love affair with the Christian mystics, beginning in 1960, led to the birth of this book. The author, an electrical engineer who had read almost nothing religious since his grammar school catechisms, read his first mystical text, St. John of the Cross' *Dark Night of the Soul.* The book stirred him deeply and convinced him that the church's pastoral life suffers from benign neglect of its enormously rich Christian mystical heritage because the mystics could be seen as pioneers of a transformed and totally authentic humanity. They are powerful amplifiers of the experience of God; of the faith, hope and love in every human heart; and of the full flowering of Christian life. In due course his teaching and priestly experience led to a strong desire to put together his own anthology. The result is this excellent selection of the works of fifty-five mystics and/or mystical theologians from Origen to Karl Rahner. While the author admits that there is no substitute for reading the primary texts, he believes that everyone should read Pascal's experience of God as fire; Francis of Assisi's "Canticle of Brother Sun"; Julian of Norwich's hazelnut vision; and Merton's remarks about "masked contemplatives." Reading these texts not only refreshes us inwardly; it also convinces us that mystical literature has literary value and that it can also be life-changing.

Eiseley, Loren. *All the Strange Hours.* Magnolia, MA: Peter Smith, 1983.
In this autobiographical narrative, the author covers the span of time from his formative, adventurous years into the most creative period of his life as a writer and a thinker. He concludes with the expression of his philosophy as a scientist and humanist. Devastatingly honest, but always with the selective eye of a man who sees beyond the obvious to the mystery beneath all things, the text can be, by turns, as harsh as the badlands Eiseley once knew as a fossil hunter or as tender as the lover of simple people, nature, and animals he became.

Eiseley, Loren. *The Immense Journey.* New York: Random House, n.d.
With an unusual blend of scientific knowledge and imaginative vision, the author tells a universal human story and reveals, in the process, life's endless mysteries. He departs from his own experiences in their immediacy into meditations on the distant past, wandering on the paths and byways of time and then returning to the present. While this text is a work of science, it surely is also literature, delving with the delicate touch of poetry into the mysteries of nature and human existence. (See Reading Program III)

Eiseley, Loren. *The Night Country.* Magnolia, MA: Peter Smith, 1988.
In a book of poignant beauty, the author, a paleontologist by profession, draws out of the shadows of a strange and lonely boyhood and the darkness of forgotten civilizations, a tale of haunting fears and hopes, failures and triumphs. Through the life of one man is woven the story of all of us in all times who know the night country even when the sun is shining. (See Reading Program I)

Eiseley, Loren. *The Unexpected Universe.* New York: Harcourt, Brace, 1972.
In a highly personal book, the author writes about a naturalist's response to the unexpected and symbolic aspects of the universe, ranging from seeds and the hieroglyphs on shells to such disparate subjects as the microscopic components of our bodies, the Ice Age, lost tombs, the goddess Circe, city dumps, and Neanderthal Man. Through all these perspectives, with a blend of scrupulous scholarship and magical prose, runs the theme of desolation and renewal in our planet's history, evoking in author and readers alike a sense of wonder.

Eliot, T.S. *The Complete Poems and Plays, 1909-1950.* New York: Harcourt, Brace, 1952.
The collected poems of T.S. Eliot (1909-1935) include *Prufrock* (1917), *Poems* (1920), *The Waste Land* (1922), *The Hollow Men* (1925), *Ash Wednesday* (1930), the *Ariel Poems,* unfinished poems, *Choruses from "The Rock," Four Quartets,* and *Old Possum's Book of Practical Cats.* The plays include *Murder in the Cathedral, The Family Reunion,* and *The Cocktail Party.*

Eliot, T.S. *Four Quartets.* New York: Harcourt, Brace, 1968.
This poem in four movements is the last major verse Eliot wrote and the culminating work in his distinguished career as a poet. It is a poetic and religious masterpiece.

Emerson, Ralph Waldo. *Selections from Ralph Waldo Emerson: An Organic Anthology.* Ed. Stephen E. Whicher. Boston: Houghton Mifflin, 1972.
The aim of this volume is to shift our attention from Emerson as a teacher, preacher, and writer of essays to the "active soul" to be found in his neglected masterwork, the journals. He stressed not his doctrine but his spirit and method, his enactment of the self-created role of the "thinking Man." For Emerson, thinking was not only the contemplation of final Truth; it was the daily encounter of an active mind with its environment. It was not a special activity but life itself.

Everyman and Medieval Miracle Plays. Ed. A.C. Cawley. Boston: Charles E. Tuttle, 1991.
This important collection contains the famous morality play *Everyman* and a completely new selection of fifteen biblical pageants derived from the Latin liturgical drama of the medieval Church. These pageants are just as religious in origin and inspiration as the Church architecture, painting, and sculpture of the Middle Ages. Most of these are Corpus Christi pageants or guild pageant short plays acted by the trade guilds as episodes of the Corpus Christi cycle, which dramatizes the whole Christian scheme of salvation.

Franck, Frederick. *Zen Seeing, Zen Drawing: Meditation in Action.* New York: Bantam Books, 1993.
Seeing/drawing is a way of contemplation by which all things are made new, by which the world is freshly experienced at each moment. It is the opposite of looking at things from the outside or taking them for granted. "What I have not drawn I have never really seen," says the author, and he goes on to show that "once you start drawing an

ordinary thing, a fly, a flower, a face, you realize how extraordinary it is—a sheer miracle...." For him seeing/drawing is a spiritual discipline, a "Zen method" admirably suited to the active temperament of western people. Even if a reader has never thought of drawing, even if he or she claims to be one of those people who cannot draw a straight line, this book may make one want to pick up a pencil and begin *to see.*

Friedman, Meyer and Ray H. Rosenman. *Type A Behavior and Your Heart.* New York: Alfred A. Knopf, 1974.
In this important book, two medical doctors explain their startling finding that the primary cause of heart disease is a distinct behavior pattern, a particular complex of personality, lifestyle, and attitude, which they call "Type A" behavior. This pattern of behavior bears an extremely close correlation to the incidence of heart disease—indeed according to their findings more than ninety percent of heart attack victims are "Type A's." The pattern is marked by a compelling sense of time urgency—"hurry sickness"—aggressiveness and competitiveness, usually combined with a marked amount of free-floating hostility. "Type A's" engage in chronic, continuous struggle against circumstances, against others, against themselves. Though the authors do not make this correlation, they indirectly reveal many obstacles to spiritual living in their description of the "Type A" pattern.

Frost, Robert. *Selected Poems.* Avenal, NJ: Outlet Books, 1992.
A poet of wit and wisdom, Robert Frost has written on almost every subject, but his central topic is humanity. His poetry lives with particular vitality because it expresses living people. His poems are not *about* people; they *are* the people who live and work and tell stories with the freedom of common speech and without "company manners."

Greene, Graham. *The Power and the Glory.* New York: Viking Penguin, 1991.
In a particular Mexican state where the church has been outlawed and priests driven underground, there is still one priest, Father Montez, who moves from village to village carrying on the work of the Church by administering the sacraments and saying masses. Though in a moment of weakness (for he was a "whiskey priest" who would "do anything for a drink") he had fathered a child by a woman in an inland village, he was still determined to carry on the work of the Church as long as he could, not because he wanted to be a martyr, but because there was no one else to do it. In the evening of the day on which he died (shot without benefit of the Church's last rites), another priest made his way, in secret, into the town where the execution took place. Father Montez was dead but not the Church's presence.

Hawkins, Peter. *The Language of Grace: Flannery O'Connor, Walker Percy, and Iris Murdoch.* Cambridge, MA: Cowley, 1983.
This book explores the huge problem of religious communication today: how to portray the transforming action of the divine in human life for readers who no longer have a powerful sense of God, much less a world of symbols by which to understand religious experience. Turning to the work of three contemporary novelists—Flannery O'Connor, Walker Percy, and Iris Murdoch—the author shows their diverse attempts to portray the reality of grace across the chasm of unbelief. Among the works he con-

siders closely are O'Connor's *A Good Man is Hard to Find*, Percy's *The Second Coming*, and Murdoch's *Word Child*. Although his focus is literary, the issues his study raises concern the crisis in our present spiritual and imaginative lives. He presents three novelists struggling to bridge the gap between ourselves and those mysterious realities about which we can no longer talk.

Herbert, George. *The Poems of George Herbert*. London: Oxford University, 1961. See also *George Herbert: The Country Parson, The Temple*. Ed. John N. Wall, Jr. *The Classics of Western Spirituality*. NewYork: Paulist, 1981.
Herbert's poetry is recognized as a supreme contribution both to poetry and to the literature of devotion. Herbert speaks to God like one who really believes in him and whose business in the world is most with God. The desire to know that one is serving God, that one is being of use and is not an unprofitable servant, is the "last infirmity" of the religious mind—what Herbert calls "this deare end...my power to serve thee." The source of struggle in *The Temple*, his best known work, does not lie in a conflict between the world and a call to serve God at his altar, but in the difficulty of learning to say truly in any calling, "Thy will be done." His best poems are those in which his art enables him, whether he speaks to us or to his God, to speak in the accent of absolute sincerity, in the tone of one opening his heart to a friend.

Hesse, Hermann. *Siddhartha*. Trans. Hilda Rosner. Cutchogue, NY: Buccaneer Books, 1983.
The spirituality of East and West meet in this novel that matches deep human wisdom with a rich and colorful imagination. As a youth, the young Indian Siddhartha meets the Buddha but cannot be content with a disciple's role: he must work out his own destiny and solve his own doubt—a tortuous road that carries him through the sensuality of a love affair with the beautiful Kamala, the temptation of success and riches, the heartache of a struggle with his own son, to final renunciation and self-knowledge.

Hopkins, Gerard Manley. *Poems and Prose*. Ed. W.H. Gardner. Baltimore, MD: Penguin, 1953.
The permanent worth of Hopkins as a writer is threefold. Firstly, he is one of the most powerful and profound of our religious poets and also one of the most satisfying of the so-called "nature poets" in English; secondly, he is one of the acknowledged masters of original style—one of the few strikingly successful innovators in poetic language and rhythm; thirdly, the publication of much of his prose—notebooks, journals, letters, sermons—has given us a body of autobiographical and critical writing which, apart from its broader human interest, sheds needed light on the development of a unique artistic personality, on those interests which inform and shape his poetry—namely, his religion, his personal reading of nature, his love of people, and his critical approach to art.

Hurnard, Hannah. *Hinds' Feet on High Places*. Ed. Darien Cooper. Shippensburg, PA: Destiny Image, 1993.
This is an allegory of Much-Afraid, who follows the Shepherd to the High Places where perfect love casts out fear. The High Places of victory and union with Christ

cannot be reached by any mental reckoning or ascetical discipline as such. The only way to go there is by learning to accept day by day the actual conditions and tests permitted by God, by a repeated laying down of our own will and an acceptance of the Divine Will as it is presented to us in the people with whom we have to live and work and in the things which happen to us.

Jacobson, Edmund. *You Must Relax.* Chicago: National Foundation for Progressive Relaxation, 1991.
In this famed text, a medical doctor presents a practical guide to reduce the strain of modern living. Writing for the average reader, the author describes the nature and source of bodily tension in easily understood terms. The text gives a well-defined method of *active* relaxation, which tells basically how one can learn to relax even while doing work and keeping busy. Related topics include sleep, relaxing the mind, and frequent problems associated with the digestive and circulatory systems.

Kazantzakis, Nikos. *Report to Greco.* Trans. P.A. Bien. New York: Simon & Schuster, 1975.
The *Report* is a mixture of fact and fiction—a great deal of truth and fancy in which the author tells not just what he did but rather what he wanted to do: to go ever higher, to ascend and reach the summit he promised himself he would climb before abandoning the tools of labor because night had begun to fall. He writes in the introduction: "...in these pages you will find the red track made by drops of my blood, the track which marks my journey among men, passions, and ideas. Every man worthy of being called a son of man bears his cross and mounts his Golgotha. Many, indeed most, reach the first or second step, collapse pantingly in the middle of the journey, and do not attain the summit of Golgotha, in other words the summit of their duty: to be crucified and resurrected, and to save their souls. Afraid of crucifixion, they grow fainthearted; they do not know that the cross is the only path to resurrection. There is no other path."

Kazantzakis, Nikos. *St. Francis.* Trans. P.A. Bien. New York: Simon & Schuster, 1971.
Writing a work of fiction about St. Francis, which for the author is truer than truth itself, he relates how overwhelmed he was by love, reverence, and admiration for Francis, hero and martyr. For him the saint is the model of the dutiful man, the man who by means of a ceaseless, supremely cruel struggle succeeds in fulfilling the highest obligation, something higher even than morality or truth or beauty: the obligation to transubstantiate the matter which God entrusted to us and turn it into spirit.

Lewis, Sinclair. *Babbitt.* Cutchogue, NY: Buccaneer Books, 1987.
George Babbitt lives in a small town in the United States, but it could be a small town anywhere. He is a hustling prosperous property dealer—a dull little man blown about by prejudice and ignorance, "extremely married and unromantic." But Babbitt dreams. He dreams about beauty, love, romance, and an unattainable girl who loves him. George Babbitt, the realist, seeks happiness in the unreality of dreams. This thoroughly conventional businessman lives in a respectable suburb, owns the right kind of car, gives agreeable little dinner parties for the right sort of people, and belongs to all the appropriate clubs and lodges. Efficiency and productivity are the twin gods of his

existence, but piercing through that defensive armor is the vague awareness of some indefinable lack, a loneliness, a restless discontent. Babbitt's prosaic lifestyle is heading for a big change.

Lynch, John. *A Woman Wrapped in Silence.* New York: Paulist, 1976.
Written like a profoundly dramatic, narrative, and contemplative poem, this book presents a touching and human portrait of the woman who was the mother of Christ. The story of Mary mounts in beauty and power as her life proceeds from Bethlehem to Calvary where the woman wrapped in silence becomes magnificent in her own last agony and tremendous majesty. (See Reading Program II)

*Martz, Louis L. (ed.). *The Meditative Poem: An Anthology of Seventeenth-Century Verse.* New York: Doubleday, 1963.
The meditative poem (exemplified in the writings of Robert Southwell, John Donne, George Herbert, Henry Vaughan, and others) bears a close relation to the practice of religious meditation in that era. The relationship is shown by the poem's own internal action, as the soul or mind engages in acts of interior dramatization. The poet accuses himself; he talks to God within the self; he approaches the love of God through memory, understanding, and will; he sees, hears, smells, tastes, and touches in imagination the scenes of Christ's life as they are represented on an inward, mental stage.

Mauriac, François. *Woman of the Pharisees.* New York: Carroll & Graf, 1988.
This highly regarded novel is a dramatic example of Mauriac's unshakable faith in our ability to overcome evil, his extraordinary gift of revealing the struggle between flesh and spirit, and his phenomenal aptitude for literally getting inside his characters. His savage portrayal of Brigitte Pian—a "good" woman who believes herself to be rationally self-righteous and passionately noble but who, in reality, is spiritually derelict, domineering, and narrow-minded—is masterful. Combining impeccable artistry with compassionate awareness of human weakness, he etches a realistic tableau of characters that will haunt the reader's memory long after one finishes the book.

McGinley, Phyllis. *Saint-Watching.* New York: Crossroad, 1982.
In this amusing book, the author succeeds in rescuing the saints from their pillars and plaster niches, honoring them instead as earthly heroes. Here, among many, are St. Paul, Augustine of Hippo, Ignatius of Loyola, Francis Borgia, Blessed Katherine Drexel of Philadelphia, and the bizarre Simeon Stylites. In "Heroes with Halos," she concludes on an ecumenical note by citing three who she thinks would have received halos, had they belonged to a church that grants them: John Wesley, Florence Nightingale, and Gandhi.

Milton, John. *Paradise Lost and Paradise Regained.* New York: Airmont, 1968.
Paradise Lost, Milton's great epic narrative, tells the story of the revolt of Satan and his banishment from heaven and the fall of man and his expulsion from Eden. *Paradise Regained* explores man's regaining of grace through the sacrifice of Christ.

Milton, John. *Samson Agonistes.* Ed. F.T. Prince. London: Oxford University, 1957.
Milton saw in the life of the Hebrew champion—as he would interpret it in this verse drama—a fitting emblem of his own active life during the interval, his "race of glory" and his "race of shame." *Samson* must be read first as a self-sufficient work of art and only secondarily as having autobiographical overtones. The poem is perhaps Milton's most convincing presentation of the theme of temptation. In *Samson,* the hero's life and death include both fall and redemption, and redemption comes, as in *Paradise Regained,* through temptations overcome. Milton's ideal of heroic poetry takes intransigence of judgment, firmness of faith and the acceptance of both action and suffering as its foundation.

Michener, James A. *The Source.* New York: Fawcett Book Group, 1986.
The author weaves a fascinating story around a fictional archeological site in Israel called Makor, whose name, meaning the "source" refers to the hidden spring of water that accounts for the constant human habitation at this spot. The time element extends from 12,000 years ago to the days when the modern state of Israel was established. Fifteen "layers" of civilization are identified by artifacts and potsherds, beginning with Ur, a cave dweller. Around these "finds" amplified by the scriptural and historical records of actual persons and events, the novelist weaves a story for each period. The book sheds light on the history of Judaism and the movement of humankind in general to search for and live in obedience to the Sacred. Told with remarkable erudition and moving detail, the novel is not only entertaining; it is a monumental and imaginative study of the ancient and new state of Israel.

Paton, Alan. *Cry, The Beloved Country.* Cutchogue, NY: Buccaneer Books, 1991.
This is a beautiful and tragic story of racial unrest centering on the crime, arrest, trial, and execution of Absalom, son of the Reverend Stephen Kumalo. In searching for his son, the poor Zulu clergyman also searches for answers to the meaning of his life and the fate of his people.

*Péguy, Charles. *Basic Verities: Prose and Poetry.* Trans. Anne and Julian Green. Chicago: Henry Regnery, 1965.
One of France's greatest modern poets, a convert to Catholicism and a patriot, Péguy writes with a simplicity of language that defies translation. What characterizes the speeches in this collection, particularly those spoken by God the Father, is a sort of supernatural common sense—an internal rhythm of thought which lends them majesty and pathos. Charity and intellect go hand in hand. Intellect is always ready to efface itself before charity which is, after all, nothing but a superior form of understanding. His prose and poetry reveal that the deepest spiritual truths are approachable only through the heart and can be grasped only when they are embodied in the realities of this world.

Potok, Chaim. *The Chosen.* New York: Fawcett Book Group, 1987.
This absorbing novel captures the warmth and pathos of dealings between fathers and sons, between generations and religious traditions among Hasidic and Orthodox Jews in modern Brooklyn. An understated odyssey from boyhood to manhood, it offers

sympathetic insight into the variety and profundity of Jewish tradition and heritage. It is as interesting a story as it is a social commentary.

Potok, Chaim. *In the Beginning*. New York: Fawcett Book Group, 1986.
The narrator of this novel, set in the Bronx, is a brilliantly gifted Orthodox Jewish boy, who eventually accommodates himself to modern life. His search for the essential truth of the human condition is couched in a recapitulation of the Book of Genesis from creation to the flood. David is the son of Jewish immigrants from Poland, educated the hard way by events of the late twenties and thirties that convulsed his people and the world. Though ordained a rabbi, bit by bit he becomes a secular scholar of the Bible in an effort to discover a more comprehensive foundation for his belief. The novel brings to the fore the problem of maintaining religious faith in an apparently meaningless world. There is no easy solution to this journey of a soul. It seems in the mind of the author that ambiguity is perhaps the only response of an intelligent religious sensibility to life.

Potok, Chaim. *My Name Is Asher Lev*. New York: Fawcett Book Group, 1984.
In this novel the author traces the making of a great contemporary painter from the time when an ordinary Brooklyn boy responds to the first stirrings of a commanding talent to the triumphant exhibition that wins recognition for his art and marks his final, heartrending estrangement from the world in which he was born. Asher's extraordinary talent leads him away from his family and his faith into a painful maturity and a perilous success.

Potok, Chaim. *The Promise*. New York: Fawcett Book Group, 1985.
In this novel, the two boys of *The Chosen* are portrayed through the crucial testing time of their young manhood. The author offers readers a subtle, warm, suspenseful sojourn into the mirth and misery of growing up with a fierce concern for moral righteousness.

Prayers and Poems of Inspiration. Nashville: Ideals, 1992.
In the 2,000 years since its advent, Christianity has spread across the globe and found unique expression in every culture it has touched. One thing, however, has remained constant: Christians of all eras, all nations, and all churches have recognized their need for prayer. Prayer is a common bond that unites Christians across time, space, and denomination. The lives included in this volume represent a variety of Christian voices; their poems and prayers rise above the specific circumstances of their lives and speak to all persons who seek a closer communion with God.

Richards, Mary Caroline. *Centering in Poetry, Pottery, and the Person*. Hanover, NH: University Press of New England, 1989.
This is the spiritual testament of a woman who found her creative expression in pottery and poetry. From these disciplines, as from the total process of living, she draws the principles that guide her both in her role as teacher and, more fundamentally, as person. "Centering," the image taken from the potter's craft, expresses the author's most felt necessity: to be on center. The clay brought into a spinning, unwobbling

pivot is free to take shape as it and she press against each other. Her ideal is to be on center as a person, in her poetry, in the classroom, in her daily encounter with the great spinning universe and all the forces of life and spirit that flow and counterflow. Centering is a severe and thrilling discipline, often acutely unpleasant yet essential if one would be whole.

Rilke, Ranier Marie. *Poems from the Book of Hours.* Trans. Babett Deutsch. New York: New Directions, 1975.
Rilke's poem falls into three parts: *The Book of Monkish Life* (1899), *The Book of Pilgrimage* (1901), and *The Book of Poverty and Death* (1903). Although these poems were the work of Rilke's youth, they contain the germ of his mature convictions. The poet felt that Russia, which he had visited just prior to the writing of the first section, is his spiritual home, and so the monk, who is the imaginary author of the poems, is represented as an adherent of the peculiar faith that Rilke ascribed to his spiritual kinsmen—a faith in a God remote from the august if benign Father of western Christianity, a God waiting to be born of the artist's alert and sensitive consciousness.

Salinger, J.D. *Franny and Zooey.* New York: Little, Brown, 1991.
Franny is a college girl and Zooey, a successful television actor of twenty-five. Like the rest of the children in their family, they are prodigies. Despite numerous advantages, Zooey has an ulcer and Franny an incipient nervous breakdown; both have a sense of profound dissatisfaction with the world, with people, and with themselves. Franny's difficulties form the central concern of the novel as she withdraws from the self-centered, pseudo-intellectual qualities of her peers, from drama and allied activities, to seek grace and sustenance in the "Jesus Prayer." This move proves ineffectual to forestall the malaise she feels. The segment of the book bearing her name ends with her recovering from a fainting spell. Zooey's search for meaning leads him to eastern religions but he, too, suffers disappointment. The novel is and remains a *search for,* not a *finding of,* spiritual advancement.

Schaeffer, Edith. *Hidden Art.* Wheaton, IL: Tyndale House, 1985.
"Hidden art" is that found in the ordinary areas of everyday life. Each person has some talent which is unfulfilled in some hidden area of his or her being—a talent which could be expressed and developed. This book is not a call to housewives and bank clerks to leave their kitchens and desks to produce great works of art, but a portrayal of what anyone, anywhere, can do to develop that "unfulfilled" talent and transform the here-and-now situation with a touch of true creativity. Serving a meal, setting a table, decorating a room, reading a story to the children, gardening outdoors or in a window-box, painting, singing, or playing an instrument, writing letters, choosing clothing, arranging flowers—in each of these commonplace activities of life the author sees an opportunity for modern people to express themselves as individuals in an increasingly monochrome society. She not only offers encouragement to find these opportunities but also makes practical suggestions as to how creative self-expression can be achieved.

Selected Poetry of Jessica Powers. Eds. Regina Siegfried and Robert F. Morneau. Kansas City: Sheed & Ward, 1989.

The poems in this collection draw readers into the mystery of God's presence in each individual, in the church, in all of humanity, and in nature. Jessica (Sister Miriam of the Holy Spirit) Powers' lifelong desire as a poet was to lead readers to feel the experience of God's mercy. Her words and images are clear, profound, and precise. They tantalize the imagination, and in that process, evoke a spirit of prayer. Simone Weil once wrote: "We need poetry as much as we need bread." If such be the case, then Powers provides much nourishment for a century in need of a renewed imagination. Following the tradition of St. John of the Cross, appreciative of the blatant beauty of nature, in touch with the radical rawness of the human condition, these selected poems provide spiritual sustenance for all the seasons of life. A style that is deceptively direct and simple characterizes her poetry. It is at once immanent and transcendent, displaying a synthesis seldom found in contemporary verse.

Selye, Hans. *The Stress of Life*. New York: McGraw-Hill, 1978.

The main purpose of this book is to tell, in a generally understandable language, what medicine has learned about stress. The author provides basic insights into the stress syndrome, which can be related to the vital dimension of the self and can either hinder or facilitate spiritual experience. Throughout the book, examples demonstrate the author's belief in the mutual influence of body and mind and the costly affair mental stress is for the body, to say nothing of its effect upon our response to the world.

Shakespeare, William. *The Complete Works of William Shakespeare*. Ed. G.B. Harrison. Stamford, CT: Longmeadow, 1990.

The spiritual reader may find much enrichment in a meditative reading of the tragedies of Hamlet, Othello, King Lear, and Macbeth.

Silone, Ignazio. *Bread and Wine*. Trans. Harvey Fergusson II. New York: New American Library, n.d.

Pietro Spina, the hero of this novel, a "revolutionary saint," returns to his homeland after fifteen years of exile—a revolutionary disguised as a priest. His journey takes him from the pavements of Rome to the lovingly tended earth of the impoverished countryside, where he rediscovers a way of life attuned to the eternal rhythms of planting and harvesting, the enduring pulsebeat of birth and death. Slogans and political dogma fade beside the blossoming of a vision in which flesh and spirit are as inseparably joined as the bread and wine that give this masterpiece its title and its theme.

Solzhenitsyn, Alexander. *Cancer Ward*. Trans. Nicholas Bethell. New York: Random House, 1989.

This a deeply moving novel in which people from all walks of Soviet life are thrown together by the accident of malignant disease and in which their world undergoes a searching examination. For all their diversity, the people in this environment have two things in common: the hospital environment and the ubiquitous presence of cancer. These factors give an intense sincerity to their thoughts and arguments; they speak frankly because they are beyond human retaliation. Men facing death have no time for the luxury of complicating issues; they have to come to the heart of questions about life and death. The result is not merely a fascinating novel but a penetrating inquiry into morality, ideology, social relationships, humane principles, and concepts of the individual in relation to the state.

Solzhenitsyn, Alexander. *The First Circle.* New York: HarperCollins, 1990.
The author spent years in exile and in prison. Therefore, the men and women in this novel of prison camp revelations are flesh and blood. They love; they hate; they laugh; they cry; they gossip; they dream.... And suddenly we see that prison, terror, corruptibility and sadism refine and purify the human ethos. In the end, it is not the prisoners who are destroyed, even though they may lose their lives. It is the jailers, the oppressors, who are doomed. The human spirit lives on in all its grandeur and dignity.

Solzhenitsyn, Alexander. *One Day in the Life of Ivan Denisovich.* New York: Farrar, Straus & Giroux, 1992.
This is the terrifying story of an almost unbelievable man-made hell, the Soviet work camps, and of one man's heroic struggle to survive in the face of the most determined efforts to destroy him.

Thomas, R.S. *Mass for Hard Times.* Great Britain: Bloodaxe Books, 1992.
R.S. Thomas has always posed difficult questions in his poems and forced readers to confront uncertainties, ambiguities, and the equivocal and paradoxical nature of our experience of life. In *Mass for Hard Times*, he has drawn together a collection that encompasses all his major areas of questioning. Here are poems about time and history, about the self, about language and the writing of poetry, about love, the machine, the Cross and prayer. In many of the poems, clusters of these concerns are movingly and unforgettably imaged in both familiar and new ways: the sea and ships, journey and travelers, painting, mirrors, science and geological time are intertwined as he questions and reflects on our own unvoiced concerns.

Thompson, Francis. *The Poems of Francis Thompson.* Westport, CT: Greenwood, 1979.
The theme of God's pursuit of the soul echoes throughout the religious poetry of Francis Thompson but most powerfully in his justifiably famous vision of *The Hound of Heaven.*

Tolstoy, Leo. *The Death of Ivan Ilyich and Other Stories.* New York: Viking Penguin, 1989.
"The Death of Ivan Ilyich" offers unmistakable proof that a selfish life, spent in the pursuit of material things, pleasure, and power, is a wasted life whereas a life motivated by a compassionate feeling for one's fellowman is rich and rewarding: the first a life of darkness, the second, a life of light. These generalizations are worked out in fine detail as the narrator describes the reactions of the various characters to Ilyich's terminal disease and death. The more serious his illness grows, the greater is the indifference to him and the greater his sensitivity to this indifference. Toward the end he is engulfed by a terrible loneliness and only then can he make the unqualified admission that his

life of possession and power was all wrong. On the threshold of death, a happy Ivan has begun a life of light.

Traherne, Thomas. *Centuries.* Two Volumes. Ridgefield, CT: Morehouse, 1986.
These works justify Traherne's title as the "poet of felicity." He tells of his "felicity" as an infant, of his temporary loss of it, and of his paradise regained with a richness unknown in infancy. He did, however, become a child again, in the sense that was necessary for one seeking to enter the kingdom of heaven. The "adult" of the poet is aware that the phenomenal world is not all; it is not even primary or infinite. Primary and infinite is Spirit, that is, God, a Trinity of Love. This double awareness of enjoying the phenomenal world and of belonging to a God-fearing community is the foundation of his philosophy of life. His works witness to the marriage of sense and spirit, leaving the objects of sense undimmed and showing the potencies of spirit in a pure and perceptive soul.

West, Jessamyn. *Hide and Seek: A Continuing Journey.* New York: Harcourt, 1987.
In pursuit of solitude, the author lived by herself for three months in a travel trailer on a remote bank of the Colorado River. Hiding? Yes, in a way. Seeking? Of course, yet the quest was uncertain. There were distant neighbors and a small town within reach by car. So, as intended, she was alone. But to say "alone" is to deny the embrace of this remarkable memoir of her experiences, observations, and thoughts during those months. Hers is a mind intimately aware of the moment, yet able to reach out beyond time and place to find companionship from all life, past and present, her own as well as others'. Hers is a spirit responsive to the beauty and wonder of all things. Throughout this unconventional adventure, there is an abiding kinship with nature, whether in awe of its force or in affection for its loneliness. This memoir is in fact not an egocentric celebration of the author but of life and its possibilities. Whether or not that is what she sought, it is what she found. (See Reading Program III)

Whitman, Walt. *Leaves of Grass.* The First (1855) Edition. Ed. Malcolm Cowley. New York: Random House, 1993.
The long opening poem ("Song of Myself") is one of the great masterpieces of modern times, numbered among certain inspired, even prophetic works that have appeared at intervals in the western world. It records the poet's rapt feeling of union or identity with God (or the Soul or Humankind or the Cosmos), a sense of ineffable joy leading to the conviction that the seer has been released from the limitations of space and time and has been granted a direct vision of truths impossible to express. God, for the poet, is that principle of energy that is manifested in every living creature as well as in "the grass that grows wherever the land is and the water is." The central image of the poem is the grass, symbolizing the miracle of common things and the divinity of ordinary persons.

Afterword

At the conclusion of this revised edition of *A Practical Guide,* it would seem that we are only beginning to understand how much ordinary Christians living in the world want to integrate sacred and secular values, faith and functionality, worship and work. Many, though well on the way, are still disinclined to call themselves "formative readers" or "mediators" or "contemplatives." While they report a growing, often unsatisfied hunger for spiritual deepening, they may be inclined instead to associate formative reading, meditative reflection, or contemplative prayer only with the formation process undergone by monks or nuns. Yet the desire for a deeper relationship with God persists despite the obstacles of materialism, consumerism, hedonism, and individualism so prevalent in our world. St. Augustine put words to these feelings when he said, "Our heart is restless until it rests in you, O God." Especially in the light of Vatican Council II, more and more laity wonder not only about the universal call to holiness[1], but about their personal response to and implementation of this call. The exact teaching of the Church is illuminating in this regard:

> The Gospel of Christ constantly renews the life and culture of fallen man; it combats and removes the errors and evils resulting from the permanent allurement of sin. It never ceases to purify and elevate the morality of peoples. By riches coming from above, it makes fruitful, as it were from within, the spiritual qualities and traditions of every people and of every age. It strengthens, perfects and restores them in Christ. Thus the Church, in the very fulfillment of her own function, stimulates and advances human and civic culture; by her action, also by her liturgy, she leads [all] toward interior liberty.
>
> For the above reasons, the Church recalls to the mind of all that culture is to be subordinated to the integral perfection of the human person, to the good of the community and of the whole society. Therefore, it is necessary to develop the human faculties in such a way that there results a growth of the faculty of wonder, of intuition, of contemplation, of making personal judgment, of developing a religious, moral and social sense.[2]

Common Ways of Spiritual Formation in Christian Life

Our Christian tradition offers to all believers basic paths to spiritual awakening that are both unique and communal. These are the so-called "common ways" of spiritual formation. They are practiced by the community as a common whole while helping each person to pursue his or her call to spiritual deepening and a life devoted to meditation, prayer, love, and service in Christ's name. In cooperation with the initiating and transforming grace of God, these ways may become avenues to intimacy with the Trinity and a lived commitment to the Gospel. Briefly, they are:

1. *Liturgy.* Many denominations of Christianity (Roman Catholic, Orthodox, Lutheran, to cite some examples) teach the fundamental importance and centrality of liturgy, ritual, and symbol in the worship experience. The quality of our coming before God in reverence and adoration depends in great measure on the overall quality of the spiritual life of presiders and participants alike. The findings of the Second Vatican Council are significant in this regard:

> Our union with the Church in heaven is put into effect in its noblest manner especially in the sacred liturgy, wherein the power of the Holy Spirit acts upon us through sacramental signs. Then, with combined rejoicing we celebrate together the praise of the divine majesty.[3]

Properly understood and devoutly followed, the liturgy offers the Christian community an opportunity to enter into the mystery of a God who has loved us first (cf. 1 Jn. 4).[4] According to Jacques Maritain, the liturgy is itself ordered to contemplation.[5] While contemplation of the saving mystery of God in Christ in itself remains ineffable, it is toward it, in Maritain's thought, that the liturgy wishes to lead souls, and it is from it that the liturgy superabounds.

In *Sacrosanctum Concilium*, the Second Vatican Council's *Constitution on the Sacred Liturgy*, it is written that "the liturgy is the summit toward which the activity of the Church is directed; it is also the fount from which all her power flows."[6]

According to Cyprian Vagaggini, it is not a contradiction to contend that participation in the liturgy and the mystical life go hand in hand. It is his contention that there can be a fruitful interaction among liturgy, liturgical spirituality, and ascetical effort—all leading toward Christian perfection.[7] In fact, as Vagaggini reminds us, the official spirituality the Church proposes to her members is liturgical. Thus it is no surprise that many today are discovering anew the depth and richness of the spirituality of the liturgy. They find it to be an answer to their aspirations for a holy and harmonious life individually and communally. Indeed, as the Church teaches:

> Zeal for the promotion and restoration of the sacred liturgy is rightly held to be a sign of the providential dispositions of God in our time and as a movement of the Holy Spirit in his Church. It is today a distinguishing mark of the life of the Church, and indeed, of the whole tenor of contemporary religious thought and action.[8]

For this reason the Second Vatican Council has reaffirmed that the principal epiphany of the Church is the liturgy.[9]

2. *Word of God.* The people of God are led to a fuller awareness of their faith through hearing and reading the Word of God in scripture and in the texts of our tradition, some of which are identified as the classics of spirituality. The Word of God is compared to a seed which is sown in a field; those who hear this Word with faith become part of the flock Christ came to call (cf. Mt. 13:1-9). They receive, through the Word, entrance to God's reign. Then, by its own power, the seed sprouts and grows until harvest time.[10]

It is impossible to calculate or predict the power of God's word to convert hearts, transform lives, evoke repentance, and encourage prayer. Catholic teaching holds that Christ himself is present in his Word since it is he himself who speaks when the holy scriptures are read in the church.[11]

It is clear from this teaching and from personal practice that the ministry of the liturgical rite and the ministry of the word are complementary. In the words of Vagaggini:

> Without the ministry of the word the rite runs the risk of remaining unfruitful for the faithful who do not understand the meaning of it and do not approach it with the necessary moral dispositions.... But without the ministry of the rite...the ministry of the word is of no avail...that is why, from its very first day, the Church has built herself on the ministry of the word, followed immediately by the ministry of the liturgical rite.[12]

For the word of God to bear solid fruit in daily life, it must be heard with the inner ears of the heart. If one is to "go into the whole world and preach the Gospel to every creature" (Mk. 16:15), the Word has to be the center of thought, decision, and action. In former ages it was common practice for one to commit the Bible to memory so that passages were ready at hand when one engaged in meditation. The Word of God was literally food for the soul. Through the power of the Holy Spirit, it could draw one to the threshold of contemplative prayer.

St. Teresa of Avila, for instance, said that for eighteen years, while she was learning about her life call, she could not pray without a book in hand.[13]

There is perhaps no more "common way" to foster Christian contemplation than that of *lectio divina* or prayerful, affective listening to a text we believe to be divinely inspired.

3. *Sacramental Life.* Our tradition as represented by the so-called "mainline churches" further teaches that it is only through the sacramental economy, only through worthy reception of the sacraments, that what is proclaimed in the Word of God is fulfilled. Frequenting of the sacraments is a common means toward Christian perfection. The sacraments and the proclamation of the Word are the Church's two great means of transmitting the divine life to the world. All of the sacraments in turn are ordered to the Eucharist. The Eucharist, together with Baptism, is the principal means of formation of the people of God. Such is the teaching of Vatican Council II. The Eucharist is the fountain of all graces, a truth that was stated already at the Council of Trent. From the earliest Church teachings to those of the present day, the sacraments have been seen as powerful means of salvation, so much so that "all the faithful, whatever their condition or state, are called by the Lord, each in [their] own way, to that perfect holiness whereby the Father himself is perfect."[14]

A. *Baptism.* To be baptized in the name of the Father, the Son, and the Holy Spirit is to become a participant in the life of the Trinity itself. Baptism is an opening to this ineffable communion. That is why contemplation is seen as the final fruit of baptism, available to all. It confers upon us the privilege of universal priesthood, fully realized in participation in the worship and priesthood of Christ. Through Baptism we are formed in the likeness of Christ, "For in one spirit we were all baptized into one body" (1 Cor. 12:18). In this sacred rite, a oneness with Christ's death and resurrection is both symbolized and brought about.[15]

B. *Eucharist.* Reconciled with God, forgiven of sin, invited to receive Christ bodily and spiritually in the Holy Eucharist, we begin to taste something of what it means to have our hearts set afire with love. We are drawn into a lived experience of intimate, contemplative union. All St. Francis of Assisi could say as he beheld the uplifted host was "My God and my all!" Toward the end of her life, St. Catherine of Siena took the bread of Christ's Body and the wine of his Blood as her only food and drink. No contemplative life is thinkable without the action and intervention of the Holy Spirit, who teaches us what and who it is that we receive. "By partaking of the body of the Lord in the breaking of the eucharistic bread, we are taken up into communion with Him and with one another."[16]

C. *Confirmation.* We are then more perfectly bound to the Church by the Sacrament of Confirmation, which together with Baptism, confers upon us the universal priesthood of the faithful. The Holy Spirit endows us with special strength so that we are more strictly obliged to spread and defend the faith, both by word and deed, as true witnesses of Christ.[17]

The sacrament of Confirmation signifies in a new way that we are children of God and heirs of heaven. It is through the Spirit that we are able to say, "Abba, Father," and that we are readied by grace to receive the virtues and gifts that enable us to make a renewed commitment to Christian action. There is no more "common way" to follow Christ than to combine in a graceful rhythm the depths of contemplation and the heights of effective apostolic and social action. Confirmation seals this commitment that is then lived out in a variety of life states and relationships in accordance with a diversity of gifts.

> Therefore all the disciples of Christ, persevering in prayer and praising God, should present themselves as a living sacrifice, holy and pleasing to God. Everywhere on earth they must bear witness to Christ and give an answer to those who seek an account of that hope of eternal life which is in them.[18]

4. *Devotions and Devotio.* It is, of course, the responsibility of every believer to personalize these common ways, to find the link between their efficacy and our effectiveness as followers of Christ. Not to be underestimated is the importance of devotional practices and renewal programs like the Rite of Christian Initiation of Adults. Such practices and programs enter into our Catholic religious consciousness like seeds planted in fertile soil awaiting the time to bloom and bear fruit. Praying the rosary, venerating icons, choosing patron saints, participating in processions on holy days, following the stations of the cross, pilgrimaging to sacred places—all of these symbols, images, and acts comprise in great measure what many believers mean by their spiritual life. Persons who leave the Church have been known to return to it because they are drawn by memory traces implanted through such expressions of the common ways. These are for many Catholics, for example, the main staging area of their personal encounter with a personal God.

In this regard, it might be well for us to remember the ancient meaning of the concept of *devotio*. This word is derived from the Latin, *devovere*, meaning to devote oneself to, to give oneself entirely to, even unto death. Those who are called "devout" devote themselves to God in such a way as to be entirely subject to the Divine Will in contemplative love. *Devotio* can thus be seen as a certain ready will to give oneself to whatever concerns the service of God.[19]

Devotio, according to Vagaggini, is thus a total vowing of oneself to God, an engaging in whatever concerns God's honor. He calls *devotio* a basic psychological attitude, the fruit of the virtue of religion (or contemplation), a disposition that permeates one's life, giving orientation and form to subsequent acts in which this service may be realized. Vagaggini's point is that "devotions" are of value insofar as they are means to nurture and express *devotio*. It is thus possible to suggest that *devotio* is like the soil in which the spiritual exercises stemming from liturgy, word, and sacrament can bud and flower. It suggests a disposition of openness to the Sacred that makes one ready and eager to receive and use for the good of all the foundational disciplines I shall now discuss.

Common Disciplines of Spiritual Deepening

The classical spiritual disciplines and the exercises related to them are resources for contemplative prayer in our tradition. To practice the disciplines of silence (*silencio*), spiritual reading (*lectio*), meditation (*meditatio*), prayer (*oratio*), contemplation (*contemplatio*), and action (*incarnatio*) presupposes the need for purification from self-centeredness and from the inordinate attachments that account for the triple disorientation typical of one who would make pleasure, possession, and power ultimate. The spiritual disciplines not only redirect our energy toward the transcendent; they also create, with the help of grace, an inner climate of openness to divine directives. Sin and death lose their hold on a humble, converted heart.

The Church Fathers, notably St. Augustine of Hippo and St. Gregory of Nyssa, as well as such influential spiritual writers as St. Bernard of Clairvaux, Hugh and Richard of St. Victor, William of St. Thierry, St. John of the Cross, and St. Teresa of Avila, are all concerned with the attainment of the heights of contemplation understood as God's free gift. As our tradition teaches, grace operates hand in glove with free will. The decision to live a spiritually disciplined life enables one to climb the ladder of love that leads from knowing about God (*sapere*) to knowing God (*sapientia*). St. John of the Cross summarizes this great tradition in one short sentence, saying, "Seek in reading and you will find in meditation; knock in prayer and it shall be opened to you in contemplation."[20]

For our purposes we shall focus on *lectio*, *meditatio*, *oratio*, and *contemplatio* as the four main disciplines taught by our tradition.[21] These are basic ways in which the people of God can personalize the foundational truths of their faith through the intentional practices of reading, meditation, prayer, and contemplation. Let us begin with the two disciplines at either end of the scale, *silencio* and *incarnatio*.

Maintaining a certain inner, if not outer, silence is a preliminary disposition readying one to hear the word with ears of the heart. The same readiness might be fostered for some by fasting from certain foods, for others by choosing to chant psalms or prayers aloud, for still others by keeping a spiritual journal or making a retreat. At issue here is the awareness that it is necessary, considering the noise and speed of modern life, to prepare consciously to practice the spiritual disciplines. One has to create, at least inwardly if not outwardly, a climate of quiet, of stillness and centering.

Someone may choose, for example, to make a silent retreat. Being in *silencio* enables them to create symbolically an inner space in which to encounter themselves and God on a deeper level. Their exchange is, in a sense, beyond words. These four disciplines, like the devotions that may surround and sustain them, are to be understood not as privatized expressions of an emotive kind of piety but as pointers to the highest goal of union with God. They may be seen as means to this end, never as goals in their own right or as guarantors of sanctification, for this is from beginning to end a gift of grace.

The disciplines are not something we "do" to gain holiness but ways in which we listen, as disciples, to what God is doing in us. In this sense, it is not we who master the mystery but the mystery that masters and teaches us. What we are being taught is that a disciplined life is meant to make us better disciples, people who are more socially present to others in acts of justice, peace and mercy, people for whom the test of contemplation is not the contemplative experience as such but the charity that flows from it.

Just as silence and solitude ready us for formative reading, meditation, prayer, and contemplation, so Christian action (*incarnatio*) is the outreach of a loving heart overflowing with the grace of nearness to God. One is eager to share with others what one has so generously received.

1. *Lectio*. One can distinguish formative reading or *lectio divina* from conceptual study or informational exegesis. This manner of approaching the text refers mainly to the scriptures but, as we have seen, it applies especially to the essential reading of the classics as well. It seeks, in the words of Guigo II, a Carthusian monk of the twelfth century, "for the sweetness of a blessed life."[22] He compares taking up a text in this way to putting a ripe grape into one's mouth. Nourishing the body is analogous to feeding the soul with solid truths. Now is the time for listening to the text with appreciation, humility, and attentiveness. One wants to hear the slightest whispers of the Holy Spirit, who stirs the heart and enlightens the mind.

Appreciation suggests that we care for the Word of God disclosed in the text at hand as a mother cares for her child. *Humility* implies our acceptance of the fact that the practice of formative reading challenges us to remain docile and willing to be taught. *Attentiveness* helps us to go beyond the words on the page to the Word himself. We allow the Word to draw us beyond the surface meaning of the text to the intimacy of understanding shared by friends. In other words, we appreciate the timeless intention of the text rather than being distracted by some of its time-bound accretions. We wait humbly upon the word, trusting that a deeper meaning will be disclosed to the degree that we resist modes of mastery. We pay attention not only to the words on the page but to what God may be saying in the happenings that comprise our life.

Lectio is an uplifting discipline precisely because new ranges of significance light up. It stimulates our powers of memory, imagination, and anticipation. We go beyond superficial interpretations, discovering in the process that formative reading really means rereading a text several times in a slow and abiding manner at different stages of our life to draw all the "juices" from it.[23]

2. *Meditation*. Guigo describes meditation as "the busy application of the mind to seek with the help of one's own reason for knowledge of hidden truths." He says that meditation "perceives" the sweetness of a blessed life.[24] If reading puts food whole into the mouth, then meditation chews it or ruminates upon it. Meditation is a combined exercise of the imaginative, cognitive, and affective faculties of the mind to seek the meaning of what God may be telling us in a significant text. To meditate is to reflect with regularity upon the Word of God, on our response or resistance to God's will, and on our calling in this life.

This reflection is not an external exercise that relies on grappling with new information but an internal process of ruminating on the text or narrative at hand with the intention of going to the heart of the matter. We take careful note of what the text does not say in order to examine what it does say and to connect this meaning to God's will for our life.

There is obviously a close connection between *lectio* and *meditatio* in our tradition. To seek in reading, as the saying of St. John of the Cross suggests, is to find in meditation. It is to discover the word of God not only in the background of our Christian life but also in the foreground of a person-to-Person relationship. In ruminating upon the word, we wonder why we resonate with it or why we feel some resistance. *Meditatio* might then be fleshed out in the related discipline I recommend in this book of keeping a spiritual reading notebook or journal. This becomes a further aid to understanding the meaning of the text in the context of our current situation. Such a style of reading-reflection may lead us to assess our failings as well as to affirm our gifts.

In these moments of receiving insight from the disciplines of *lectio-meditatio*, we may sense God's self-communication to us. We are aware that the Holy Spirit is using the vehicle of the text to reveal more of the transcendent for which we are so ardently thirsting. The text becomes a friendly companion, reminding us of the infinite ranges of God's mercy. By releasing us from mere intellectualizing about God, by drawing us closer to the sweetness of tasting and seeing God as God, we are moved by *meditatio* a step further along the path of prayer, contemplation, and Christian action.

3. *Oratio*. The Carthusian master, Guigo II, defines prayer as "the heart's

devoted turning to God to drive away evil and obtain what is good." It is a sighing to God, prompted by the Holy Spirit, that "asks for" the sweetness of a blessed life.[25] If reading puts food into our mouth, if meditation chews it and breaks it up, then prayer extracts the flavor. It does so in a variety of ways: praise, petition, intercession, thanksgiving, conversation. This longing can be expressed non-verbally as well as verbally, mentally as well as vocally.

To pray unceasingly is to live in worship, adoration, and awe. It is not merely a question of saying prayers but of oneself becoming a living prayer.[26] St. Bernard of Clairvaux compares prayer to a reservoir of divine energy continually being refilled inside of us so that we can share its power with others in the world.[27] Prayer means being able, as St. Teresa of Avila would say, to converse familiarly with the God who loves us, not only asking for what we need but living always in a posture of self-sacrifice and surrender.[28] Prayer sustained by reading and reflection enables us to behold, as it were, the invisible order of reality behind the visible order of creation.[29]

Prayer understood in this light is not a complicated procedure but an exercise in simplicity. It is that which renders us open, receptive, and abandoned to the mystery, majesty, and mercy of God. It is comparable to breathing, to beholding the wonder of things with the eyes of a child, to believing in the Most High, who lovingly holds us in the palm of a mighty and mothering hand. Prayer is the realization that we are in God's omnipresence as a fish is in the ocean. This is a favorite image of St. Catherine of Siena, who attuned herself in a refined and exquisite way to the symphony of transformation enfolding and energizing her at all times.[30]

Prayer, as a way of being, expresses itself in many ways. It can be a longing for sweetness, a cry for mercy, a song of joy, a wordless exchange of love between friends, an awareness of affinity, a plea for another's need, a gasp of gratitude when the ordinary suddenly becomes extraordinary.

Prayer is many ways of presence, yet it is one. It is the soaring of the human spirit to meet and be one with the Spirit of God. It is heart calling to Heart, the alone with the Alone, the finite before the Infinite, the temporary at home with the Eternal. Prayer in the end is loving God with our whole heart, soul, mind, and strength; it is becoming the fully alive persons God intends us to be.

4. *Contemplatio*. In Guigo's words, contemplation occurs when "the mind is in some sort lifted up to God and held above itself, so that it tastes the joys of everlasting sweetness." Contemplation, he says, "tastes" the sweetness of the blessed life we have found. It is as if God runs to meet the soul at prayer in all haste, as if Divine Mercy itself sprinkles the mind with "sweet heavenly dew," and anoints the heart with "the most precious perfumes."[31] It is now God who takes the initiative to restore the weary soul, slake its thirst, feed its

hunger. As Guigo says, God "makes the soul forget all earthly things; by making it die to itself He gives it new life in a wonderful way, and by making it drunk He brings it back to its true senses."[32] In fact, contemplation is often compared in the classical tradition upon which we have been drawing to inebriation. If reading puts food into the mouth, if meditation chews it and breaks it up, if prayer extracts its flavor, then as Guigo says, contemplation "is the sweetness itself which gladdens and refreshes."[33] It delights us, as does a glass of fine wine, in the sweetness we have found.

The previous disciplines (seeking, finding, knocking) have made us ready and receptive to the infused openings to grace we now experience. God takes the initiative to enlighten, elevate, restore, and renew our life of faith, hope, and love. It is now no longer we who seek to grasp the Mystery through *silentio, lectio, meditatio, oratio*, but the Mystery that grasps us. It draws us beyond ourselves to depths of intimacy understood abstractly but now known experientially. The language of contemplation is the language of love: "I adore you, hidden God" (Thomas Aquinas); "Ah! the sheer grace" (John of the Cross); "My all!" (Francis of Assisi).

God to the contemplative is a ray of darkness, a wonder unspeakable, an Other incomprehensibly beyond us and yet intimately near to us. The contemplative experience is admittedly paradoxical. Though of short duration, its effects are lasting. It is an experience of dying and rising. What has to die is not our deepest self, our being made in the form and likeness of God, but the illusion that our functional ego is all-powerful. Contemplation is seemingly inseparable from the dark nights of sense and spirit in which we are invited, if not impelled, by grace to shed the imprisoning restrictions of self-centeredness and to acknowledge our call to sacrificial love and dependency on God. In this time of dying and rising, we are asked to give up our desires for things or relations that can never satisfy us fully so that we can attend to the Triune God in whose presence we alone can find rest.

In these dark nights we are given the strength to relativize whatever we may have turned into an idol or a substitute for the Transcendent. There is pain to be sure in this parting from the self-deceptive ways in which we have been living, but there is also joy in the awareness that we are now letting go of the baggage that prevents us from soaring freely to our Divine Source. It is this freedom to be always with God and for God that enables the contemplative heart to become a charitable heart, showing to others the justice, peace, and mercy that are the marks of Christians who accept the command to love their neighbors as themselves and who know, in the words of St. John of the Cross, that in the evening of life, they shall be judged on love.[34]

Summary of the Spiritual Disciplines. Guigo, the Carthusian, sees these disciplines joined to each other not only in the order of time but in the order of causality. Reading, as we have seen, comes first and is, as it were, the foundation because it provides, as Guigo observes from experience, the subject matter we must use for meditation. Then it is the role of meditation to consider more carefully what is to be sought after. It, so to speak, "digs...for treasure which it finds and reveals."[35] However, since it is not in meditation's power to seize upon this treasure, it directs us to prayer. Then, says Guigo, prayer lifts itself up to God with all its strength and begs for the treasure for which it longs, and this is, of course, the sweetness of contemplation. This gift rewards the labors of the other three disciplines beyond our expectations. It "inebriates the thirsting soul with the dew of heavenly sweetness."[36] Quoting the monk directly we learn:

> Reading is an exercise of the outward senses, meditation is concerned with the inward understanding, prayer is concerned with desire; contemplation outstrips every faculty. The first degree is proper to beginners, the second to proficients, the third to devotees, the fourth to the blessed.... From this we may gather that reading without meditation is sterile, meditation without reading is liable to error, prayer without meditation is lukewarm, meditation without prayer is unfruitful, prayer when it is fervent wins contemplation, but to obtain it without prayer would be rare, even miraculous.... The man who has worked in this first degree, who has pondered well in the second, who has known devotion in the third, who has been raised above himself in the fourth, goes from strength to strength by this ascent on which his whole heart was set, until at last he can see the God of gods in Sion (cf. Ps 83:8)...[where] His chosen enjoy the sweetness of divine contemplation, not drop by drop, not now and then, but in an unceasing flow of delight which no one shall take away (cf. Jn 16:22), an unchanging peace, the peace of God (cf. Ps 4:9).[37]

Spiritual Direction

A key discipline and practice associated with the common ways and spiritual exercises developed thus far is spiritual direction. It cannot help but play a significant role in implementing the findings and recommendations of this book. Thus I need to say a few words about it. This art and discipline encompasses three interrelated aspects, defined by Adrian van Kaam as spiritual self-direction, direction-in-common, and private or one-on-one direction.[38] The latter way is especially necessary at crisis moments in one's faith journey or when one is led by grace to higher regions of prayer and contemplation. To offer private direction in these delicate matters, one has to be, in the words of Teresa of Avila, wise, learned, and experienced.[39] He or she cannot be a "blacksmith" of the spiritual life. St. John of the Cross depicts such a guide as unwise, ignorant, and inexperienced.[40] He or she may unwittingly retard the work of the Holy Spirit by advising directees to return to regions of imagination and discursive meditation from which they have already been weaned by grace. The worst possible direction occurs when a "blind guide leads the blind."[41] Wise directors are ones who embody the common wisdom of the Church. They have learned from the study of the masters to understand the life of the spirit in the light of ascetical-mystical theology. They are experienced enough to avoid building dependency relations in the name of spiritual direction. They also know when to refer someone to other experts in counseling, psychiatry, or psychotherapy for the help they need.

The way of direction-in-common is the most universal form of guidance offered by the Church. It imitates Christ's own way of teaching gatherings of believers and unbelievers. People representing all walks of life came together to listen to the Teacher. What he said made sense to many of them both personally and communally. The word of God became the guiding light of their life.

Direction-in-common invites us to remain open to divine directives emanating from such reliable sources as spiritual conferences, homilies, and lectures, from shared reading groups, prayer and Bible study sessions. Such occasions deepen and strengthen our commitment to Christ and teach us how to grow in intimacy with God through the common ways and disciplines discussed thus far. We learn to hear and heed the appeals, invitations, and challenges of the Spirit received in communal direction. It complements private direction and helps us to foster the dynamics of Spirit-inspired self-direction in the situations of everyday life. For example, the Holy Spirit can and often does use a text read formatively as a means to communicate a message that can be life-transforming.[42] In reference to this point, W.A. Barry and W.J. Connolly write:

> A spiritual direction that stems from the heart of the Christian tradition has no axes to grind, no pet theories on which its efficacy depends. It is primarily concerned with helping individuals freely to place themselves before God who will communicate himself to them and make them more free. The focus of the direction is on the Lord and on the way he seems to relate to each person.[43]

This truth—that the Director of directors is the Lord through the power of the Holy Spirit—enables directors-in-common and in-private to grow in spiritual maturity. By helping those seeking guidance to root their inner motivations and dispositions in their faith and formation tradition, directors enable directees to renew their commitment to Christ, to the Church, and to all those entrusted to their care. Good direction always makes us more receptive to the forming, reforming, and transforming presence and action of the Trinity. Rather than focusing narrowly on either consolations or desolations, we desire most of all to experience the slow but steady emergence of what Barry and Connolly call a "contemplative attitude"[44] or what Adrian van Kaam names the disposition of "transcendent self-presence."[45] Speaking of this level of awareness in relation to contemplative prayer, van Kaam writes:

> This [presence] is not divisive but unitive. It is transcendent. It makes whole; it attunes us to a mysterious totality that already is. It is a healing reflection...[that] pushes us beyond the limited here and now meanings of our own particular problems, childhood traumas, sensitivities, faults and projects. In and beyond all of these, it integrates our lives contextually, that is, it helps us [to] live in the context of the whole of reality, of which we are part, and with its divine all-pervading source. We begin to see ourselves in the loving and redeeming perspective of Divine Presence.[46]

Knowing that they stand under the loving gaze of God, good directors understand that they can neither push directees beyond the pace of grace nor make decisions for them. Ultimately, the process of moving toward a life of contemplative prayer and presence is a matter of grace. Directees have to be helped to respond to grace and to take responsibility for their own lives. All of us must strive over a lifetime to be faithful to our unique-communal life call. Another person can facilitate our efforts, but only God can lead us to loving knowledge of our faith or what St. John of the Cross calls the "secrecy of...dark contemplation."[47]

Approaches to Contemplative Prayer

Keeping in mind this overview of the common ways of faith formation, I would like to say something in closing about five classical schools or methods of spiritual formation frequently mentioned in the reading programs I outlined and in the annotated bibliography. They are: 1) The Benedictine Way and Centering Prayer; 2) The Orthodox Way and the Jesus Prayer; 3) The Franciscan Way and the Prayer of Praise; 4) The Ignatian Way and the Spiritual Exercises; 5) The Carmelite Way and the Threefold Path of Purgation, Illumination, and Union.

The Benedictine Way and Centering Prayer

The Rule of St. Benedict from its inception to the present age constitutes one of the most formative and formidable influences on western civilization as such, as well as on the unfolding of both the eremitical and the cenobitical life.[48] In spite of the changing ways and altered conditions of modern monastic life, the Benedictine ideal, like the Gospel, remains unchanging: to integrate the love of God with the works of charity owed to one's neighbor. A true Christian community in the Benedictine sense is always a "school of charity." *The Rule* embodies the wisdom of the Desert Fathers, notably St. Anthony of Egypt[49] and John Cassian.[50] A typical trait of Benedictine spirituality is its stress on contemplation as the source of Christian action. It is clear to clergy, religious, and laity that the love of learning must be subordinated to the desire for God and that the acquisition of spiritual knowledge and discipline begins with obedience to Christ.[51] One adopts a posture of discipleship in relation to one's spiritual father or mother or the person invested with legitimate authority. Conversion and submission, perseverance in the common life and confidence in God—all strengthen moral conduct and ready one for conformity to Christ.

This way of Christian spirituality proposes that Christ's life within us is a living power. Hence a "monk's" essential life is to be ordered not by customs or rules as such, but by Christ. According to Dom Hubert van Zeller:

> When by sanctifying grace the soul has been introduced to this life in Christ, the monastic vocation comes along to develop it. Thereafter, in the monastery and as a member of this particular body within the mystical body, the monk's union with Christ is furthered by fidelity to every custom, rule, vow, prayer, work, penance, human contact and act of submission.[52]

The offshoots and branches of the original Benedictine charism form a litany of sanctity and formation extending over one thousand years. One important contemporary revival of a method of prayer some would say is as old as Christianity itself is that of "centering prayer." It was first taught in the West by John Cassian, who wrote about a method of coming to rest in God in his *Conferences* early in the fifth century.[53] It has been reintroduced in our times by M. Basil Pennington,[54] whose work has been inspired by the teaching of the late Thomas Merton. In Merton's own words:

> Christian contemplation [is] an experiential contact with God, in and through Christ, beyond all knowledge, in the darkness of the mystery of divine charity, in "unknowing."[55]

This way of prayer indeed traces its roots to a medieval text by the anonymous author of *The Cloud of Unknowing* where it is said that few words and firm love lead us most swiftly to God.[56] "Centering Prayer" has perhaps received its most significant thrust to date from the writings and teachings of Abbot Thomas Keating.[57]

Important in this tradition is its insistence that contemplative prayer is meant for all and not only for a chosen few. To ready ourselves to receive this grace, we must:

1. turn in faith and love to God present in the inmost center of our being;
2. abide there in rest and simplicity, trusting that Christ is as near to us as if he were standing before us;
3. accept whatever God allows to happen during this time of prayer, remaining present to the Divine Presence in faith, hope, and love.

In regard to judging the authenticity of this or any form of contemplative prayer, its practitioners would agree with Pennington that contemplation should overflow into action and the action has to be rooted in contemplation. We behold the sacredness of our environment because of this graced opening to the Sacred. Contemplation then becomes not an occasional happening but a constant stance. As Thomas Merton says:

> The life of contemplation is...not simply a life of human technique and discipline, it is the life of the Holy Spirit in our inmost souls. The whole duty of the contemplative is to abandon what is base and trivial in his [her] own life, and do all he [she] can to conform...to the secret and obscure promptings of the Spirit of God. This...requires a constant discipline of humility, obedience, self-distrust, prudence and above all of faith.[58]

The Orthodox Way and the Jesus Prayer

According to many experts, there are several elements that distinguish the Orthodox way. Among these are: the scriptural, the primitive Christian, the intellectual, the early monastic, the liturgical, and the contemplative. For our purposes the development of the contemplative element in the Orthodox Church is due mainly to the movement called "hesychasm." The tradition of the "hesychasts" (from *hesychia* or "quiet") has its roots in the work of great mystics like St. Symeon the New Theologian (949-1022).[59] From the eleventh century on, Mount Athos in Greece became the center of hesychasm.[60] Hesychasm was further identified with the theories of St. Gregory Palamas on the "uncreated light."[61] The hesychast tradition centers on four main points:

1. the striving toward a state of total rest or quiet that excludes for the duration reading, psalmody, meditation, etc.;
2. the repetition of the "Jesus Prayer" ("Lord Jesus, Son of God, have mercy on me, a sinner" or simply "Jesus, mercy");
3. practices designed to help the concentration of the mind, such as physical immobility, control or suspension of breathing, fixation of the eyes of the mind on the heart;

4. feeling at times an inner warmth or perceiving an epiphanic radiance like the "light of Tabor."[62]

It is important to note that the hesychasts themselves never dreamt of proposing an infallible technique. They did not offer "recipes" that would automatically bring one to contemplation nor do they sever their contemplative disciplines from the joys and obligations of charity. The inner endeavor to come closer to God remained their foremost concern, as we read in the following commentary:

> Hesychasm in the Orthodox Church may be compared with the great Spanish school of mystics in the Latin Church of the sixteenth century. In both cases we find a remarkable endeavor to simplify and systematize the spiritual ways, to make them more practical and accessible. But St. Teresa, St. John of the Cross, and St. Ignatius Loyola do not surpass and still less supersede St. Augustine, St. Benedict, St. Gregory the Great, St. Bernard and St. Thomas. In the same way Symeon the New Theologian...and Gregory Palamas neither surpass nor supersede St. Basil, St. Chrysostom, St. Gregory of Nazianzus, and St. Gregory of Nyssa—the Fathers and most authorized interpreters, not only of Orthodox thought but of Orthodox piety as well. And beyond the contemplative mystics, beyond the Fathers themselves, the simple and pure Gospel remains central.[63]

As to the essentials of Orthodox Spirituality, they are, in brief:

1. The aim of human life is union of God and deification, a union that cannot be achieved without the mediation of Jesus Christ; hence the redeeming action of our Lord constitutes the Alpha and Omega as well as the center of Christian spirituality.

2. Incorporation into Christ and union with God require the cooperation of two unequal but equally necessary forces: divine grace and the human will, because it is our will, not our intellect or our feelings that is the chief human instrument of union with God; there can be no intimate union with God if our own will is not surrendered and conformed to the Divine Will.

3. There is a commingling in the spiritual life of ascetical and mystical elements: "asceticism" is generally understood as an "exercise" of the human will on itself in order to improve itself; "mysticism" or the "mystical life" is a life in which the gifts of the Holy Spirit are predominant over human efforts and in which "infused" virtues are predominant over "acquired" ones. To use a classic comparison: between the ascetic life, in which human action predominates, and the mystical life, in which God's action takes the initiative, there is the same difference as between rowing a boat and sailing it: the oar is

the ascetic effort, the sail is the mystical passivity or receptivity unfurled to catch the wind of the Spirit.

4. Prayer is a necessary instrument of salvation, the prayer of supplication (for oneself), of intercession (for others), and of thanksgiving or praise (for God). In contrast with prayer, contemplation is not necessary to salvation, but as a general rule, assiduous and fervent prayer becomes contemplative. Contemplation begins with the "prayer of simplicity" or the "prayer of simple regard," consisting of placing ourselves in the presence of God and maintaining ourselves in this presence for a certain time in an interior silence that is as complete as possible. One concentrates upon the Divine Object, reducing to unity a multiplicity of thoughts and feelings and endeavoring to keep ourselves quiet without words or arguments. Contemplation is "acquired" if the acts of contemplation are the results of personal effort; it is "infused" if these acts are produced by divine grace without, or almost without, human effort. Acquired contemplation belongs to the ascetical life, infused to the mystical life.

5. The "holy mysteries" or in the Latin Church the "sacraments" are means and only means, of grace toward which one must maintain a disposition of awe and reverence, so that what is mysterious remains a mystery, the depth of which no human mind can pierce.

6. A sense of the communion of saints (veneration of saints and icons) is second in Orthodox spirituality only to the veneration of the Theotokos, the blessed Virgin Mary and Mother of God incarnate, whose icons are especially precious in this tradition. Concerning this devotion in orthodoxy, it is important to note that an icon to the East is understood as a means of communion, an objective presence opening one to grace, a meeting place between the believer and the heavenly world. An icon is not that which one worships but that through which worshippers can encounter the Holy.

7. The stages of the spiritual life—purgative, illuminative, unitive—that have become classical in the West originated in the East under the influence of Pseudo-Dionysius. The tradition discriminates between beginners, proficients, and the perfect and mentions three types of Christians: (1) those introduced to or approaching contemplation who are mainly concerned with the practice of virtues (*praxis*); (2) those in the middle way to whom contemplation (*theoria*) and the suppression of passions (*apatheia*) are particularly suitable; and finally (3) the perfect, to whom is made known true experimental knowledge of God (*theologia*). These various stages are understood to interpenetrate one another; the soul rises and falls back from one to the other without following any rule. They mark moments of our own human existence open to divine transformation.[64]

Suffice it to say, in these memorable words attributed to St. John Chrysostom, "No matter where we happen to be, by prayer we can set up an altar to God in our heart." Chief among these prayers is the one Jesus taught to his disciples, the Lord's Prayer, the wellspring of Christian devotion. It ranks supreme among all the prayers of the Christian Church.

Together with the "Our Father," there is another prayer that is focal in the Christian tradition, this being the Prayer of the Publican, asking for mercy. In the Eastern Church, the practice of this prayer is outlined in detail in *The Philokalia, The Way of the Pilgrim,*[65] and a multitude of minor texts that address the mystery and meaning of the name of Jesus.

A contemporary exponent of this way of prayer, Kallistos Ware, has said that the invocation of the name of Jesus, while being a prayer of utmost simplicity, accessible to every Christian, "leads at the same time to the deepest mysteries of contemplation" and that the more this prayer becomes a part of ourselves "the more we enter into the movement of love which passes unceasingly between Father, Son , and Holy Spirit."[66]

The Franciscan Way and the Prayer of Praise

The spirituality of St. Francis permeates the teachings of his order and in the writings of saints like Clare of Assisi and Bonaventure.[67] The doctrine most identified with a Franciscan theology of formation centers on Christ, the Second Person of the Blessed Trinity, that is to say, it is "Christocentric" through and through.[68] Francis is universally recognized as a Christ-figure. He lived in the flesh the mystery of incarnation, adoption, redemption, and restoration. He saw all of creation as a revelation of the eternal designs of a loving Creator. His love of creation overflows in frequent prayers of praise and thanksgiving. His canticles summarize his abandonment to Christ and his conviction that Jesus not only draws repentant sinners to a new order of relationship but turns the entire order of creation into one long hymn of praise. The hallmarks of Franciscan spirituality are, therefore:

1. that we are called to see with a contemplative gaze the marvelous unity in all the works of God;
2. that every facet of human life reflects this unity, including temporary trials and touches of glory;
3. that as innumerable and detailed as our activities might be, they find themselves, in and through Christ, wholly concentrated on God's love for us and on our love for him and one another;
4. that all human efforts originate in grace and are supported by grace;
5. that the principal of universal love is the force ruling and directing all things from beginning to end;

6. that Christ is both the immediate object of contemplation and the means by which we know the Father and the Trinity;

7. that rather than trying to bring more of the supernatural into our life, as though this were something superimposed from the outside, a follower of Francis seeks to know by revealed teaching that every life, that all our actions and sufferings, have supernatural implications; that we are essentially dependent on God; that we come to know the will of Christ day by day in the duties imposed by our vocation as inspired by the Spirit of Jesus, as found in the Gospels, and as under the direction of the Church; and that to accomplish God's will with joy, confidence, humility, and generosity restrains the aimless rambling of our own selfishness and self-will.[69]

Praise of the Triune God is a form of contemplative prayer characteristic of the Franciscan way since it draws us to adore, love, and serve God and to see brotherly/sisterly goodness in every creature. It inclines us to act with the Spirit of Jesus in contrast to every form of violence. For these reasons the Franciscan way is often associated with an ecological spirituality, centered on caring for things as an expression of the care of the Divine for creation.

Some essential exercises of Franciscan spirituality are: reception of the Eucharist; the imitation of Christ; reliance on the Holy Spirit, who vivifies and activates the soul, thus making possible our transformation into Christ; a love for and a keen devotion to the Virgin Mary and the Mystical Body of Jesus; reception of the sacraments and participation in the liturgical life of the church; and adherence to various ascetical practices such as meditation, not as ends in themselves, but as openings to the mysteries and revelations of the life of Christ—all drawing us toward appreciative abandonment to the Paschal Mystery and a contemplative style of prayer.[70]

The Ignatian Way and the Spiritual Exercises

The wisdom of Ignatian Spirituality and its methods of discernment continue to be sought as a trusted source of guidance to contemplative prayer. At the core of the Ignatian way is Ignatius' own story, for he was blessed through suffering with a a change of heart that made him an intense lover of God and others, a man of faith as eager as the bride in the Canticle of Canticles to tell of the wonders of divine love.[71] He felt an inner urge to communicate his contemplative experience in some form, though nothing verbal could match the force and power of the non-verbal exchange he had undergone. The sum total of these factors resulted in *The Spiritual Exercises* that record Ignatius' extraordinary openness to God, his religious experiences of conversion and contemplation, and his awareness of the need for competent direction to help one discern, for example, the meaning of consolation and desolation, good and evil movements of the spirit, and the way to devote one's whole life to the love and service of God. While the *Exercises* occupy a preeminent place in the formation of members and affiliates of the Society of Jesus, increasingly in our time lay men and women have participated in directed retreats of eight to thirty days in forms reflecting a Vatican II theology without impeding the authority and efficacy of the authentic *Exercises*.[72]

At the heart of the *Exercises* is the process of Ignatian discernment in which one must prayerfully reflect upon the concrete situation as the living word of God. All that one is and does must be seen in the light of God's revealed Word in Jesus Christ, in the Bible, and in the tradition of the church. This process consists in attending to the personal and spiritual experiences that are part of every life situation. One then reflects on them in dialogue with directives present in the prophetic Word of God. The end result is a listening stance toward our world as Spirit-filled in a way that renders us both free and objective, able to view life with a contemplative eye and to act according to the command of love.

In *The Spiritual Exercises*, Ignatius shows that to discover one's true identity in Christ is not a self-centered process resulting in self-fulfillment in a functional sense. It is an ongoing process of self-transcendence resulting in self-giving love in a transcendent sense.

Discernment in this way of prayer entails:

1. being receptive to the dynamics of God's active love in history and its presentation of new and unexpected challenges;
2. reflecting prayerfully on the concrete circumstances of our lives as well as on our own interior reactions and responses to them;
3. striving to go beyond appearances to a profound confrontation with what the following of Christ seems to demand of us here and now;
4. coming to a kind of felt-knowledge (*sentir*) or an effective, intuitive knowing that is more than an intellectual grasping of abstract propositions but is rather a total human experience of understanding whether or not a decision or action will lead us to an authentic response to the word of God;
5. making a final act of determination or decision in the light of the Gospel and according to the norm of personal identity with Christ, in short, responding wholeheartedly to the Word of God here and now.[73]

In this process, we are to pray ceaselessly for the light of the Holy Spirit, for interior understanding, for illuminating touches that are from God, in God, and for God. We are to seek through prayer a lived resonance with Jesus Christ and an ongoing creative fidelity to the call of the Spirit, no matter the cost.

A sign of confirmation of our chosen direction, a "testing of the Spirit," can be found in Ignatius' constant use of words like "contentment," "peace," "quiet," "rest." These words refer to the importance of felt-knowledge grounded in spiritual liberty and the desire to serve Christ alone.[74] This is the peace that leads to profound joy and its fruits of patience, kindness, and self-control. This is the sign of Jesus' own "yes" to the Father that is to be imitated by each follower and by the Christian community as a whole.

The aim of the *Exercises* is thus complete openness to the Spirit and an unconditional "yes" to God. Throughout the four weeks of contemplation, this aim never wavers. It may be approached with different, increasingly intense experiences of communion, but the goal of growth in real love of Jesus is our constant guide. In this light, there can be no separation between contemplation and action, for the aim of being and doing is oneness with the Lord, glorifying God's name, and therein not only winning souls for Christ but finding our own salvation.[75]

The Carmelite Way and the Threefold Path of Purgation, Illumination, and Union

Contemplative prayer in the Carmelite tradition is best understood in the light of the four ways of prayer described by Teresa of Avila in her autobiography as the "four waters":[76]

1. The prayer of discursive meditation is compared to laboriously drawing water up from a well and transporting it in a bucket. This stage of beginners often includes bouts of aridity and distaste since it depends heavily upon the activity of the intellect but in the midst of it one may derive great comfort and benefit from considering the power and greatness of God and the love God shows us in all things.

2. Working a windlass and bucket is comparable to the second method of irrigation or the prayer of quiet. This presupposes that one has grown in an ability to relax in God and to avoid excessive use of the reasoning faculties. This second stage is a gift one cannot acquire or procure by means of one's own efforts alone; it is God who draws one to inner recollection and new feelings of affection in a relationship akin to "spiritual courtship."

3. The third method of irrigation is the employment of water from a stream. This is comparable to a kind of suspension of the sense faculties in which one experiences incomparable sweetness and delight and finds oneself immersed in contemplation and the enjoyment of one's Beloved, a stage of prayer akin to "spiritual betrothal."

4. The fourth method of irrigating is quite easy; it is under the care of Divine Providence and is comparable to watering by rain. This signifies a state

of union in which the soul is apparently passive, a recipient of the graces of transforming union, comparable to "spiritual marriage." One lives now in a habitual state of union as opposed to moments of brief, but intense, duration, that are, in fact, life-transforming. The effects of "spiritual marriage" are an awareness of the divine indwelling in the soul, a great tenderness and a courage to perform in Christ's name deeds of heroism and deep humility.

What Teresa experienced as a contemplative, John of the Cross was able to explain as a mystical theologian.[77] He, too, enjoyed the highest graces of union while being gifted with the ability to describe in detail the threefold path of purgation, illumination, and union. The purgative way was a gift of grace, given precisely to disclose the poverty of our existence. It implied passing through "dark nights" of sense and spirit in which we learn to fasten our eyes on Christ alone. This midnight hour can only be endured in faith, which for St. John is the only "proximate means of ascent to union with God."[78] Under the guidance of grace, we may be led toward the dawning of a new day of understanding (illumination) and a new life of union with God, who alone can satisfy our spiritual hunger.

John's teachings, like those of Teresa, are as comprehensive as they are convincing. They cover all facets of our relationship with the Lord from the childhood of dependency on consolations to the adulthood of carrying the cross. The saint identifies with the accuracy of an experienced guide the characteristics of beginners, proficients, and the perfect. He traces the movements of the mind from discursive meditation to the secret wisdom of the heart only God can teach.[79] In the teachings of both Teresa and John, the following dispositions foster a life of contemplative prayer.

1. *Attention*: mental prayer is a matter of being aware of and knowing to whom we are speaking; it involves focusing our memory, imagination, and anticipation, our faith, hope and love, on God alone.

2. *Affection*: this prayer is intimate, comparable to conversation between friends who experience great affinity for one another; it is an experience of communion with God, rooted in a great desire to be with the Beloved.

3. *Christ-centeredness*: Christ is the direct object of both mental and affective prayer; he is the Way, the Truth, and the Life. In and through his humanity and his divinity we are led to intimacy with the Trinity and to transformation of the highest degree possible in this life.

4. *Contemplation*: it is to contemplative prayer that we are oriented by virtue of our Baptism. This grace is not produced by our own efforts; it is wholly gratuitous; it is an infused experience of the presence of God that gives light and warmth to our mind and heart; it is a habitual state of receptive recollection, of mystical attraction to God in the depths of our being, and of a willingness to act in God's name and to obey only God's will.

Conclusion

In this Afterword, I have tried to present a sampling of the ways of spirituality found in the two thousand-year treasury of our faith and formation tradition. Though not mentioned here, I also have in my mind the varied and laudable contributions to the field of formative spirituality to be found in the Dominican school, in the mystics of the English School (notably Richard Rolle, Walter Hilton, the anonymous author of *The Cloud of Unknowing*, and Julian of Norwich); in the Rhineland School (John Ruusbroec, Henry Suso, Johannes Tauler; and, of course, in the French School (Pierre Cardinal de Berulle, Jean-Jacques Olier, John Eudes), the influence of which cannot be underestimated. The impact of the latter school extends to the Salesians, the Christian Brothers founded by Jean Baptiste de la Salle, the Spiritans under the leadership of Venerable Francis Libermann, and the members of the St. Vincent de Paul Society. Of interest here is the French School's stress on *adoration*, a state of adoring love proceeding from the core of one's being; *abnegation* or profound surrender to God implying annihilation of self-interest; and a desire to fulfill in God's name one's *apostolic* duty.[80] Once again in these representative schools we see the emphasis that characterizes a truly Christian way of life: openness to the inspirations of the Spirit and a willingness to incarnate what one receives in the marketplace of the mundane, in the "Nazareths" of daily life.

Though each school of spiritual deepening brings with it a distinctive emphasis or way of responding to the Word of God, all center on the common ways of reading, meditating, praying and contemplating discussed previously. All respect the forming, reforming, and transforming power of intentional spiritual disciplines or practices that guide us on our journey homeward to God.

As I hope this book has made clear, whether we read Benedict, Symeon the New Theologian, Francis of Assisi, Ignatius of Loyola, Catherine of Siena, or Teresa of Avila, we shall find concurrence on the point that contemplative prayer transforms the particulars of one's emotional, cultural, political, and social life. It involves becoming so interiorly liberated that no suffering, no material restraint, no incident of failure or defeat can deter us from pursuing the way that leads to God and that lends transcendent significance to the smallest act. Contemplative prayer thus allows the radical restlessness of the human heart to culminate in a mystical experience of resting in God, momentarily on earth and forever in eternity.

Endnotes

1. See *Lumen Gentium*, 39-42. All references to the Vatican II Council Documents can be found in Walter M. Abbott, gen. ed., *The Documents of Vatican II* (Chicago: Follett, 1966). References are cited by Article numbers. Much of what I write here is based, of necessity, on my own Roman Catholic faith and formation tradition.

2. *Gaudium et Spes*, 58-59.

3. *Lumen Gentium*, 50.

4. All references to Holy Scripture incorporated into this text are taken from *The New American Bible* (Wichita: Catholic Bible, 1992/93).

5. See Jacques and Raissa Maritain, *Liturgy and Contemplation*, trans. Joseph W. Evans (New York: P.J. Kenedy, 1960), pp. 19-23.

6. *Sacrosanctum Concilium*, 9-10.

7. See Cyprian Vagaggini, *Theological Dimensions of the Liturgy: A General Treatise on the Theology of the Liturgy*, trans. Leonard J. Doyle and W. A. Jurgens (Collegeville, MN: Liturgical, 1976).

8. *Sacrosanctum Concilium*, 43.

9. *Ibid.*, 41.

10. See *Lumen Gentium*, 5.

11. See *Sacrosanctum Concilium*, 7.

12. Vagaggini, *Theological Dimensions of the Liturgy*, pp. 882-883.

13. See *The Book of Her Life* in *The Collected Works of St. Teresa of Avila*, Volume One, trans. Kieran Kavanaugh and Otilio Rodriguez (Washington DC: Institute of Carmelite Studies, ICS Publications, 1976), p. 44.

14. *Lumen Gentium*, 11.

15. *Lumen Gentium*, 71.

16. *Ibid.*, 71.

17. *Ibid.*, 11. See Article 11 for the Church's teaching on the other sacraments. Here I am only commenting on the "Sacraments of Initiation," Baptism, Confirmation, Eucharist.

18. *Ibid.*, 10.

19. See Vagaggini, *Theological Dimensions of the Liturgy*, pp. 132-133.

20. *The Sayings of Light and Love* in *The Collected Works of St. John of the Cross*, trans. Kieran Kavanaugh and Otilio Rodriguez (Washington, DC: Institute of Carmelite Studies, ICS Publications, 1991), p. 97.

21. See Susan Muto, *Pathways of Spiritual Living* (New York: Doubleday, 1984; rpt. Petersham, MA: St. Bede's, 1991).

22. Guigo II, *The Ladder of Monks and Twelve Meditations*, trans. Edmund Colledge and James Walsh (Kalamazoo, MI: Cistercian, 1978), p. 68.

23. *Ibid.*, p. 69.

24. *Ibid.*, p. 68.

25. *Ibid.*, pp. 68-69.

26. See Anthony Bloom, *Living Prayer* (Springfield, IL: Templegate, 1966).

27. See Bernard of Clairvaux, *Sermon on the Song of Songs*, I, *Works of Bernard of Clairvaux*, Vol. 3, Cistercian Fathers Series, trans. Killian Walsh (Kalamazoo, MI: Cistercian, 1971), pp. 95-101.

28. *Teresa of Avila: The Interior Castle*, trans. Kieran Kavanaugh and Otilio Rodriguez, *Classics of Western Spirituality* (New York: Paulist, 1979).

29. See E. Underhill, *Practical Mysticism* (Columbus, OH: Ariel, 1991 rpt.).

30. See *The Dialogue of Catherine of Siena*, trans. Suzanne Noffke, *Classics of Western Spirituality* (New York: Paulist, 1980).

31. Guigo II, *The Ladder of Monks and Twelve Meditations*, p. 68.

32. *Ibid.*, p. 74.

33. *Ibid.*, p. 69.

34. *The Sayings of Light and Love* in *The Collected Works of St. John of the Cross*, p. 90.

35. Guigi II, *The Ladder of Monks and Twelve Meditations*, p. 79.

36. *Ibid.*

37. *Ibid.*, pp. 80-86.

38. See Adrian van Kaam, *The Dynamics of Spiritual Self-Direction* (Pittsburgh: Epiphany Books, 1991); see also Susan Muto and Adrian van Kaam, *Divine Guidance: Seeking to Find and Follow the Will of God* (Ann Arbor, MI: Servant Publications, 1994).

39. *The Book of Her Life* in *The Collected Works of St. Teresa of Avila*, pp. 46-47.

40. *The Living Flame* in *The Collected Works of St. John of the Cross*, pp. 684-701.

41. *Ibid.*, pp. 698-699.

42. See Susan Muto, *Womanspirit: Reclaiming the Deep Feminine in Our Human Spirituality* (New York: Crossroad, 1992).

43. *The Practice of Spiritual Direction* (San Francisco: Harper & Row, 1982), p. 44.

44. *Ibid.*, pp. 45-64.

45. *In Search of Spiritual Identity* (Denville, NJ: Dimension, 1975), pp. 172-196.

46. *Ibid.*, pp. 175-176.

47. *The Dark Night* in *The Collected Works of St. John of the Cross*, pp. 435-438.

48. The best sourcebook of information outlining *The Rule*, its history and continuing influence, including a detailed listing of Benedictine monks and nuns of North America and centers where Benedictine spirituality thrives, can be found in the 1980/81 definitive translation of *The Rule of St. Benedict*, ed. Timothy Fry (Collegeville, MN: Liturgical, n.d.).

49. See *Athanasius: The Life of Anthony and the Letter to Marcellinus*, trans. Robert Gregg, *Classics of Western Spirituality* (New York: Paulist, 1980).

50. See *John Cassian: Conferences*, trans. Colm Luibheid, *Classics of Western Spirituality* (New York: Paulist, 1985).

51. Jean Leclercq, *The Love of Learning and the Desire for God: A Study of Monastic Culture*, trans. Catharine Misrahi (New York: Fordham University, 1985).

52. Hubert van Zeller, *The Benedictine Idea* (Springfield, IL: Templegate, 1959), p. 29.

53. *John Cassian: Conferences*, pp. 125-140.

54. See M. Basil Pennington, "Thomas Merton and Centering Prayer," *Review for Religious* (January-February, 1989), 119-129.

55. "The Inner Experience: Christian Contemplation," *Cistercian Studies*, Vol. 18, No. 3 (1983), 207.

56. See Anonymous, *The Cloud of Unknowing*, ed. James Walsh, *Classics of Western Spirituality* (New York: Paulist, 1981).

57. Further information on Abbot Keating's work can be obtained by writing to: Contemplative Outreach, 1591 Gateway Road, Snowmass, CO 81654. See his book, *Open Heart, Open Mind: The Contemplative Dimension of the Gospel* (Rockport, MA: Element, 1986).

58. "The Inner Experience: Christian Contemplation," p. 210. See also Thomas Merton, *Seeds of Contemplation* (New York: Dell, 1949).

59. *Symeon: The New Theologian, the Discourses*, trans. C. J. de Catanzaro, *Classics of Western Spirituality* (New York: Paulist, 1980).

60. See M. Basil Pennington's book, *O Holy Mountain!: Journal of a Retreat on Mount Athos* (Garden City, NY: Doubleday, 1978) for a contemporary look at an ancient and still flourishing way of life centered in the hesychast method of contemplative prayer.

61. *Gregory Palamas*, ed. John Meyendorff, *Classics of Western Spirituality* (New York: Paulist, 1983).

62. For further information, consult *Orthodox Spirituality: An Outline of the Orthodox Ascetical and Mystical Tradition* by a Monk of the Eastern Church (London: SPCK, 1968).

63. *Ibid.*, p. 21.

64. For further insight into Orthodox Spirituality, see Andrew Ryder, *Prayer in the Eastern Tradition* (Locust Valley, NY: Living Flame, 1983); and *The Jesus Prayer* (Philadelphia: Fortress, 1975).

65. See Anonymous, *The Way of a Pilgrim*, trans. R. French (San Francisco: Harper, 1991); and *Early Fathers from the Philokalia*, trans. E. Kadloubovsky and G. Palmer (London: Faber and Faber, 1954).

66. See Kallistos Ware, *The Power of the Name: The Jesus Prayer in Orthodox Spirituality* (Fairacres, Oxford: SLG, 1976).

67. *Bonaventure: The Soul's Journey into God; The Tree of Life; The Life of St. Francis*, trans. Ewert Cousins, *Classics of Western Spirituality* (New York: Paulist, 1978). See also *Francis and Clare*, trans. Regis Armstrong and Ignatius Brady, *Classics of Western Spirituality* (New York: Paulist, 1982).

68. See Valentine-M. Breton, *Franciscan Spirituality: Synthesis/Antithesis*, trans. Flavian Frey (Chicago: Franciscan Herald, 1957).

69. *Ibid.*, pp. 31ff.

70. Recommended for further study as the most authoritative compendium of Franciscan spirituality is *The Omnibus of the Sources*, ed. Marion A. Habit (Chicago: Franciscan Herald, 1973). This essential text also contains an extensive research bibliography, index of writings, and further resources.

71. A good introduction to Ignatius' life and a contemporary translation of the *Exercises* is that by David L. Fleming (St. Louis: Institute of Jesuit Sources, 1978).

72. See George E. Ganss, "The Authentic Spiritual Exercises of St. Ignatius: Some Facts of History and Terminology Basic to Their Functional Efficacy Today," *Studies in the Spirituality of Jesuits*, Vol. 1, No. 2 (Nov. 1969).

73. See John Carroll Futrell, "Ignatian Discernment," *Studies in the Spirituality of Jesuits*, Vol. 2, No. 2 (April, 1970).

74. *Ignatius of Loyola*, ed. George Ganss, *Classics of Western Spirituality* (New York: Paulist, 1991).

75. Retreats based on the *Exercises* are offered at many centers, for example, Loyola House in Guelph, Ontario, and the Mercy Center, in Burlingame, California. Several universities and schools offer courses in Ignatian spirituality, notably Creighton University, St. Louis University, the University of San Francisco, Fordham, and Georgetown, to mention only a few.

76. *The Book of Her Life* in *The Collected Works of St. Teresa of Avila*, pp. 80-144.

77. See Sebastian V. Ramge, *An Introduction to the Writings of Saint Teresa* (Chicago: Henry Regnery, 1963); see also Richard Hardy, *The Search for Nothing: The Life of John of the Cross* (New York: Crossroad, 1982).

78. *The Ascent of Mount Carmel* in *The Collected Works of St. John of the Cross*, pp. 154-155.

79. See Susan Muto, *The Journey Homeward* (Denville, NJ: Dimension, 1977); and Susan Muto, *John of the Cross for Today: The Ascent* (Notre Dame, IN: Ave Maria, 1991); and Susan Muto, *John of the Cross for Today: The Dark Night* (Notre Dame, IN: Ave Maria, 1994).

80. See *Berulle and the French School*, ed. William M. Thompson, with a Preface by Susan Muto in *Classics of Western Spirituality* (New York: Paulist, 1989).

Appendix

A Practical Guide to Spiritual Reading

How to Follow a Three-Part, Twelve-Month
Cycle of Readings in the
Classics of our Christian Faith and Formation Tradition
For Classroom or Home Study Purposes*

---

1. Select six texts per cycles A and B from the essential classics (totaling over the year twelve books, or one per month, and over three years, thirty-six books).

    A. Ancient to Medieval (c. 100 - 1200)
    (January to June)

    B. Medieval to Modern (c. 1300 - 1900)
    (July to December)

2. Set aside sacred reading time every day.
3. Do background reading of any secondary material you deem necessary at another time during the month.
4. Read the selected classics formatively following the directives found in *A Practical Guide to Spiritual Reading.*
5. Do foundational theme tracing according to the guidelines also found in *A Practical Guide to Spiritual Reading.*
6. Follow-up personal formative readings with optional small reading groups that meet once a month to share their walk with the masters.

---

*Audio tapes by Dr. Susan Muto on the works of many of these masters are available from the Epiphany Association. Call (412) 661-5678 for further details pertaining to featured authors and rental fees.

Purpose of Planning Cyclical Reading Programs (Ancient to Medieval and Medieval to Modern)

The cycles I have outlined for you offer a first-hand encounter with representative authors, texts, and schools of spirituality from classical and contemporary resources in the pre- and post-Reformation literature of spirituality. These selections feature the world's great faith and formation traditions with a special emphasis on ancient, medieval, and modern Western and Eastern Christian masters.

Followers of the cycles read and meditate on the formationally relevant themes found in seminal texts of timeless validity from the ancient to the medieval era and from medieval to modern times, potentially encountering over a three-year period a total of thirty-six texts.

These cycles aim, first of all, to help you to trace foundationally the steps and stages necessary for growth in the life of the spirit and to disclose formative directives that represent, in effect, conditions for the possibility of any spiritual progress whatsoever.

Readers strive to personalize these themes, indicated at the start of each suggested cycle, by making them relevant for their own and others' human and Christian formation in today's world. They reflect on these rich treasures of wisdom in the light of St. Paul's words to Timothy:

> Take as a model of sound teaching what you have heard me say, in faith and love in Christ Jesus. Guard the rich deposit of faith with the help of the Holy Spirit who dwells within us. (2 Tim. 1:13-14)

Secondarily, you will discover as you read in a foundational way the paths, steps, stages, rules, patterns, and experiences that describe in concrete terms the journey of the soul to God—the way of purifying formation, illuminating reformation, and unifying transformation.

As distinct from a mainly historical or literary-critical treatment of texts, readers strive in their reflections on the writings of the masters to disclose foundational formative directives that suggest obstacles to and conditions for the possibility of spiritual progress. Strive to personalize these themes by linking them as closely as possible to your unique, communal formation journey, to the God who guides you on the way, and to the words of sacred scripture.

Above all, take your time. If you want to spend more months with one book, do so. Spread the cycle over as much time as you need to imbibe the wisdom of the masters. If you do not finish one book, but want to go on to the next, commit yourself to return to your original selection when you can. Make these books your "friends," a part of your library of spiritual literature. Let the themes they offer become your openings to divine guidance.

YEAR ONE

A. First Year Cycle: Ancient to Medieval
Theme: *Our Likeness to God*

1. Origen
(185-254)

Origen has been called the most influential and seminal theologian, biblical scholar, and master of souls in the early Greek Church. He succeeded Clement of Alexandria as head of the Christian Catechetical School (hence his interest in the spiritual or allegorical *vs.* the strictly literal meaning of the text). He is largely responsible for the early synthesis of Platonism and Christianity and is a major contributor to the theology of the *image of God.*

Read: *Origen: An Exhortation to Martyrdom, Prayer and Selected Works,* trans. Rowan A. Greer in *The Classics of Western Spirituality.* New York: Paulist Press, 1979.

2. Antony the Great
(c. 400)

Abba Dorotheus
(c. 500)

St. Isaac of Nineveh
(c. 600)

These three belong to the common heritage of East and West, to the undivided Church. They not only treat the sublime themes of the relation of God to cosmos and humankind; they also reveal a profound understanding of human nature, of the obstacles that mar our *likeness to God*, and of the personal and social conditions that facilitate solitude and community in Christ. The texts that best represent the teachings and practices of the Early Eastern Fathers are: St. Antony's *Directions on Life in Christ*; Abba Dorotheus' *Directions on Spiritual Training*; and St. Isaac's *Directions on Spiritual Training.*

Read: *Early Fathers from the Philokalia, Together with Some Writings of St. Abba Dorotheus, St. Isaac of Syria and St. Gregory Palamas*, trans. E. Kadloubovsky and G.E.H. Palmer. London: Faber and Faber, 1954.

3. Augustine
(354-430)

St. Augustine of Hippo was the dominant personality of the Western Church of his time. Some scholars rank him as the greatest thinker of antiquity, others as among the greatest of mystics. Undoubtedly he is a powerful, often controversial theologian, influencing with equal vigor Bernard of Clairvaux in the twelfth century and Martin Luther in the sixteenth.

Augustine dialogued the religion of the New Testament with the Platonic tradition of Greek philosophy (Neoplatonism), and he struggled throughout his life to overcome the dualistic tendencies engendered by the early influence of Manichaeism in his life.

At the heart of Augustine's theology (and thus at odds with Neoplatonism) is the doctrine of the Incarnation. Christ is the mediator by whom, and alone by whom, we come to God.

Christocentricity is thus the keynote of Augustinian spirituality. It helps to explain the intensely personal note of the *Confessions*, the work which, above all others, gives an insight into Augustine's mind. In his *Confessions*, he is mainly a man of prayer, moving from painful conversion to the heights of mystical vision. Despite his emphasis on the primacy of love, Augustine's spirituality is intellectual as well as affective and emotional. His *Confessions* is one of the finest spiritual autobiographies ever written; its formative influence on fellow Christians is unsurpassed in the literature of spirituality. In this text, reformation of the deformed *image of God* in the sinful soul is accomplished by *participation in God*, made possible by the *mediation of Christ*.

To understand his foundational contribution to our Christian formation tradition, read: *The Confessions of St. Augustine*, trans. John K. Ryan. New York: Doubleday, 1960.

4. Maximus the Confessor
(c. 580-662)

St. Maximus has been called the last great theologian of Greek patristics. From the time that he entered monastic life in 613, he spent most of his energy in the defense of orthodox doctrine against the heretics preaching various forms of separation of the divine and human nature of God in the second Person of the Trinity. Ultimately he was arrested in Rome and sent into exile. In 662, he was again in Constantinople where heretics condemned him to be scourged and to have his tongue and right hand cut off. He died in that year as a result of his sufferings for the faith.

In addition to his dogmatic and polemic writings, Maximus expounded a doctrine of charity and commented on the works of Pseudo-Dionysius, for whom he had the greatest reverence. He centers his entire doctrine on Christ, on love for him as our Savior versus any form of self-love. Above all, it is charity that deifies the soul, enables it to experience its *adoptive filiation*, and unites it to God in the bond of mystical marriage—all of which comes through Christ Jesus.

Read: *Maximus Confessor: Selected Writings*, trans. George C. Berthold in *The Classics of Western Spirituality*. New York: Paulist Press, 1985.

5. William of St. Thierry (1085-1148)

Born at Liège, France, of noble parentage, William left there to study at Rheims; hence he was a well-educated man when he entered the Cistercian abbey of Signy where he died in 1148. Prior to that, he became abbot of the Benedictine monastery of St. Thierry near Rheims around 1121. He served as abbot for at least fourteen years, providing exemplary discipline and spiritual leadership. During this time there developed the close and lasting friendship between William and St. Bernard of Clairvaux, whom he met around 1118, and who was influential in his later decision to become a Cistercian monk. Most of the time he spent at Signy was devoted to writing due to an illness that left him unable to share fully the rigors of monastic life.

In 1135, William resigned his abbatial office and withdrew to the meditative life of the Cistercian monastery of Signy. There he wrote his more formative works on questions pertaining to the spiritual life and the problem of faith, including *The Enigma of Faith*, *The Mirror of Faith*, and *The Nature and Dignity of Love*.

In 1144, after visiting the charterhouse (a hermitic form of monasticism) of Mont-Dieu near Rheims, he composed *The Golden Epistle*, one of the most significant medieval works on the value of the contemplative life.

William remained an active critic of the primarily rational expositions of Christian doctrine on the Trinity, proposed by his contemporary, Peter Abelard, attacking especially what he perceived as the latter's moral relativism. William's main interest, however, centered on mysticism versus theological debate. He proposed that the soul, although estranged from God due to original sin, is also empowered intrinsically to experience a mystical return to its *divine origin* during its earthly existence.

William believes that this return is effected in stages analogous to the archetype of God's inner Trinitarian structure: that is to say, humans are progressively liberated from material and temporal impediments to union and eventually undergo, as God's gift, an experiential knowledge of him by a process of (1) *Reminiscence* (the ascetical stage, relative to the Father); (2) *Understanding* (the intellectual stage, relative to the Son); (3) *Love* (the unitive stage, relative to the Spirit). This direct participation in the life of the Spirit is held to be an anticipation of the eternal existence in the life to come.

Read: *William of St. Thierry, The Golden Epistle, A Letter to the Brethren at Mont Dieu.* Spencer, MA: Cistercian Publications, 1971; *William of St. Thierry: On Contemplating God.* Spencer, MA: Cistercian Publications, 1971.

6. Richard of St.-Victor
(+1173)

Richard of St.-Victor's treatises profoundly influenced medieval and modern mysticism. He entered the Abbey of Saint-Victor in Paris and studied under the famous scholastic theologian and philosopher, Hugh of Saint-Victor. Richard represents the school of Saint-Victor centered at the Abbey where, at an early age, he became superior in 1159 and prior in 1162.

The Victorines were erudite in Holy Scripture and the Latin Fathers and interested in theology and mysticism. Richard's thinking was not dry and abstract but profoundly biblical. Using the Bible in a spiritual sense, he found in it the basis of his theological thought. In this regard, he enjoys an affinity with St. Augustine, St. Anselm of Canterbury, and St. Bonaventure, all of whom focused on a loving contemplation of God rather than on a strict scholastic approach.

For Richard, the act of contemplation is a function of faith, searching after insight and *unification with God.* Starting from an analysis of the natural abilities of the soul and the different forms of knowledge and love, he describes the six different stages of contemplation.

To each of these corresponds a spiritualization of knowledge and a higher form of love, starting from an initial desire via the love of oneself to utter oneness with the Beloved.

An astute director of formation, Richard's mystical theology had great influence through St. Bonaventure and the Franciscan School. Employing in his mystical works an extensive symbolism reminiscent of the Alexandrian School, he made the School of Saint-Victor famous throughout the twelfth and into the thirteenth century.

According to Richard, the soul proceeds from sense perception to ecstasy through imagination, reason, and intuition. The soul must employ secular learning as well as divine revelation until it is finally united through grace with God in divine contemplation. His *Benjamin Major* and *Benjamin Minor* became standard manuals on the practice of mystical spirituality in medieval times.

Read: *Richard of St. Victor: The Twelve Patriarchs, The Mystical Ark, Book Three of the Trinity,* trans. Grover A. Zinn in *The Classics of Western Spirituality*. New York: Paulist Press, 1979.

B. First Year Cycle: Medieval to Modern
Theme: *Our Call to Love*

1. Jacopone da Todi
(1230-1306)

Like all spiritual seekers, Jacopone descends into the depths of his soul and struggles to *respond fully to God's love* in a world always inclined to give other relations and responsibilities primacy. Jacopone found, as did St. Francis, that in repentance and poverty, one possesses all things.

His *Lauds* offer an excellent example of the poetry of spirituality, but, more significantly, they movingly introduce us to the foundations of Christian spirituality as lived in the spirit of St. Francis of Assisi.

Read: *Jacopone da Todi: The Lauds*, trans. Serge Hughes and Elizabeth Hughes in *The Classics of Western Spirituality*. New York: Paulist Press, 1982.

2. Richard Rolle
(1300-1349)

Richard Rolle, an English mystic, grew disillusioned with his studies at the University of Oxford, especially theological disputation, and left without a degree. He then established himself as a hermit on a private estate.

Later he moved to other hermitages, probably leading a wandering life while offering occasional spiritual direction to a group of nuns at Hampole in South Yorkshire.

In his writings Richard exalts the life of solitude and contemplation, urging strict, at times excessive, physical self-control. He realizes, however, that spiritual progress consists mainly in the development of the *love of God*, not in excesses of mortification. This *life of love*, he assures us, is consummated in mystical union.

His method involves essentially a concentration on and a direction of the affections toward the person of Christ, with a resulting experience of intense joy. To appreciate Rolle's ascetical and affective spirituality, read *The Fire of Love and the Mending of Life*.

Read: *Richard Rolle: The English Writings*, trans. Rosamund S. Allen in *The Classics of Western Spirituality*. New York: Paulist, 1988.

3. Walter Hilton (c. 1343-1396)

Walter Hilton is considered one of the greatest English mystics of the fourteenth century. Following study at Cambridge, he joined an Augustinian Priory and later became a hermit, composing at the Priory his masterwork, *The Scale* (or *Stairway*) *of Perfection*.

This text contains two main books, written separately. The first teaches the *means* by which a soul may advance toward perfection by destroying the image of sin and forming the image of Christ through the practice of virtue and the *works of love*. The second distinguishes between the active or ascetic life and the contemplative or mystic life. Here we find a description of the early stages of mystical contemplation, apparently based on Walter's own experience.

His theological basis resembles the Dominican spirituality of the Rhineland School of Eckhart, Tauler, and Ruusbroec and anticipates the teaching of the Spanish mystics of the sixteenth century, notably St. John of the Cross.

The Scale became and remained a popular devotional classic in the following centuries. It is regarded as one of the finest treatises on contemplation of the late Middle Ages.

Read: *Walter Hilton: The Scale of Perfection*, trans. John P.H. Clark and Rosemary Dorward in *The Classics of Western Spirituality*. New York: Paulist Press, 1991.

4. St. Catherine of Siena (1347-1380)

To meet Catherine is to meet a woman whose *love for the Lord* transformed her personality and enabled her to be a channel through which he could communicate his basic message to the world. Her sensitivity to people's needs and her spirituality go hand in hand. There is no separation in her life between action and contemplation, service and silent adoration. She pierces through the illusions of selfish sensuality and challenges us to become mirrors of Christ's own peace and joy.

The Dialogue is the crowning achievement of the only woman besides St. Teresa of Avila to be granted the title Doctor of the Church.

Read: *Catherine of Siena: The Dialogue*, trans. Suzanne Noffke, O.P., in *The Classics of Western Spirituality*. New York: Paulist Press, 1980.

5. St. Catherine of Genoa (1447-1510)

Catherine's achievement in this poetic outpouring of the soul's *longing for union with God* matches her ability to reconcile polarities of life often thought to be conflicting, for she is at once a mystic and a humanitarian, a contemplative and a servant immersed in care for the physically ill and destitute. In her life and works she is a model of her Divine Master in whose presence our restless souls, with their "instinct for beatitude" come to rest.

Purgation and Purgatory represents one of the finest texts ever composed on the way of purification both in this life and in the next.

Read: *Catherine of Genoa: Purgation and Purgatory, The Spiritual Dialogue*, trans. Serge Hughes in *The Classics of Western Spirituality*. New York: Paulist Press, 1979.

6. John of the Cross (1542-1591)

St. John of the Cross' analysis of mystical experiences is invaluable. His meeting with St. Teresa of Avila in 1567, the year of his ordination, proved decisive, for she enlisted him to promote her reform of the Order by returning to the rigorous primitive rule among the friars. St. John, like St. Teresa, spent the rest of his life in service of the Reform. However, the hostility of the "unreformed" led to his arrest and solitary confinement in the Carmelite monastery at Toledo in December, 1577. When he escaped on a dark night eight months later, he brought with him a number of poems; more followed, with commentaries on the three most important: the *Spiritual Canticle*, the *Ascent of Mount Carmel* and the *Dark Night*, in reality a single unfinished treatise, and the *Living Flame of Love*. Further disputes resulted in his banishment to a remote Andalusian monastery, where he died in 1591.

St. John was widely read in medieval mystical literature. His works, which he never intended for publication, make constant and searching use of the Bible. His poems are among the supreme lyrical creations of Spanish literature, haunting, and passionate, with an exuberance of imagery unequaled in his time.

Both the *Spiritual Canticle* and the *Living Flame* follow the poetic text closely while the *Ascent-Dark Night* is a more formal, systematic treatise on mystical prayer. The active nights of sense and spirit deal with the soul's own preparation for contemplation and action; the corresponding passive nights ponder what God alone can work through the infusion of these gifts. The passive night of the spirit, in which the absence of God is most grievously experienced, becomes nonetheless the threshold of union, the darkest part of the night which precedes the dawn.

The *Canticle* was begun during St. John's imprisonment (1577-1578) and completed after his escape. Later he revised and completed the commentary so that it would more closely accord with the traditional threefold way of purgation, illumination, and union. The *Living Flame* completes his teaching on the *love between God and the soul* and the transformation of the soul in God.

Read: *John of the Cross: Selected Writings*, ed. Kieran Kavanaugh, O.C.D., in *The Classics of Western Spirituality*. New York: Paulist Press, 1987.

YEAR TWO

A. Second Year Cycle: Ancient to Medieval
Theme: *Our Struggle for Perfection*

1. Gregory of Nyssa
(c. 332-c. 395)

St. Gregory of Nyssa was born in Cappadocia, Asia Minor. A Cappadocian Father, who epitomized post-Nicaean patristic thought, he abandoned wealth and family connections to take up a life of ascetic solitude. With companions, among them Gregory of Nazianzus, he formed a cenobium, a community of monks in separate dwellings who observed the rule of silence. In 371 he was appointed bishop of Nyssa. In his mystical doctrine, he describes the spiritual life as an ascent *from darkness to light to deeper darkness*. The true enjoyment of the soul consists in never ceasing to ascend toward the "kindred Deity," who draws that which is his own to himself.

Gregory is one of the three Greek Cappadocian Fathers, the other two being his brother, St. Basil the Great, and their mutual friend, St. Gregory Nazianzus. Of the three, Gregory of Nyssa is considered the most profound mystical teacher and has been called the founder of mystical theology in the church.

The Life of Moses reflects his spiritual sense of the scriptures, that is, the capacity of the Bible to elevate the soul to God. He saw the spiritual life as a continual growth, a straining ahead for what is to come. The spiritual ascent takes place in three stages, symbolized by the Lord's revelation of himself to Moses, first in light, then in the cloud, and, finally, in the dark. In the words of Father John Meyendorff, an authority on Orthodox spirituality, "...Gregory, while being Greek, transcends the Greek mind itself and indicates to his contemporaries and to future generations, including our own, the path to the Living God."

Read: *Gregory of Nyssa: The Life of Moses*, trans. Abraham Malherbe and Everett Ferguson in *The Classics of Western Spirituality*. New York: Paulist Press, 1978.

2. St. Gregory the Great (540-604)

St. Gregory the Great was born in Rome, founded, though without becoming its abbot, St. Andrew's, a Benedictine monastery, and established six additional monasteries on family property. He was papal nuncio to Constantinople and served there until 584. After sincere efforts to evade his election, he became Pope in 590, determined to be a pope of the people and referring to himself as the "servant of God's servants," a title still used today.

Drawing upon St. Augustine of Hippo's *City of God* for his views of the ideal Christian society, Gregory initiated administrative, social, liturgical and moral reforms, which provided the model for the medieval Church. He was a gifted author and one of the great masters of the spiritual life.

Gregory's spirituality is marked by two interdependent characteristics: biblical and monastic. The prime source of his vast knowledge of the Bible was the *lectio divina* that was part of *the monk's daily duty*. This habit of reading and meditating ensured that the meaning of the scriptures sank deeply into the reader's mind.

In his *Moralia in Job*, he made no secret of his preference for the contemplative life and the personal conflicts to which this gave rise. In his *On Pastoral Care*, which became a spiritual and practical guide for medieval bishops, he does admit that both the *vita contemplativa* and the *vita activa* are valid ways of discipleship for Christian preachers/teachers. He makes clear in the text that a man called to the office of bishop must not neglect his neighbors on account of his love of contemplation.

Gregory's teaching on contemplation derives in the Western tradition from Augustine and Ambrose and in the Eastern tradition from St. Basil, Evagrius Ponticus, and St. John Chrysostom, mediated through the writings of Cassian and other Eastern Desert Fathers. Like Cassian, Gregory stresses the need for compunction before contemplation as well as the need for contemplation before action.

Read: *Gregory the Great: Pastoral Care*, trans. Henry Davis. New York: Newman Press, 1950.

3. John Climacus (c. 579-c. 649)

John Climacus entered the monastery of St. Catherine on Mt. Sinai around 600, where he lived as a hermit. He was chosen abbot around 639 and ruled until shortly before he died. *The Ladder of Divine Ascent*, from whence he derived his name, "John of the Ladder," is a handbook on the ascetical and mystical life, most widely used in the ancient Greek Church and still an enduring Christian spiritual classic.

John's "Ladder" symbolizes the Old Testament patriarch Jacob's dream of a climb to heaven. The work is divided into thirty chapters describing the steps in *the spiritual struggle to moral perfection*, culminating on the highest rung in passive contemplation and the mystical ecstasy of divine union. Its thirty steps, instructing the aspirant in a virtue to be acquired and a vice to be surrendered, reflect the hidden life of Christ, whose perfection we are called to imitate.

Although he was influenced by earlier Egyptian and other Eastern monastic writers, John exhibits psychological and spiritual insights with a distinctive, terse style. Translation of the "Ladder" into almost all classical and modern languages attests to its perennial popularity. It has a fundamental influence on the development of Christian monasticism generally and particularly on the Hesychast (Jesus Prayer or Prayer of the Heart) movement among Greek Orthodox and Russian contemplatives.

Read: *John Climacus: The Ladder of Divine Ascent*, trans. Colm Luibheid and Norman Russell in *The Classics of Western Spirituality*. New York: Paulist Press, 1982.

4. Bernard of Clairvaux (1090-1153)

Bernard of Clairvaux, the "Last of the Fathers," stands at the end of a long tradition which saw reason and faith as fused together in a single intuitive loving act. To be "reasonable" was to activate (or allow to be activated) in oneself the image of God, that capacity for *conformity to the divine archetype*, the eternal Word and Wisdom, which is alone truly rational. In his life and teaching and in his writings, Bernard proposed, with fervor and clarity, a mystical theology of love and knowledge, which established a school of spirituality (the Cistercian) of immense power and lasting influence.

The contemplative life, as he understood it, must nourish the entire church in compassion and charity. His texts, *On Loving God* and *The Steps of Humility and Pride*, are invaluable for our spiritual direction and formation.

Read: *Bernard of Clairvaux: Selected Works*, trans. G. R. Evans in *The Classics of Western Spirituality*. New York: Paulist Press, 1987.

5. Hadewijch (c. 1200)

Hadewijch, a Flemish Beguine (a contemplative lay women's movement of her day and country), follows the tradition of love mysticism that is both Christological and trinitarian—a tradition brought to such lofty heights by Bernard and continued in the Rhineland School by John Ruusbroec (1293-1381). Her letters, poems, and "visions" are strongly emotional and ecstatic and yet, like Teresa of Avila, she is able to analyze with reasoned faith and keen powers of personal observation the *steps and stages on the way of love.*

Read: *Hadewijch: The Complete Works*, trans. Mother Columba Hart, O.S.B. in *The Classics of Western Spirituality*. New York: Paulist Press, 1980.

6. Clare of Assisi (c. 1193-1254)

Born in Assisi of a noble family, Clare refused two offers of marriage, but did not finally make up her mind to leave the world until she came under the influence of St. Francis. When she was eighteen, she left home secretly and was placed by Francis in the care of a local convent of Benedictine nuns. Her family tried to induce her to return home, but in vain. She was joined by her sister and later by her widowed mother. St. Francis installed them as the nucleus of a community in a house by the church of San Damiano, drawing up a way of life for them. Thus began the order of Poor Ladies, Minoresses, or, simply, Poor Clares. In 1215, Clare obtained from Pope Innocent III the privilege of poverty, i.e., permission for the nuns to live wholly on alms, without possessing any personal or communal property. Their mode of life was harder than that of any other nuns at the time, and Clare had to resist attempts at moderation in order to practice what she called "the most authentic expression of *evangelical perfection* as understood by St. Francis of Assisi." Clare guided her community with discretion for forty years, during many of which she suffered severe ill health—though she was glimpsed at night tucking in the bedclothes of her nuns and wrote to a Poor Clare who started a convent in Prague not to overdo her austerities, "for our bodies are not made of brass." She died twenty-seven years after St. Francis, having left a powerful spiritual legacy in the form of a letter, the *Rule* of St. Clare, and most of all her own interior life.

Read: *Francis and Clare: The Complete Works*, trans. Regis J. Armstrong, O.F.M. Cap. and Ignatius C. Grady, O.F.M. in *The Classics of Western Spirituality*. New York: Paulist Press, 1982

B. Second Year Cycle: Medieval to Modern
Theme: *Our Fidelity to Christ*

1. Francis of Assisi
(1182-1226)

Born in Assisi, Italy, of a wealthy merchant family, as a youth Francis led a frivolous, carefree life; then an experience of sickness and civil war settled and steadied him. One day in the church of San Damiano he seemed to hear Christ saying to him: "Repair my falling house." Taking the words literally, he sold some goods from his father's warehouse to pay for the repair work. Before long he had been disinherited and disowned. Penniless, he wed "Lady Poverty." Three years later in 1210, Pope Innocent III authorized him and eleven companions to be roving *preachers of Christ in simplicity and lowliness*. Thus began the Friars Minor.

In 1212, he founded with St. Clare the first community of Poor Clares. In 1221 he produced a revised version of his rule, which reiterated his example of poverty, humility, and evangelical freedom. In 1224 Francis received the gift of stigmatization. He suffered increasingly until he apologized to his body, "Brother Ass," and welcomed "Sister Death" two years later.

Francis is universally admired as a man of tremendous spiritual insight and power, whose consuming love for Jesus Christ and redeemed creation found expression in all he said and did, as witnessed in the compelling appeal of his *Canticle of Brother Sun* and in his ability to capture the imagination of believers and non-believers alike.

Read: *Francis and Clare: The Complete Works*, trans. Regis J. Armstrong, O.F.M. Cap. and Ignatius C. Grady, O.F.M. in *The Classics of Western Spirituality*. New York: Paulist Press, 1982

2. Bonaventure (1217-1226)

Little is known of Bonaventure's family life, but it seems that when he fell gravely ill in his youth, he was saved from death through the intercession of St. Francis of Assisi. Bonaventure's *Life* of the Saint manifests eloquently his *devotion to the poor man of God*, in whom he saw Christ, and his personal fidelity to the Franciscan spirit. His own gifts flowed in the direction of mystical theology, university teaching, and spiritual writing—all of which were rooted in his studies of Holy Scripture and the masters. In due course he was drawn into the strife between mendicants and scholars, but as Superior General of the Order (1257), he did all he could to combine scholasticism, mysticism, and ministry.

His visit to LaVerna (1259) had a profound effect on him. It resulted in his famous text on the soul's journey to God. Bonaventure became deeply interested in Francis' life and allowed it to set the tone for his future reflections and legislative decisions, especially in matters of poverty understood in both the material and spiritual sense. In the midst of much ecclesiastical and formative activity, Bonaventure suddenly died on July 15, 1274. In 1588 he became the sixth Doctor of the Church after St. Thomas Aquinas.

Read: *Bonaventure: The Soul's Journey into God; The Tree of Life; The Life of St. Francis*, trans. Ewert Cousins in *The Classics of Western Spirituality*. New York: Paulist Press, 1978.

3. Ignatius of Loyola (1491-1556)

Born in Loyola, Spain, founder of the Society of Jesus, Ignatius was the youngest son of a Basque nobleman. As a young man he was a soldier. During a long convalescence, following a siege in which he was wounded, he did much *reading of the life of Christ* and the saints. After a time he determined to give himself wholly to God's service. After a year's retirement at Manresa, which influenced his whole life, he went on pilgrimage to Jerusalem. Then, from 1524 to 1534, he gave himself to study in Barcelona and the University of Paris.

From time to time, Ignatius did evangelical work among the people, but such an activity by a layman aroused suspicion among Spanish church authorities. In Paris he inspired a group of seven students, among them St. Francis Xavier, to vow to be missionaries to the Moslems in Palestine. Slowly the group increased in numbers and—since war made it impossible for them to journey to Palestine—they offered their services to Pope Paul III in any capacity.

At the age of forty-seven, Ignatius was ordained a priest. Various tasks were assigned to members of the group. Soon they organized into a regular religious order, with the usual vows and an additional one, to be at the Pope's disposal. His composition of the *Spiritual Exercises* left a distinctive mark on the formation of the Jesuits and on countless others who, following the *Exercises*, seek contemplation in Christ.

Read: Tetlow, Joseph, A., S.J. *Ignatius Loyola: Spiritual Exercises*. New York: Crossroad, 1992.

4. Johann Arndt (1555-1621)

Known as the "Father of German Pietism" and the "Prophet of Interior Protestantism," Arndt gave up plans for a medical career and began to read theology and mystical authors. He became a Lutheran pastor and theologian whose mystical writings were widely circulated in Europe in the seventeenth century. He was also a major figure in the 1575 controversy at Wittenberg within Lutheranism over the meaning of the Eucharist. Arndt sided with those who were known as crypto-Calvinists, because they had come to see the ceremony of the Eucharist largely as a symbolic observance. The Eucharist thus came to be considered a remembrance of the Lord's Supper rather than an acceptance of the Real Presence of Christ's body and blood in the consecrated bread and wine.

Later in 1590 he offended the Calvinist concept of strict purity and simplicity by refusing to remove pictures from his church (he became pastor at Badeborn in 1584) and by refusing to discontinue the use of exorcism in Baptism. He also aroused Calvinist hostility by his *spirituality of Christ in the heart of man*. Despite these theological debates, he followed in his famous books on *True Christianity* the medieval mystical insights of St. Bernard of

Clairvaux, Angelo of Foligno, Johann Tauler, and Thomas à Kempis. The book was translated into most European languages and served as the basis of many Roman Catholic and Protestant devotional books. It was also a chief influence on the life of Philip Jakob Spener (1635-1705), founder of Pietism as a movement that stressed simple Christian living and a reform of life that was to follow Luther's reform of doctrine.

Read: *Johann Arndt: True Christianity*, trans. Peter Erb in *The Classics of Western Spirituality*. New York: Paulist Press, 1979.

5. Francis de Sales (1567-1622)

Bishop and writer, Francis was born in the Chateau de Sales at Thorens, France, studied at Paris and the University of Padua, and in 1593—after some opposition from his father—was ordained a priest. His first mission was to the people of his own country, who had left Catholicism for Calvinism. Francis went out to them in a spirit of love and most returned to the church of their baptism. In 1602 he became bishop of Geneva, reorganizing a difficult diocese, preaching tirelessly, and writing. During a Lenten course at Dijon in 1604, he met St. Jane de Chantal with whom he founded the Order of the Visitation six years later. He died at the Visitation convent at the age of fifty-five.

A Calvinist minister in Geneva said of him, "If we honored any man as a saint, I know no one since the days of the apostles more worthy of it than this man." In controversy he was a model of good manners, sensitive to others, moderate in judgment, clear in expression, dignified, modest. One of his main gifts was in the realm of spiritual direction, where he made as a basic aim to help people see how ordinary life in the world—in *imitation of Jesus of Nazareth*—can be holy. One ought not to exclude devoutness of life from shops and offices, from royal courts and the homes of the married. His famous *Introduction to the Devout Life* was appreciated by such diverse readers as King James I and John Wesley. This book, in addition to his treatise on the *Love of God*, has entitled him to being named a Doctor of the Church.

Read: *Francis de Sales, Jane de Chantal: Letters of Spiritual Direction*, trans. Péronne Marie Thiebert, V.H.M. in *The Classics of Western Spirituality*. New York: Paulist Press, 1988.

6. Thomas Merton (1915-1968)

Born in France in 1915, Merton traveled between there and America during the first years of his life. His mother died of cancer when he was six and he was taken by his father to Bermuda while his younger brother, John Paul, remained on Long Island with his maternal grandparents. At the age of ten, his father brought him to Europe to live with him, and he was enrolled subsequently in French and English schools, matriculating in 1933 from Clare College, Cambridge. In 1934 he returned to live permanently in the United States, enrolling for graduate studies at Columbia, where he became a popular figure on campus, a tireless activist.

In 1938 he converted to Catholicism, an event which was to change his life. Soon thereafter he applied for admission to the Franciscan order, but was asked to detain, perhaps indefinitely, his novitiate. Though crushed, he accepted the decision with courage, vowing that if he could not live in a monastery he would become a monk in the world. He taught English at St. Bonaventure University and worked for a while with Catherine de Hueck Doherty in a settlement house in Harlem. In 1941 he gave up teaching and followed his call to be a Trappist monk at the Abbey of Gethsemani, Kentucky. His life thereafter was marked by prayer, work, and, despite ongoing conflicts with his calling and his community, by publication, including the autobiography that brought him fame, *The Seven Storey Mountain*.

Merton made solemn vows in 1947, became an American citizen in 1951, and was appointed to the position of Master of Novices in 1955, a post he held until 1965 when, after many years of trying, he obtained permission from his abbot to live as a hermit in a wooded area about a mile from the main buildings. There he spent most of the remaining three years of his life. In the fall of 1968, he embarked on an extensive trip to the Far East to attend a conference on monasticism in Bangkok and to visit several Trappist monasteries. He gave a morning talk at the conference on the relationships between Marxism and monasticism and, on that day, December 10, 1968, at the age of fifty-three, was killed accidentally, electrocuted by a defective electric fan.

Above all, Merton was a man of faith, a person of almost limitless expansiveness, whose writings witness to the continuing *validity of Christian spirituality in the modern world.*

Read: Merton, Thomas. *The Sign of Jonas*. New York: Doubleday, 1953.

YEAR THREE

A. Third Year Cycle: Ancient to Medieval
Theme: *Our Resistance to Evil is a Gift of Grace*

1. St. Athanasius of Alexandria
(c. 295-373)

St. Athanasius of Alexandria was Bishop of Alexandria from 328. He battled the Arian heresy with his conviction that Christ is the eternal Son and Word of God who had taken a human body to rescue humankind from moral and physical corruption (cf. *Orations against the Arians* and *On the Incarnation*).

In this way he effected a lasting shift in Christian doctrine, guaranteeing that Christian spirituality should subsequently have as its theme for contemplation not a god-like hero winning for himself divine honors in his *struggle with evil*, nor a creating angel inhabiting a human frame, but the Son of God in flesh. In the *Life of St. Anthony* he presents his doctrine of Christian asceticism.

Read: *Athanasius: The Life of Antony and the Letter of Marcellinus*, trans. Robert C. Gregg in *The Classics of Western Spirituality*. New York: Paulist Press, 1980.

2. Evagrius Ponticus
(c. 345-400)

Evagrius Ponticus was a disciple of the Cappadocian Fathers (Basil the Great [330-379]; Gregory of Nyssa [c. 330-395]; and Gregory of Nazianzus [329-389]). As a monk he came into contact with the first generation of the Desert Fathers and with their spirituality in its purest form. He himself went to Egypt in 383 and spent the remaining years of his monastic life there. His "speculative" writings rely heavily on Origen (c. 185-254) while on the "practical" side he draws upon the living experience of the Desert Fathers of Egypt. His gifts of psychological insight and vivid description enable him to analyze and define with precision the various stages on the spiritual way.

Evagrius' reputation was exalted in his time, darkened after his death under the suspicion of heresy, and restored in our time to the status of Church Father and founder of monastic mysticism. He had a profound influence in the East through St. John Climacus, Maximus the Confessor,

Dorotheus of Gaza, and the Hesychasts, and in the West through John Cassian. Evagrius was ordained a deacon by Gregory of Nazianzus in 379; he journeyed to Jerusalem in 382 and resided in the monastery founded by Melania the Elder on the Mount of Olives. In 383 he became a monk in Egypt and subsequently settled in the Nitrian Valley with Macarius and Ammonius as spiritual fathers.

Notwithstanding the possible errors in his theology due to the gnostic trends of the times, one can gain a great deal, formatively speaking, from his twofold description of the soul's return to God.

The *ascetical* way aims to purify the passionate part of the soul, thereby *removing obstacles to contemplation* and drawing the soul into a state of *apatheia* or tranquillity. The main obstacles are the "eight" capital vices, namely, gluttony, lust, avarice, sorrow, anger, despondency (*acedia*), vainglory and pride.

The *contemplative* way proceeds by degrees from natural contemplation using the senses and reason to progressive contemplation in which the intellect empties itself of all forms and comes to see in itself the light of God. His works can be found in *The Philokalia* and in the Ancient Christian Writers Series. Of eminent importance is *The Praktikos*.

Read: *The Mind's Long Journey to the Holy Trinity: The Ad Monachos of Evagrius Ponticus*, trans. Jeremy Driscoll. Collegeville, MN: Liturgical Press, 1993.

3. John Cassian (c. 365-435)

John Cassian was a disciple of Evagrius. The way to God, for Cassian, was a perpetual spiritual combat, a *struggle to divest the soul of "vices,"* of all transient, egocentric, and material interests, by means of the "virtues" *facilitated first of all by God's grace* and nurtured by solitude, repentance, and uninterrupted communion with God. He insists, as will Benedict, that the essence of perfection is charity and that the perfection of charity is reached by way of asceticism—not as a goal in itself but as a means toward greater love and above all unceasing contemplative prayer.

A pupil of St. John Chrysostom, he entered a monastery in Bethlehem before leaving to study monasticism in Egypt along with his friend and fellow monk, Germanus. In him we have the greatest exponent of the monastic life and the most influential figure prior to St. Benedict. With his background and experience in Eastern monasticism and his firsthand acquaintance with the various types of monastic life, Cassian was able to found a monastery near Marseilles for men and one nearby for women.

The *Conferences* insist that the essence of perfection is charity and that the perfection of charity is reached by way of asceticism—not as a goal in itself but as a means toward greater love and, above all, unceasing contemplative prayer. His text, "On the Eight Vices" can be found in the *Philokalia*.

Read: *John Cassian: Conferences*, trans. Colm Luibheid in *The Classics of Western Spirituality*. New York: Paulist Press, 1985.

4. Benedict (480-547)

St. Benedict of Nursia is the father and legislator of western monasticism. Born of an illustrious family and educated in Rome, he retired to a life of solitude at Subiaco, about forty miles from Rome. There he attracted followers and within a short time organized twelve monasteries of twelve monks each. For our knowledge of him, we are entirely dependent on a single source, the *Dialogues* of Pope Gregory the Great. Yet his *Rule* is the most influential document in all of western monasticism, drawing as it does on such sources as Pachomius, Basil, Cassian, and Augustine. Benedict synthesized the essentials of these sources to create a Rule at once inspirational and practical, emphasizing that the monastery is a *school for the Lord's service*, a place where one lives and learns the fundamental value of obedience, silence, humility, *lectio*, prayer, and labor.

Read: *St. Gregory the Great: Pastoral Care*, trans. Henry Davis. New York: Newman Press, 1950. See also Joan Chittister. *The Rule of Benedict: Insights for the Ages*. New York: Crossroad, 1993.

5. Pseudo-Dionysius (c. 500)

Pseudo-Dionysius is an enigmatic figure who writes under the pseudonym of Dionysius the Areopagite. He had a profound influence on a broad range of mystical writers from the middle ages on due to his formulation of a method of "negative theology" that stresses the utter *inability of the human mind to penetrate the impenetrable abyss of the mystery of God.* His influence on the author of *The Cloud of Unknowing* is obvious.

Dionysian spirituality finds echoes in Gregory of Nyssa as well as in John of the Cross. The writings of Dionysius all have a single ultimate aim: the union of the whole creation with God by whom it was created, a union in which the created order will attain perfection, i.e., divinization or deification by participation in the saving mystery of God's love. This union is the final stage of a threefold process of purification, illumination, and union—the famous three ways of the mystical tradition, first found in our author.

In the *Divine Names*, Dionysius tells how our praise of God may be perfected and the various ways in which God manifests himself. This knowledge of God through affirmations about him drawn from creation and the scriptures is called *cataphatic* theology. However, all affirmations fall short of God and point beyond themselves, as the short but powerful treatise, the *Mystical Theology*, makes clear, to that which is *apophatic* in which the soul passes beyond anything it can perceive or know into the darkness where God is.

Read: *Pseudo-Dionysius: The Complete Works*, trans. Colm Luibheid in *The Classics of Western Spirituality*. New York: Paulist Press, 1987.

6. Author of *The Cloud of Unknowing* (c. 1399)

The author of *The Cloud of Unknowing* is an anonymous English monk, who presents in a fresh, concrete, joyful style—characteristic of English spirituality of the period—a vivid example of apophatic or negative theology. The text also relies on closely reasoned arguments, faculty psychology, and Augustinian theology, especially in its appreciation of the *reciprocal action of grace and the human will.*

The *Cloud* contains a detailed and practical explanation of the author's views on the method of contemplative prayer understood as a work of grace and a miracle of love. In spite of its emphasis on seeking God by way of unknowing, the *Cloud* has a distinctively Christological focus, for it is the Lord Jesus Christ himself who calls us in the Gospel to the perfection of every human virtue, especially that of humility (for the "most divine knowledge of God is that which is known by not-knowing").

Read: *The Cloud of Unknowing*, trans. James Walsh, S.J. in *The Classics of Western Spirituality*. New York: Paulist Press, 1981.

B. Third Year Cycle: Medieval to Modern
Theme: *Our Ongoing Commitment to Conversion*

1. Meister Eckhart
(1260-1327)

Meister Eckhart, German Dominican and speculative mystic of the Rhineland School, contributed to the future development of Protestantism, Idealism, and Existentialism. He was a controversial figure in his own time but today the essence of his contribution to the Christian formation tradition is more clearly understood. His main activity was not teaching or writing as such but preaching to a group of contemplative nuns in Strassburg, Germany. Hence many of his texts were reproduced without his specific editing of them —perhaps the cause of much misunderstanding in his lifetime, culminating in a charge of heresy in his sixtieth year.

Eckhart's main interest centered on *the foundational human quest for union with God*. He described this union in four stages occurring between the soul and God. These were: *dissimilarity*, *similarity*, *identity*, and *breakthrough*. In his lifetime he published a reply to the list of errors of which he was accused by the Franciscan Archbishop of Cologne. When faced with new charges, he relied on the testimony of his personal mystical experience to justify his position. After his death, at least twenty-eight propositions of his were condemned by Pope John XXII—but the validity of this condemnation still remains in question today. One can begin to know Eckhart by reading *The Essential Sermons* and any good collection of his writings.

Read: *Meister Eckhart: The Essential Sermons, Commentaries, Treatises and Defense*, trans. Edmund Colledge, O.S.A. and Bernard McGinn in *The Classics of Western Spirituality*. New York: Paulist Press, 1981.

2. Blessed Jan van Ruusbroec
(1293-1381)

Also in the Augustinian tradition, Blessed Jan van Ruusbroec was born in Brabant in the Low Countries. He knew the masters of Latin mystical theology, including St. Augustine, Pseudo-Dionysius, and Aquinas. Despite his lack of formal education, he was a man of great intellectual energy, at home in the didactic presentation of mystical speculation. He saw the spiritual life in terms of a graduated *procession toward deification*. In every soul, he taught, the eternal image of God dwells as its roots and essence. This image is trinitarian, for humans are a "created Trinity." The spiritual life also proceeds according to three stages: the active, the inward, and the contemplative.

Read: *John Ruusbroec: The Spiritual Espousals and Other Works*, trans. James A. Wiseman, O.S.B. in *The Classics of Western Spirituality*. New York: Paulist Press, 1985.

3. John Tauler
(1300-1361)

A Dominican preacher and mystic, Tauler, along with Henry Suso, his contemporary, came under the influence of Meister Eckhart at the University of Cologne. Unlike Suso, who bitterly lamented Eckhart's condemnation, Tauler adopted an equable, gentler tone that placed this event within the limits of time and the limitless, revealing possibilities of eternity. Strictly speaking, Tauler wrote nothing himself, but his sermons were transcribed by his usual audience, the nuns of Dominican houses of the Rhineland, and these texts survived.

The style and brevity of pulpit discourse suited Tauler as an artist and theologian. The power of his preaching is evident. By avoiding rhetorical effect, he was able to make his points directly, plainly, with common sense freed from hyperbole. Tauler insists on the need for humility and simplicity, cautioning us not to be overawed by the subtleties of scholars. Yet he reminds us that *we are called by God to employ all our faculties in the effort to reach him.* Always balanced in his views, he tells us that there is a time to cease from action and suffer God to act within us and a time to serve him with zeal. We must be replenished by union with God if we are to use wisely the gifts we have received. Spiritual suffering is a welcome part of life for anyone who is truly Christian and who believes that we shall be drawn out of sorrow into divine peace.

Read: *Johannes Tauler: Sermons*, trans. Maria Shrady in *The Classics of Western Spirituality*. New York: Paulist Press, 1985.

4. John Wesley
(1703-1791)

The writings of John and the hymns of Charles Wesley combine to communicate the founding intuitions of the Methodist revival that swept through England in the early nineteenth century, a revival that synthesized into a unique blend the intuitions of the Eastern Fathers, the mystics of the undivided Church, notably Augustine and à Kempis, and the Protestant Reformers.

The essence of their vision pertains to the *integration of spirituality and social presence in imitation of Christ's divine and human mission* and to our desire to live united with the Lord through love. In an age where spiritual formation seems on the wane, the Wesleys offer a powerful reminder that "We shall not in the desert stray; / We shall not...miss our providential way; / ...While love, almighty love, is near.

Read: *John and Charles Wesley: Selected Writings and Hymns*, ed. Frank Whaling in *The Classics of Western Spirituality*. New York: Paulist Press, 1981.

5. Søren Kierkegaard (1813-1855)

Søren Kierkegaard described himself as a poet in service of Christianity, but instead of poems he wrote in a variety of forms including psychology, literary and social criticism, ethical discourse, philosophical polemics, Bible exposition, and edifying discourses, the latter written under his own name. The single purpose of all of this was, in his words, to "reintroduce Christianity to Christendom." He saw his Christian task as one of reminding individuals that they are responsible to God as spiritual creatures, dependent on grace, and *called to inner awakening and conversion to Jesus as savior*. The goal sought is conformity of mind and heart to the upward call of God in Christ.

Read: Kierkegaard, Søren. *Purity of Heart Is to Will One Thing*, trans. Douglas V. Steere. New York: Harper Torchbooks, 1956.

6. Elizabeth of the Trinity (1880-1906)

Born at the military camp of Avor where her father was an officer in the French Army, Elizabeth was seven years old when he died, leaving her, her mother, and her sister Marguerite. The three of them moved to Dijon. Around the time of her first communion (April 19, 1891), Elizabeth made a vow of virginity and became aware of a vocation to Carmel. Her mother agreed, though reluctantly, insisting that she finish her education. During the intervening years, Elizabeth devoted herself to the usual pursuits of a young member of a pious Catholic family—helping with the parish choir and teaching catechism. Her proficiency as a pianist increased and she won several prizes at the Dijon Conservatory of Music.

At the age of nineteen, Elizabeth read St. Thérèse's *Story of a Soul* and made her profession two years later. She cultivated a deep *devotion to the mystery of the indwelling of the Trinity.* In 1905 she experienced the first symptoms of the illness from which she died on November 9, 1906. She was beatified on November 25, 1984 at St. Peter's in Rome.

Elizabeth is best known through her posthumously published prayers, letters, notes, and diaries, of inspiration to countless believers who identify with her conviction, based on the Epistle to the Ephesians, that *every Christian is "predestined" through baptism to be a "praise of glory."* Particularly attractive is the trinitarian character of her spirituality, her rediscovery of the New Testament as the fundamental charter of Christian life, and her stress on the common call to holiness of all the baptized.

Read: *Elizabeth of the Trinity: The Complete Works*, trans. Sr. Aletheia Kane, O.C.D. Vol. One. Washington, DC: Institute of Carmelite Studies, ICS Publications, 1984.